King Arthur's Voyage to the Otherworld

KING ARTHUR'S VOYAGE
to the
OTHERWORLD

Was Arthur killed in America?

Robert MacCann

IMPERATOR

PUBLISHER
Imperator Press, Sydney Australia
PO Box 41 Broadway NSW 2007

www.kingarthursvoyagetoamerica.com

Copyright © Robert G. MacCann, 2016

The right of Robert MacCann to be identified as the author of this work has been asserted by him in accordance with the Copyright Amendment (Moral Rights) Act, 2000. This work is copyright. Apart from any use permitted under the Copyright Act, 1968, no part may be reproduced, copied, scanned, stored in a retrieval system, recorded, or transmitted, in any form or by any means, without the prior written permission of the publisher.

First published in Australia in 2016.

NATIONAL LIBRARY OF AUSTRALIA
CATALOGUING-IN-PUBLICATION DATA

AUTHOR:	MacCann, Robert
TITLE:	King Arthur's Voyage to the Otherworld: Was Arthur killed in America? / Robert MacCann
ISBN:	9780994510211 (softcover)
NOTES:	Includes bibliographical references and index
SUBJECTS:	Arthur, King
	Arthur, King--Death
	Arthur, King--Travel
	Voyages and travels
	Civilization, Ancient
	Britons--History
	Great Britain--Antiquities, Celtic
	Great Britain--History--To 1066
DEWEY NUMBER:	942.014

Book cover by the Scarlett Rugers Design Agency.

Front cover map adapted from Sarah Dunning Park.

Back cover Welsh script: folio 26 recto, manuscript Peniarth 2 (Llyfr Taliesin), part of a poem about the sea voyage of Arthur to Annwfyn. By permission of Llyfrgell Genedlaethol Cymru/National Library of Wales.

CONTENTS

	List of Figures	viii
	Acknowledgements	ix
	Preface	
	The Rise and Fall of Arthur	xi
	A British Overking in Gildas	xiv
	Eyewitness Data from Poetry	xvi
1	**Overview of Arthur**	
	An Expedition to America in Welsh Poetry	1
	Portrayals of Arthur	4
	Medieval Beliefs in Arthur's Voyages	8
	Dating the Three Welsh Poems	10
2	**Historical Context for Arthur**	
	The Post-Roman Period	13
	Gildas: *The Ruin of Britain*	14
	Arthur's Battles in the *Historia Brittonum*	18
	Language Change: from British to Neo-Brittonic	23
3	**Medieval Beliefs in Arthur's Atlantic Voyages**	
	Arthur's Death Overseas in Geoffrey's history	27
	Mercator's Letter to John Dee	32
	The Arthurian Voyages in *Gestae Arthuri*	33
	The List of Northern Lands under Arthur	38
	Did the Northern Lands List precede Geoffrey?	39
	A Dating for the Northern Lands List	41
	Conclusion	43
4	**Sixth-Century North America**	
	The Hopewell	47
	The Mounds and their Enclosures	48
	Hopewell Artifacts	57
	What did the Native Americans look like?	59
	Native American Weapons	61
	Unrest After the Hopewell Period	62
5	**Arthur's American Voyage**	
	A Disastrous Historical Expedition	65
	Stanza 1: Conflict at Kaer Sidi	68
	Stanza 2: Four-peaked Camp and Cauldron with Pearls	71
	Stanza 3: The Camp of Extreme Coldness	76
	Stanza 4: Meeting the Inhabitants	78
	Stanza 5: The 'Brindled Ox'	80

	Stanza 6: Tamed Animal with Silvery Head	83
	Stanza 7: The Lords who Know the Secret	85
	Stanza 8: Arthur's Death in Annwfyn Revealed	86
	Arthur as a Christian	88
	The Mystery of Arthur's Grave	88
	Attempts to Truncate the Poem	90
	The Complete Poem	92

6 Death of Arthur in America
  The Annwfyn Section in *Kat Godeu* 97
  Translation of the Annwfyn Section 99
  The Fighting 99
  The Death of Arthur 100

7 Interpreting the 'Battle of the Trees'
  The 'Battle of the Trees' 107
  Who was the Enemy? 108
  An Environmental Downturn AD 540 109
  Rocky 'Hail' from Space 111
  Arthur Fighting a Dragon 112
  Summary 113

8 The Aftermath of the Voyage
  The Chair of the Sovereign 115
  A Eulogy to Arthur 116
  An Implication that Arthur was Overseas 120
  The Bard's Beliefs 122
  A Successor to Arthur 123
  Wild Weather Conditions 125
  The Poem's Ending 125
  Summary 126

9 Dating the Three Poems
  Overview of the Dating 129
  Dating from Historical Context 130
  The Bard's Anger at the Monks 132
  Was the Bard an Eyewitness? 133
  Dating via *Historia Brittonum* 137
  Dating via *Voyage of Bran* 139
  Dating via *Echtrae Chonnlai* 141
  Dating via *Dún Scáith* 142
  Dating via *Bricriu's Feast* 144
  Comparing *Kat Godeu* to *Dún Scáith* 145
  Comparison of the Three Poems 147
  Archaic Language Remnants 148
  Summary 150

10 An Attempt to Reconstruct the Voyage
Early Voyages in the North Atlantic 153
Celtic Ships 157
Speculation on Arthur's Route 159
America 164
The Four-Peaked Camp – Montreal 166
Exploring North America 168
Entering the Ohio Eastern Woodlands 170
Conclusion 179

11 A Reappraisal of the Traditional Arthurian Evidence
The Traditional Evidence for Arthur 181
Men named after Arthur 182
Arthur in *Y Gododdin* 184
Arthur in *Marwnad Cynddylan* 189
Arthur in *Geraint son of Erbin* 190
The *Historia Brittonum* 192
The *Annales Cambriae* 193
Summary of the Traditional Evidence 196

12 Who Was Arthur?
An Overking in Gildas 199
Gildas' Hatred of the Military 205
Evidence for a North Wales Location 208
Arthur's North Wales Kingdom 213
Speculation on Arthur's Family 217
The Superstition surrounding Arthur's Name 219
Evidence pointing to Southwest Scotland 222
The Novantae Region 224
Arthur's Northern Achievements 226

13 Who Was Arthur's Bard?
The *Book of Taliesin* Poems 231
The Bard's Mixture of Beliefs 235
Talhaearn as Arthur's Bard? 237

14 Review of the Claims
Review of the Evidence usually considered 241
New Evidence concerning Arthur 243
Evidence for a Voyage to America 248
Inadequacy of the Non-Historical Interpretations 255
Conclusion 257

Notes 261
References 307
Index 327

LIST OF FIGURES

4.1	Hopewell mounds with their core region centred on Ohio	50
4.2	Newark Earthworks Plan, from Squier and Davis, 1848	51
4.3	Newark: top of Great Circle wall	52
4.4	Newark: Great Circle wall, viewed from inside	52
4.5	Newark: Great Circle entrance	52
4.6	Newark: two Octagon walls joining at right	53
4.7	Newark: circular wall leading to Observatory Mound	53
4.8	Newark: circular wall with elliptical Observatory Mound	53
4.9	Hopewell Earthworks Plan, from Squier and Davis, 1848	54
4.10	Mound City Plan, from Squier and Davis, 1848	55
4.11	Mound City: four mounds of varying shapes and sizes	56
4.12	Mound City: posthole remains for a submound building	56
4.13	Seip Mound, southwest of Chillicothe	56
4.14	Hopewell carving of a head, from Squier and Davis, 1848	61
10.1	Arthur's possible route to America	160
10.2	Mont Royal, the first of the Four Peaks	167
10.3	Mont St-Bruno, Mont St-Hilaire and Mont Rougemont	167
10.4	The 'Brindled Ox'	174
10.5	North American river otter – with 'silvery head'	176
10.6	Hopewell carving – river otter with fish	177
10.7	Rivers of Ohio showing important Hopewell earthworks	178
12.1	Nameplate for Stone of Huail	207
12.2	The stone on which Huail was said to have been beheaded	207
12.3	Dinarth: looking east	208
12.4	Dinarth: looking north	208
12.5	Dinarth: looking northwest towards Little Ormes Head	209
12.6	Dinarth: looking west towards Anglesey and Puffin Island	209
12.7	Dinarth: looking southeast	209
12.8	Sea routes from north Wales to Rheon and Hadrian's Wall	227

ACKNOWLEDGEMENTS

I wish to thank all the people who have contributed to improving this book. I am greatly indebted to Glen Thomson, who carefully read the entire book and made many helpful comments which made the presentation clearer. At his suggestion, a rather dry chapter was deleted and its contents dispersed into the Notes. He also designed the companion website for the book at: www.kingarthursvoyagetoamerica.com

Thanks are due to Helen Fulton, Professor of Medieval Literature at the University of York, who read through an early draft of the book and made thoughtful comments on a number of issues. These helped me to revise and strengthen my arguments. I am also grateful to Professor John Koch of the Centre for Advanced Welsh and Celtic Studies. While at Oxford University as a Research Fellow, I had the time to drive across to Aberystwyth to spend an afternoon with him discussing Welsh poems from the *Book of Taliesin*. His arguments that *Preideu Annwfyn* was probably an early poem (c. AD 750 is defensible in his view) gave me the motivation to thoroughly study it and compare it with certain Irish texts of an early date. Thanks are also due to Dr Ken MacMillan of the University of Calgary who promptly responded to my question on his work regarding John Dee's manuscript in the British Library, *Brytanici Imperii Limites* (Limits of the British Empire). Others who have helped by reading chapters are Dr Robert Hynson, Beth Everitt, and Bill and Felicity Lawson. My adult children Jennifer MacCann, James MacCann and Dr Carolyn MacCann all read and critiqued chapters and made a number of valuable suggestions.

I would of course add that none of the people thanked above are in any way responsible for the arguments or conclusions in the book and that any errors of fact or interpretation are mine alone.

At Oxford University I was able to obtain many important references not easily available elsewhere. The librarians in the Taylorian, Sackler, History Faculty Library and the English Faculty Library were very helpful. When back in Australia, I greatly appreciated the help of the librarians at the University of Sydney, the University of NSW, Macquarie University and the Australian National Library.

I thank the Ohio Historical Society for permitting me to use a photo of a Hopewell smoking pipe carved in the form of an otter (shown in Figure 10.6). In my book, the North American river otter is identified as the tamed animal with the 'silvery head' referred to in *Preideu Annwfyn*.

I also acknowledge the superb photos taken by Jack Dykinga of the buffalo (shown in Figure 10.4) and Dimitry Azovtsev of *Lontra canadensis* (the two otters shown in Figure 10.5). The Dykinga photo is from the US Agricultural Research Service and appears at:
http://en.wikipedia.org/wiki/File:American_bison_k5680-1.jpg

Dimitry Azovtsev holds the copyright of the otters photo and licensed it under Creative Commons Attribution-ShareAlike 3.0 Unported licence. See http://creativecommons.org/licenses/by-sa/3.0/legalcode The photo is at: http://en.wikipedia.org/wiki/File:LutraCanadensis_fullres.jpg The usage of this photo is not meant to imply that the copyright holder endorses the content or views expressed in this book. Both photos are in colour but in the book are reproduced in greyscale.

I thank Sarah Dunning Park, based in San Francisco, for her expert drawing of the maps and for permission to have one of her maps adapted for use on the front cover. Sarah had previously drawn the maps in the *History of the Ancient/Medieval World* books by Susan Wise Bauer.

I also thank the Scarlett Rugers Design Agency for producing the book cover and the National Library of Wales (Llyfrgell Genedlaethol Cymru) for permission to use a folio image from manuscript Peniarth 2 which appears on the back cover.

Last but not least I thank my wife, Ann, a wonderful partner. She read drafts of each chapter, made thoughtful comments, queried ambiguities and suggested simplifications of the text. She also persuaded me to change the author/date/page references in the body of the text to the far less obtrusive superscript system to improve readability. For her love and support at every stage I am most indebted.

PREFACE

THE RISE AND FALL OF ARTHUR

The ideas in this book have been developed over many years of informal reading, my interest in the Arthurian legends having begun in the early 1970s. This period and the decade preceding it were a time of renewed interest in Arthur's historicity. He had been a controversial figure from the time he was popularised in Geoffrey of Monmouth's pseudo-history in the twelfth century and belief in him as a historical figure has continued to wax and wane over the centuries. In the 1960s and 70s, belief in Arthur had peaked again. Even the political administration of John F. Kennedy had associated itself with the Camelot aura. The musical *Camelot* was an outstanding success in New York, London and Australia and was followed by a film version, while the books of Geoffrey Ashe were beautifully written and highly effective in generating an interest in Arthur.

In 1965 the Camelot Research Committee was formed with the eminent archaeologist Sir Mortimer Wheeler as president. Money was then raised to excavate the massive hillfort at South Cadbury on the grounds that an old tradition from the 1500s had held that it was Camelot. Leslie Alcock led the excavation and in 1972 concluded that it had been fortified in the post-Roman period over a large area, sufficient to house a war band of record size. He gave the impression that Cadbury could be Camelot by entitling the book '*By South Cadbury is that Camelot...*', based on a quotation from the old tradition. In fact, there was really nothing to link the hillfort to Arthur. Inside the book, Alcock had correctly noted that Camelot was a twelfth-century creation of French poet, Chrétien de Troyes. Alcock also produced a fine academic book called *Arthur's Britain*, based on his expert knowledge of archaeology and the sources on Arthur.

However the Arthurian bubble was about to burst. The catalyst for this was the publication in 1973 of John Morris' book, *The Age of Arthur*. This book was outwardly an impressive work of scholarship but scholars familiar with the sources were dismayed by some of the arguments within it. Morris had confidently made numerous strong claims that simply could not be justified from the sources. A critical reaction was building in the academic world. In 1977 David Dumville wrote an important paper heavily criticizing Morris' book, noting his overuse of very late sources and claiming that his book (and that of Alcock) provided a medieval view of Arthur. Dumville criticized the use of Welsh sources and the use of poetic sources, the latter of which would include the hypothetical Welsh poem thought to underlie the battle list of Arthur in the *Historia Brittonum*. If these are excluded, then the only source remaining is the Welsh Annals, a Latin source giving the dates of Arthur's victory at Badon and his death at Camlann.

Alcock had thought that these entries had been originally recorded into an Easter table close to the time the events occurred and that this table was the source for the Annals entries. While this has not been disproved, the work of Kathleen Hughes has demonstrated that there is no need for the Easter table idea and that the entries may have been added to the Annals centuries after the events they describe. These entries could even have been based on legends. It left no evidence for Arthur's historicity rigorous enough to satisfy Dumville. In a sweeping conclusion he writes:[1]

> ...there is no historical evidence about Arthur; we must reject him from our histories and, above all, from the titles of our books.

False Negative or Type 2 Error

Dumville has strongly influenced current historians who now tend to omit Arthur from their history books. He advocates strict criteria for accepting a figure as historical, placing reliance on valid contemporary sources and also a secure line of transmission of such information. When such sources exist, all would agree. The problem arises where such sources do not exist. In the latter case, scholars had previously sought out the sources that were available and, where possible, tried to assess their validity for examining the historicity of a given figure. However Dumville rejects this kind of procedure. The result is Arthur's exclusion from history.

Historians are not infallible. There are two broad categories of error that hypothetically can be made in judging whether a figure was historical. These are shown below, using Arthur as an example.

Reality for Arthur	Historians' Judgements	
	Arthur: not historical	Arthur: historical
Not historical	True	False Positive (Type 1 error)
Historical	False Negative (Type 2 error)	True

In two of these states, the historians' judgements are false as they differ from reality. In one, Arthur was not historical but historians thought that he was, known as a False Positive in fields such as medicine. In hypothesis testing in mathematical statistics this is known as a Type 1 error. In the other, Arthur was historical but historians thought he was not. This is called a False Negative or Type 2 error.[2] Dumville's approach is to avoid a False Positive. It would be embarrassing to admit a non-historical figure into the historical canon, but the use of overly strict criteria for making the judgement runs the risk of creating a False Negative. In this book it will be argued that historians have made a massive False Negative or Type 2 error in rejecting Arthur from their history books. The implications of using Dumville's approach are briefly discussed below.

Although Arthur was the target, the emphasis on contemporary data and the rejection of Welsh poetry results in other casualties. If strictly followed, it eliminates other figures formerly regarded as historical, including the kings Urien, Owain and Gwallawg, the poets Taliesin and Aneirin, Maelgwn's son Rhun and wife Sanant. Even Vortigern, the king who invited the Saxons into Britain, must be rejected. He was not a contemporary of Gildas, so a sceptic could argue that the tale of his hiring the Saxons may have been only a legend which Gildas had accepted as history. My belief is that all these people were historical figures and their rejection from history resulting from Dumville's stringent approach results in a serious loss of information. They are probably False Negative or Type 2 errors.

What are the consequences of making a Type 2 error? In Arthur's case it discourages further enquiry into whether he was actually a historical figure. In addition, it encourages implausible theories that he was non-historical; for example, that he was originally a folkloric figure or Celtic god who over the centuries became 'historicized'. These theories are beginning to become the default position on Arthur. However they too are being rendered invalid by Dumville's strict requirements.

The Prolific Use of Late Sources in the Folkloric Theories of Arthur
The folkloric theories, like the historical theories, rely for their evidence on the same late texts that Dumville dismisses and hence are subject to the same criticism. Amazingly no one seems to object to this use of very late sources by the mythological theorists, not even Dumville. If an advocate of these theories employs a twelfth-century text to infer that Arthur was originally viewed as a folkloric figure in an earlier period, say the sixth century, then it is an invalid inference. It provides no evidence on how Arthur was actually viewed 600 years earlier. Arthur may have been regarded correctly as a historical figure in the sixth century, while the twelfth century text merely reflects the legends that developed around him.

Note Dumville's inconsistencies, in his 1977 paper, on using late texts. He correctly criticises John Morris for his usage of late sources but approves of John Rhŷs' view that Arthur was a figure of mythology, a view Rhŷs asserted in *Studies in the Arthurian Legend*. However Rhŷs is far worse than Morris in employing late sources. He uses the twelfth-century story on Guinevere's kidnapping for his case that Arthur was viewed from an early stage as a divine 'culture hero'. He even employs the pseudo-history of Geoffrey of Monmouth. In 1927 the great literary scholar, Sir Edmund Chambers, wrote an accurate assessment of Rhŷs' works:[3]

> A similar uncritical use, not only of Geoffrey, but also of the later elaborations of the romance-writers, renders valueless much of the work of the late Professor Rhys. He is even capable of quoting the fifteenth-century Malory as an authority for mythological *data*.

In contrast, Dumville writes approvingly of Rhŷs' work:[4]

> The totality of the evidence, and it is remarkably slight until a very late date, shows Arthur as a figure of legend (or even – as Sir John Rhŷs pointed out last century – of mythology).

The evidence in Dumville's quote also includes the dubious 'evidence' about Arthur from *Studies in the Arthurian Legend* (which Dumville cites below the quote) but unfortunately Dumville makes no mention of Rhŷs' prolific use of late sources.

Dumville's demands destroy the Folkloric Theories of Arthur

The fact of the matter is that there is not a shred of sixth-century evidence that Arthur was seen as mythical, folkloric or a divine 'culture hero'. We must therefore reject notions that Arthur was regarded as any of the above in the sixth century and accept that the first legendary material on Arthur appeared 300 years after his purported floruit, in the *Mirabilia* (Marvels) appendix of the *Historia*. Even this late material is useless as evidence for inferring that the figures in it must be myths. By this stage, legends were developing around historical figures of the fifth and sixth centuries. The historical battle leader, Ambrosius, appears in the *Historia* in legendary form as a boy wizard, the product of a virgin birth, who prophesies the future. Further, two almost certainly historical persons, St Illtud and King Meurig of Gwent, appear in the *Mirabilia*. As historical people are appearing in this material, one cannot reasonably infer that it points to Arthur as a non-historical figure.

A BRITISH OVERKING IN GILDAS

Dumville's emphasis on contemporary texts directs our attention to *The Ruin of Britain* by sixth-century British cleric, Gildas. This work gives lurid detail on the lives of five British kings – Constantine, Aurelius 'Caninus', Vortipor, Cuneglasus and Maglocunus. Opponents of a historical Arthur often state that Gildas did not refer to him. However a reanalysis of Gildas in this book reveals items that, when considered jointly, suggest that he may have indeed referred to Arthur, though not specifically by name. In Section 37, Gildas makes the surprising statement that there is a Pharaoh (overking) above the five kings. They are described in the following metaphor:[5]

> ...these five mad and debauched horses from the retinue of Pharaoh which actively lure his army to its ruin in the Red Sea.

Who was this Pharaoh who had Cuneglasus and the others as part of his retinue? He was probably the figure noted in Section 33 when Gildas twice suggests that there is a more powerful king than Maglocunus, the strongest of the five kings.[6] Furthermore, in Section 32 Cuneglasus is called the 'chariot driver of the Bear's Stronghold'.[7] Here 'chariot driver' is a metaphor in which Cuneglasus is being likened to Pharaoh's chariot drivers who were killed in the Exodus. Apparently Cuneglasus was subordinate to a powerful overking whose name allowed the punster Gildas to call him 'the Bear'. If Cuneglasus were subordinate to both 'the Bear' and 'Pharaoh', this would imply that these figures were the same overking. As *Arth* meant 'bear' in the Neo-Brittonic language, and Arthur lived in the sixth century, it suggests that this overking was Arthur.

Vortigern and Arthur are treated Similarly by Gildas

John Morris has remarked how few British figures were actually named by Gildas. Even Vortigern, who invited the Saxons into Britain as mercenaries, is not named by Gildas. Instead Gildas speaks in code in the three times he mentions him, calling him 'arrogant tyrant', 'Pharaoh' and 'ill-fated tyrant'. Similarly Gildas refers to Arthur as 'the Bear' and 'Pharaoh'. Why does he suppress the real names of these figures? He answers this himself when he refers to the bloody military men whom he detests. In his eyes they are:[8]

> enemies of God, if chance so offers, who ought, together with their very name, to be assiduously destroyed.

Bede, who used Gildas extensively, approved of this practice of suppressing names. He writes:[9]

> the name and memory of those apostates ought to be utterly blotted out from the list of Christian kings and that no year should be assigned to their reign.

It would seem that Gildas did refer to Arthur after all, but spoke in code to suppress his name, just as he did with Vortigern.

Arthur's Location in Britain

If Arthur were punned as 'the Bear' by Gildas, then he was located at 'the Bear's Stronghold', equivalent to *Din Eirth* in early Welsh, and modernised later to *Dinarth*. It is an impressive hillfort at Colwyn Bay, with spectacular views along the north Wales coast.

This deduction from Gildas is supported by several sources. The poems *Preideu Annwfyn* and *Kadeir Teÿrnon* both link Arthur to north Wales, with the former linking him to the meadows along the River Dee and the latter associating him with *Lleon* (Chester). Further, the Welsh Triads name one of his mistresses as Garwen, daughter of Hennin. The *Stanzas of the Graves* state that Garwen was buried on the *Morfa*, the long beach at Llandudno, quite close to Dinarth, while Hennin was buried at Dinorben, a few miles to the east of Dinarth.[10]

EYEWITNESS DATA FROM POETRY

Does other contemporary material on Arthur survive? Despite Dumville's mistrust of poetry, a search of all Arthurian poetry was made. If any early material on Arthur had survived it would most likely have come from his bard. There are three *Book of Taliesin* poems that are in the voice of Arthur's bard – *Preideu Annwfyn* (Spoils of Annwfyn), *Kadeir Teÿrnon* (Chair of the Sovereign) and *Kat Godeu* (Battle of the Trees).[11] They are currently thought to deal with only legendary material. It is argued that this is a mistake and that they are genuinely early poems by Arthur's bard. They were probably orally transmitted initially and then were progressively modernized as the language evolved from Neo-Brittonic to Old Welsh to Middle Welsh.

Preideu Annwfyn is a difficult work with obscure allusions. The current academic view is that it is a fantasy, based on conceptions of a Welsh/Irish Otherworld. This book argues that it reflects a real journey to a distant land where Arthur was killed. Not only is the fantasy interpretation implausible, its elements do not cohere in any meaningful way, as can be seen from the outline below. In contrast, the historical view gives a coherent account of the poem's features, including the identity and location of the inhabitants, and also its emotional content comprising the bard's repeated expressions of distress, his hatred of the monks and his grieving over Arthur's death. These starkly opposing interpretations are now summarised.

Preideu Annwfyn – the Fairyland Fantasy Approach

Arthur and his men set sail to a Celtic Otherworld to steal a magic cauldron which is decorated with pearls. The sailors see a 'glass fortress', interpreted as a glass fairy castle. The Annwfyn inhabitants are fairies or immortals who are associated with earthen mounds. It is a perfect existence where they live forever without sin, strife, sickness, decay or death, as in the Irish Otherworld stories. At one point the Britons meet the fairies who are standing on a wall of the glass castle. Contrary to their depiction in the Irish stories, the fairies and the Britons cannot understand each other.

The Britons see an 'ox' with a huge head and neck, and a tamed animal having a silvery head. These are sometimes explained away as just 'magical' animals. At *kaer sidi* ('mound fortress') the mounds are thought to be fairy mounds where the fairies live. Kenneth Jackson and John Bollard translate it to mean 'Faery City' and 'fairy fortress' respectively.[12]

One of Arthur's men, Gweir, is captured by the fairies. This is reported by Pwyll and Pryderi, whom John Rhŷs calls 'dark divinities', while Kenneth Jackson sees Pryderi as an Otherworld divinity.[13] The Britons are decimated by the fairies, with only a few survivors. Arthur's fate is unknown. The bard who survived is overwhelmed with grief at the losses and turns to Christ for comfort. However this clear Christian feature is usually viewed as a later interpolation made by monks who were eager to insert Christian references into a 'magnificently pagan' poem.[14]

In stanzas 4-8 the bard excoriates the British monks, calling them 'little men' and cowards, having no manly resolve, and derides their ignorance of what happened in Annwfyn. This is viewed as the bard trying to upstage the monks by showing his superiority in learning.[15]

A Historical Voyage to North America

It is argued that this poem was composed by Arthur's bard and gives an eye-witness account of a sea voyage to Annwfyn, interpreted here as North America. The bard's abuse of the monks, noted above, was an overflow of rage at the slanders published by Gildas in his *Ruin of Britain*. Gildas refers to the British military as cowards and 'like women', calls the bards liars, raving hucksters and parasites, and lashes the British kings for their sins.[16] This would date the poem to shortly after the publication of Gildas' work, circa AD 540. An outline for the historical view is given below.

Arthur and his men sail 'across the shores of the world' to a distant land. No one before him had visited it. On the way the sailors see a 'glass fortress', the same object as the 'glass tower in the middle of the sea' in the related story from the *Historia Brittonum*. It is called a 'crystal pillar' in the sea in the *Navigatio* of St Brendan. These three instances suggest it is a metaphor for a large iceberg.[17] Annwfyn's people are Native Americans at the start of the Late Woodland period, the successors to the renowned Hopewell culture. Long ago, the Hopewell had built a huge number of earthen mounds, and mound walls in various geometric shapes, across the Eastern Woodlands. At some point on the mainland, the Britons meet the inhabitants who are standing on a wall, perhaps one of the earthen walls that enclose their mounds. As the two groups have different languages, they cannot understand each other.

While in the Eastern Woodlands, the Britons see an 'ox' with a huge head and neck (the buffalo) and a tamed animal with a silvery head (the North American river otter). These animals were flourishing in this region. In a skirmish with the Native Americans, the Britons capture a ceremonial clay pot (cauldron) which was decorated with pearls, a contrast to its dark rim. The Native Americans made extensive use of pearls where in one site alone 100,000 pearls were found. At *kaer sidi* (a camp near the mounds) conflict arises and Gweir is captured, which was reported by Pwyll and Pryderi who are two of Arthur's men. The Britons are decimated in the fighting. Back in Britain as one of the few survivors, the bard describes a scene where the lords who know about Arthur's death are clashing with the monks. A few lines later he announces Arthur's death, stating that his grave and body are lost. He then turns to Christ for comfort.

Support for this naturalistic view of *Preideu Annwfyn* comes from a 16-line section of *Kat Godeu*. These two poems are the only works that portray Annwfyn as a disaster rather than a paradise. In *Kat Godeu*, the bard states that the inhabitants of Annwfyn gathered for battle by means of the rivers and streams, quite apt for the Native Americans, but rather preposterous for fairies. This section refers to heated fighting between the Annwfyn warriors and the Britons and describes an enigmatic incident where the dying Arthur gives an honour to his bard.

The Structure of the Book

It is a huge claim that Arthur explored eastern North America and was killed there. However, whether a claim outruns its evidence can only be determined by actually examining the evidence, which is discussed in detail in this book. If Arthur were 'the Bear' and 'Pharaoh' of Gildas, a powerful overking above the five kings, there is no reason to doubt that that he was able to make such a journey. The technological capabilities of these early seafarers have often been underestimated. In modern times, Tim Severin and his crewmen were able to sail in a small leather curragh from Ireland to North America.

This book sets out the case for Arthur leading an expedition to sixth-century North America and outlines his sphere of influence in Britain. The first chapter gives an overview of Arthur, the legends he accrued and the later romances which form our image of Arthur today. The second chapter gives the historical context based on Gildas and discusses Arthur's battle list from the *Historia Brittonum*.

The third chapter analyses medieval legends showing widespread beliefs that Arthur had discovered a land in the west Atlantic. In one of these legends Arthur settles Grocland (a land beyond Iceland), which probably means 'wild pasture land'. In his innovative wall-map of 1569, Mercator places Grocland close to Canada, to the west of Greenland. In Chapter 4, the sixth-century Native Americans are introduced, successors to the Hopewell culture, and the Hopewell earthworks and artifacts are described.

Chapters 5-9 deal with the three poems *Preideu Annwfyn*, *Kat Godeu* and *Kadeir Teÿrnon*. In each case, the poems are given in the unemended Welsh with an English translation. They reveal some astonishing facts about Arthur: his location in Britain, where he fought, his remarkable exploration of North America and how he died there.

Chapter 9 is devoted to dating the three poems. In *Preideu Annwfyn*, the bard's anger at the monks is evident in the last five of the eight stanzas, an emotional response to Gildas' insulting of the kings, bards and military. It is argued that the grieving bard returned to Britain after the Annwfyn disaster at the time that the slanders of Gildas were being discussed. This would date it to circa 540, the exact date depending on when Gildas wrote. This early date for *Preideu Annwfyn* is supported by a comparison with early Irish texts, whereby incidents or features in *Preideu Annwfyn* appear in the Irish texts in a modified form, either being misunderstood or elaborated, indicating that they were derived from *Preideu Annwfyn*.

Chapter 10 speculates on the expedition's route, both across the ocean and within America, based on clues from the poems. Chapter 11 re-examines the traditional evidence on Arthur and provides a new argument that the poetic reference to Arthur in Y Gododdin is unlikely to be a late interpolation and that the Arthurian stanza was probably composed in the mid-sixth century.

In Chapter 12, the home base and role of Arthur are discussed. Arthur is argued to have been a seafarer who from his north Wales site was able to easily reach harbours in southwest Scotland and the Solway Firth. *Kadeir Teÿrnon* calls him governor of *Rheon*, an obscure site identified with Loch Ryan in Galloway. This site is very close to Ireland, being the most direct way for the northern Irish to cross over to Britain. It suggests that Arthur's huge reputation in Scotland may have been won by his controlling the influx of the Irish into Britain. Gildas relates that the bloodthirsty Irish and Picts had at one time controlled northern Britain down to Hadrian's Wall.

In Chapter 13 Arthur's bard is tentatively identified as Talhaearn (Iron Brow) on the basis of placenames in north Wales, the main one being a few miles from Arthur's hillfort at Dinarth. From the *Historia Brittonum* list of bards Talhaearn seems to have been the leading bard, being called 'father of inspiration'. The theme of inspiration (*awen*) is also prominent in two of the Arthurian poems. Finally in Chapter 14, all the arguments are summarized.

It is intended that the book be accessible to a wide audience. Referencing uses the superscript to refer to a place in the end Notes so that the reader is not interrupted by intrusive references in the main text. The language is simple and direct and the arguments are logically organised into sections with headings to remove the tedium of reading large blocks of text. The key poetic text is given in the unemended Welsh with an English translation beneath. A discussion of the translation is then provided. In this way, every stage of the argument can be checked and evaluated. The book sheds new light on the enigmatic Arthur and investigates the exciting idea that he led a disastrous expedition to the eastern part of North America around the mid 530s and was killed there by the Native Americans.

1
OVERVIEW OF ARTHUR

AN EXPEDITION TO AMERICA IN WELSH POETRY

Three Ancient Welsh Poems

This book argues that King Arthur led an expedition to North America in the sixth century, perhaps in the mid 530s, and was killed there. The expedition was a disaster, with the fighting described as 'woeful conflict'. The Britons moved from camp to camp in the new country and encountered appalling difficulties. Eventually only a small number survived who were able to escape back to Britain. The disaster is described in an ancient Welsh poem, *Preideu Annwfyn* (The Spoils of Annwfyn) that has been fortunately preserved in the *Book of Taliesin*, whose 14th-century manuscript, Peniarth 2, is held in the National Library of Wales at Aberystwyth.[1] The mainstream view is that the poem is a fantasy in which Arthur sails to a Celtic Otherworld that is inhabited by fairy-like creatures and steals a magic cauldron, a quest where most of his men are killed. Beyond this summary, little is understood about the poem and the cryptic allusions within it. In this book, it will be shown that the fairy-tale interpretation of the poem is fundamentally incorrect and that Arthur's expedition to Annwfyn was real and that the mysterious Annwfyn can be identified with sixth-century America.

A second ancient Welsh poem in the *Book of Taliesin* called *Kat Godeu* (The Battle of the Trees) also contains a section on the voyage to Annwfyn. This enigmatic poem was composed by an old man, formerly a bard, who is recounting the most significant events of his life, among them his disastrous experiences in Annwfyn. The old bard describes ferocious fighting and the death of a lord he calls 'the boar', whom he reveres. The bard refers to the lord's last moments alive and how he died. It is argued in this book that the lord was Arthur.

A third early poem from the *Book of Taliesin* called *Kadeir Teÿrnon* (The Chair of the Sovereign) is set in the aftermath of Arthur's death. It refers to a eulogy for the dead Arthur and notes the fierce, battle-hardened qualities his successor will need. It also provides interesting information about Arthur's achievements and provides important clues to both his home location and a significant area where he fought.

These three poems, *Preideu Annwfyn*, *Kat Godeu* and *Kadeir Teÿrnon* have traditionally been thought to deal only with legendary or mythological material. It is argued here that this is a major misconception and that they contain important factual information. Never before have they been closely analysed from a historical perspective. They are interpreted and discussed in Chapters 5 to 8 and a variety of arguments suggesting an early dating are given in Chapter 9.

Sixth-Century America in the Ancient Poetry

The allusions from *Preideu Annwfyn* correlate remarkably well with what is known of sixth-century America. The expedition sails past a 'glass fortress', the same object as the 'glass tower in the middle of the sea' (*turrim vitream in medio mari*) in the related Latin work, the *Historia Brittonum* – that is, a large iceberg. An iceberg zone is present in the northern route from Britain to America, where the icebergs are conveyed down the coasts of Labrador and Newfoundland. In 1912, one of these icebergs travelling further south than expected, sank the Titanic.

From their northern route, the Britons probably entered the Gulf of St Lawrence and sailed partway up the St Lawrence River. It seems that Winter set in before they could travel far enough south and they endured a 'camp of extreme coldness', as Jacques Cartier did in the Winter of 1535-6. They seem to have reached Montreal, the 'four-peaked camp', with its four striking peaks – Mont Royal, Mont St-Bruno, Mont St-Hilaire and Mont Rougemont. At the time of the Britons' arrival in the sixth century, these peaks would certainly have dominated the campsite.

The expedition continued south, past the Great Lakes, and entered the area of the Eastern Woodlands where the Hopewell culture had built their most complex earthworks. Here the Britons encountered man-made earthen mounds at a place called *kaer sidi* in the poem, translated as 'mound fortress' by Sarah Higley.[2] The Hopewell had built numerous mounds enclosed by earthen walls in an extraordinary variety of geometric patterns. The bard refers to the capture of a 'cauldron' (a decorated clay pot) belonging to the Annwfyn inhabitants which was decorated with pearls. These had been used in abundance by the Hopewell, where one site alone produced about 100,000 freshwater pearls.[3] He comments on the bravery of the inhabitants, the owners of the cauldron, that 'it does not boil the food of a coward'.

Buffalo herds grazed along the rivers there and were still plentiful in the 1700s according to missionary David Zeisberger.[4] The bard was interested in these beasts unknown in Britain and notes their huge head and neck. He also states that the people had tamed an animal with a 'silvery head', an apt description of the North American river otter, whose head, chin and throat give a silvery sheen when the fur is wet. The focus on the 'head' probably stems from the bard watching it swimming where it holds its head above water. This otter was plentiful in the Eastern Woodlands and the inhabitants made very realistic carvings of it, often depicted carrying a fish in its mouth.

Numerous rivers and streams in the region allowed the Native Americans to travel freely in their canoes. Before the fighting began, the poetry describes them mustering for battle by means of the streams. Great conflict occurred near *kaer sidi*, with the bard vowing to pray until Judgement Day for one of his companions who had been captured. The poetry seems to give no further sign of progress by the Britons. It appears that they were nearly destroyed there by the conflict with the Native Americans. A small remnant survived to return to Britain.

That Arthur led an voyage to America almost 500 years before the Norse and nearly a millennium before Columbus seems extraordinary. However it was certainly possible for the shipping technology of the time, as indicated by the shipping knowledge provided in the *Etymologies* of Isidore of Seville. This information was probably written in the early 600s and thus would have been only about 80 years after Arthur's death.[5]

Indeed, over half a millennium before, Julius Caesar had expressed his admiration for the impressive ships of the Veneti of Brittany in his *Gallic War*.[6] The Britons had knowledge of these ships as they were allies of the Veneti and close contact with Brittany had been maintained in Arthur's day. Further, as will be later discussed, by Arthur's time there had probably been a number of journeys exploring the islands north of Britain which were the stepping stones to America.

The Current Views of Scholars

The idea of Arthur sailing to America is all the more astonishing in view of scepticism about his historical existence by modern scholars. Those willing to entertain his historical existence may say that, even if he existed, one can say little about him, a view expressed by Kenneth Jackson and Thomas Charles-Edwards.[7] Two important Arthurian texts, the battle-listing section of the *Historia Brittonum* (History of the Britons) and the *Annales Cambriae* (Welsh Annals) have been strongly criticised from a historical perspective. Further, it is now known that the *Annales* reference to Arthur's victory at Badon Hill is not independent of the *Historia* battle list, which reduces the value of the former.

Other scholars are more forthright in their rejection of Arthur, preferring the 'safe' procedure of relegating him to the 'legendary' category and omitting him from their histories.[8] One archaeologist, Nowell Myres, has stated that 'no figure on the border-line of history and mythology has wasted more of the historian's time.' The last occasion any historian argued that Arthur was a significant historical figure was in 1973, by John Morris, but he was severely criticised for his over-generalizations and his frequent use of late sources by David Dumville and others.[9]

Another level of rejecting an historical Arthur comes from those who think that he was originally a mythical folkloric figure or Celtic god who came to be thought of as historical; that is, he became 'historicized'. These views have been argued recently by Oliver Padel and Caitlin Green.[10] Such theories are heavily criticised in this book, as they tend to use very late texts to make their inferences about Arthur.

These sceptical views in the scholarly world may be a source of surprise to the general public who would assume that behind the legendary King Arthur lies a more primitive historical figure. In this book, the historical existence of Arthur as a powerful king and peerless battle commander is strongly argued and new information from the ancient Welsh poetry will be used to give a fuller picture of this enigmatic figure.

PORTRAYALS OF ARTHUR

Early Evidence for Arthur

Scholarly scepticism towards Arthur manifests in a more critical view of texts than formerly. Arthur appears as a heroic figure from the past in the Welsh poem *Y Gododdin* (The Gododdin). Scholars now tend to view this reference with scepticism and some list it as a possible late interpolation. In this book a new argument is presented that an interpolation is unlikely and that the reference is probably from the sixth century, perhaps within a few decades of Arthur's death.

Other references in the Welsh poems *Marwnad Cynddylan* (Deathsong of Cynddylan) and *Geraint son of Erbin* give a similar heroic view of Arthur. It is argued here that these are probably seventh century and eighth century respectively and support the heroic picture of Arthur given in *Y Gododdin* as a military paragon.

Further evidence for Arthur's historicity comes from the cluster of 'Arthur' names in the approximate period 560-600. The name 'Arthur' was almost unknown before this, a fact noted by Hector and Nora Chadwick. This sudden cluster of naming babies 'Arthur' in a short time period is hard to explain unless there was a hero of this name who had lived earlier in the sixth century or late fifth century.[11]

The *Historia Brittonum* of 829-30, a Latin text giving a list of Arthur's battles, has been heavily criticised as a historical source. Some claim that it is 'inadmissible evidence'. However, the battle list itself appears to derive from an underlying Welsh poem in which the battle names are part of the rhyming scheme. If so, then the general criticisms applied to the *Historia* would probably not affect this self-contained source. The existence of such a poem would suggest that Arthur was seen as a great military figure before the *Historia* was compiled.

This summary indicates that Arthur was viewed as a historical figure in the sixth century and up to the ninth century. It is discussed in more detail in later chapters. New evidence will also be presented from *Preideu Annwfyn*, *Kat Godeu* and *Kadeir Teÿrnon* which will substantially enlarge our view of Arthur's achievements.

The Accrual of Legends

In later centuries, Arthur's fame spread rapidly across Britain and overseas, as discussed by Rachel Bromwich and Caerwyn Williams.[12] The main text of the *Historia Brittonum* of 829-30 presents him in his familiar role as warrior and battle commander. However, he had begun to accrue legendary features. Our first evidence of these appears in two historically worthless marvels in the *Mirabilia* (Marvels) appendix to the *Historia*.[13] This accrual of legendary features was also occurring for Arthur's near contemporary, the historical Ambrosius. He was the Briton who initiated the fightback against the Anglo-Saxons. In the *Historia Brittonum* Ambrosius is portrayed as a boy wizard, born of a virgin mother, who prophesied the future. His identity with the historical Ambrosius is confirmed when he tells Vortigern that his father was a Roman consul.[14] This imagery was later used by Geoffrey of Monmouth to create his fictional character of Merlin.

In some of the later texts (from c. 1000 and onwards), Arthur's opponents include more exotic creatures, his fame being such that ordinary warriors were no longer considered sufficiently challenging. These texts, biased to the weird and exotic for entertainment value, have him fighting creatures such as witches, dogheads, giants and dragons.[15] Arthur had also become associated with features of the landscape: e.g. Arthur's Seat near Edinburgh; Arthur's Stone in Herefordshire. On the continent, the Arthurian tales were beginning to be elaborated with the familiar themes that we associate with him, as will be discussed later in this chapter.

Geoffrey of Monmouth

About 1138, Geoffrey of Monmouth completed an influential book entitled *History of the Kings of Britain* (Historia Regum Britanniae) in which Arthur was a dominant figure. However his pseudo-history resembles an historical novel, in which he uses historical data where he can, but also employs his imagination to tell an exciting story of the Britons from pre-Roman times to the time of the Saxon domination.

He maintains that he actually did not write it but merely translated from Welsh into Latin a book shown to him by Walter, Archdeacon of Oxford. Few believe him on this point. On the contrary, he appears to have been extremely diligent in gathering data from many sources and weaving it into his story. These included Gildas' *Ruin of Britain*, Bede's *Ecclesiastical History*, the *Historia Brittonum*, the *Annales Cambriae*, the *Book of Taliesin* poems, the Welsh prose tale *Culhwch and Olwen*, material from the *Lives* of the Welsh saints and Welsh genealogical data.[16]

Although he was able to get access to this data, he was often indifferent to its accuracy and he modified it when necessary to improve his story and to disguise his reliance on the known sources. His imaginative storytelling then gave the colour, excitement and detail that other sources lacked.

Merlin

After his *History*, Geoffrey also wrote a poem, *The Life of Merlin*. He created the composite character Merlin from a fusion of the boy wizard Ambrosius in the *Historia Brittonum* and a Scottish seer and wild man of the forest called Lailoken who, if he were historical, lived after Arthur's time.[17]

The main role of Merlin in the *History* was to change the shape of Uthyr Pendragon into that of Gorlois so that Uthyr can sleep with Gorlois' wife, Ygerna. From this union, based on magic and deception, Arthur was born. The exciting climax of the *History* was the glorious reign of Arthur and his battles against the Saxons, adventures in Gaul and his anachronistic battles against the Romans.

Popular imagery and Dark Ages reality

As Geoffrey lived in the twelfth century, his portrayal of Arthur has many twelfth-century features, bearing little resemblance to the primitive Arthur of 600 years earlier. Arthur's 'battle horsemen' of the Welsh Triads have become knights. Geoffrey also introduces the new ideal of chivalry into the court of Arthur which he places at Caerleon-on-Usk, an unlikely location. He portrays Arthur's court as the ultimate in refinement and sophistication.

Arthur's knights who were famed in battle wore their own unique colours on their livery and arms. Some womenfolk also wore the same colours to identify with the knights.[18] The imagery we have today of Arthur's knights comes from the twelfth and later centuries: the heavy armour, helmets with visors, large shields exhibiting the insignia of each knight, and the powerful lances for jousting.

In reality, Arthur's horsemen were much more primitively equipped and perhaps they did not even have stirrups. Lynn White estimates that stirrups did not appear in Western Europe until the early 700s, about 200 years after Arthur, while Wilfred Seaby and Paul Woodfield give a similar estimate for the appearance of stirrups in the Frankish cavalry across the Channel. How did the horsemen fight? Jenny Rowland argues that the Gododdin Britons (contemporaries of Arthur) may have mounted attacks from horseback, by throwing spears and then slashing with swords. Without stirrups this would have required great skill and agility.[19]

For body protection, some men may have had a lorica, a tough leather vest that was reinforced with metal. The wealthy possibly had helmets and chain-mail armour, the latter being laboriously constructed. Elite warriors probably had a spear, a sword and a shield, similar to the weapons of the Saxon king in the Sutton Hoo ship-burial, as discussed by Leslie Alcock. Their shields were probably round or oval, made from thick wooden boards, reinforced around the rim with iron or bronze mountings. At the centre of the shield was an iron boss. Swords were high-status items that were made by specialist craftsmen. They were probably like the Roman spatha, much smaller than the huge swords often depicted.[20]

Gerald of Wales' view

Despite the Uthyr Pendragon shapeshifting incident, and other improbable events in the *History*, Geoffrey generally kept his story within the bounds of believability so that it was accepted as an authentic history. However there were some critics, such as Gerald of Wales. Gerald in his *Journey through Wales* (1191) relates a story he heard about Geoffrey's *History*. A prophet, Meilyr, was plagued by evil spirits which he could actually see. He knew when a person spoke falsely, as he saw the demons leap onto the tongue of the liar and exult. To gain relief from these demons, a copy of St John's Gospel was placed on his bosom whereupon the demons would quickly flee. However when a copy of Geoffrey's *History* was placed there, the evil spirits would instantly return in great numbers and remain a longer time than usual on the body and the book. Such was Gerald's low opinion of the truthfulness of the pseudo-history of Geoffrey.[21]

Despite the dissent of a few, Geoffrey's pseudo-history was a great success and was believed as the true history of Britain for over four centuries, but its success tended to overwhelm more primitive Welsh traditions, making them conform with it. Hence the sources which have followed have been regarded as possibly 'tainted' by the overpowering success of Geoffrey's work.

This has led to a division of sources as pre-Galfridian (before Geoffrey) and post-Galfridian (after Geoffrey), Galfridus being the Latin for Geoffrey. The pre-Galfridian sources are more valued for the task of investigating the historical Arthur and will be the focus of study in this book.[22]

Familiar Additions to the Arthurian Story

Following Geoffrey's pseudo-history, later poets and writers continued the story, introducing the concepts we associate with Arthur today, these being non-historical.

The Round Table

In 1155 the Norman poet Wace wrote his verse history of Britain, *Roman de Brut*, basing it on Geoffrey's pseudo-history. He introduces the concept of King Arthur's Round Table, possibly derived from Breton legends. In the late thirteenth century, Edward I made a model of this fictional Round Table which was later painted by Henry VIII.[23] It now hangs in the Great Hall of Winchester Castle.

Lancelot

In France, Chrétien de Troyes composed a series of sublime works during the approximate period 1160-90 which added to the richness of the Arthurian tales.[24] In the poem *Lancelot: the Knight of the Cart*, he features Lancelot, a character he had briefly mentioned in his earlier works, *Erec and Enide* and *Cliges*.[25] This poem is the first to present the love affair between Guinevere and Lancelot. This is in contrast to Geoffrey of Monmouth's pseudo-history, written approximately 40 years earlier, in which the liaison was between Guinevere and Mordred.

Camelot

Contrary to popular beliefs, Arthur's magnificent court at Camelot was not historical, again being a creation of Chrétien de Troyes. It is mentioned in the *Lancelot* poem where the impressive court at Camelot is noted in a passing comment. Geoffrey of Monmouth had placed Arthur's court at Caerleon, and *Lancelot* does refer to Caerleon, but of course Camelot has now supplanted the latter in popular belief.

The common depiction of Arthur's residence as a massive stone castle is also not historical, such castles generally appearing from the time of William the Conqueror, the eleventh century, and later.[26]

The Holy Grail
Chrétien is the first to describe the Holy Grail (*Graal*) in his *Perceval*, a graal being a serving vessel. It was part of a mysterious procession observed by Arthur's knight, Perceval. The Graal was golden, with precious stones, and held a mass wafer which sustained the life of an old man, the Fisher King's father. About two decades later, around 1200, Robert de Boron wrote the poem *Joseph of Arimathea* in which he reinterpreted the Holy Grail as the cup shared at the Last Supper and used by Joseph (in the poem) to catch the blood of Christ at his crucifixion.[27]

Excalibur
Chrétien's *Perceval* had also described Arthur's knight Gawain carrying the sword *Escalibor* which later became Arthur's sword *Excalibur*. In the earlier Welsh tale *Culhwch and Olwen*, Arthur's sword is called *Caledfwlch*. This Welsh name parallels the Irish name, *Caladbolg*, the sword of Fergus mac Róich in *Táin Bó Cuailnge*, a tale from the early Ulster cycle of stories.[28]

The Sword in the Stone
Robert de Boron also wrote *Merlin* which gave the first account of Arthur pulling the sword from an anvil on top of a stone, the famous 'sword in the stone' tale.[29]

From the above outline it can be seen that many of the familiar elements of the Arthurian stories have no historical basis. While some may have derived from Welsh or Breton legends, their final form is the result of the creative energy of writers 600 or more years after the time of Arthur.

MEDIEVAL BELIEFS IN ARTHUR'S VOYAGES

In Geoffrey of Monmouth's Works
Although the proposition that King Arthur led an expedition to America may create astonishment, the idea was present from before the time of Geoffrey of Monmouth. America would not be discovered by Columbus for another three and a half centuries, but Geoffrey himself was aware of a tradition that Arthur had died in an unknown land over the seas. He was also aware of the *Annales Cambriae* tradition that Arthur had died in battle at Camlann, thought to be located in Britain. To incorporate these two incompatible traditions into his pseudo-history, he was forced into constructing a clumsy, contrived ending to Arthur's life. Instead of Arthur being killed at Camlann, Geoffrey described him as only severely wounded. He then inserted the 'death overseas' tradition by having the wounded Arthur being taken on an improbable long sea voyage to a place he called Avalon.

In 1150 Geoffrey expanded on this theme in his poem, *The Life of Merlin* (Vita Merlini), where he links this Avalon voyage to one taken by the sixth-century Irish saint, Brendan the Navigator, in the *Navigatio*. Several authors have suggested that Brendan's sea voyages could have included a journey to America or reflect general knowledge of such a journey.[30] Geoffrey links the Avalon voyage to the Brendan voyage through the character Barinthus who in the *Navigatio* had sailed west over the Atlantic to an unknown land. When Barinthus told Brendan of this new land, Brendan then resolved to sail there himself. In his *Life of Merlin*, Geoffrey has Barinthus as the crewman who guided Arthur's ship to Avalon, implying that Avalon was the same place as that reached by Brendan.

A Source from Holland

Other material from Europe that is apparently independent of Geoffrey's source, indicates that people thought that Arthur had discovered a new land in the northwest Atlantic. This material was assembled in the 1500s by John Dee, mathematician, astrologer and adviser to Queen Elizabeth I. It was used in a political context to encourage Elizabeth to claim possession of parts of North America, citing several British explorations, which included those of Arthur and Brendan.

It has not been taken seriously by most scholars. However, the use of this material in a political context does not necessarily invalidate its truth. Dee did not manufacture it. His friend, the celebrated cartographer, Mercator, unearthed an account of Arthur's sea voyages in the northwest Atlantic. It came from Jacob Cnoyen who lived in Holland. Mercator sent this account to Dee in a letter dated 1577, the letter being translated and discussed in 1956 by Eva Taylor.[31]

The material contains extracts from a lost source *Gestae Arthuri* (Deeds of Arthur), outlining two Arthurian voyages that ventured to Iceland, then possibly beyond Greenland to an unknown land called *Grocland*. Mercator places Grocland to the west of Greenland in his famous wall-map. James Enterline convincingly argues that Grocland means 'wild pasture' land, which would probably exclude Greenland.[32] In documents presented to Elizabeth in August 1578, Dee argues that around AD 530 King Arthur led an expedition to North America.[33]

A Source from Northern Europe

Dee also presented Arthurian material that had been published in 1568 by William Lambarde in his *Archaionomia*. This material appears to originate from northern Europe. It contains a long *Northern Lands List* comprising 16 countries or areas (plus many other unnamed lands) outside Britain which were under Arthur's dominion. This list includes Norway, Iceland, Greenland and a place called (in Latin) Wynelandiam that Lynette Muir equates with Vinland.[34] By circa 1000, the Norse had reached Vinland, located in North America, probably south of the Gulf of St Lawrence. Vinland's existence was known to some scholars from its mention in Adam of Bremen's *History of the Archbishops of Hamburg-Bremen* (i.e. Gesta Hammaburgensis Ecclesiae Pontificum), written around 1075.

It is argued in Chapter 3 that the *Northern Lands List* preceded Geoffrey of Monmouth, which would give a northern European source untainted by his pseudo-history. Moreover, it is argued that Geoffrey actually borrowed from the *Northern Lands List* to create his own account of Arthur conquering some northern lands, including Iceland. Further, it is argued that this list probably provided the justification for Geoffrey's rather puzzling statement that Arthur had conquered 30 kingdoms.[35]

All these sources will be discussed in detail in Chapter 3. Unfortunately, the 'death overseas' tradition used by Geoffrey and the other two sources are of unknown provenance and appear at too late a stage. By themselves, they can't be used to develop a case that Arthur reached America. However all these sources seemingly from Wales, Holland and northern Europe give a similar picture, that Arthur was thought to have explored distant, unknown lands in the Atlantic, a fact that itself requires explanation.

DATING THE THREE WELSH POEMS

The key data for the argument that Arthur reached America comes from the three Welsh poems *Preideu Annwfyn*, *Kat Godeu* and *Kadeir Teÿrnon*. It is argued that these poems were composed in the sixth century and had their language progressively updated over the centuries, as the language evolved from Neo-Brittonic to Old Welsh to Middle Welsh. Given their content, it is probable that they were composed by Arthur's bard and thus give eyewitness accounts of what happened in Annwfyn.[36] Hence Chapter 9 which attempts to date these poems is one of the most important in the book.

The dating of *Preideu Annwfyn* is primarily based on fitting the content of the poem into the historical context. About AD 540, a British cleric named Gildas wrote a malicious work, *The Ruin of Britain*, in which he slandered the British kings, their bards and the military. This book created a poisonous atmosphere between the monks and the bards.

Arthur's bard was one of the few survivors of Annwfyn and returned to Britain grieving for his king and his brave comrades who had been killed in the disastrous expedition. He composed *Preideu Annwfyn* as a tribute to the dead Arthur but his anger at the monks was unleashed in the poem, where he called them 'little men' and cowards, attacking them in the last five of the eight stanzas. Therefore the poem's date would be shortly after *The Ruin of Britain* was being widely disseminated. If Gildas wrote in approximately 540, then *Preideu Annwfyn* was composed not long after.

A second approach to dating *Preideu Annwfyn* compares certain features in the poem to similar features in five early Irish works and an incident in the early Latin work, *Historia Brittonum*. These features appear in the other works in a way that suggests the source is *Preideu Annwfyn*. They are either misunderstood, or taken literally where a metaphor was given, or elaborated (often in a cartoonish manner). In addition, the *Kat Godeu* poem describes an incident that appears to have been copied in the early Irish poem *Dún Scáith*, implying that *Kat Godeu* was the earlier.

A third approach to dating notes the remnants of archaic language in the three poems, particularly *Preideu Annwfyn* and *Kat Godeu*. These linguistic features were identified by leading Celtic scholars John Koch and Marged Haycock. They are suggestive rather than conclusive, as archaic language can persist in poetry long after it has generally died out and also may have been deliberately used by poets to strike an archaic note.[37]

Each poem appears to be in the voice of Arthur's bard, suggesting that his bard composed all three. A series of pairwise comparisons is conducted, that shows the features in common between pairs of poems. Although this type of approach can hardly be conclusive, it does indicate sufficient commonality to suggest the hypothesis of a common poet is not unreasonable.

Concluding Comments

The case for Arthur leading an expedition to America is primarily based on the three Welsh poems. It is therefore vital to the argument that these poems were early, as part of the *Cynfeirdd* poetry that was composed by the first or earliest poets. If it could be firmly established that the poems were composed hundreds of years after the time of Arthur, then the case made in this book would be gravely weakened. However if a plausible case can be made that they were composed in the sixth century, and modernised as the language evolved, then the central questions of Arthur's historicity and achievements should be reconsidered.

In this book the arguments derived from the poetry will be presented directly: the old poetry will be given in the unemended Welsh followed by an English translation. The meaning of each translated line will be discussed and, where relevant, related to the hypotheses being considered. The rival hypotheses will also be discussed and their relative merits evaluated. Where the latter material would overload the text or obscure the argument, it will be presented in the Notes appendix. The aim is to present the evidence as clearly as possible to facilitate study by scholars and the general reader.

It is argued that if one is prepared to put aside an emotional response and study the evidence with a cool-minded rationality, then there is a convincing body of data supporting the proposition that Arthur did voyage to America and was killed there. This poetic evidence also supports the traditional view of Arthur, that he was a powerful king and was renowned as an unsurpassed battle commander.

2
HISTORICAL CONTEXT FOR ARTHUR

THE POST-ROMAN PERIOD

The Britons

Arthur probably lived during the late fifth and the early sixth centuries in a period formerly known as the Dark Ages, a term that vividly indicates the scarcity of reliable contemporary written sources. The period has also been termed post-Roman Britain, sub-Roman Britain and the Brittonic Age.[1] It was a turbulent time, when the Britons were under threat from various foreign peoples: the Irish, the Picts and a newer threat, the Anglo-Saxons. The term 'Briton' had a different meaning in this context than it does today. The Britons were the Celtic-speaking peoples who had inhabited Britain from before the time of Christ.[2] They were organised into tribes, each with their own king, and spoke a common Celtic language, *British*, which was an Indo-European language with close ties to Latin.[3]

In AD 43 the Britons began to lose political control of the island when the Romans invaded under Claudius. When they came under Roman control, the British kings lost their power and Latin became the language of government and administration. Their Celtic language, British, lost prestige. It was almost certainly not a written language during this period but remained the spoken language of the people in their home life, as argued by eminent Celtic linguist Kenneth Jackson.[4]

The Romans kept control of Britain for about three and a half centuries, eventually leaving by 410 to defend their crumbling empire on the continent. With the Romans gone, Britain came increasingly under attack from the Picts and the Irish. But the main threat to their future lay elsewhere. A significant number of Anglo-Saxons had been settling in Britain from near the beginning of the fifth century, but at some point more were officially invited over as mercenaries to help fight the Picts and the Irish. Eventually they revolted against the Britons, being continually reinforced from their European homelands, and threatened to take over the island. Such is the traditional view of the Saxon takeover.

Traditional Dates for Arthur

Arthur has been dated by two references in a set of annals, known as the *Annales Cambriae* (that is, the Welsh Annals), which comprised part of the Harleian 3859 manuscript in the British Library. These annals do not have AD dates – they have to be calculated, as will be shown below. In Year 72 of the annals, Arthur is said to have been the victor at the Battle of Badon, a battle mentioned by Gildas. In Year 93, Arthur is said to have died with Medraut (Mordred) at the Battle of Camlann.

To convert these annal dates to the AD dates, Year 9 (when the annals record Pope Leo changing the date for Easter) can be equated to AD 455, the known date for this event.[5] In this scheme, Year 72 becomes AD 518 (Badon) and Year 93 then becomes AD 539 (Arthur's death). However this equating scheme gives datings for some later events in the annals which are two years too late which could then imply an alternative equating of 516 for Badon Hill and 537 for Arthur's death.[6] Hence the date of Badon is often written as 516/518 and Arthur's death as 537/539, as approximations for these events. These key dates have been heavily contested by scholars, most regarding them as later estimations retrospectively inserted into the annals, rather than a contemporaneous recording of events against a given year.

GILDAS: THE RUIN OF BRITAIN

The main source for this period is a fascinating work in Latin by a Briton called Gildas. Its title is *The Ruin of Britain*, in Latin, *De Excidio Britanniae*. It is unique, being the only surviving account of sixth-century Britain written by an eyewitness. Gildas was a British cleric whose writings became highly influential in the church. He states that he delayed writing his work for ten years and that many others in the church with similar critical views to him had urged him to write it. He provides a blatantly one-sided account of the shortcomings of his fellow Britons, detailing the sins of five contemporary kings (about whom he was very well informed), and referring to the British warriors as cowardly on the one hand, but constantly waging war amongst themselves on the other. He also berates the British clergy for their ungodly way of living.[7]

The Ruin of Britain was not primarily written as history, but it does have a 'historical' section which is somewhat inaccurate, but which presumably becomes more accurate as it approaches Gildas' time. It covers the history of Britain from early Roman times, based mostly on foreign works and the oral traditions of Britain, as Gildas indicates that any British written material had either been burnt by their enemies or removed overseas when the Britons fled the country, in particular to Brittany.

Time of Writing

According to the dates in the *Annales Cambriae*, Gildas should have been a younger contemporary of Arthur. His date of writing is not known but is often taken as circa 540, as indicated by John Morris. A date in the quarter from 525 to 550 is estimated by David Dumville. A possible upper limit of 540 may apply, as Michael Baillie identifies severe environmental conditions from 540 to 545 where the trees were affected, their rings showing minimal growth, as will be discussed in a later chapter. Given his providential view of history, Gildas could have referred to this as a chastisement from God, but apparently he does not mention it, suggesting that he may have written a little earlier than 540.[8]

He died in 570 according to the *Annales Cambriae* and states that he was writing at age 44. Assuming these details are correct, if Gildas wrote c. 540, then he was born around 496 and died aged 74 in 570. These values are not unreasonable. Gildas probably wrote not far from the 537/539 death date of Arthur.[9] If Arthur existed as a historical figure, Gildas would surely have known about him. Yet he does not mention him explicitly and does not credit him with the decisive victory at Badon, as later works do, such as the *Historia Brittonum* and the *Annales Cambriae*. This point will be discussed in detail in a later chapter.

Location

The most interesting and accurate part of the book is the attack by Gildas on five contemporary kings, whom he personally addresses. In blistering prose he excoriates the kings, lashing them for their sins and urging them to repent. The kings (or tyrants, as he prefers to call them) are all located in south west Britain which gives a clue to Gildas' location – Constantine from Dumnonia (Devon/Cornwall); Vortipor from Demetia in southwest Wales; Cuneglasus from north Wales; Maglocunus, probably from the island of Anglesey in north west Wales, and Aurelius 'Caninus', perhaps from the old British kingdom called Powys.

Gildas seems remarkably well informed about these kings, listing many vivid details about their personal lives, their marriages, family and even their appearance (for example, that the hair of Vortipor was starting to whiten), but he writes nothing about the kings in the north of Britain. He also writes with the perspective of someone from the south – he refers to the Picts as being in the north of Britain (Section 14) and as being in the far end of the island (Section 21). As the Saxons controlled large parts of southeast Britain it appears that he lived in southwest Britain (possibly in Wales) but after his publication probably lived at a location where he could not be found by the kings, possibly overseas. Alternatively, Gildas may have written in hiding by perhaps using a false name, as 'Gildas' does not appear to be British or any other language, as discussed by Patrick Sims-Williams.[10]

Threats from the Irish and Picts

The Ruin of Britain relates that for many years before Arthur's time, Britain was being terrorised by raiding from the north. One threat was from the Scotti, Irish people from the Dál Ríata clan in the north of Ireland who had been raiding across the Irish Sea. Over time, they settled in the Argyll area in western Scotland, there founding the kingdom of Dalriada. Eventually they became the Scots, giving their name to Scotland. A second threat came from the Picts (the painted ones) who had settled mainly in central and east Scotland, north of the Firth of Forth. These threats had been occurring during the time of Roman occupation, but the disciplined Roman soldiers had kept them in check. Gildas states that after the Romans left, the Irish and the Picts had at one stage captured northern Britain down to Hadrian's Wall (*The Ruin of*

Britain, Section 19.1). There had also been Irish incursions from the Déisi, a people from southeast Ireland, who had settled in north Wales and in south west Wales. The *Historia Brittonum* (Section 62) describes how Cunedda and his sons, Britons from the Manau Gododdin region in southern Scotland (around modern Stirling), had moved to north Wales to expel the Irish there. David Dumville and Geraint Gruffydd provide quite contrasting discussions on the historical validity of this event.[11]

Vortigern hires Saxon Mercenaries

The Romans had left Britain by 410, with Rome itself being sacked in that year by the Visigoths led by Alaric. The terrifying raids of the Picts and the northern Irish continued. In Section 23, Gildas gives a fascinating historical account of how the Saxons came to Britain. The earliest manuscript of *The Ruin of Britain* in which this story survives was written in the 900s at St Augustine's, Canterbury. Gildas refers three times to the British overking, whom he does not name but calls 'arrogant tyrant', 'Pharaoh' and 'ill-fated tyrant'. In two of Bede's works and later manuscripts of *The Ruin of Britain*, the proud tyrant is called Vortigern, a name meaning 'overlord'.[12] Faced with threats from the Picts and Irish, Vortigern consulted his advisers and decided to bring in paid fighters from the continent, the Saxons, to help control the northern invaders. To Gildas, this was insane. He remarks: 'How desperate and crass the stupidity! Of their own free will they invited under the same roof a people whom they feared worse than death'.[13] The Saxons were settled on the east side of the island and were given supplies by the Britons, which initially satisfied them.

The Saxon Revolt

Over time, the Saxons were reinforced by more fighters arriving from their homelands. It is usual to use the generic terms, Anglo-Saxons or Saxons (as will be used here), to describe the invaders from the continent, although they can be differentiated into distinct peoples. To the Saxon priest Bede, writing 200 years after Gildas, there were three main groupings: the Saxons (from northern Germany), the Angles (from central and lower Denmark), and the Jutes (from the Jutland peninsula in Denmark). At the time of the initial Saxon settlements, this differentiation into ethnic groups would have been of little consequence to the Britons.

After an indeterminate 'long time' the Saxons began to complain that their provisions were insufficient and deliberately set out to provoke discord with the Britons, threatening to plunder the whole island unless they received more lavish payment. The Saxons were soon in revolt and thus the Britons were now faced with fighting the Picts, the Irish and the Saxons.

Gildas vividly presents the conflict between the Britons and the Saxons in dramatic and lurid terms. He describes the Saxons smashing the walls of towns with battering rams, the crackling of flames as buildings burned, and the mangled bits of corpses with congealed blood, looking as though they had been through a wine-press. Many bodies were not buried but were left in the ruins of buildings or were eaten by animals and birds. Some Britons fled to the mountains and were finally captured and then ruthlessly slaughtered by the Saxons. Others, desperate from hunger, had offered themselves as slaves. Still others fled overseas by boat, in particular to the Brittany region across the Channel.[14]

The Fightback by the Britons

Eventually the Britons fought back, led by Ambrosius Aurelianus, a Briton who had rallied his countrymen and won an initial victory. Typically, Gildas did not give any credit to the Britons for this fightback, but emphasised the Roman characteristics of Ambrosius. Gildas described him as a 'gentleman' who almost alone of the Romans had survived the initial onslaught of the Saxons. However, his parents had been killed. They are described as having 'worn the purple', presumably referring to their aristocratic Roman heritage. Gildas points out that the descendants of Ambrosius, at the time of writing, were greatly inferior to him, their illustrious ancestor. It is clear that Gildas greatly admired Ambrosius, from the detail he gives on his background and the fact that Ambrosius is the only Briton named from the fifth century in the main manuscript of his work.[15]

Victory at Badon Hill

From the time of this significant victory, both sides had mixed fortunes as victory went first to one side and then the other. In this period of inconclusive battles, Gildas refers to God as making a trial for the Britons, a period in which their faith in God is being tested. It seems that a considerable time elapsed during this trial period, for two reasons. The first is that for God's trial to completely test the Britons' faith (in the eyes of Gildas), an extended period of time would be required. The second is that the Saxons would not be likely to withdraw before making protracted attempts to establish their own territories. Eventually the Britons won a decisive victory at the siege of Badon Hill which ushered in an extended period of peace, free from Saxon harassment, at least on the western side of the island. In later texts, the *Historia Brittonum* and *Annales Cambriae*, this victory is attributed to Arthur, but Gildas does not name the victor.

An Extended Peace

The extended period of peace which followed the British victory at Badon Hill eventually led to complacency among the Britons. When under external threat from the Saxons, everyone had kept to their 'own stations', but this generation died off and was replaced by a new one that had known mainly peace. Over time, the Britons fell into a state of complacency, corruption and sin. Brutal civil wars had replaced external wars, with the Britons launching plundering raids against their neighbours. This was the setting for Gildas writing *The Ruin of Britain*, in which he launched an intemperate attack on almost everything British, the kings, their bards, the warriors and the clergy. John Koch refers to it as 'the bias of the one-dimensional misanthrope'.[16] It is argued that the furore created by *The Ruin of Britain* was the setting for the composition of *Preideu Annwfyn*, the poem being a counterattack against the monks by Arthur's bard who was still grieving over the loss of Arthur and his comrades in Annwfyn.

At this time, around AD 540, Britain was partitioned. A large part of south east and eastern central Britain was under Saxon control, as shown by the distribution of Anglo-Saxon cemeteries. Nonetheless, as Kenneth Dark has argued, Saxon control of these areas may have been very uneven, with large regions within Saxon territory where Britons predominated.[17] Outside this patchy area, the Britons controlled the southwest, Wales, the west midlands and northern England/southern Scotland.

This account, based on Gildas, does not discuss the many problems and uncertainties concerning the timing of the Saxons' arrival, their numbers, and how they managed to dominate. A discussion showing the diversity of views on these and other issues is provided in the Notes.[18]

ARTHUR'S BATTLES IN THE HISTORIA BRITTONUM

Background to the Historia

Where does Arthur fit into the above context? He is placed in a historical setting, victorious in twelve battles, in the *Historia Brittonum*, a Latin work written in 829-30. About 40 manuscripts still survive today. There are eight recensions, each one comprising a family of related manuscripts. The most comprehensive recension is the Harleian, of which the key manuscript is MS Harleian 3859, which is held in the British Library. The *Historia* has long been attributed to Nennius, a cleric writing from north Wales, but the careful research of leading historian David Dumville has shown the attribution to Nennius to be lacking in foundation.[19]

In the first half of the 20th century, scholars sought to use the *Historia* as a prime source for the events of the fifth, sixth and seventh centuries. But now, following the studies of Dumville from the late 1960s, the text is viewed sceptically as a possible source. Robert Hanning calls it a 'dangerous text from which to draw conclusions about actual happenings of British history'. Dumville thinks that the *Historia* is a synchronising history, a type of work in which the author attempts to combine all material (however contradictory) into a coherent official whole, and considers that it was written in a uniform latinity. He regards it as being of little historical value for events from the fifth to the seventh centuries.[20]

In total contrast, Wendy Davies describes it as 'an ill-synthesized and ill-digested work' and concludes that it is not possible to generalize about its value. Other scholars such as Kenneth Jackson, John Koch and Peter Field also appear to have taken a less pessimistic view of the worth of the *Historia* than Dumville.[21]

As will be argued below, the Arthurian section appears to be mostly a self-contained unit (apart from its introduction), probably deriving from a Welsh praise poem which lists Arthur's battles.

The Battle List

Harleian recension

In the Harleian recension, Arthur's battles appear in Section 56, where the role of Arthur is described in the context of the growing threat presented by the Saxons. The following translation records Arthur's battles in point form for greater clarity:

> Then Arthur fought against them in those days, along with the kings of the Britons, although he was the leader in battle.
>
> - The first battle was at the mouth of the river which is called Glein.
> - The second, and third, and fourth, and fifth were on another river which is called Dubglas, and is in the region of Linnuis.
> - The sixth battle was on the river which is called Bassas.
> - The seventh battle was in the forest of Celidon, that is Cat Coit Celidon.
> - The eighth battle was at the fortress of Guinnion, in which Arthur carried the image of Saint Mary, perpetual virgin, on his shoulders, and the pagans were put to flight on that day, and there a was great slaughter of them through the power of our Lord Jesus Christ and the power of the holy Virgin Mary, his mother.
> - The ninth battle was fought in the City of the Legion.
> - The tenth battle was fought on the bank of the river which is called Tribruit.
> - The eleventh battle occurred on the mount which is called Agned.
> - The twelfth battle was on mount Badon, where in one day there fell 960 men to one assault of Arthur; and no one felled them except he alone, and in all the battles he was the victor.

In a different family of manuscripts, the Vatican recension, the *Agned* battle is replaced by another name, the variants being Breguoin, Breuoin, Bregion and Bregomion. Kenneth Jackson convincingly argues on linguistic grounds that Breguoin was Bremenium, a former Roman camp. This site is at High Rochester in Northumberland, not far from the Scottish border. Bregion, which is mentioned as *Cat Bregion*, appears to be a gloss giving an alternative name for the battle at Breguoin.

Jackson can find no sensible derivation or meaning for Agned, which may be a corruption. Geoffrey of Monmouth identified Agned with Edinburgh but this has received little support. The Vatican recension also differs from the Harleian in some other Arthurian details, one of which implies that Arthur had a pedigree that was undistinguished.[22]

The Poetic Origin of the Battle List

Although the *Historia Brittonum* has been heavily criticised, the Arthurian section may be unaffected by these general criticisms as it seems to derive from a single source. There is evidence that the battle list, which is written in Latin in the *Historia*, was derived from a Welsh battle-listing poem, an idea first proposed by Hector and Nora Chadwick.[23] As shown below, there are several reasons for supporting the Chadwicks' proposal.

The terseness of the information

This list has an obvious late embellishment about the Virgin Mary, possibly from the late 700s/early 800s. The Badon battle is also embellished with hyperbole on Arthur's heroism, but the only 'data' given is the site and the number killed. If one disregards these elaborations, the list is terse, giving little data on the battles apart from their names and a geographical setting. It is typical of the sparse data generally derived from Welsh poetry, which by its nature is succinct and tends to dwell briefly on particular elements before moving on to the next.

Poetic exaggeration of numbers killed

The 960 men killed by Arthur would sound like an extreme exaggeration if written in a prose document. It can be rationalised by arguing that these were the total number slain by the whole of Arthur's army, with the total being attributed to Arthur alone. While this is not impossible, the battle list is more likely to have come from a poem where exaggerated figures of the opponents killed were made in praising the heroes. In the northern poem, *Y Gododdin*, Hyfaidd killed 250 men, while Neithon's son killed a hundred gold-torqued chieftains. In *Kat Godeu*, the warrior bard claims that he slew 900 picked warriors. Further, the number 3 and its multiples were often used in poetry ($960 = 3 \times 3 \times 100 + 3 \times 20$). The claim that Arthur slew 960 men is much more likely to have come from a Welsh poem praising him.

Welsh poem with rhyming battle names

There is some linguistic evidence suggesting an underlying Welsh poem. In his 1949 paper, Kenneth Jackson is adamant: 'All through these names, Nennius is obviously translating Welsh phrases into Latin', while in a later work in 1959 he remarks that the phrase '*in ostium fluminis Glein*' is not a natural Latin expression, and hence is presumably derived from rendering its Welsh equivalent ('*in oper Glein*') into Latin. He also provides three other examples where in each case it is probable that the Latin expression was a translation of the Welsh.[24]

In 1964, an important paper of eminent Welsh scholar Thomas Jones was published in English. Jones suggests that the battle names might reflect the rhyming scheme of a Welsh poem.[25] Further, as has long been recognized, it is probable that the poem mentioned a shield (*scuit*), which would have rhymed with the battle at *Tribruit*. Shields are mentioned extensively in the early poetry. The reference to Arthur's shoulders (*scuid*) in the eighth battle is incongruous and may derive from a confusion with shield (*scuit*) in the poem. David Dumville states that the poem must have been in the form of a written source when the confusion occurred.[26]

This issue will be later discussed concerning the *Annales Cambriae* where the same confusion between *scuit* and *scuid* has arisen. Ignoring other words that could have been part of the rhyme, the rhyming scheme for the poem may have included the following elements:

Dubglas / Bassas
Celidon / Guinnion / scuit / Legion / Tribruit / Bregion / Badon.

That is:

A / A
B / B / C / B / C / B / B.

Other battle-listing poems honouring kings
In the *Book of Taliesin*, battle-listing poems (thought to be sixth century by Ifor Williams) honour the British kings Cynan Garwyn, Urien Rheged and Gwallawg. They are *Trawsganu Kynan Garwyn* (Praise for Cynan Garwyn), *Ardwyre Reget* (Rheged Arise) and an untitled poem on Gwallawg, Poem 11 in Williams' book on Taliesin.[27] These kings were from the sixth century, as was Arthur. It is thus possible that the underlying poem about Arthur could have derived from the sixth century. However this cannot be established. The *Historia* battle names do not have any pre-Old Welsh features but this is not surprising as it was compiled in 829-30 in the Old Welsh period.

It appears that the *Historia* compiler did not know the location of many of the battle names. For the battles at Glein, Dubglas, Bassas, Tribruit and Agned, he uses language such as 'which is called' in contrast to expressions like 'was at/in/on...' which suggests that the places were unfamiliar to him, probably because their names were no longer in use. It may suggest that the poem was considerably earlier than the compilation date of 829-30. It is not impossible that it was orally composed in Neo-Brittonic before later being modernised into a written form of Old Welsh and finally converted to prose. The hypothesis of an underlying battle catalogue poem has been given wide acceptance, being supported by a number of eminent scholars.[28]

Implications
The fact that Badon rhymes with four of the other battles suggests that it was originally in the poem and was not an interpolation; that is, the poet himself attributed victory at Mount Badon to Arthur and this attribution preceded the compilation of the *Historia Brittonum*. Therefore it is unlikely that the anonymous compiler of the *Historia* found the battle of Badon in Gildas and for political reasons attributed it to Arthur.[29] It also indicates that there was

a tradition (prompting the poem) which preceded the *Historia Brittonum*, portraying Arthur as a victorious battle commander, famous for his many victories.[30]

Battle Locations
Plausible identifications

An authoritative discussion of the battle locations is given in three papers by Kenneth Jackson and a more recent paper by Peter Field.[31] In general, an identification with any modern place names is difficult. Jackson sums up his linguistic analysis by giving the most probable identifications – the City of the Legion is Chester and the wood of Celidon is the well known forest of British tradition in southern Scotland, apparently within easy reach of both Carlisle and Glasgow. As discussed earlier, Jackson identifies Bregion with *Bremenium*, which is High Rochester in northern England.

The river name *Dubglas* means 'blue-black' (water), which could survive under a number of variants, including Douglas, Dawlish, Dowlish, Dulas and so on. However the region where the four battles were stated to be fought, *Linnuis*, is the former British kingdom of Lindsey, located around Lincoln as argued by Caitlin Green. It was probably lost to the Saxons by the late sixth century.[32] Although there are no rivers there now with a *Dubglas* equivalent, Bernard Bachrach suggests the Humber river as a possibility, noting that it was long ago called *Umbri maris* in the *Historia Brittonum* of 829-30. It is possible that the author of the battle poem rendered the Humber name by the Welsh *dubglas* (with its black component) due to the Latin word *umbra* (shadow, darkened place).[33]

Unidentified locations

Of the other battles in the *Historia*, *Glein* means 'pure or clear' (water) and may survive today under the name 'Glen'. There are rivers of this name in Northumbria and Lincolnshire which are possibilities, particularly the latter one. *Bassas* is unfortunately quite obscure, while the fortress of *Guinnion* seems to mean the 'stronghold of the white people' according to Kenneth Jackson.[34] This would suggest a realistic but non-specific description for a battle site with the fair-skinned Anglo-Saxons. The river *Tribruit* is currently unidentified but it appears as an independent reference in *Pa Gûr*, a later Welsh poem. It may well be a genuine Arthurian battle.

Badon

The site of Badon, named by Gildas, unfortunately remains elusive. It was equated with Bath by Geoffrey of Monmouth in c. 1138 and in modern times Bath has been advocated by several scholars, but there is no universal agreement.[35] Jackson suggests that Badon was at one of the Badbury hills located near Faringdon (Oxfordshire), or Swindon (Wiltshire) or Blandford (Dorset), while Peter Field thinks that it was in the border region between Wales and England, possibly centred around Gloucester.[36]

The 516/518 dating has also been contested, with many scholars believing it was fought a few decades earlier.[37]

Distribution of the battles
These battles are widely distributed over Britain. They suggest that Arthur was an overking with considerable resources and manpower, consistent with the *Historia Brittonum* statement that he fought alongside other British kings but was the overall battle commander. It was demonstrated by Kenneth Jackson that other Dark Age kings (notably the seventh-century Cadwallon) fought battles that ranged widely across Britain.[38] The battle sites strongly suggest that Arthur's opponents were not just the Anglo-Saxons. If genuine, the Caledonian Forest battle in southern Scotland may have been against the Irish. In later chapters, it will be shown that Arthur was very active in the Galloway area of Scotland. The High Rochester battle, north of Hadrian's Wall, may have been against advancing Picts. It seems to be rather early for a significant Saxon presence to have been in that region in Arthur's time. However, the Lincolnshire sites are very plausible ones for clashes with the encroaching Anglo-Saxons.

Summary
There is no universal agreement on the location of the most famous battle, Badon, although Bath has received some support. Arthur's battle locations seem to be widely dispersed, consistent with the viewpoint that he was an overking who could mobilize his manpower to wherever they were needed. Arthur's most plausible battle locations are listed below:

City of the Legion	=	Chester
Coit Celidon	=	Forest in southwest Scotland
Dubglas in Linnuis	=	Four battles in Lindsey (Lincoln)
Bregion	=	High Rochester, Northumberland.

It is of great interest that the *Historia* placed four of the battles in Lindsey around Lincoln and possibly a fifth, if the river Glen in Lincolnshire was intended. This is where one would expect Arthur to have fought against the Saxons. It would appear that the *Historia*'s source, the underlying poem, is conveying valid information that may not have been at all obvious to the anonymous compiler writing 300 years after the battles.

LANGUAGE CHANGE: BRITISH TO NEO-BRITTONIC

It will be argued in Chapter 9 that *Preideu Annwfyn*, *Kat Godeu* and *Kadeir Teÿrnon* were composed in the sixth century and then later modernised as the language changed over the centuries. This section will outline important changes that were occurring in the language of the Britons. It may surprise the layperson that Arthur would not have spoken English, no matter how primitive. The English language did not exist in his time but eventually developed out of the Germanic language brought over by the Anglo-Saxons.

The *British* language (as distinct from English) was an Indo-European language with quite close affinities to Latin. It had been changing over the centuries as a result of the Roman occupation and had continued to change during Arthur's lifetime. By the time of Arthur's adult years it had probably dropped its final unstressed syllables in polysyllabic words and also dropped certain unstressed vowels between consonants, with the consonants tending to be softened (lenited). For example, Ifor Williams discusses the British word for 'tenth', *decametos*. In pronouncing this word, the stress was on the penultimate syllable, *met*. As time passed, the final *os* was dropped and the *a* preceding the stressed *met* was also dropped, giving *decmet*. Eventually, the consonants softened to arrive at *degfed* in Modern Welsh.[39]

At the point at which the final unaccented syllables and medial vowels were lost, British had changed to what Kenneth Jackson labelled *Primitive Welsh*. This date of transition is now estimated to be around 500, or a little later. Despite the name being *Primitive Welsh*, this language was not just confined to Wales, but was spoken by Britons all over what is now England and southern Scotland. To account for this oddity, the term *Neo-Brittonic* is used which removes the specific reference to Wales.[40] The languages that emerged from Neo-Brittonic (Welsh, Cornish, Breton) had not yet become differentiated - it was in effect just one language, but with probable regional dialects. It is the language that Arthur would have spoken.

The above point about the transition date from British to Neo-Brittonic is important. Initially, most scholars had doubted whether certain poetry that seemingly dealt with early historical incidents could have been composed contemporaneously with those events.[41] Their rationale was that poetry that rhymed in British would not rhyme when the language changed, as the final syllables would have been dropped. The rhythm of such poems would have also been affected by internal syllable loss. If this transition date were near AD 600 (rather than 500), then rhyming poems that purported to describe events in the 500s would have had to be composed after 600.

In this book, it is maintained that the three poems, *Preideu Annwfyn*, *Kat Godeu* and *Kadeir Teÿrnon* were orally composed from about the mid to later 500s, after Arthur's death. As the transition date is now estimated to be not far from AD 500, there is no impediment to the rhyming schemes in these poems being preserved as they were progressively being written in more modern forms of Welsh. John Koch makes this point directly when he states that a 'language similar enough to Welsh already existed in the 6th century for poems composed at that time to survive in copies of the Middle Welsh period without impossible linguistic barriers'.[42]

This chapter has briefly sketched the historical background of the Dark Ages period when Arthur lived, which culminated in the eventual takeover by the Saxons. It has also outlined the changes that were occurring in the *British* language that are of importance in the dating of early Welsh poetry. During this tumultuous period, Arthur had won his reputation as a supremely great military figure. It will later be argued that much of his fighting appears to have been located in southwest Scotland and northern Britain, probably against incursions from the Irish (the Scotti) and possibly the Picts. Further, from Arthur's home territory (argued in Chapter 12 to be north Wales) he was well placed to fight against the Anglo-Saxons who were settling in what is now Lincolnshire.

In later chapters, evidence from the poems *Preideu Annwfyn*, *Kat Godeu* and *Kadeir Teÿrnon* will be considered. It will be argued that the Arthurian references in these poems, currently thought of as depicting a legendary or mythological Arthur, give new and important historical information. These references, when examined in a new light, provide more detail on Arthur and suggest the astonishing conclusion that he led an expedition to north America in the sixth century and was killed there. These poems will be examined in detail in Chapters 5-8. It will be argued in Chapter 9 that the three poems were composed in the sixth century and were progressively modernised as the Welsh language evolved. In the next chapter, several strands of evidence are presented and discussed which indicate that during the medieval period there were widespread beliefs that Arthur had sailed to a distant, unknown land in the northwest Atlantic, and that some of these beliefs preceded the pseudo-history of Geoffrey of Monmouth.

3
MEDIEVAL BELIEFS IN ARTHUR'S ATLANTIC VOYAGES

ARTHUR'S DEATH OVERSEAS IN GEOFFREY'S HISTORY

Geoffrey's Reconciliation of Two Traditions

The thesis set out in this book, that Arthur sailed west to an unknown land in the sixth century, here identified as North America, is not a new one. It was present at the time that Geoffrey of Monmouth wrote his famous *History of the Kings of Britain* in c. 1138. Geoffrey drew on a wide range of material to write his book and would have been familiar with the entry in the *Annales Cambriae* that Arthur died at the battle of Camlann along with Mordred (Medraut) in 537/539. Camlann was thought to be located in Britain. In his pseudo-history, Geoffrey expands this meagre data into a story of adultery and betrayal. He falsely presents Mordred as Arthur's nephew, usurping the crown and starting a sexual relationship with Guinevere (Gwenhwyfar) while Arthur was fighting in Europe. Hearing this news, Arthur returns to Britain and engages Mordred in a series of battles until Mordred flees to Cornwall. There at the River Camblam (Geoffrey's location for Camlann) the final battle took place, where Mordred is killed.

However at this point Geoffrey inexplicably departs from the basic data of the *Annales Cambriae*. Instead of Arthur being killed at Camlann, Geoffrey presents him as only being severely wounded and abruptly states that he was then carried off to the Isle of Avalon so that his wounds might be healed. No information or explanation concerning the Isle of Avalon is given. The key question of interest is why did not Geoffrey simply allow Arthur's life to end at Camlann, as in the *Annales Cambriae*, dying a heroic death but winning the battle against the traitors and heathens opposed to him? The answer to this is that Geoffrey was aware of a different tradition that had Arthur dying at a distant place overseas.

The Life of Merlin

About twelve years after writing his *History* Geoffrey elaborates on this theme in his *Life of Merlin* (Vita Merlini), written c. 1150.[1] In this poem, the dying Arthur is taken from the Camlann battlefield to a ship, accompanied by Taliesin, who is named in the *Historia Brittonum* as a sixth-century bard. The ship then sails on a long voyage to a mysterious country overseas. That this place was not a known country is shown by the name Geoffrey created for it in his *History*, Avalon. The name is derived from the Welsh *afal* which means 'apple', as noted by Rachel Bromwich.[2] In his *Life of Merlin*, Geoffrey explicitly describes the country as the 'island of apples' and the 'Fortunate Isle'. In giving these names, he relates Avalon to legends about mysterious lands across the Atlantic Ocean, associated with apples, and described as a paradise where there is no decay or death.

Three such early Irish tales are *Echtrae Chonnlai*, *The Voyage of Bran son of Febal* and the *Navigatio* of St Brendan.[3] The first two tales refer to a magic apple and apple tree branch, respectively, associated with this paradise while the *Navigatio* also refers to the 'Promised Land of the Saints' in which there was not a tree without fruit. These lands of paradise had been discussed in antiquity. In Plutarch's life of Sertorius (in his *Parallel Lives*, written about AD 90-100), he refers to the 'Isles of the Blest', the Atlantic islands to the far west, some 10,000 furlongs from Africa and remarks 'here is the Elysian Field and the abode of the blessed, of which Homer sang'.[4]

That Geoffrey thought Avalon was a long and difficult journey (not just a journey to a familiar place like Ireland) follows from two details in his poem. The first point is the fact that the ship was to be guided by an expert to whom the seas and the stars were well known. Secondly, when Geoffrey has Taliesin reflect on whether Arthur should be brought back to expel the Saxons (after his wounds were healed), a 'swift ship' is desired, suggesting that the journey was not a trivial one.[5] Geoffrey's *Life of Merlin* has links to important Irish and Welsh traditions. It is linked to the voyages of the Irish monk, Brendan the Navigator, and is also linked to the key Welsh poem, *Preideu Annwfyn*, as will now be discussed.

The Link to Brendan the Navigator

In the *Life of Merlin*, Geoffrey names Barinthus as the expert guide who steered Arthur's ship to Avalon. In doing so, he is linking Arthur's journey to the legendary journeys of the Irish monk, Brendan. In the *Navigatio* of St Brendan, Barinthus sailed west into the Atlantic to the 'Promised Land of the Saints' and told Brendan of this land. This inspired Brendan to travel there himself, as described by his voyages in the *Navigatio*.[6] The implication is that Geoffrey thought that Arthur had been taken to the same overseas country to which Brendan had gone. America was not to be discovered by Columbus for another three and a half centuries but speculation about such a land in the west had been made in antiquity and this land appeared to be associated with Arthur before Geoffrey's time.

The voyages of Brendan were also linked to America by the Elizabethan polymath, John Dee. An outstanding scholar whose interests ranged widely, covering mathematics, astronomy, history, law, navigation, cartography and extensive studies in the occult, Dee had assembled arguably the best library in Europe at his home in Mortlake near London. He had gathered evidence for establishing a 'British Empire', in particular, a case for Elizabeth I to lay claim to the parts of America that were not under the influence of Spain and Portugal. In a package of four documents given to the queen, Dee presents a case that King Arthur had visited America in c. 530, followed by Brendan in c. 560. This package was given to Elizabeth in August 1578, as discussed by Ken MacMillan and Jennifer Abeles.[7]

Apart from Dee, several researchers argue that Brendan may have reached America or that the *Navigatio* reflected general knowledge of such westward voyages, even if Brendan did not make the full journey. These include Tim Severin, who with four others attempted to replicate Brendan's journey. They sailed in a leather *curragh* (like Brendan's) and made a one-way journey from Ireland to Newfoundland, via the Faroes and Iceland.[8]

Others such as Jonathan Wooding note that having the capacity to do the voyage is not proof that it was done. He thinks it not impossible that Brendan visited the Faroes and Iceland but that the *Navigatio* is not strong evidence for the Irish reaching America.[9] Most scholars would agree with Wooding. The *Navigatio* data is too vague and inconsistent to serve as evidence but it did influence some researchers to believe that Brendan could have reached America and, 350 years before America was known, Geoffrey appears to have thought that Arthur and Brendan had sailed to the same place in the distant Atlantic.

The Link to the Celtic Otherworld of Annwfyn

In the *Life of Merlin*, Taliesin relates that after the battle of Camlann he took the wounded Arthur to his ship and set sail for the 'island of apples' (called Avalon in Geoffrey's *History*), guided by Barinthus. Avalon was ruled by nine sisters, skilled in the magic arts, who were to care for Arthur until his wounds healed.[10] There are two elements of interest here:

- Taliesin and Arthur sailing to a distant, unknown land
- Nine maidens who practised magic.

Both these elements appear in the poem *Preideu Annwfyn* from the *Book of Taliesin*, to be discussed in Chapter 5. For Geoffrey, the mysterious land is Avalon; in *Preideu Annwfyn*, the land is Annwfyn. It seems that Geoffrey was aware of the poem (or data derived from it) and reasoned that Avalon and Annwfyn were the same place. It is even possible that he coined Avalon as a smoother equivalent of Annwfyn (in relating it to 'apples'), both three syllable names beginning with 'A' and ending with 'n'.

The Nine Priestesses

In Stanza 2 of *Preideu Annwfyn* the bard is boasting about his poetic prowess and refers to his poetry as coming from a cauldron that is kindled by nine maidens. The meaning of this imagery is debatable, but it may indicate that poetic inspiration (*awen*) could be partly conjured through the arcane arts. An alternative interpretation is that his poetry was so profound that it was as though it were conjured by magic.

The casting and lifting of spells, prophesying the future, the changing of one's shape to deceive enemies and other magical activities were part of the 'mental furniture' of sixth-century thought and the cauldron was a vehicle in which potions to effect various ends could be mixed. It had long had a value far in excess of its utilitarian function in food preparation. Cauldrons had been discovered in lakes as offerings to the gods for hundreds of years before Christ, as discussed by Barry Cunliffe.[11]

Where did the bard gain his knowledge of the nine maidens? The most likely source is Pomponius Mela who wrote *Chorographia* (Description of the World) in AD 43-44 (or stories derived from him). In Book 3, Section 48 he mentions nine priestesses who reside on the island of Sena (off Gaul) and who practise the magic arts. They can heal the incurable, predict the future, control the weather and change their shape. It seems that the bard and his audience were familiar enough with tales of this type for the bard to include the nine maidens in his poem.[12]

Geoffrey of Monmouth was also familiar with the traditions about the nine priestesses but in typical fashion elaborates them with many details from his own imagination. Instead of the isle of Sena, in his *Life of Merlin* Geoffrey locates the nine priestesses in Avalon. He makes them sisters, and creates names for each one, with Morgen the leader being more beautiful and more skilled in healing than the others.

The beautiful Morgen later became known as 'Morgan le Fay' (the fairy) in the later Arthurian romances. In addition to her skill in healing with herbs, Morgen could also change shape, developing wings which could enable her to visit any place. Thus Geoffrey includes in his poem two of the four attributes of the priestesses in the *Chorographia*, the ability to heal the sick and the ability to change one's shape.

Was Geoffrey familiar with the Preideu Annwfyn poem?

It might be objected that Geoffrey did not know *Preideu Annwfyn* because if he did he would surely have known that Arthur's ship was called *Prydwen* from its prominent mention in the poem. Instead in his pseudo-history he inexplicably makes *Pridwen* the name of Arthur's shield. However it is hard to support this argument as Geoffrey appears to have used the Welsh prose tale *Culhwch and Olwen* as a source for Arthur's weapons and this tale refers to Arthur's ship as *Prydwen* on three separate occasions. It also lists four weapons of Arthur: his sword (*Caledfwlch*), his spear (*Rhongomiant*), his shield (*Wynebgwrthucher*) and his knife (*Carnwennan*).[13]

In his *History*, Geoffrey gives a description of Arthur dressing for battle. However he chooses only three of the four weapons and then simplifies the names.[14] He simplifies *Caledfwlch* to Caliburn, then *Rhongomiant* to Ron and totally ignores *Wynebgwrthucher* for shield, replacing it with *Pridwen*. It would appear that the very complex *Wynebgwrthucher* did not appeal to Geoffrey's aesthetic instincts, so that he looked around for a suitable Welsh name for Arthur's shield and decided to substitute the far simpler name of Arthur's ship, *Prydwen*. It could be for this reason that he never refers to Arthur's ship by name. Throughout his works Geoffrey simplified names in order to give a more pleasing narrative, a notable example being his changing of *Myrddin* to Merlin.

The Ambiguity concerning Arthur's death

In his late twelfth-century work, *On the Education of a Prince*, Gerald of Wales clearly implies that Geoffrey was not the source of the stories about Arthur meeting his end at a distant land overseas. He writes that 'the legends had always encouraged us to believe that there was something otherworldly about his ending, that he had resisted death and had been spirited away to some far-distant spot'.[15] Gerald made this remark in the context of the bogus 'discovery' of Arthur's remains at Glastonbury. In around 1191 the monks were digging near the site of their ancient church (recently burned down) and found the remains of two bodies, claimed to be Arthur and Guinevere. The details of what was found vary between different accounts. It was an event managed and faked by the monks.[16]

Gerald believed strongly in the historicity of Arthur but was a vehement critic of Geoffrey's *History* – recall Gerald's ridicule from Chapter 1 about Meilyr being inundated by demons whenever the *History* was placed on his bosom. Had Gerald thought that Geoffrey was the only source of Arthur's death overseas, he would surely have treated it with scorn. Instead, he refers to legends that are known to the public (as might be inferred from 'legends... encouraged us to believe') suggesting Arthur had died or was lying mortally wounded in a far distant place.

A further source that implies a pre-Geoffrey ambiguity about Arthur's death appears in the Breton foundation legend, the *Life of St Goeznovius*. The author, a Breton priest, gives his name as Guillelm (William) and the date of his writing as 1019 which would place it about 120 years before Geoffrey's *History*. This surprising pre-Galfridian date of 1019 was strongly defended by Geoffrey Ashe.[17] It describes Arthur as reducing the Saxons to subjection and winning many victories in Britain and Gaul. However, interest centres in the way it refers to Arthur's ending – it does not say that he died but states that Arthur 'was finally summoned from human endeavour' or 'called forth from human affairs'.[18]

Summary

It would appear that Geoffrey was aware of two distinct traditions about Arthur's death: firstly, the *Annales Cambriae* death at Camlann in Britain and secondly, a death overseas in a distant land to the west. He attempted to combine the two with a contrived, improbable solution – that Arthur was only severely wounded at Camlann and was then taken overseas for his wounds to be healed. Geoffrey appears to have had knowledge of traditions or stories about the nine priestesses recorded by Pomponius Mela in AD 43-44 and incorporated them into his *Life of Merlin*, elaborated with his own details. He also seems to have had knowledge of the contents of *Preideu Annwfyn* (either directly or indirectly) as this source is the only one known to us which precedes Geoffrey and which combines the two elements of Arthur sailing overseas with Taliesin and the reference to nine maidens who were skilled in magic.

MERCATOR'S LETTER TO JOHN DEE

The Account of Jacob Cnoyen

In 1569 the great cartographer, Gerard Mercator, was working in his studio in Duisburg, completing his famous wall-map. As his new projection caused severe distortion near the poles, he included a circular inset of the regions around the North Pole. Attached to this inset was text which referred to a description of the northerly regions that had been made by Jacob Cnoyen of Holland. It related that King Arthur of Britain had sent people to settle in these regions.[19]

Several years later from London, Mercator's friend, John Dee, requested further detail on this source and Mercator responded, sending Dee a letter dated 20 April 1577. Whereas the text attached to the map's inset had been brief, the letter contained a much fuller transcript of Cnoyen's account that Mercator had copied out years before.[20] It outlined two journeys of Arthur, sailing into the northwest Atlantic via Iceland to an unknown place called Grocland. There are two versions of this letter, as discussed below.

The Discoveries version

Cnoyen wrote in the Belgic language (i.e. Old Dutch), from which Mercator had copied word for word, except where for the sake of brevity or speed he translated into Latin. Therefore the letter sent to Dee was a mixture of Old Dutch and Latin. Dee included a transcript of this letter in the final chapter of his manuscript *Of Famous and Rich Discoveries* (Cotton MS Vitellius C. VII, British Library), a manuscript he had prepared for Queen Elizabeth. This transcript has been damaged by fire and contains some missing lines. It was published in 1956, with an English translation by Eva Taylor. This copy of Mercator's letter will be called the *Discoveries* version.[21]

The Limits version

In recent times, another set of Dee's manuscripts surfaced after apparently being lost for 400 years. These were known by the title *Limits of the British Empire* (Brytanici Imperii Limites) and in 1976 were acquired by the British Library (British Library Additional Manuscript 59681). They comprise four documents, of which the last is the most extensive. The latter is written in English, but has a number of excerpts in Latin taken from other sources, one of which is a much shortened version of Mercator's letter. This excerpt will be referred to as the *Limits* version, from which Dee does mention the earlier *Discoveries* version.[22]

Although it suffered no fire damage and contains no missing lines, it is an inferior version – Dee shortens and paraphrases the *Discoveries* version and deviates from it in ways that cannot be explained by the missing lines. For example, Dee makes the inference that for Arthur's second voyage the ships were built without iron nails, a statement not in the *Discoveries* version. However it does illustrate Dee's line of thought.

The Gestae Arthuri (Deeds of Arthur)

Cnoyen's account was partly based on a lost work *Inventio Fortunatae* that was written by an Oxford friar about his northern travels through regions above latitude 54 degrees.[23] However Cnoyen also used the *Gestae Arthuri*, another lost work, with author unknown. This purports to describe two sea voyages made by Arthur to the northwest and refers to the 'Little People' who live there. The later Norse explorers called these people 'scraelings'.[24] As parts of the *Gestae Arthuri* were preserved by Jacob Cnoyen who lived in Holland, it was probably written on the continent. It has little in common with Geoffrey's *History*. While Geoffrey presents Arthur as a great military hero, mainly in Britain and Europe, the *Gestae Arthuri* portrays him more as an explorer and settler, losing thousands of men in exploratory voyages in the north and in the second voyage, taking women on board.

THE ARTHURIAN VOYAGES IN GESTAE ARTHURI

Cnoyen's Arthurian section begins with the statement that part of Arthur's army had conquered the Northern Islands but that nearly 4,000 of his people had entered the 'indrawing seas' and never returned. The indrawing seas were made a salient feature of the region around the North Pole in Mercator's wall-map. Later in the account, a description of Arthur's two voyages from the *Gestae Arthuri* is given. These are discussed below, based on the more accurate *Discoveries* version.[25]

Arthur's First Voyage (circa 530)

The *Discoveries* version begins with the great army of Arthur's wintering in the northern islands of Scotland before setting out on 3rd May. The total number of ships is not provided. Part of the fleet crossed over to Iceland. Then it appears that some of the ships from Iceland had ventured further into unknown seas on an exploratory voyage. Arthur had remained behind in an unstated location, probably Iceland. Finally, four ships returned from the exploratory voyage and warned Arthur of the indrawing seas.

Arthur heeded this warning and settled his people in islands between Scotland and Iceland and also in an unknown country called *Grocland*. The latter probably means 'wild pasture' land, as will be later discussed. In his 1569 wall-map, Mercator had placed Grocland as a large island to the west of Greenland, as did Abraham Ortelius in his 1570 map. When the four ships returned from their exploration, their sailors announced that they knew the location of the *magnetini*. There the account suddenly ends. Nothing further is provided on the *magnetini* in the *Discoveries* version but from the *Limits* version, and from other stories, they reflect the belief that magnetic rocks under the water could attract and wreck ships that contained iron.

Although a date of 530 is given for this voyage in the *Discoveries* version, there is a blank space in the Old Dutch text over which the 530 date has been inserted. Thus it seems unlikely that it was in the original Mercator letter.

Dee has probably inserted this date in his transcript as an estimate. In another Dee manuscript, *Unto your Majesties Tytle Royall* (the third document in *Limits of the British Empire*), Dee presents the date as circa 530, which suggests that it was Dee's own estimate.[26]

Arthur's Second Voyage (circa 531)

The *Discoveries* version begins with a line missing due to fire damage, so the following in the square brackets is a reconstruction: [In twelve ships, Arthur accommodated about] 1800 men and about 400 women. They set out in the following year on 3rd May (the same date given for the first voyage). Of the twelve ships, five were wrecked in a storm, being driven onto rocks. The other seven ships were apparently successful in continuing the voyage but there is no mention of the Grocland name here. The remaining seven ships made their way through a 'passage bordered by high rocks' on 18 June, 44 days after they set out. This abruptly ends the account.

Problems with the Accounts

The accounts of the voyages appear to be corrupted, incomplete and have inconsistencies. They are certainly not a polished product like the pseudo-history of Geoffrey of Monmouth. Both accounts end rather abruptly as if they were truncated. In the first voyage, the *magnetini* are not explained, while in the second, the location of the ships is not given. The first voyage mentions people who were 23 feet tall, which is apparently a corrupted element from another part of the account in which 23 people who were not above 4 feet tall were observed.[27]

In addition, the second voyage duration of 44 days has an inconsistency that Eva Taylor missed: if they left on 3rd May and arrived on 18 June, then the voyage took 46 days. In the *Limits* version, this problem is bypassed as the starting date is recorded as 5th May, probably because Dee noticed this inconsistency and emended the original 3rd May starting date.

The Magnetic Rocks

In the *Discoveries* first voyage, the sailors returning from their exploratory voyage state that they knew the location of the *magnetini*. Dee elaborates on this in the *Limits* version where he refers to eight ships foundering because they contained iron nails, being attracted to magnetic rocks under the water. In the *Limits* second voyage, the twelve ships were fitted out with no iron, a further elaboration by Dee.[28]

The notion of magnetic rocks (and later, mountains) wrecking ships that used iron nails was geographically widespread. Before Arthur's time there were written accounts of such beliefs, one from Ptolemy's *Geographia*, about AD 150, and another in the *Commonitorium Palladii* by Bishop Palladius of Helenopolis, written in the early 400s. It is possible that the wrecking of any ships on the first voyage may have been attributed to magnetic rocks by the credulous sailors conditioned with this belief.[29]

This notion of magnetic rocks under the water preventing the passage of ships also appears in *Branwen daughter of Llŷr*, the second tale in the Welsh story collection, the *Mabinogi*, written 500-600 years after *Preideu Annwfyn*. Brân's voyage to Ireland was thought by eminent scholar, Thomas Jones, to be modelled on Arthur's expedition in *Preideu Annwfyn*. In the *Branwen* story, Arthur is replaced by Brân and Annwfyn by Ireland. The parallels between Arthur and Brân are numerous and specific – both were called 'the Blessed'; both led their warriors overseas; for both the subject of 'who was minding the country' was raised; both fought a horrific battle while overseas; both were linked to a cauldron when overseas; both died in their battle; only seven men survived Arthur's conflict and seven survived Brân's; Pryderi, Manawydan and Taliesin were associated with Arthur in Annwfyn and were also with Brân in Ireland; Brân means 'crow', a bird that houses Arthur's soul in folklore. These interesting correlations are discussed in more detail in Chapter 6.[30]

In summary, Brân's expedition to Ireland was a much later rationalized and elaborated version of Arthur's voyage to Annwfyn. A further striking parallel now appears from the *Gestae Arthuri* material: the magnetic rocks in Arthur's voyage are paralleled by magnetic rocks under the water in Brân's story, which the Irish thought would stop Brân's progress. This raises the question of where the *Branwen* author found the story of the magnetic rocks impeding Arthur's ships to include in his own story. It did not come from *Preideu Annwfyn*. It would appear that the *Branwen* composer knew a version of the *Gestae Arthuri* material – that is, a *Gestae Arthuri* version of Arthur's expeditions was in existence before the *Mabinogi* story was written. Two leading scholars Thomas Charles-Edwards and Patrick Sims-Williams have dated the *Mabinogi* to the 11th or 12th century.[31]

Grocland

At first Dee identified Grocland with Greenland. In the *Discoveries* version he made some marginal notes to this effect: 'Grocland to me seemeth to be our Greenlande'. However, by the following year he had changed his mind. In his *Unto your Majesties Tytle Royall*, Dee refers to Grocland as lying 'beyond Groenland'. This was Mercator's location for it in his 1569 wall-map, where Grocland is displayed as a large island to the west of Greenland, in a similar position to Baffin Island. Abraham Ortelius also had Grocland in this position in his 1570 map. Dee's updated view is reflected in his 1580 map (Cotton MS. Augustus, I.i.1, British Library), which now placed Grocland as an island to the west of Greenland.[32]

James Enterline makes the plausible suggestion that the Old Dutch *groc* in Grocland is related to the middle Dutch *crocke*, the Flemish *krakke*, and the Modern Dutch *krok*, with all meaning approximately 'wild pasture'. If he is correct, then Grocland may well be part of Labrador or Newfoundland. This meaning would also probably disqualify Greenland itself, as 'wild pasture land' would seem an unlikely term for explorers to use to capture the predominant features of Greenland.[33]

The Hudson Strait

Two distinctive features of Arthur's first voyage are suggestive of the Hudson Strait – the *magnetini* and the indrawing seas. In its *Sailing Directions* book, the National Geospatial-Intelligence Agency gives a map listing three areas of magnetic disturbance in the Hudson Strait.[34] These are to the north of Akpatok Island, to the north of Charles Island and to the east of Coats Island. The fear that magnetic rocks could affect the navigation of ships with iron nails was evident in the 400s as shown by Bishop Palladius. How were these magnetic anomalies detected? Perhaps a needle was temporarily magnetized by stroking it against a lodestone. It could then be fixed to a straw floating in a bowl of water which gave it the freedom to respond to magnetic influences. Although this method was employed at a much later date, when it was first used in Europe is unknown. However, the lodestone's magnetic properties were known by the ancient Greeks in the sixth century BC.[35]

The Hudson Strait also has strong currents, which suggest an 'indrawing sea'. James Enterline remarks that it 'has persistent indrawing tidal flows of five to seven knots, especially along its northern edge.' In addition, Hudson Bay itself is conducive to strongly counterclockwise tidal currents that circle its shores.[36] On his 1569 wall-map, Mercator placed Grocland near Baffin Island which is adjacent to the Hudson Strait.

Another possible instance of an 'indrawing sea' concerns the east side of the Davis Strait (adjacent to Greenland) where the currents pull strongly to the north, as indicated by Eva Taylor. While Mercator's scheme, where four indrawing seas led to the North Pole, has no basis in reality there are areas of strong currents that could have contributed to these beliefs.

Are the Accounts Plausible?
Plausible features

The wintering of the fleet in the Scottish islands is not implausible. It would save travel time, allowing them to arrive earlier and get settlements set up before Winter. The departure dates in early May are also plausible as shown from later voyages. John Cabot left Bristol about 20 May on his first voyage to Newfoundland. For his three voyages, Jacques Cartier left St Malo on 20 April, 19 May and 23 May respectively, all Old-Style dates.

The travel time of either 44 or 46 days for the second journey is quite plausible. It is slow compared to the travel times of the late 15th and 16th centuries. Cabot took 35 days to reach Newfoundland in 1497. Cartier took 20 days to reach Newfoundland and 21 days to return on his first voyage in 1534. In his second voyage in 1535 he ran into foul weather and was tossed around at sea for a full month, eventually taking 50 days, but took only 21 days to return. For his third trip in 1541, Cartier again had a rough journey and took about 30 days.[37]

Arthur's slow time is consistent with the route described in the *Gestae Arthuri* which used the various islands in the northwest as stepping stones and stopovers – they would not have to face weeks of travelling through a vast expanse of unknown ocean without sighting land.[38] In contrast, both Cabot and Cartier sailed at a nearly constant latitude when crossing the Atlantic to Newfoundland, a more direct and faster route. Arthur's vessels were also probably slower than those of Cabot and Cartier.

Finally, the correlation of the Hudson Strait features with the *magnetini* and indrawing seas is quite striking. These two features do not appear in the Norse sagas.

Some surprising features

The precise numbers given for the people on board (around 1800 men and around 400 women) are a surprising feature, and one arousing scepticism. This apparent precision could have been derived from an eyewitness or was the work of one like Geoffrey of Monmouth, someone who embroidered his tales with precise but imaginary details. The total number of 2200 is hardly compatible with having only twelve ships. It is also astonishing that about 400 women are stated to have been on board. This suggests a prior plan that the expedition would be away for a long time. The impression given by the large numbers of people and the surprising presence of women is that Arthur intended to establish a settlement.

Conclusion

One's first reaction is to reject the story as a medieval fantasy. However, this brushes aside some enigmatic features of the account, in particular the fact that the *Gestae* is so different from Geoffrey in its treatment of Arthur. In Geoffrey, Arthur is the triumphant military hero, accomplishing great and important achievements like Alexander the Great, successful at everything he attempts, operating in important civilised parts of the world such as Britain and Europe. However in the *Gestae*, Arthur is not accomplishing a grand military deed but exploring little known or unknown places that were barely inhabited. In doing so, Arthur fails massively, losing 4,000 men on a quest that seems to have little payoff and hardly adds to his reputation.

The motivation of the author for writing the *Gestae* is another puzzling problem. If the whole work was a fiction, it is difficult to see the point, or even who would benefit from such a tale. Arthur's mysterious *Grocland* does not even correspond to any known land. The last sentence of the second voyage refers to the remainder of the fleet passing through a passage bordered by high rocks. It is not stated whether this place is in *Grocland* or in some other place. The account abruptly ends there. If this were simply an imaginative attempt to glorify Arthur, then one would expect a more detailed, coherent account that had a clearer purpose.

In a real voyage in the sixth century, the lands visited would obviously not have their modern names but would be described by their geographical or botanical features. Thus the representation of one of the lands as Grocland (probably 'wild pasture' land) is not implausible. With the transmission of such a story over the centuries, the modern names would eventually have replaced older names for places that were recognisable in the story. If the *Gestae Arthuri* were the only source which implied that Arthur had sailed to unknown lands in the west, then one would probably dismiss it as merely a medieval fabrication by a person who was similar to Geoffrey, someone who gave precise details originating solely from their imagination.

The difficulties are that the author of the *Gestae* is unknown, the work is of unknown date and provenance and the particular journeys cannot even be identified with any precision. It can not be used as an historical document. However, it is not a useful policy to make judgements in isolation of other evidence and there is further data that points broadly in the same direction, which will now be considered.

THE LIST OF NORTHERN LANDS UNDER ARTHUR

Dee's case to Queen Elizabeth also included material on Arthur's conquests in Scandinavia and beyond, including a long list of northern lands said to be controlled by Arthur, called here the *Northern Lands List*. Dee obtained this from William Lambarde's *Archaionomia*, a collection of 'Saxon laws' printed in Latin in 1568. An English translation of Lambarde's Arthurian material was made by Richard Hakluyt who published it in his *Principal Navigations* in 1589. This account is reproduced by John Masefield in his *Voyages*, while a modern translation is given in MacMillan and Abeles.[39]

This Arthurian material had appeared earlier in a collection on the 'laws of England' and material connected to the city of London. Felix Leibermann named it *Leges Anglorum Londoniis Collectae* and dated it to between 1206 and 1239, probably c. 1210.[40] However it will be argued later in this chapter that the Arthurian material containing the *Northern Lands List* is far earlier than the *Leges Anglorum* account and actually preceded Geoffrey's pseudo-history of about 1138.

Northern Lands List

The northern lands that were under Arthur's dominion are listed below, with their more modern equivalents in parentheses. Lynette Muir has provided the tentative identifications for the more obscure lands:[41]

- Norweya (Norway)
- Islandiam (Iceland)
- Grenelandiam (Greenland)
- Suetheidam (Sweden)
- Hiberniam (Ireland)
- Gutlandiam (Gotland)
- Daciam (Denmark)
- Semelandiam (Semland)
- Wynelandiam (Vinland)
- Curlandiam (Churland, Kurland)

- Roe   (Rugen, Riga, Ruhne)
- Fenielandiam   (Finland)
- Wirlandiam   (Virland)
- Estlandiam   (Aestland)
- Cherrelam   (Karelien, Corelia)
- Lappam   (Lapland).

The list also includes Scanciam (Scandinavia) which encompasses several of the other countries or regions, so it has not been shown above. Apart from the countries in the above list, many other unnamed lands are claimed for Arthur. The latter are recorded in Hakluyt's text as all the other lands and islands of the East Sea up to Russia (Lapland being the eastern limit) and many other islands beyond Norway, up to the North Pole.

Muir identifies Wynelandiam with Vinland, the inviting region of North America discovered by the Norse in circa 1000. Vinland was described in the *History of the Archbishops of Hamburg-Bremen* written by Adam of Bremen in about 1075. Adam derives the name as follows: 'It is called Vinland because vines producing excellent wine grow wild there'. Although Dee presented this list as part of his case to Queen Elizabeth, he missed the identification of Wynelandiam with Vinland, as Lynette Muir points out. Had Dee made this identification, he could have then argued directly that this *Northern Lands List* (distinct from Mercator's Letter) placed Arthur in Vinland and hence North America.[42]

It is not being implied here that Arthur visited all or even most of the areas listed above. The list clearly looks like an attempt to aggrandise the deeds of Arthur by listing as many northern countries as possible, no matter how insignificant, that were under his control. Nonetheless, it is not impossible that Arthur did visit some of the Scandinavian regions and fought battles there, as there are Swedish legends of Scottish warriors sailing across the North Sea in plundering raids in the AD 200-600 period.[43]

Further, in *Culhwch and Olwen* Arthur's gatekeeper Glewlwyd reminisces with Arthur about lands they had visited, including one conflict in which twelve hostages were taken from *Llychlyn*. The latter is Norway, although it may have referred to Scandinavia in general.[44] What is of interest is that the *Northern Lands List* gives places in the north and northwest, the same areas as in Mercator's Letter. Did this list precede Geoffrey's *History*? If it did, it gives a viewpoint that Arthur was associated with voyages to the north and northwest regions of the Atlantic that is unpolluted by the strong influence of Geoffrey's pseudo-history.

DID THE NORTHERN LANDS LIST PRECEDE GEOFFREY?

Although Felix Liebermann has dated the *Leges Anglorum* to c. 1210, about 70 years after Geoffrey's *History*, it is probable that the Arthurian material, including the *Northern Lands List*, was in existence before the *History*. The compiler of the *Leges Anglorum* appears to have drawn on this pre-existing passage and combined it with the laws of England and other miscellaneous material, including references to the *History*, at about 1210.

Another short text, *Insule Brittannie* (an appendix presented in Francis Tschan's translation of Adam of Bremen) also describes northern lands that were under 'British' control. Their spelling bears a close resemblance to that given in the *Northern Lands List*, as discussed by Lyn Muir. The earliest *Insule Brittannie* manuscript dates to about 1200 but could be a little earlier and may have preceded the *Leges Anglorum*.[45] It is argued below that the *Northern Lands List* preceded Geoffrey's 1138 *History* and that Geoffrey himself used the list to create his imaginative section on Arthur's northern conquests. Two sets of arguments are used: the first is based on Geoffrey's pseudo-history while the second is based on dating the political material into which the *Northern Lands List* is embedded.

Arguments from Geoffrey

Geoffrey's borrowing

Geoffrey includes a section on Arthur's northern conquests which lists only six countries: Ireland, Iceland, Gotland, Orkney, Norway and Denmark. In his typical fashion he invents names for their rulers and has them invited to Arthur's grand feast at Caerleon. The brevity of his list contrasts with that of the author of the *Northern Lands List*. It seems that the latter was trying to unearth as many countries as possible to attribute to Arthur's dominion. He names 17 places, of which 16 are specific countries or areas, some of them so small and obscure that there is doubt about their location. Further, he adds all the unnamed lands in the East Sea, Lapland being the eastern limit, and all the unnamed lands beyond Norway up to the North Pole.

If the unknown author was inspired to create his list by Geoffrey then given his desire to maximise his list, it is puzzling that he does not even use all of Geoffrey's six lands. He does not mention Orkney, one of Geoffrey's six. This omission cannot be explained on the grounds that the Orkney Islands were too far south for inclusion, as Geoffrey does include Ireland. It casts considerable doubt on the hypothesis that the unknown author borrowed his list from Geoffrey's *History*. It rather suggests that any borrowing was in the other direction.

This important point was missed by Lyn Muir who made an error in her paper on the *Leges Anglorum*. In referring to the 17 locations in the *Northern Lands List* she remarks: 'Of the seventeen places mentioned six are included among Arthur's conquests in the *Historia Regum Britanniae*' (i.e. Geoffrey's *History*). Her statement is incorrect – only five of the 17 items in the list are in Geoffrey's pseudo-history, the sixth being his own addition, Orkney. This mistake illustrates the general tendency to regard Geoffrey as the source of Arthurian material that has no clear origin. With Geoffrey assumed as the origin, any such material can be explained away as fictional, the work of an author extending the tales of Geoffrey. Muir has adopted this approach in assuming a late dating for the *Gestae Arthuri* by remarking 'it seems most improbable that the *Gestae* would have antedated Geoffrey of Monmouth'. As argued earlier in discussing the magnetic rocks under the water in the second *Mabinogi* story, it is certainly possible that the *Gestae Arthuri* material did antedate Geoffrey. In the case of Geoffrey's six Arthurian conquests in the northern regions, it is he who took most of his material from the *Northern Lands List*.[46]

Futile 'Arthurian conquests'
Given Geoffrey's portrayal of Arthur as an all-conquering military hero, it seems improbable that he would invent such far-away conquests, lacking in any credibility, as Iceland and Gotland – unless he found them in another source. What is the point of Arthur conquering Iceland, a difficult place to survive at that time, possibly uninhabited or inhabited by only a few settlers struggling to meet the basic necessities? Given his inventiveness, he could have expanded Arthur's conquests in a grander manner, perhaps striking at the heart of the Saxons in Germany. The hypothesis of Geoffrey inventing the northern conquests as a way of glorifying Arthur (without knowledge of a prior source) is not a very plausible one.[47]

A source for Arthur's 30 kingdoms
There is an odd reference in Geoffrey's *History* to Britain having conquered 30 kingdoms. This number of kingdoms conquered is preposterous and is given no explanation by Geoffrey. However it could be explained if he had seen the *Northern Lands List* with its 17 countries (and many other unnamed lands) and added the 9 distinct battle regions given in the *Historia Brittonum* which would give well over 26 regions. He may have rounded the total out to 30 to create his 30 kingdoms.[48]

He could then have employed a strategy that he had used elsewhere in his *History*. He would select a few instances from the extended list, pad them out with his imaginary details and make some small changes to ensure that his version did not look like a copy of an existing text. In this scenario he selected Norway, Iceland, Ireland, Gotland and Denmark; that is, he selected five of the first seven items from the *Northern Lands List*. He then added Orkney as his unique contribution and wrote up the fictitious details of Arthur gaining tribute from each.[49]

A DATING FOR THE NORTHERN LANDS LIST

A dating for the *Northern Lands List* may be estimated from the historical context with which it is associated. The list is merely a way of emphasising Arthur's greatness, but is not the main aim of the passage. It is integrated seamlessly into a political text called here a *Plea from the Norse*. The text is translated in MacMillan and Abeles.[50] Having set up the grand Arthur as a second Alexander the Great, Arthur's authority was then used to drive home the political point – that the Norse have the right to live in peace in Britain as brothers to the English. Assuming that the lands list and political text were written at the same time as part of the one document, then a dating of the political context would also date the *Northern Lands List*.

A Plea from the Norse to live in Britain

This account was written after the reign of Edward the Confessor (who died in the first week of 1066) and from the perspective of the 11th century English. However the sixth-century differentiation between the Britons and Saxons (who became the English) is blurred. It has no historical basis, being purely a political argument invoking the authority of both Arthur and at the conclusion, Edward the Confessor.

After introducing Arthur as a great king with extensive Scandinavian conquests (the *Northern Lands List*), it describes how he arranged for the Norse to be baptised and ensured that the Christian God was worshipped throughout Scandinavia. It refers to the Norse kings of Arthur's time taking wives from the noble families of Britain and hence the Norse of the current time (when the document was written) claim that they are of British blood. Arthur assisted this bonding process by petitioning the Pope and Roman Curia for Norway to be then annexed to the British crown in perpetuity, a complete nonsense.

Then commences an argument that the Norse are of British blood, they belong to the crown of Britain and thus should be able to dwell in Britain as brothers to the English. On five occasions in the text this general theme is emphasised. To add further authority, a fictitious account is then given of Edward the Confessor making an agreement with the consent of the whole realm that the Norse should have the right to live in Britain as the sworn brothers to the English.

In referring to Edward, the unknown author of the plea calls him 'our last king', as translated by Elisabeth Leedham-Green in the book by MacMillan and Abeles.[51] Thus the author is setting the writing of the *Plea from the Norse* in the reign of William the Conqueror, which agrees with the argument set out below. The alternative date of c. 1210 given by Liebermann for the *Leges Anglorum* would set the writing in the reign of King John, when there was no threat at all to the Norse in Britain. It would thus bypass the reigns and laws of John, Richard the Lionheart, Henry II, Stephen, Henry I, William II and William the Conqueror to appeal to a non-existent agreement of Edward the Confessor, an improbable proposition.

The Norse and William the Conqueror

In seeking to date the *Plea from the Norse*, one should look for a period when the Norse were under threat in Britain. This had to have occurred after the reign of Edward the Confessor and most probably occurred under the brutality of William the Conqueror, when William sought to suppress the English resistance. Peter Rex notes that in the period of English resistance to

William, the English 'were in constant negotiation with the Danes' who aided the English.[52]

During this period of resistance, William and his agents were effective and brutal. His response to the English revolt in Northumbria was the infamous 'harrowing of the north' in 1069-70 which instilled fear and insecurity. This murderous rampage annihilated all opposition in Yorkshire and destroyed property, tools, livestock and harvests, laying the land waste. A large region of 1,000 square miles was converted into a wilderness, with no habitation between York and Durham. The aftermath was a famine which led to widespread food shortages in Britain and desperate times for the Britons in the Yorkshire region. The land did not fully recover for many years. This brutal suppression then continued with the later revolts. Although it is difficult to estimate precisely when the *Plea from the Norse* was written, the most likely time would appear to be after William's 'harrowing of the north' and before 1087 when he died.[53]

The Assimilation of the Norse

When were the Norse effectively assimilated into the English population so that their different ethnicity was no longer an issue? An effective endpoint would surely be the close of William's reign in 1087. Hugh Thomas notes that a chronicler in the north of England, writing a decade after the Conquest, had thought that the English and Danes had become one people long before. Thomas concludes: 'After the conquest any remaining separate Scandinavian identity rapidly disappeared' and gives a rationale:[54]

> I suspect that in large measure Danish identity disappeared so quickly after the conquest because assimilation and acculturation had proceeded sufficiently far that the remaining ethnic boundaries easily dissolved under the shock of the Norman Conquest and the common oppression at the hands of the Normans.

Given this viewpoint, it is difficult to see how the *Plea from the Norse* could have been written after Geoffrey's *History* in 1138. The period from about 1070 to 1087 would seem to be a suitable time for the document to have emerged. It is here argued that the constant threat from Denmark and their assistance to the English rebels may have made life difficult for the Danes living in England during the Conquest. They may have been threatened or harassed by William's men and other English supporters of William which produced the feeling of insecurity that gave rise to the document.

CONCLUSION

The belief that Arthur had sailed to a distant land in the northwest Atlantic was present from before the time of Geoffrey of Monmouth. In his *History* (c. 1138) Geoffrey acknowledges this belief by reconciling it with Arthur's death at Camlann (*Annales Cambriae*) in a clumsy, contrived ending to his Arthurian account. His Arthur was only wounded at Camlann and was then taken by ship to a distant land called Avalon for his wounds to be healed. In his *Life of Merlin* (c. 1150) Geoffrey has Barinthus steer Arthur's ship to Avalon, Barinthus being the guide who told Brendan the Navigator about the distant country in the west. Brendan's voyages have been linked with America by a number of writers.

Geoffrey may also have been familiar with the poem *Preideu Annwfyn* (or data derived from it) which relates Arthur's sea voyage to a mysterious land called Annwfyn. That poem has Arthur's bard (who was ostensibly Taliesin) sail with Arthur and refers to nine maidens skilled in magic, two features that Geoffrey includes in his *Life of Merlin*. It would seem that Geoffrey was not the source of the legends linking Arthur with the land to the west. If he were not directly familiar with *Preideu Annwfyn*, his source for these beliefs was probably from Wales.

The other sources for these beliefs seemingly derive from the continent, perhaps from Holland and Scandinavia. These were collected by John Dee who used them to argue for a British claim on parts of North America. In his documents given to Queen Elizabeth in 1578, Dee argues that Arthur had sailed to America in about 530. One part of his evidence comes from the notes of Jacob Cnoyen, from 's-Hertogenbosch in Holland. These refer to the lost Arthurian work, *Gestae Arthuri*, which describes two voyages of Arthur's fleet to lands in the northwest Atlantic, sailing via Iceland. Arthur's fleet reached an unknown land called *Grocland* ('wild pasture' land) which was placed on the western side of Greenland by Mercator in his 1569 wall-map and by Ortelius in his 1570 map.

The details in the voyages have some plausible features and some very surprising features. They seem to indicate that a long term settlement was intended. If it were a purely fictional account, it is difficult to explain why it portrays the all-conquering Arthur in such a strange role and is worded so vaguely that its intent is difficult to fathom. These voyages of exploration are claimed to have carried a very heavy loss of life, with 4,000 people who never returned.

Dee also presents a second source for beliefs that Arthur had sailed into the northwest Atlantic, possibly derived from Scandinavia. It gives a long list of northern lands under Arthur's dominion, plus many other unnamed lands. The list looks like a way of aggrandising Arthur's deeds, but it is of interest that the lands include Iceland, Greenland and apparently Vinland in North America. Several arguments are then given which suggest that the northern lands list preceded Geoffrey's *History*.

Unfortunately, these accounts cannot be used as historical evidence to demonstrate Arthur's voyages. They are too late, of unknown provenance and are uncorroborated. Nevertheless, it has been argued that at least two of the three sources have arisen without Geoffrey's overpowering influence, as they preceded him – the Scandinavian account linking Arthur to lands in the northwest Atlantic and the Welsh material that Arthur was lying wounded in a distant land across the ocean.

The third source, the *Gestae Arthuri*, could also have preceded Geoffrey. It appears to have preceded the story of Brân's expedition in the *Mabinogi*, based on Arthur's voyage in *Preideu Annwfyn*. The Brân author introduces a feature appearing in the *Gestae Arthuri* – the magnetic rocks under the water which were a hazard to Arthur's ships. The inclusion of this unusual detail in the *Mabinogi* is unlikely to be a coincidence. It suggests that the Brân author included it because he was already familiar with the *Gestae Arthuri* tale. The *Mabinogi* collection is not dated very precisely: if it were 11th century then the earlier *Gestae* would have preceded Geoffrey's 1138 book. If it were 12th century, then there is a possibility that the *Gestae* did precede Geoffrey but without a precise dating this cannot be determined. If there were no core of truth in Arthur's voyages into the northwest Atlantic then these three seemingly independent strands present a puzzle that requires an explanation.

In later chapters it is argued that there is genuine sixth-century material which provides solid evidence that Arthur sailed to America. Evidence based on the ancient Welsh poems will be considered, most importantly the *Preideu Annwfyn* poem. It will be argued that this poem was originally composed not long after the few survivors had returned to Britain and was the work of an eyewitness who accompanied Arthur on the expedition.

4
SIXTH-CENTURY NORTH AMERICA

THE HOPEWELL

Introduction

During the time the Romans were ruling in Britain, across the Atlantic Ocean Native Americans of superb artistic and geometric talent were flourishing. They are now known as the Hopewell culture by archaeologists, being named after an archaeological site a few miles northwest of Chillicothe, Ohio. The site was owned by Mordecai Hopewell at the time it was excavated in 1891-92 by Warren Moorehead. It produced 'one of the largest, most unusual, and most significant collections of artifacts' representing the richness of the Hopewell culture according to Susan Woodward and Jerry McDonald.[1] The flowering of the Hopewell began about 150 BC and ended about AD 500 in what is called the Middle Woodland period.[2] In this interval they built a huge number of earthen ceremonial mounds enclosed by earthen walls of varying geometrical shapes.

The Hopewell were not the first mound builders as they were preceded by the Adena culture which lasted from about 1000 BC and continued into the Hopewell period. They were named after Governor Worthington's estate 'Adena', close to Chillicothe. It contained a large conical burial mound which was representative of other Adena sites. The two groups, Adena and Hopewell were not necessarily different peoples but had different cultures or traditions that overlapped in time, with some groups pursuing an Adena way of life and others a Hopewell way of life in this period. The earlier Adena culture laid the foundations for the Hopewell, which was a richer culture that built larger and more complex earthworks.

The Hopewell lived in the Eastern Woodlands of North America. Their culture began in southern Illinois where the oldest Hopewell artifacts are found. Although their mounds were spread widely across eastern North America, their core area is considered to be central to southern Ohio. Two outstanding areas of interest are the river valleys around Chillicothe and at Newark, east of Columbus. Here the earthworks were densely clustered and reached an extraordinary degree of complexity.

To build these structures must have required the co-operation of many Hopewell groups. Apart from the earthworks themselves, exotic goods that were buried in the mounds command interest. Some of these came from far afield in North America which implies that the Hopewell had a wide sphere of influence. If the ideas in this book are correct, then Arthur's expedition would have travelled southwards into the Eastern Woodlands and there encountered the extraordinary mound complexes that are referred to in the *Preideu Annwfyn* poem.

Hopewell Communities

Before European settlement, eastern North America was covered by forest which was broken by grasslands and areas for villages and land cultivation. Large areas of land had been cleared by the Native Americans through their deliberate use of fire and their girdling of trees. This use of fire removed the underbrush, allowing them to make their way through forests and creating zones for the animals to browse.[3] Game animals were in plentiful supply – white-tailed deer, wild turkey, beaver and bear. The rivers and streams were key sources of food. At the McGraw site, two miles south of Chillicothe, Ohio the bones of nine species of fish were found, along with the bones and shells of a variety of turtles and the shells of 25 species of mollusc. The Hopewell also ate a variety of nuts (including hickory nuts, walnuts and acorns) and the hackberry and wild plum.[4]

In some Hopewell areas, such as Illinois, large villages were near the earthworks according to Olaf Prufer. However in the Ohio heartland the Hopewell did not live inside the enclosures or next to them. In one model, they lived in small, scattered hamlets in surrounding areas and grew native weedy crops such as maygrass, sunflowers, goosefoot and knotweed by using the 'slash and burn' method of cultivation.[5] Brad Lepper suggests that after some years at the same place, as the soil nutrients became depleted and firewood became harder to find, they probably moved on to a nearby location, allowing the resources to regenerate.[6]

There is some debate on the extent to which the Hopewell lifestyle was sedentary. Richard Yerkes argues against the notion that they had sedentary agricultural chiefdoms. Rather, they were a fairly mobile people whose main subsistence was through hunting, fishing, gathering nuts and wild plants, which was supplemented by the cultivated native crops. Their construction of earthworks and participation in the rituals and feasts held there helped to integrate these mobile tribes.[7] Their houses were generally squarish with a frame of logs set upright in the ground. Small branches and twigs were interlaced through the logs and covered with suitable material such as bark or mud mixed with grass. They were probably roofed with thatch, reeds or bark.[8] These Hopewell houses are to be differentiated from the large wooden framed buildings erected within the earthen enclosures themselves. These buildings were sometimes very large, as shown by the posthole pattern of the large building under the Edwin Harness mound in Ross County. These were probably used for a diverse range of purposes, one being as charnel houses, where the dead were prepared for cremation or burial.

THE MOUNDS AND THEIR ENCLOSURES

In the ancient Welsh poetry, Arthur's expedition sailed over the seas to a new country, where no Briton had been before. They moved through a series of camps one of which was associated with earthen mounds. This camp, *kaer sidi*, is rendered as 'mound fortress' by Sarah Higley in her translation of

Preideu Annwfyn. It is the most important camp in the poem, featuring in the opening stanza and being the setting for conflict.[9] In the later chapters, it is argued that the expedition probably entered the Gulf of St Lawrence, sailed partway up the St Lawrence River and camped at Montreal, before moving southwest past Lakes Ontario and Erie. They then probably entered the Eastern Woodlands where they saw the mound complexes, which had been built long ago. When Arthur arrived in the 530s, it was after the Hopewell culture had ended, around AD 500. So the Native Americans they encountered would have been post-Hopewell, Native Americans at the start of the Late Woodland period. But the Hopewell had made their mark with the complex earthworks and had left their successors with a rich set of skills and traditions.

This route can be visualised by inspecting Figure 4.1 below.[10] It depicts the main influence of the Hopewell by the encircled area centred on Ohio, where the densest concentration of man-made earthworks is found. The river valleys of the Scioto and Muskingum Rivers and the tributaries of these rivers contain many complex earthworks. If the expedition did sail partly up the St Lawrence after suffering from a cold Winter, as related in the poem, then it would be a natural inclination for them to follow the river south to seek a more comfortable climate.

The Distribution of Mounds

Figure 4.1 shows that the Hopewell mounds were widely distributed across eastern North America. There are a sprinkling of Hopewell mounds around Lake Ontario; to the west of Lake Erie; on both sides of Lake Michigan; as far west as Kansas and all the way south to the Gulf of Mexico. Many of the earthworks have been damaged or destroyed by European settlement. However, it is fortunate that a systematic survey of such earthworks was performed in the nineteenth century by Ephraim Squier and Edwin Davis, when archaeology was in its infancy. Their book was the first publication of the Smithsonian Institution.[11] The maps in their book show the distribution of the earthworks in certain areas and their impressive complex structures, preserving images of what they would have looked like.

The mounds vary from the dome-shaped mounds to elliptical mounds or even truncated pyramids. The earthen enclosures comprise walls arranged in a variety of shapes and sizes, including circles, squares, rectangles, octagons, even a rhombus, with these shapes being joined together in various combinations. In addition, 'avenues' formed by the building of parallel earthen walls were created, sometimes of short length connecting the various geometric enclosures but also running for a considerable distance to connect to other earthworks. The complexity of the Hopewell earthwork designs is most easily appreciated by studying the plan views in the book by Squier and Davis. To illustrate these, three earthworks will now be briefly described – the Newark site (which is east of Columbus), the Hopewell site (northwest of Chillicothe) and Mound City (just north of Chillicothe). Many of the features shown in these diagrams are no longer in existence.

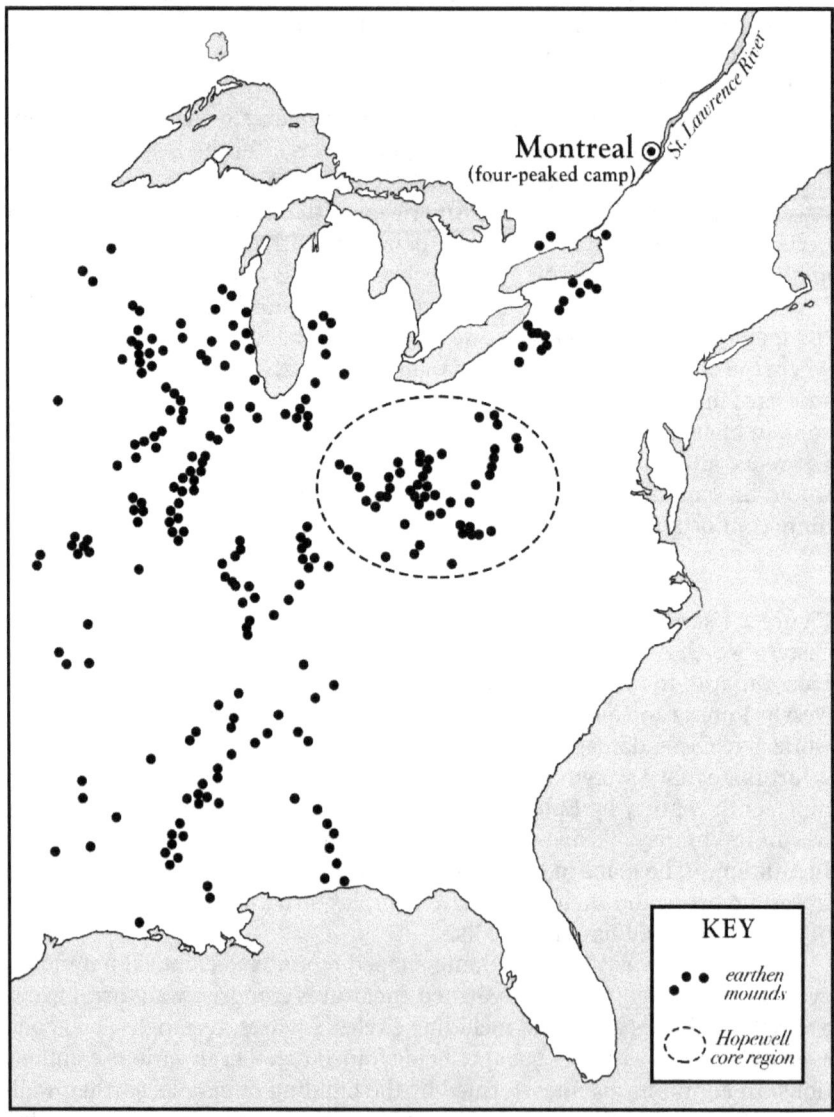

Figure 4.1 Hopewell mounds with their core region centred on Ohio (Map: Sarah Dunning Park)

The Newark Earthworks

These are in Newark, Ohio and comprise three sections: the Great Circle, the Wright Earthworks and the Octagon Earthworks.

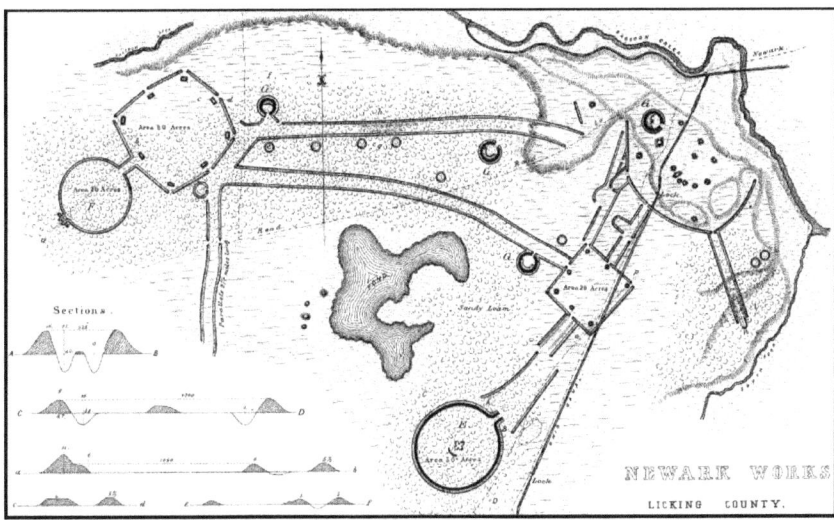

Figure 4.2 Newark Earthworks Plan, from Squier and Davis, 1848

Great Circle
The south of the complex contains a large circular enclosure with an inside concentric ditch. At the centre of the circle there are four elliptical mounds that join together to form an eagle's shape: two for the wings, one for the head and one for the body – the set known as the eagle mound.

Wright Earthworks
The gate from the Great Circle meets a wide avenue with narrowing walls. They lead to an entrance to the Great Square. Inside the square are seven dome-shaped mounds, four at the corners and three at the side midpoints.[12] To the northeast of the Great Square is an irregularly shaped complex that contains a number of mounds: most are dome-shaped, one is elliptical and one appears to be pyramidal with the top truncated.

Octagon Earthworks
From the eastern part of the earthworks, two long avenues head west to join an octagon enclosure. At each point of the octagon is a gate and inside at each gate is an elliptical shaped mound. A short avenue joins the octagon to a circle enclosing 20 acres. At the southwest side of the circle is a small loaf-shaped mound – the Observatory Mound. From here one can look through the circle into the octagon and to the far gate of the octagon. Such alignments may have had an astronomical function, as has been argued by Ray Hively and Robert Horn.[13]

The Great Hopewell Road

Parallel walls running south from the octagon may have continued all the way to Chillicothe, almost 60 miles. Bradley Lepper refers to it as the Great Hopewell Road.[14] If true, it would constitute an extraordinary achievement and would link the two main Hopewell centres in Ohio.

Newark: Great Circle (Photos: R. MacCann)

Figure 4.3 Top of Great Circle wall, with concentric inside ditch on right

Figure 4.4 Great Circle wall viewed from inside the circle

Figure 4.5 Great Circle entrance; walls visible at sides

Newark: Octagon Earthworks (Photos: R. MacCann)

Figure 4.6 Two octagon walls joining at right

Figure 4.7 Circular wall leading to Observatory Mound in distance on right

Figure 4.8 Circular wall with elliptical Observatory Mound

The Hopewell Site

Before this site received its current name, Squier and Davis referred to it as Clark's Work, after the Clark family who owned the land at that time. It is on the north fork of Paint Creek, a stream running off the Scioto River and is a few miles northwest of Chillicothe.

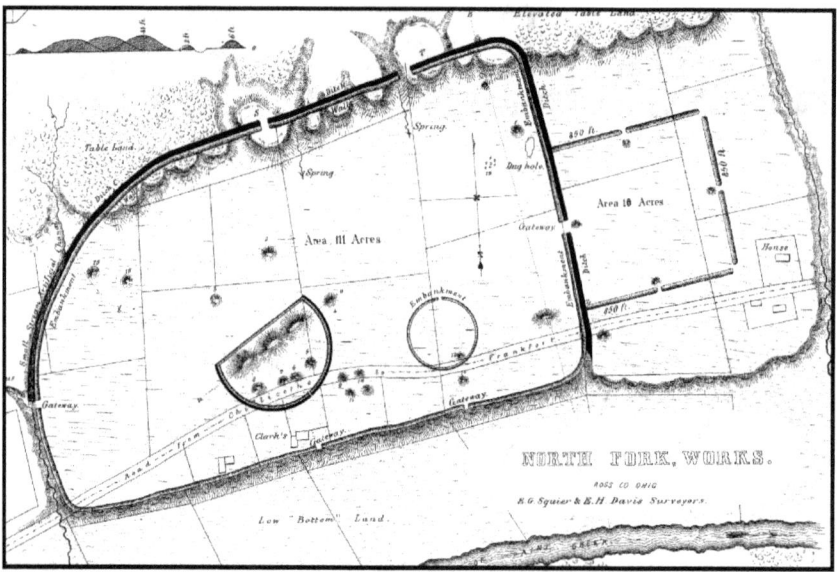

Figure 4.9 Hopewell Earthworks Plan, from Squier and Davis, 1848

Great enclosure

This earthwork contains the biggest Hopewell enclosure of all, consisting of 111 acres. It is roughly rectangular in shape but follows the contours of the plateau on which it sits, thus having a rounded corner on the northwest side. A ditch extends around the outside of the enclosure where the terrain allows it. It has two gates on the northern side, two on the southern, and one gate on each of the eastern and western sides. There are 13 mounds within this great enclosure that are not within the other enclosures, one of these being an elliptical-shaped mound.

Truncated circle

Within the Great Enclosure are two other enclosures, one which comprises two thirds of a circle joining a straight edge, an unusual enclosure even by Hopewell standards. It has a small gate to the south. Within this shape are three large elliptical mounds that are joined together to form an elongated mound, which (if considered as a single mound) was the largest Hopewell mound of all. It was roughly 500 ft long, 180 ft wide and 30 ft high when examined by Squier and Davis in the 1800s. Apart from this, there are four dome-shaped mounds in this unusual enclosure.

Circular enclosure
Within the Great Enclosure is a second enclosure that consists of a perfect circle, which has a small gate facing north. This circle contains one dome-shaped mound.

Square enclosure
Attached to the eastern wall of the Great Enclosure is a huge square, of side length about 850 ft, the square sharing part of the wall of the Great Enclosure. At the midpoint of each side of the square is a gateway. Inside the square and aligned with each gateway is a mound, with each of these mounds appearing to 'guard' the corresponding gateway. The gateway on the western side of the square allows access to the Great Enclosure.

Mound City and the Seip Mound
About three miles north of Chillicothe lies a dense cluster of mounds known as Mound City, shown in the Figure 4.10 plan below. It has 23 ceremonial mounds of varying sizes, 22 dome-shaped mounds and one large mound in the shape of an ellipse. See also the photo in Figure 4.11. The mounds are enclosed by a square earthen wall with rounded corners which encloses 13 acres. Although it is not shown in Figure 4.10 (and no longer in existence), about 440 yards south of Mound City there was a large circular enclosure that contained a concentric ditch on the outside, which enclosed 28 acres. At the centre of this circle was a dome-shaped mound.

About 14 miles southwest of Chillicothe, the Seip Mound may still be seen, a remnant of the complex Seip earthworks. The plan of the original earthworks is displayed in the Squier and Davis book.[15] A photo of the Seip Mound is shown in Figure 4.13.

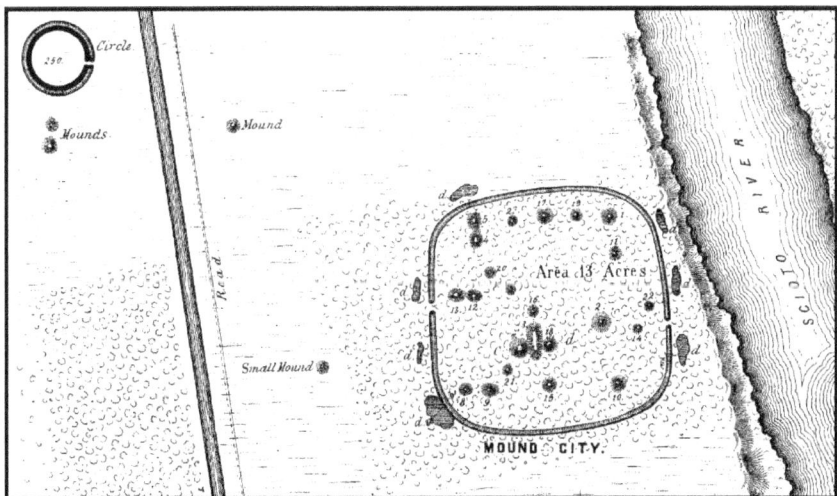

Figure 4.10 Mound City Plan, from Squier and Davis, 1848

Mound City and Seip Mound (Photos: R. MacCann)

Figure 4.11 Mound City: four mounds of varying shapes and sizes

Figure 4.12 Mound City: posthole remains for a submound building

Figure 4.13 Seip Mound, southwest of Chillicothe

The Purposes of the Earthworks
Mortuary rituals
Under some of the important mounds, post holes for buildings were found as shown in Figure 4.12 from the Mound City site. These buildings were used for mortuary rituals and other functions, as will be outlined below. For example, in the 'Mica Grave' mound in Mound City a wooden building was constructed in which a shallow clay basin was created. This basin was lined with sheets of mica. Inside the basin were the cremated remains of four or more Hopewell people. Associated with the remains were important grave goods, including their smoking pipes skilfully carved in the shape of various animals or birds, obsidian tools and large obsidian points, bear teeth, elk teeth, about 5000 shell beads and two copper headdresses, one having antlers. Apart from the cremations in the basin, 16 more Hopewell were laid to rest on the floor of the building.[16]

Eventually such wooden buildings were either burned to the ground or dismantled after a suitable time had elapsed. An earthen mound was then built over everything. The complexity of the floor plans for Hopewell sites may be seen from the work of N'omi Greber and Katharine Ruhl and other papers by Greber.[17]

A diverse range of functions
Although rituals for the dead were an important feature of the earthworks, they appear to have served a diverse range of functions. Bruce Smith makes four broad classifications – (1) mortuary programs, (2) corporate building projects, (3) craftsmen on site producing ceremonial items for burial and exchange, and (4) feasting. To this list, Paul Pacheco adds the creating of kinship ties through marriages between different territorial groups. Warren DeBoer also suggests that feasts, games, dances, gambling and foot races along the causeways may have taken place.

Chris Carr, Beau Goldstein and Jaimin Weets argue that the functions probably changed over time. The earlier gatherings were probably small and involved gift giving by individuals to build alliances. Later, the gatherings grew larger and were dominated by regional leaders aiming to build and maintain alliances. These alliances would have been further consolidated by the burying of Hopewell from separate communities in each other's charnel houses.[18]

HOPEWELL ARTIFACTS

Animal Effigy Pipes and Figurines
The Hopewell showed superb craftmanship in creating animal effigy pipes, generally carved from Ohio pipestone. These pipes were for smoking but were carved in the shapes of various animals and birds – bears, beavers, toads, otters, birds and so on, with outstanding skill and attention to detail. They also skilfully carved human heads or complete figures. These figurines were

sometimes ritually broken or 'killed' when placed in their mounds according to Olaf Prufer.[19]

Pearls

The Hopewell also collected a huge number of freshwater pearls from the shellfish of local rivers. Such pearls were found in the mounds as mortuary offerings. In the Hopewell site alone there were found 100,000 pearls, while the Turner site yielded over 48,000 pearls, as discussed by Olaf Prufer. The Seip-Pricer Mound yielded about 18,000 pearls, according to Brad Lepper. Pearls were also used for necklaces and inserted into holes for the 'eyes' in the animal effigy pipes.[20]

Prufer states that pearls were also frequently inlaid into the canine teeth of grizzly bears. He displays a photo of such a bear canine tooth with two round holes where the pearls would have been. Adjacent to this tooth the photo shows a fragment of Hopewell pottery with two identically-sized round holes which are also now empty.[21] Given the similarity in shape and size, it would be reasonable to infer that these holes in the pottery also held pearls. If this inference is correct, then it is consistent with the description given in the Welsh poetry in the next chapter. This describes a 'cauldron' (ceremonial pot) that had been captured in the new country overseas, which had been decorated with pearls.

Other Materials

The Hopewell imported large quantities of mica from the mountains of Virginia, North Carolina and Alabama. These were used in the form of flat sheets to line burial pits within mounds. They were also cut into abstract shapes and the shapes of people or animals. For example, mica cutouts of a large human hand and a snake effigy are displayed by Olaf Prufer, while Bradley Lepper shows mica cutouts of two human torsos.[22]

Copper was highly sought by the Hopewell, being obtained from the Lake Superior area. They used it to make axes and adzes, earspools, rings, breastplates and headdresses. It was also used to create the shapes of living things. Prufer and Lepper each show superb copper representations of two falcons, both of which were discovered at Mound City.[23] Silver was highly prized and was also obtained from the Lake Superior region. It was often juxtaposed with copper in the Hopewell artifacts, probably because of the pleasing visual contrast between the two metals. The Hopewell made silver panpipes, as shown by Gina Turff and Chris Carr, and they also used silver for ornaments such as bracelets and earspools, as shown in the paper by Michael Spence and Brian Fryer.[24]

In Mound City, several hundred pounds of obsidian were found in one mound. This beautiful volcanic glass was highly prized and was used to make ceremonial projectile points. The Hopewell's extraordinarily wide sphere of influence made it possible for this obsidian to be brought all the way from a site in present day Yellowstone Park, 1500 miles away.

Large conch shells were brought up from the Gulf of Mexico and were then gouged out to form drinking vessels while smaller shells from the Gulf were used for strings of beads. Sharks' teeth were also prized as decoration, brought from the Atlantic Ocean coast.

Hopewell Sphere of Interaction

The above outline indicates that the Hopewell had a 'sphere of interaction' over widely dispersed regions. Material came from near Lake Superior (to the north), Yellowstone National Park (to the west), the Gulf of Mexico (to the south) and the Atlantic Ocean (to the east). While this material could have been brought to Ohio as a result of trading, Bradley Lepper indicates that very little material from Ohio has been found at these far flung parts.[25] One might have expected flint tools from Flint Ridge in Ohio to have been found at these distant regions as a result of trading. Their apparent absence could suggest that the material brought to the Ohio core may have been from pilgrimages, or perhaps the Hopewell even took extended journeys to gain the materials. From this very brief review of the various functions held at the earthworks, it would appear that there was much co-operation from widely distributed Hopewell territorial groups and that the era was generally one of peace and prosperity.

WHAT DID THE NATIVE AMERICANS LOOK LIKE?

One of the best ways to visualise the Native Americans is to examine the oil painting by Louis Glanzman entitled *A Hopewell Indian Burial Ceremony*. It is located within the Interpretive Center of the Hopewell Culture National Historical Park at the Mound City site, three miles north of Chillicothe.[26] It shows a group of Hopewell males inside one of the wooden framed houses built within the mound enclosures.

Body Decoration

The picture is dominated by the shaman who is dancing with a dagger in one hand and a effigy rattle in the shape of a human head in the other. The shaman is wearing a white robe with geometric designs created by sewing shells onto the garment. His face and the crown of his head are completely covered by a pale leather mask with holes for the eyes. Copper decorations shaped like small feathers are attached to the mask below each eye. Around his neck there swings a long shell-beaded necklace with an ornament on the end. Material extends from his upper arms, feathers being attached, which sway as he dances.

The shaman is surrounded by twelve men, each strong and muscular. Their hair and eyes are dark, their complexion reddy-brown, and their faces solemn. Each wears a loin cloth and all except one wear a necklace. These vary from simple shell beads with a pendant on the end to more elaborate versions. A high status man wears an impressive necklace of large animal claws attached to a shell bead necklace, with a pendant at the end. On his head is an impressive deer antler headdress, made of copper. Another man of high status wears a fur headdress with animal ears, with the headdress being draped over his shoulders and down to his thighs. Around his neck is a necklace containing animal teeth and he is holding a long staff. Two of the men hold spears with the projectile points made of sharpened flint, probably from Flint Ridge in Ohio.

Hair in Mohawk Style

The Hopewell warriors and their Late Woodland successors would have presented a fearsome appearance in battle. Their hair is shown as variants of the 'mohawk' style, where most of the black hair is plucked out to create a ridge of hair on the top of the head. This hairstyle is displayed in a sample of the terracotta artwork found in the village associated with the Mann earthworks in Indiana, as reproduced by Chris Carr and Troy Case.[27]

During the late 18th century, the Moravian missionary David Zeisberger described the Native Americans he lived with in Ohio, his manuscript being translated from the German by Archer Hulbert and William Schwarze.[28] Writing in 1779-80, he describes their custom of rooting out their hair from the forehead towards the back of the head, so that the head was bald up to the crown. Only a circular remnant remained, which was commonly worn with feathers.

Body Paint and Tattoos

Glanzman's painting also displays the use of body painting. Two men have red ochre that bisects the face down the forehead, nose and chin. Another man has three red ochre stripes on the upper arm, while others appear to have red ochre on the cheeks. This use of ochre paint is shown in a ceramic sculptured head found in the Seip Mound No. 1 in 1927, which appears to have red pigment on parts of the head.[29]

It is also highly probable that the Hopewell tattooed their bodies. N'omi Greber reproduces a carving of a human head on a smoking pipe found in the Edwin Harness Mound in Ohio.[30] The whole face, chin and side of the head is covered in an intricate design with the pattern drawn in a very fine detail. This elaborate detail probably would indicate tattooing rather then ochre paint. Similar fine-detailed artwork (but less densely distributed) is shown on a carving of a man wearing a cat headdress, found in Mound 8 at Mound City. This is shown in Figure 4.14, from Squier and Davis.[31]

In his 1779-80 notes from Ohio, David Zeisberger records that the Native Americans tattooed their faces, arms and legs with a variety of designs. They pricked their skin with a needle and then rubbed powder or soot into the punctures.[32] It is clear from the very fine-detailed artwork on items such as bears' teeth that the Native Americans had the sufficiently sharp instruments to do such tattooing.

Figure 4.14 A Hopewell carving of a man wearing a cat headdress, found in Mound City: from Squier and Davis, 1848

NATIVE AMERICAN WEAPONS

Susan Hughes identifies four weapon systems that were used by the Native Americans: the throwing spear, thrusting spear, spear thrower (known as the atlatl) and dart, and the bow and arrow. The 'dart' referred to here is not a small instrument like those used today in the game of darts, but a spear-like object propelled by the atlatl. The atlatl effectively extends the length of the thrower's arm. Photographs of modern-day throwers using the atlatl and dart are shown by Bradley Lepper.[33]

The date of the introduction of the bow and arrow has been extensively discussed with differing opinions. A major problem is that it is difficult to distinguish between a projectile point that may have belonged to a dart (with atlatl) and an arrow, as their wooden shafts have usually rotted away. The classification as one or the other then rests on an evaluation of the projectile point itself, with larger points tending to be classified as darts and smaller ones tending to be classified as arrows.

There is a general consensus that projectile points in the form of small triangular bifaces represent arrow heads and hence the adoption of the bow and arrow. However, it was recently thought that the native Americans centred in Ohio did not use these points until around AD 700 of the Late Woodland period.[34] On this view, they would not yet have adopted the bow and arrow when Arthur arrived at the beginning of the Late Woodland period in the mid 530s.

However contrary arguments have been made by George Odell who had suggested early use of the bow and arrow, but with arrow heads that may have been unstandardized. Andrew Bradbury also suggests that the dart and atlatl and the bow and arrow were used simultaneously at the time of the Hopewell with the atlatl/dart fading out when the small standardized arrow heads were widely adopted.[35]

The statistical technique of discriminant analysis has been employed by several researchers to help distinguish arrow points from dart points. Using discriminant analysis, Michael Shott has shown that the most important discriminating variable is the shoulder width of the point.[36] Recently John Blitz and Erik Porth used a reduction in the shoulder width and the weight of the point to argue that the bow and arrow was adopted in the Eastern Woodlands around AD 300-400.[37] The atlatl probably persisted in use while the Native Americans experimented with the arrow points. Several scholars have suggested that the bow and arrow would confer an advantage to the group possessing it in warfare.[38] It is now likely that the Native Americans did employ the bow and arrow with the larger unstandardized arrow heads at the time Arthur's expedition entered their lands, along with other weapons such as clubs, axes, thrusting spears and darts thrown with the atlatl.

UNREST AFTER THE HOPEWELL PERIOD

Evidence of violence among Native American groups, such as scalping and decapitations, date as far back as the Archaic period, well before the Middle Woodland period in which the Ohio Hopewell lived.[39] However, during the Middle Woodland period itself, skeletons with conflict-related wounds were uncommon. As noted previously, the Hopewell period was one of peace and prosperity, with George Milner stating 'This state of relative harmony lasted for many hundreds of years'.[40] However, after about AD 500 the long-lasting Hopewell harmony came to an end, with a cessation of mound-building in open valleys and a reduction in the co-operative goods exchange between different groups. The reasons for this are not well understood.

In seeking reasons for the change, it is natural to consider explanations that offer some continuity, building on the known attributes of the existing culture. Bradley Lepper offers one such explanation, postulating a growing rivalry in building the earthworks, these requiring larger labour pools, and the subsequent depletion of resources. These factors may have created the need for a more centralised leadership within each area and hence conflict with other areas, this resulting in a cessation of the widespread regional co-operation.[41]

Blitz and Porth offer another scenario in which the introduction of the bow and arrow increased the hunting efficiency of individuals and their kinship group so that they did not need to co-operate with a larger group to catch game. Further, an increased production of native seed crops may have increased household autonomy. These factors may have eventually broken down the level of co-operation among groups to the extent that the major building projects ceased to exist and rivalries developed.[42] In addition to reasons such as these, the Welsh poetry suggests another cause of conflict for the Native Americans, an external threat from the Britons.

The Native Americans in Danger

Given the main thesis of this book, that Arthur led the Britons to America in the sixth century and probably entered the Eastern Woodlands, the thoughts of Hopewellian scholar, Olaf Prufer, are of interest. Prufer, of course, had no inkling of any external invasion force. In his paper in *Scientific American* he argues that the Hopewell seemed to have been in danger at this time. Until around AD 550, they had felt secure enough to leave unguarded the treasures they buried with their dead, but that after about 550 no more elaborate earthworks were built in the open valleys. Prufer's dating for the unrest reflects the time that he wrote and could well have been considerably earlier, perhaps 50 years earlier. He also states that 'every inaccessible hilltop in southern Ohio was suddenly crowned by earthworks that appear to have served a defensive function'. He speculates that the hilltop earthworks were the places of refuge to which the Hopewell fled in times of danger and points to the evidence of fires and massacres at the Fort Hill, Fort Ancient and Fort Miami sites in Ohio. Prufer also notes that later, in the Late Woodland Period, the Native Americans began to protect their villages by building stockades.[43]

A defensive function had long been attributed to the hilltop earthworks by Squier and Davis who classified the earthworks into the categories of 'defensive' and 'sacred'. More recent interpretations have challenged some of Prufer's beliefs. Some of the hilltop enclosures are now known to be coeval with the lowland earthworks. Others have challenged the view that the hilltops were defensive, (or at the least, solely defensive) pointing to the many gates in such enclosures and the presence of ditches built inside the walls rather than outside.[44] This is the current view of many scholars. While it is clear that the hilltop earthwork constructions were not built to optimise defence, it is the case that the very positioning of these structures on sites that were difficult to access would have made them far easier to defend than the mounds built in the open river valleys.

Concluding Comments

It has been proposed that Arthur led an expedition to North America not far from the time that Gildas wrote *The Ruin of Britain*, which could have been in the late 530s, just before the severe environmental downturn of AD 540. Arthur's death is given as 537/39 in the *Annales Cambriae* which could imply that his expedition left in the early to mid 530s. This is of course speculation but it is not far from the time that the Native Americans were in danger according to Olaf Prufer. He asks the direct question 'What was the nature of the danger?' but has no answer, merely commenting that 'Unrest of some kind appears to have been afoot throughout eastern North America'.[45] The Hopewell Newark site appears to have been occupied around 540, as shown by the radiocarbon mean dating given in the paper by Bret Ruby, Chris Carr and Douglas Charles.[46] It appears that the Britons had arrived in America after the cultural traditions of the Hopewell had ended and the long run of peaceful relations was over.

The violence perceived in sixth-century America is consistent with the Welsh poetry. The derivation of the speculative dating for Arthur's expedition given above is completely independent of the dating for the Native American conflict following the breakdown of the Hopewell culture, but gives a similar answer. The poems *Preideu Annwfyn* and *Kat Godeu* refer to the new land as Annwfyn and describe terrible conflict with the inhabitants that destroyed most of the men in the expedition. Only a small remnant survived to make it back to Britain. In the next chapter, a full analysis of the *Preideu Annwfyn* poem will be given.

5
ARTHUR'S AMERICAN VOYAGE

A DISASTROUS HISTORICAL EXPEDITION

Introduction

Preideu Annwfyn (usually translated 'Spoils of the Otherworld') is a superbly composed Welsh poem, appearing in the *Book of Taliesin*, whose manuscript is held in the National Library of Wales in Aberystwyth. *Preideu* probably means 'spoils' or 'booty' but could also mean 'herds'. *Annwfyn* could mean 'unworld' or 'opposite world',[1] the latter possibly a geographical reference, being reminiscent of Plato's 'opposite continent' in his *Timaeus*. The poem describes an expedition led by Arthur which sails to a distant unknown land where they encounter a series of disasters. Eventually only a small number of the crew survived to make it back to Britain. It will be argued below that this represents a historical sixth-century journey to North America that resulted in Arthur being killed.

Annwfyn, the country Arthur visited, is usually identified with the Celtic Otherworld. The latter is a loosely conceived world, varying according to the input of the particular writer, but in the early Irish stories it is reached by sea voyages. In *Echtrae Chonnlai* (Connlae's Adventure), it is inhabited by the people of the *síd*, a people associated with earthen mounds. They are usually thought of as fairy beings and are also portrayed as immortals where death, sickness and decay are non-existent, the land being a Celtic paradise. Roger Loomis has argued that it does not appear to be a place where souls go to after death.[2] Rather, the inhabitants are seen as immortals living forever in a state of happiness and incorruptibility.

This viewpoint of the Otherworld as a paradise is sharply at odds with the experiences of Arthur and his men in Annwfyn. The journey appears to start well as there is imagery of Arthur's bard singing his poetry to the men and receiving great acclaim. There is a camp of the mead-feast where the men are enjoying themselves. However, disaster then looms. In a superb metaphor, Arthur and his men are before the door of the gate of Hell with their lamps burning – they are about to enter Hell. The expedition moves through a series of disastrous camps, with the first six of the eight stanzas ending with the refrain that only seven people (meaning a small number) survived from the particular camp mentioned. Apart from this, there are concise expressions of misfortune. These are translated here as 'renowned tribulation', 'disastrous visit' and 'woeful conflict'. There is a stark contrast between the Otherworld as a place of perfect happiness, where death is unknown, and the terrible loss of life of Arthur's men.

Further, the people of Annwfyn are not portrayed as having the powers of immortals or fairy beings. They do not visit the Defwy meadows in Britain, apparently because of the long distance, which should not defeat the powers of fairies who can appear anywhere. They also have problems understanding the language of the Britons. But this is never a difficulty for the fairies or immortals in the very early Irish Otherworld stories, for example, *Echtrae Chonnlai* and *The Voyage of Bran*. In addition, large numbers of the people of Annwfyn were killed in the fighting, according to the poet who composed the Annwfyn section in Kat Godeu. This should clearly be an impossibility for people who are immortals.

All these considerations suggest that the traditional mythological view of the poem may be badly misconceived. As discussed later in Chapter 11, early references to Arthur (pre c. 800) portray him as a historical figure. When a historical interpretation is adopted, puzzling features of the poem can be readily explained, features for which the mythological viewpoint has given no plausible explanation. It is worthy of note that the poem can be explained without any of the cartoonish features that appear in the Irish and Welsh mythological literature. There are no cauldrons full of gold and silver; no shape-shifters changing their shape to trick their enemies; no dead warriors being restored to life by a magical cauldron; no monsters emerging from a pit of Hell to attack the warriors; no men crumbling to dust when they return home after their overseas journeys; and above all, no magical escape for Arthur's men. The expedition was an unmitigated disaster, and as will be shown later in this chapter, resulted in Arthur's death.

Mythological v Realistic interpretations of Preideu Annwfyn

The *Preideu Annwfyn* poem has been considered baffling on the whole by most commentators.[3] Nearly all scholars give it a mythological interpretation. This fits well with the view that Arthur was not a historical figure, but a Celtic god or folkloric figure. In 1905 Charles Squire wrote *The Mythology of the British Islands* in which he viewed Arthur and his knights as Celtic gods. He interpreted *Preideu Annwfyn* as providing a revealing glimpse of the Celtic Otherworld and commented that the poem 'contains the fullest description that has come down to us of the other world as the Britons conceived it.' He then gives us his dramatic interpretation of the Otherworld as inferred from the poem:[4]

> ...it gives glimpses of a grandeur of savage imagination. The strong-doored, foursquare fortress of glass, manned by its dumb, ghostly sentinels, spun round in never-ceasing revolution, so that few could find its entrance; it was pitch-dark save for the twilight made by the lamp burning before its circling gate; feasting went on there, and revelry, and in its centre, choicest of its many riches, was the pearl-rimmed cauldron of poetry and inspiration, kept bubbling by the breaths of nine British pythonesses, so that it might give forth its oracles.

One can easily see where Squire obtained the individual elements from the poem for this description, but from the perspective of this book the effect is nonsensical, even comical. Not long after Squire's work, William Babcock (1913) wrote *Early Norse Visits to North America*, a book published by the Smithsonian Institution. He remarks that there may have been many pre-Columbian voyages to America of which no record has been discovered and that the voyages of the Celts had begun far back beyond the twilight of history. In this context he refers to *Preideu Annwfyn*:[5]

> Perhaps the first...which can possibly have any significance in this connection is Arthur's mysterious and disastrous foray into some northern Gaelic region, in quest of "The Spoils of Annwn." The ancient poem in the Book of Taliessin, bearing that title, seems to have a nucleus of reality.

Babcock does not develop this idea further, but he does suggest that *Preideu Annwfyn* may have caused Geoffrey of Monmouth to create his Arthurian conquests of Ireland and Iceland. Like Babcock, it will be argued here that the poem is describing a real voyage – that the Otherworld they visited was actually a real world, sixth-century North America. Several incidents in this poem would seem to be consistent with characteristics of Native Americans of the Hopewell culture (or their immediate successors), one which had built a large number of earthen mounds over a period of some 550 years.

As will be shown below, the bard's language suggests that he regarded the Annwfyn inhabitants as ordinary people with human limitations, not fairies or immortals. It will be shown below that the historical interpretation gives a coherent explanation. It is the simplest, most plausible view and can most naturally explain the various incidents in the poem without the need to force any mythological interpretations.

The Translation and Interpretation of Preideu Annwfyn

This translation provides the unemended Welsh in bolded text. However for clarity it has been given modern punctuation, including the capitalization of names, and distinct words that are joined by the scribe have been separated. Leading scholar, Marged Haycock, indicates certain emendments needed which are usually followed here. An important exception is her emending of *Cwy* to *Dwy* (God). Here it is argued that *Cwy* should be kept as the Britons' name of the inhabitants of Annwfyn.[6]

In interpreting *Preideu Annwfyn* it is important to note that it is a *poem*, so that a logical, orderly unfolding of events in correct temporal sequence should not be expected. The thoughts of the bard seem to dart from one image to another in an abrupt fashion, each image conveying a brief picture of part of the expedition. *Preideu Annwfyn* has relationships to a wide range of Welsh and Irish literature. Rather than viewing these instances as derived from other sources, or as manifestations of common themes whose origins are lost, the thesis argued here is that *Preideu Annwfyn* is the very source of many of these relationships.

The relationships of *Preideu Annwfyn* to other works are of importance in estimating the date of the poem and are discussed in detail in Chapter 9. There it will be argued that *Preideu Annwfyn* was composed shortly after the dissemination of *The Ruin of Britain* and was partly a response to Gildas' work. His biased tirade slandering the Britons in general and in particular, its kings, bards and military men, created a poisonous atmosphere that is manifested in the bard's counterattack on the monks in *Preideu Annwfyn*. Its date would therefore have been circa 540, the exact date depending on the date assigned to Gildas' publication.

1 CONFLICT AT KAER SIDI

1 Golychaf wledic, pendeuic, gwlat ri,
   I praise the sovereign, prince, king of the land,
2 py ledas y pennaeth dros traeth mundi.
   who has enlarged his dominion across the world's shores.
3 Bu kyweir karchar Gweir yg kaer sidi
   The prison of Gweir was prepared in the mound fortress
4 trwy ebostol Pwyll a Phryderi.
   according to the account of Pwyll and Pryderi.
5 Neb kyn noc ef nyt aeth idi,
   Nobody before him went into it,
6 yr gadwyn trom las – kywirwas ae ketwi.
   into the heavy blue chain – it restrained a loyal servant.
7 A rac preideu Annwfyn tost yt geni.
   And for the sake of the spoils of Annwfyn bitterly he sang.
8 Ac yt Urawt parahawt yn bardwedi.
   And till Judgement (Day) our bardic prayer shall endure.
9 Tri lloneit Prytwen, yd aetham ni idi.
   Three fullnesses of Prydwen, we went into it.
10 Nam seith, ny dyrreith o gaer sidi.
   Except seven, none returned from the mound fortress.

Discovery of a Distant Land over the Ocean
1 I praise the sovereign, prince, king of the land,
2 who has enlarged his dominion across the world's shores.

Stanza 1 commences with the bard praising a great king, later revealed to be Arthur. The technique of not immediately naming the main subject of the poem is used elsewhere in Welsh poetry, for example in *Kadeir Teÿrnon*. Here Arthur is indirectly introduced through the naming of his ship *Prydwen* in Line 9 and explicitly introduced in Line 21, 'when we went with Arthur'. In Line 2, Arthur has extended his sovereignty across the world's shores, a major achievement.⁷ Later, Line 5 mentions that nobody before Arthur had made this voyage to the unknown land. It indicates the major discovery of a distant land across the ocean.

The Capture of Gweir

3   The prison of Gweir was prepared in the mound fortress
4   according to the account of Pwyll and Pryderi.
5   Nobody before him went into it,
6   into the heavy blue chain – it restrained a loyal servant.
7   And for the sake of the spoils of Annwfyn bitterly he sang.
8   And till Judgement (Day) our bardic prayer shall endure.

A loyal servant named Gweir figures significantly in Stanza 1. He has been taken prisoner in the new land at a place the bard calls *kaer sidi*, translated as 'mound fortress' by Sarah Higley. This capture was reported by Pwyll and Pryderi, who are considered here to be Arthur's men. They appear together in the first story of the *Mabinogi* collection where they are father and son. Given the overwhelming disaster that engulfed the expedition and the small number of people who survived, the focus on Gweir indicates that he was personally known to the bard.⁸

Lines 5-6 state that 'Nobody before him [Arthur] went into it, into the heavy blue chain', the latter being the vast expanse of ocean. This word usage is identical to that in Line 9, where in Arthur's ship, Prydwen, they 'went into it'. It is Arthur who is intended here, not Gweir. In Line 6 Gweir is described as a loyal servant or loyal youth, depending on the translation, one who was too insignificant to be credited with leading the expedition.⁹

The bard is worrying about Gweir who has been left behind. The ocean is likened to a heavy blue chain which effectively imprisons Gweir over and above his *kaer sidi* prison, as the distance makes rescue virtually impossible. In Lines 7-8, the bard visualises him singing bitterly in his prison and states that he will be prayed for till Judgement Day.¹⁰

The Mound Fortress and the Hopewell Culture

Sidi (in *kaer sidi*) is a borrowing from Old Irish *síde* as argued by Patrick Sims-Williams. The latter Irish word is the genitive singular and plural (and nominative plural) of *síd*, which means 'fairy mound' or 'abode of the gods /fairies'. Kenneth Jackson translates *kaer sidi* as 'Faery City' while John Bollard translates it as 'fairy fortress'.¹¹ Sarah Higley notes its importance by wondering why it was not made the title of the poem: 'Why not "Kaer Sidi" ('Mound Fortress')?' she asks.¹² It is argued later that much of the conflict occurred at *kaer sidi*, an area dominated by earthen mounds.

Is such a scenario historically reasonable? As noted in Chapter 4, such a scenario is perfectly consistent with what is known about the Eastern Woodlands of sixth-century North America. The Hopewell had built their complex earthworks in a very dense concentration in the river valleys of central and southern Ohio. Between about 150 BC to AD 400 they had constructed a huge number of earthworks comprising mounds of various shapes and sizes and mound walls of various geometrical shapes that enclosed them.

Given that Gweir is described in a positive way as a 'loyal servant' and that the bard prays for him, it is clear that his imprisonment at the mound fortress was at the hands of the inhabitants rather than Arthur's men. The bard devotes most of the first verse to Gweir. If the poem were only a fairyland fantasy in which nearly all the people in the expedition were killed, then why would the bard express such concern over just one more fictional person who died? Why pray for this fictional character of low rank until Judgement Day? The bard is profoundly worried at what will happen to Gweir which implies something about the ferocity of the inhabitants. The deep worry over Gweir suggests that he was not a fictional person but an actual person known to the bard and that the expedition was a real journey to a new land.

Prydwen
9   Three fullnesses of Prydwen, we went into it.

Prydwen was Arthur's ship as was mentioned three times in the later tale of *Culhwch and Olwen*. We are told in Line 9 that 'three fullnesses' of Prydwen went into it, the meaning of which is uncertain. There appear to be three possibilities: (i) a shuttle service with three trips; (ii) the capacity of Prydwen was employed as a measure, so that three times this capacity went on the journey; (iii) Prydwen was packed to three times its normal capacity. Given that the journey appears to be a long one, (i) seems improbable. Option (ii) is possible, given that it is part of a poem, but it does seem unnecessarily complicated. Why would not the bard simply say that X ships went on the journey? If Prydwen, being the king's ship, had a larger capacity than the other ships, this would introduce further problems of interpretation.

Probably the most natural interpretation is that Prydwen was packed to three times its usual capacity, with a number of other ships unspecified, but this is uncertain. If so, then one must not take the 'three times' literally as three and its multiples were revered numbers, in which case it would simply mean that the ship was extremely crowded.

The Camps
10   Except seven, none returned from the mound fortress.

The expedition moves through a succession of camps in the new land, but sometimes it is uncertain whether a single camp is being given multiple names. The first six stanzas end in the mournful refrain that only seven people survived from the camp mentioned. The number 'seven' should also not be taken literally as it was a significant number, as were 'three' and 'nine' and their multiples. It just means a small number. The last line in its various forms is taken here to mean that only a small number survived who were able to return to Britain.

2 FOUR-PEAKED CAMP AND CAULDRON WITH PEARLS

11 **Neut wyf glot geinmyn, cerd ochlywir**
I am honoured abundantly, song was heard
12 **yg kaer pedryuan – pedyr ychwelyt.**
in the four-peaked camp – turning (to face) the four (peaks).
13 **Yg kynneir, or peir pan leferit.**
My poetry, from the cauldron it was spoken.
14 **O anadyl naw morwyn gochyneuit.**
By the breath of nine maidens it was kindled.
15 **Neu peir pen Annwfyn: pwy y vynut?**
The cauldron of Annwfyn's chieftain: what is its form?
16 **Gwrym am y oror a mererit.**
Dark around its rim and pearls.
17 **Ny beirw bwyt llwfyr: ny ry tyghit.**
It does not boil the food of a coward: it was not so destined.
18 **Cledyf lluch Lleawc idaw ry dyrchit,**
The flashing sword of Lleawc was thrust into it,
19 **ac yn llaw Leminawc yd edewit.**
and in the hand of Lleminawc it was left.
20 **A rac drws porth Vffern llugyrn lloscit.**
And before the door of the gate of Hell lamps burned.
21 **A phan aetham ni gan Arthur, trafferth lechrit.**
And when we went with Arthur, a renowned tribulation.
22 **Namyn seith, ny dyrreith o gaer vedwit.**
Except seven, none returned from the camp of the mead-feast.

The Bard's Poetry

11 I am honoured abundantly, song was heard
12 in the four-peaked camp – turning (to face) the four (peaks).
13 My poetry, from the cauldron it was spoken.
14 By the breath of nine maidens it was kindled.

The stanza opens with the bard boasting about the quality of his poetry which was drawing praise from the audience. This boasting was part of a bard's role to try to differentiate himself from other poets and ordinary men in order to enhance his professional reputation. In Lines 13-14 he likens his poetry to having been produced from a cauldron kindled by nine maidens skilled in the arts of magic. That is, his poetry was so good that it was seemingly produced by magic.[13] Stories about nine maidens practising magic must have been well known for the allusion to be understood by the audience. As noted earlier, such stories were in existence from AD 44 or before, appearing in the work of Pomponius Mela.

This part of the journey appears to have been successful, as Arthur's men were enjoying themselves by listening to the poetry and possibly singing themselves. Given the men's enjoyment, it seems that this camp was early in the expedition before they were engulfed by disasters.

In Line 12, the bard refers to the camp where he was singing his poetry as the four-peaked camp, from *ban*, meaning 'peak' or 'top'. Sarah Higley calls it the four-peaked fortress.[14] Under the historical view, it would seem that from near the campsite they could see four mountain peaks, prominent enough for the bard to name the camp after them.

The 'Revolving Fort' Misunderstanding

12   in the four-peaked camp – turning (to face) the four (peaks).

The second half of Line 12 has caused much confusion. Marged Haycock has translated it as 'revolving (to face) the four directions', noting that *chwel* can mean 'turn'.[15] But what was revolving or turning? As the only explicit noun in Line 12 is the fort or camp, nearly all interpretations have the fort doing the revolving, a view adopted by Marged Haycock and Sarah Higley. This interpretation fits well with a mythological approach to the poem that would allow wonders like revolving forts.

However, this approach gives an inconsistency in the use of the word 'four' (*pedry*), the word appearing in both the first and second half of the line. The second 'four' does not indicate what there are 'four' of. Haycock deals with this by making the first 'four' refer to the four quarters of the fort and the second one refer to the four directions of the compass. Higley has the first 'four' refer to the number of peaks and the second one refer to the number of times the fort revolved.[16]

As the second 'four' does not indicate what there are 'four' of, and then immediately follows 'four-peaked', it is highly probable that the two 'fours' refer to the same objects – the four peaks. Here, following the structure of Haycock, the second half is translated 'turning to face the four peaks'. In Lines 11 and 13, the bard is referring to himself, his acclaim as a bard and the quality of his poetry. He is probably also referring to himself in Line 12, the middle line. It seems likely that it is the bard, an eyewitness to events, who is turning to face the four peaks. In Line 12, he is remembering himself doing this. The camp or fort is not itself turning.

Revolving forts derived from Preideu Annwfyn

This misunderstanding suggests that *Preideu Annwfyn* may be the source of instances of the 'revolving fort' that appear in other literature. Early writers familiar with the poem may have associated the 'turning' or 'revolving' with the fort, as Haycock and Higley do, as it is the only explicit noun in the line. The novel idea of a revolving fort may have made it an attractive concept for other composers. It appears in the Irish tale, *Voyage of Mael Dúin's Boat*, which was probably composed in the 800s. Here the sailors approach an

Otherworld island enclosed by a revolving rampart, with the rampart being described as 'fiery'. There is an open doorway in the rampart allowing the sailors to look inside every time the door revolves in front of them. The fiery nature of the rampart (denoting the flames of Hell) and the associated door have also been copied from *Preideu Annwfyn*, as later in the same stanza (in Line 20) Arthur's men are described as standing before the door of the gate of Hell. This is a metaphor in the poem but the author of *Mael Dúin* has taken it literally.[17]

A revolving fort also appears in the early Irish tale *Bricriu's Feast* (Fled Bricrenn), composed probably in the 700s, as discussed by Thomas Cross and Clark Slover. It belonged to the Irish hero, Cú Roí, who chanted a spell over it every night so that it revolved as swiftly as a mill-stone. Here the door or entrance to the fort is again a focus, as in *Mael Dúin*, being unable to be found after sunset.[18]

Thirdly, the revolving fort appears in *Le Voyage de Charlemagne*, where it belonged to King Hugo the Strong of Constantinople. When Charlemagne visits Hugo he is impressed with the revolving palace that rotates with the blowing of the wind.[19]

Location of the four-peaked camp
In the 'four-peaked' camp, the peaks must have been unusually striking in order for them to be noticed and worthy of comment. The poem also implies that the camp was located such that they would not be able to be viewed all at once, like four peaks on a distant ridge. One would have to turn to be able to view all four. In Chapter 10 it is argued that the campsite was at Montreal, a location consistent with exploring America from a northern sailing route. The four similar peaks there are Royal, St-Bruno, St-Hilaire and Rougemont. With the absence of modern buildings, these would have dominated the site in the sixth century.

The Cauldron of the Chief of Annwfyn

15 The cauldron of Annwfyn's chieftain: what is its form?
16 Dark around its rim and pearls.
17 It does not boil the food of a coward: it was not so destined.
18 The flashing sword of Lleawc was thrust into it,
19 and in the hand of Lleminawc it was left.

After employing the imagery of his poetry coming from a cauldron of poetic inspiration, the bard then reflects on a real cauldron they had captured as spoils of a raid – the cauldron of the chief of Annwfyn. In Line 15 he asks what it was like, for the benefit of the audience, and then proceeds to answer. It was dark around its rim and was decorated with pearls. Lleawc thrust his sword into the cauldron and it was left in the possession of Lleminawc. Given the similarity of their names and the possibility of minim stroke confusion by scribes, these two men could in fact be the same person. A third possibility, as Lleawc means 'destroyer', is to translate Line 18 as 'The flashing, death-dealing sword was thrust into it' which would leave Lleminawc as the only man associated with the cauldron. It is difficult to decide between these three alternatives.[20]

Under the interpretation that the journey was a real one, there is nothing 'magical' about this cauldron – it was just a large decorated clay pot. Given the pearls on the pot, it was probably used for ceremonial purposes by the Native Americans. The Hopewell culture made extensive use of pearls, with thousands of them being found in their mounds. They made an abundance of pearl necklaces and also used inset pearls as decoration for 'eyes' in their numerous animal effigy pipes and in other ornaments. The leading Hopewell scholar, Olaf Prufer, states that bear teeth were frequently decorated with pearls. As noted earlier, he provides a photo of a pottery fragment containing two round holes, alongside a bear tooth containing similar round holes. It appears that both the pottery fragment and the bear tooth had been decorated with pearls. Pearl decoration would seem to be highly improbable for a metal cauldron in Britain.[21]

Cauldron derivatives from Preideu Annwfyn

Sometimes scholars holding a mythological view conflate the cauldron in the bard's imagery in Line 13 (used to describe his poetic inspiration) with the real cauldron taken as spoils of the fighting in Line 15. This conflation results in a single 'magical' cauldron that is associated with nine priestesses. Roger Loomis, who believed that Arthur's knights were 'gods of sun and storm', reflects this viewpoint.[22]

Under the mythological interpretation, it is sometimes inferred that the actual purpose of the journey was to seize this magical cauldron, a claim suggested by the language of several scholars.[23] It is clear that aspects of the cauldrons in quite late literature are influencing the cauldron interpretation in *Preideu Annwfyn*. Like the 'revolving fortress', the cauldron from *Preideu Annwfyn* was the basis for derivative stories in later literature that contain cartoonish features. The following incidents appear to have been influenced by *Preideu Annwfyn*.

An early poem describes an Otherworld raid on *Dún Scáith* (Fortress of Shadow) by an Irish hero, Cú Chulainn. After fighting off beasts emerging from a Hell-like pit in the fortress, he captures a cauldron full of gold and silver. This cauldron has the magical property that it serves as the 'calf' for three cows, but they are able to fill it with the milk of 30 cows. The poem appears in *The Phantom Chariot of Cú Chulainn,* while part of it appears in *The Tragic Death of Cú Roí mac Dáiri*, both reproduced in the book by Thomas Cross and Clark Slover.[24]

Another magical cauldron features in *Branwen daughter of Llŷr* from *The Mabinogi*, having the power to restore to life dead corpses that were placed in it. In their fight with the Britons, the Irish kept putting the dead bodies of their warriors into the cauldron and the next day they were returned to life.

This greatly prolonged the war, causing massive losses on both sides, with the victorious Britons having only seven survivors (the very same number as in *Preideu Annwfyn*), two of them being Pryderi and Taliesin.[25]

A third cauldron event appears in *Culhwch and Olwen* where Llenlleawg, who bore a similar name to Lleminawc, seizes Arthur's sword and kills the Irish giant Diwrnach and his entire retinue, enabling Arthur and his men to take the cauldron, full of Irish treasure, to Arthur's ship.[26] This scene has been adapted from Lines 15-19 of *Preideu Annwfyn*.

Another cauldron, appearing in *The Tale of Gwion Bach*, belongs to the witch, Ceridwen. She creates a magical brew designed to impart knowledge to her son, Afagddu. However, it is the fire stoker, little Gwion, who tastes a few drops of the brew and gains far-reaching knowledge. He flees from the furious Ceridwen, transforming himself into various shapes in trying to escape, but Ceridwen does likewise. Gwion finally changes into a grain in a pile of wheat, but Ceridwen changes into a hen and eats him. Nine months later she gives birth to him, a boy of exceptional knowledge who grows up to be Taliesin.[27]

'It does not boil the food of a coward'

Line 17 is now famous in Welsh tradition although its original meaning has not been understood. It refers to the courage of the owners of the cauldron by using the expression: 'it does not boil the food of a coward'. That is, the owners of the cauldron were not cowards. It is respect for the valour of the Annwfyn inhabitants (the owners) in their fighting with the Britons. This implies that the bard viewed them as people with human limitations – they could be badly wounded or killed and their willingness to face such dangers in battle prompted the bard's comment. Clearly, they were not supernaturally endowed opponents like fairies who could use magic to remove themselves from danger or immortals who could not be killed. This unexpected respect for the courage of the Native Americans also appears in the *Kat Godeu* poem where the bard states that he did kill many of the inhabitants.

The clear derivative nature of one of the above cauldron stories is further illustrated by the later mangling of this superb figure of speech. Diwrnach's cauldron from *Culhwch and Olwen* is given an exalted status in *The Thirteen Treasures of the Island of Britain*, as recorded by Rachel Bromwich.[28] There it is interpreted literally as an instrument for detecting cowardice. Although it would not boil the meat of a coward, it would boil the meat of a brave man, a travesty of the striking expression in *Preideu Annwfyn* that acknowledges the bravery of the Native Americans.

Impending Tribulation

20 And before the door of the gate of Hell lamps burned.
21 And when we went with Arthur, a renowned tribulation.
22 Except seven, none returned from the camp of the mead-feast.

The stanza ends with three lines emphasising disaster. The first is another superb metaphor, with Arthur and his men before the door of the gate of Hell with their lamps burning. They are about to enter Hell.

The second line is part of a repeating pattern (shared with Lines 41 and 47) according to the formula 'And when we went with Arthur, ...' where each line finishes with various disasters. A literal translation of *trafferth lechrit* would give something like 'brilliant difficulty'. It has been translated here as 'a renowned tribulation' which gives a parallelism with the hardships in the other lines. The final line has only seven returning from camp *vedwit*, which is translated here as the camp of the mead-feast, based on the discussion by Marged Haycock.[29]

3 THE CAMP OF EXTREME COLDNESS

23 **Neut wyf glot geinmyn, kerd glywanawr**
   I am honoured abundantly, songs are heard
24 **yg kaer pedryfan, ynys pybyrdor.**
   in the four-peaked camp, isle of the strong door.
25 **Echwyd a muchyd kymyscetor.**
   Flowing water and jet are mingled.
26 **Gwin gloyw eu gwirawt rac eu gorgord.**
   Bright wine their liquor before their retinue.
27 **Tri lloneit Prytwen yd aetham ni ar vor.**
   Three fullnesses of Prydwen we went upon the sea.
28 **Namyn seith, ny dyrreith o gaer rigor.**
   Except seven, none returned from the camp of extreme coldness.

What was the Strong Door?
23 I am honoured abundantly, songs are heard
24 in the four-peaked camp, isle of the strong door.

This stanza introduces the 'strong door', viewed here as the entrance to the new land. Chapter 10 argues that this was the St Lawrence River, with the 'four-peaked' camp being Montreal. Although this river was the gateway to this unexplored country for the Britons, its strong currents and dangerous obstacles would have made upstream sailing very difficult, these difficulties prompting the 'strong' adjective. Although the 'isle' could refer to an island in the river it is more likely to be a general term for the new land, conceived as an island. Marged Haycock also gives a metaphorical translation, not one where there is literally a strong door.[30]

It appears likely that the author of *The Phantom Chariot of Cú Chulainn* copied this feature from *Preideu Annwfyn*, but he does take it literally. In the raid to capture the cauldron in the overseas Otherworld fortress, *Dún Scáith*, he refers to the fort as being protected by 'doors of iron on each side', as recorded in Cross and Slover.[31]

Flowing Water and Jet are Mingled
25 Flowing water and jet are mingled.

Line 25 contains an extremely difficult allusion. Here *echwyd* has been taken to mean 'fresh or flowing water'. A literal translation would be 'Flowing water and jet are mingled', a translation favoured by several prominent scholars. However another interpretation is possible which translates *echwyd* to mean 'noonday', which also has several advocates.[32] The jet here (*muchyd*) is not a spray of water but the solid coal-like material – lignite. Marged Haycock suggests that this could refer to the belief that adding water to jet creates fire, from Isidore of Seville's *Etymologies* (XVI, iv, 3). She argues that the bard is displaying his arcane learning in contending for superiority in learning with the monks.[33] However this explanation does not explain why the water should be 'flowing' or 'fresh' and is not favoured here.

However there are other possibilities that could point to Iceland. In the *History of the Archbishops of Hamburg-Bremen* Adam of Bremen mentions a 'remarkable fact' about Iceland – that black-coloured ice can be found there which burns when fire is set to it. Francis Tschan, the translator of Adam's work, suggests that *surtarbrand* (lignite) may have been mixed with the ice. When such ice melted in Summer, the dark lignite dust and other impurities may have created the effect the bard is describing. Dark volcanic dust in ice may also have given a similar effect.[34]

If 'jet' is not to be taken literally as lignite, but as a proxy for something dark, then the waterfall *Svartifoss* (Black Fall) may be a possibility. Located in southeast Iceland, it plunges over columns of volcanic basalt, a contrast of flowing water and dramatic black rock columns. It is argued in a later chapter that the expedition probably followed the 'stepping stones' route to America, passing through Iceland.

Camp of Extreme Coldness
26 Bright wine their liquor before their retinue.
27 Three fullnesses of Prydwen we went upon the sea.
28 Except seven, none returned from the camp of extreme coldness.

In Line 28 the camp is translated as one of 'extreme coldness', following the suggestion of Patrick Sims-Williams that *rigor* should be connected with the Latin *frigus, frigoris*. John Koch also agrees with Sims-Williams, translating it as the 'Frigid Fort'.[35]

The presence of the very realistic line 'Bright wine their liquor before their retinue' suggests that the bard was not singing a fantasy involving Arthur fighting fairy creatures. This routine activity would seem an incongruous element to include in such an Otherworld fantasy. Moreover, if the camp were one of extreme coldness, it would make sense if the bright (*gloyw*) wine were *glühwein*. This wine would be served heated, a highly appropriate drink for Arthur's men in the freezing cold.

4 MEETING THE INHABITANTS

29 Ny obrynafi lawyr, llen llywyadur.
I set no value on little men, (merely) concerned with scripture.
30 Tra chaer wydyr ny welsynt wrhyt Arthur.
Beyond the glass fortress they did not see Arthur's valour.
31 Tri vgeint canhwr a seui ar y mur:
Three-score hundred men were standing on the wall:
32 oed anhawd ymadrawd ae gwylyadur.
it was difficult to speak with their watchman.
33 Tri lloneit Prytwen yd aeth gan Arthur.
Three fullnesses of Prydwen went with Arthur.
34 Namyn seith, ny dyrreith o gaer golud.
Except seven, none returned from the camp of obstruction.

The Bard's Contempt for the Monks
29 I set no value on little men, (merely) concerned with scripture.

In the first three stanzas, the perspective of the poem was on incidents in Annwfyn. In Stanza 4, the perspective suddenly shifts back to Britain. The bard is one of the few survivors and is back in Britain, devastated at the losses and furious at the monks following the publication of *The Ruin of Britain*. In every stanza thereafter he directs what seems close to hatred at the monks. This emotion goes far beyond a striving for superiority over the monks in learning. In the last five of the eight stanzas the bard's rage is fully unleashed as he expresses his contempt for the monks.

Sarah Higley captures the bard's emotions perfectly in her translation of *lawyr* as 'little men', from a compound of *llaw* (small, like the hand) and *gwŷr* (men).[36] The bard directs this insult to the monks in the opening line of Stanzas 4, 5 and 6. In Line 29 he states that he has no respect for the little men whom he regarded as living the 'soft' ordered life of the scribe. He then ridicules their ignorance of what happened in Annwfyn and, in doing so, provides us with more images of events in that new land.

Beyond the Iceberg
30 Beyond the glass fortress they did not see Arthur's valour.
31 Three-score hundred men were standing on the wall:
32 it was difficult to speak with their watchman.

On the journey the sailors observe a glass fortress – poetic imagery for a large iceberg. The use of glass or crystal to describe icebergs also appears in other early works, the *Historia Brittonum* and the *Navigatio* of St Brendan.[37] It is well known that there is a close relationship between the *Historia Brittonum* account and these *Preideu Annwfyn* lines, as argued by Kenneth Jackson and Marged Haycock.[38] In the *Historia* the sailors encounter a 'glass tower in the middle of the sea', where the men standing on it don't respond to the sailors' attempts to communicate. Compare this with Line 32 in *Preideu Annwfyn* given above. The sailors then mount a pointless attack on the glass tower (the iceberg), but all were killed.

In contrast, Line 30 in *Preideu Annwfyn* states that it is beyond (*tra*) the glass fortress that Arthur's valour was exhibited, not on the iceberg itself, but beyond it. There is a dangerous iceberg region where the icebergs drift down the eastern side of Labrador and Newfoundland, as occurred in the Titanic disaster of 1912. To reach North America they would have to sail beyond these. It will be later argued in Chapter 9 that the *Historia Brittonum* gives a vacuous scenario which appears to be a garbled version of Lines 30-2 from *Preideu Annwfyn*.

On the mainland, Arthur's expedition met the Annwfyn inhabitants in a dramatic incident. There was a very large group of them standing on a wall above the Britons. The poem gives three-score hundred men, which would simply mean a large number. It was hard to communicate with their watchman, something that would be entirely expected for two groups of people with radically different languages.

Such an encounter would hardly be implausible as the Hopewell mounds were frequently enclosed by earthen walls. The Native Americans may have been standing on such a wall to prevent their mounds and their treasures from being desecrated. If they felt threatened by the newcomers, they may have mustered their warriors and assembled to confront the Britons. In *Kat Godeu* the bard describes them as coming ready for battle by means of the streams of Annwfyn, as translated by Marged Haycock.[39]

Three elements of the above imply that the inhabitants were not viewed as fairies. The first is that they assembled in a large group to intimidate the Britons through their physical strength, rather than by magic. The idea of fairies massing to physically intimidate the Britons gives an absurd picture. Secondly, the failure of communication implies that the bard saw them as humans with another language, not fairies. In the Irish Otherworld stories, the fairies can easily converse with the humans. Thirdly, their gathering for battle by means of the streams suggests that they were Native Americans, not fairies. It is hardly a mode of transport associated with fairies who are able to use magic to appear or disappear at will.

Concluding Stanza 4

33 Three fullnesses of Prydwen went with Arthur.
34 Except seven, none returned from the camp of obstruction.

The stanza concludes with the usual haunting formula that three 'fullnesses' of *Prydwen* went with Arthur to Annwfyn, but only seven returned from the camp of obstruction. The camp's name probably gives an indication of the stubborn resistance provided by the Native Americans as the Britons moved from camp to camp in the new land.

5 THE 'BRINDLED OX'

35 **Ny obrynaf y lawyr, llaes eu kylchwy.**
I set no value on little men, loose their shield straps.
36 **Ny wdant wy py dyd peridyd pwy,**
They do not know who was created on which day,
37 **py awr y meindyd y ganet Cwy,**
what hour of the slender day the Cwy were born,
38 **pwy gwnaeth ar nyt aeth doleu Defwy.**
who made them who did not go to the Defwy meadows.
39 **Ny wdant wy yr ych brych, bras y penrwy,**
They do not know the brindled ox, thick his headring,
40 **seith vgein kygwng yn y aerwy.**
seven-score joints in his collar.
41 **A phan aetham ni gan Arthur – auyrdwl gofwy.**
And when we went with Arthur – disastrous visit.
42 **Namyn seith, ny dyrreith o gaer vandwy.**
Except seven, none returned from the camp of God's Peak.

The Monks are Cowards
35 I set no value on little men, loose their shield straps.

Here the bard shows his utter contempt for the monks by virtually accusing them of cowardice ('loose their shield straps'). He is now contrasting the monks and himself on the issue of martial valour. This goes well beyond what one would expect from a court poet from the ninth or even later centuries composing a poem to entertain his lord. If he were merely trying to upstage the monks with his learning, as discussed by Marged Haycock, it can hardly account for his implication that the monks were cowards. As was discussed earlier and argued later in Chapter 9, the bard's rage was a reaction to the cleric Gildas who (amongst other insults) described the British military as 'cowards' and 'like women'.[40] The bard then continues ridiculing the monks for their ignorance of what happened in Annwfyn.

Interest in the origin of the Native Americans
36 They do not know who was created on which day,
37 what hour of the slender day the Cwy were born,
38 who made them who did not go to the Defwy meadows.

Here the bard wonders about the origin of the Native Americans – to him a strange new people from a distant part of the world. They were known as the Cwy to the Britons. The bard believed that his people (the Britons) were descended from Adam and Eve who were created on the Sixth Day. In Line 36 he asks whether the new people were derived from this creation or were part of another creation on a different day. Whatever the creation day of the

Cwy, Line 37 continues this theme by asking what hour of this slender day (*meindyd*) they were created. Perhaps the bard thought of the 'slender day' as a fleeting or insignificant unit of time in relation to the long span of history. In Line 38 he further speculates on their origin. Who made them? If not God, then perhaps one of God's agents, a powerful enchanter. As the monks knew nothing of the Annwfyn people, they would hardly know the answers to these questions. The bard's repeated interest in their origin, expressed over three lines, would not make sense if the people were mere fictions he had created. It implies that they were real people, seen as vastly different to the Britons, rather than part of an imaginative fantasy.

Cwy – the Name given to the Native Americans
37   what hour of the slender day the Cwy were born,

Cwy (pronounced as in 'we', as inferred from the rhyme scheme) is taken as the Britons' name for the Annwfyn inhabitants, perhaps a sound used by the people themselves. The following similar sounding name (*Quii*) appears in other references to American inhabitants. On the circa 1537 globe of Gemma Frisius, the Latin expression 'Quij populi' begins a sentence placed next to a strait that shows a 'northwest passage' to Asia through north Canada. Arthur Newton translates the text as 'Quii people, of whom John Scolvus the Dane reached in 1476'. Further, the 16th century L'Ecuy globe contains a similar sentence beginning with 'Quii populi'. Newton remarks that this voyage was probably a visit to Greenland. However, given the lack of data on Scolvus, it is not really known how far he went.[41]

Further south, the Qui sound occurs in the Quiripi language of eastern American tribes, including the Quinnipiac. This language has been extinct for about 200 years. It is part of the Algonquian language family which may have retained the Qui sound in the last part of its name.

The Defwy Meadows in Britain
38   who made them who did not go to the Defwy meadows.

Here the bard notes that the Annwfyn inhabitants did not go to the *Defwy* meadows in Britain (pronounced 'Devwy'). This suggests that he sees them as people with human limitations who were restricted in where they could travel, not fairies of the Otherworld. The latter had no limitations on where they could visit, as shown by the Irish Otherworld stories.

The name *Defwy* gives an important clue to the bard's home territory in Britain. It could derive from *Deva*, the Roman name for Chester and thus refer to the meadows along the River Dee. In *The Spoils of Taliesin* poem, the same word *Deuwy* appears in the 'It is pleasing...' section and is tentatively translated as *Dee* by leading scholar John Koch.[42] It is thus possible that Arthur's expedition left from the mouth of the River Dee which prompted the bard to say that the inhabitants of Annwfyn do not ever visit there.

The American Bison (Buffalo)

39 They do not know the brindled ox, thick his headring,
40 seven-score joints in his collar.

The bard seemingly had not seen the 'brindled ox' before the ill-fated voyage to Annwfyn. In Line 36 he begins the 'they do not know' sequence and then repeats these words for emphasis in Line 39 for the brindled ox. As a result of its mention in *Preideu Annwfyn* it became famous (although no one really knew what it was) featuring in Triad 45 of the Welsh Triads, as recorded and discussed by Rachel Bromwich.[43] In composing the poem, the bard had to be economical with his words within the constraints of rhyme and syllable count in a line. His expressions are not a literal statement of shackles on the animal but a concise and vivid way of describing it. It has three main features: (i) a huge head (from 'thick his headring'); (ii) a massive neck (from 'seven-score joints in his collar'); (iii) a coat of unusual colour variation ('brindled' from *brych*).

The 'brindled ox' is almost certainly the American bison (Bison bison) commonly known as the buffalo. As Alexander Banfield remarks, the name 'buffalo' is a misnomer but it is used here as it is in common use.[44] The bard would not have seen an ox in Britain of this size and power. The huge head and forequarters consist of a thick dark brown shaggy hair which sharply contrasts with the shorter-haired 'yellow-ochre cape' on the upper back, as noted by Hal Reynolds, C. Cormack Gates and Randal Glaholt. This cape gives a patchy yellow-brown appearance in the two periods of moulting in Spring and Autumn each year.[45]

The buffalo observed by the bard would have been the plains bison, that was distributed widely west of the Appalachian Mountains. It is significant that even in historical times the bison were observed in the region where the complex earthworks were densely distributed. David Zeisberger, the Ohio missionary, noted in 1779-80 that large numbers of buffalo were seen along the banks of the Muskingum and Scioto Rivers.[46] As discussed previously, these rivers were associated with many large mound complexes.

Concluding Stanza 5

41 And when we went with Arthur – disastrous visit.
42 Except seven, none returned from the camp of God's Peak.

The haunting formula for misery continues, revealing the bard's heartfelt distress. This time Arthur's voyage is described as a 'disastrous visit'. Here the camp from which few survived is called 'God's Peak'. The latter name is inferred from the compound word *vandwy* (*ban* + *dwy*), which combines 'peak' and 'God'. It would appear to be a mountain peak of such grandeur that it would be appropriate for God to reside there. This translation is tentatively given by Sarah Higley, while John Koch translates it similarly as the fort of the divine place.[47]

6 TAMED ANIMAL WITH SILVERY HEAD

43   **Ny obrynafy lawyr, llaes eu gohen.**
     I set no value on little men, weak their resolve.
44   **Ny wdant py dyd peridyd pen,**
     They do not know which day the chief was created,
45   **py awr y meindyd y ganet perchen,**
     what hour of the slender day the owner was born,
46   **py vil a gatwant, aryant y pen.**
     what animal they keep, with its silvery head.
47   **Pan aetham ni gan Arthur – afyrdwl gynhen.**
     When we went with Arthur – woeful conflict.
48   **Namyn seith, ny dyrreith o gaer ochren.**
     Except seven, none returned from the enclosed camp.

The Monks are Weak in Willpower
43   I set no value on little men, weak their resolve.

Stanza 6 opens with the bard again pouring his contempt upon the monks. Following the pattern in earlier stanzas he taunts them as having no manly resolve. The idea seems to be that the monks are too timid to take risks or do adventurous things. They lack the strength of will to overcome the difficulties that tougher men face.

Again the hypothesis of a court poet entertaining his lord and trying to upstage the monks with his superiority in learning is exceedingly inadequate. Here the bard is contrasting the resolve he had to demonstrate in dangerous situations with the 'soft' and ordered life of the monks. He is presumably thinking of the extreme hardships that Arthur's men had endured in their expedition to Annwfyn.

The 'Animal they keep, with its Silvery Head'
44   They do not know which day the chief was created,
45   what hour of the slender day the owner was born,
46   what animal they keep, with its silvery head.

The bard continues with things the monks do not know about Annwfyn. In the first line 'They do not know which day the chief was created' the bard again speculates on the origin of this new people from a distant part of the world. On what day of Creation did God make them? This line is a variant of Line 36 in the previous stanza.

Line 45, 'what hour of the slender day the owner was born', is also a variant of Line 37 in the previous stanza, but introduces the new concept of 'the owner' (*perchen* in the text). Who was this owner? This is clarified in Line 46, where it is stated that the Annwfyn people keep a particular animal – with a silvery head.

The North American river otter

This animal is to be identified with the North American river otter (*Lontra canadensis*) which was plentiful in the streams of North America before the European colonisation. It has a glossy dense coat, generally of a brownish colour, while the 'chin and throat are silvery'.[48] In the older otters the fur may become white tipped.[49] When the coat is wet, which is often, the lustrous sheen on the coat gives a silvery appearance.

If the bard were watching the river otter swimming in the streams of Annwfyn, he may have observed the silvery head carried above the water. When swimming, the otter keeps its head above water so that the nostrils, ears and eyes are exposed.[50] The bard's description is of interest for two reasons. The first is his claim that the animal was partly domesticated, a claim that is quite plausible as will be argued below. The second is that to observe this interaction between the Annwfyn inhabitants and the otter, the Britons must have come into close contact with them.

Training the otter

It is well known that the clever otter can be trained by humans. Otters are intelligent, playful, sociable and inquisitive, and are perfectly adapted to catching fish. In 1927 Eugene Gudger wrote that training otters to catch fish for humans has been proceeding since early times to the twentieth century, particularly in Asia.[51] He quotes from a Chinese writer of the Tang Dynasty on how otters are trained to fish and concludes that otter fishing in China goes back to a remote past, prior to about AD 600. He notes the wide range of countries in which otter training has occurred and provides details of some of the different training methods used. Gudger reproduces two photographs, each showing an otter resting in the stern of the Chinese fishing boat of his master. Some aquariums today train otters to respond to key commands to help monitor their state of health; for example, at the Tennessee Aquarium in Chattanooga.

The Hopewell and the otter

The Hopewell and their successors left no writings that can confirm that they trained the otter to help them fish. However, there is evidence that they were respectful of the otter. It should be noted that the Hopewell centre of influence in southern Ohio has an abundance of streams and rivers in which the North American river otter would have flourished.

The Hopewell are well known for the carving of animal effigy pipes which expertly depict the animals with which they interacted. At Mound City, a few miles north of Chillicothe, the visitor centre displays such a pipe in the shape of an otter that was found during excavation of the mounds there. Similarly the British Museum in London displays another Mound City effigy pipe in the form of an otter (North America section, Room 26). Slight damage to the pipe suggests that this otter originally had a fish in its mouth. Four more otter effigy pipes have been found in the Hopewell Tremper mound, of which three show the otter carrying a fish in its mouth, as shown on the Ohio Historical Society website.

Further, Squier and Davis provide drawings of two more otter effigy pipes found in Hopewell mounds, one badly damaged pipe showing little more than the head, with the captured fish prominently displayed.[52] In summary, of the eight otter pipes noted here, five had the otter carrying a fish in its mouth. If the arguments presented earlier are correct, it would be a remarkable fact that knowledge of the sixth-century Hopewell culture could have come from a sixth-century Welsh poem.

Concluding Stanza 6
47 When we went with Arthur – woeful conflict.
48 Except seven, none returned from the enclosed camp.

Line 47 gives another expression of disaster – the Britons endured 'woeful conflict'. Then the repeating end line follows with the camp here being the 'enclosed camp'. Perhaps *ochren*, the word translated as 'enclosed', may refer to the enclosed earthwork walls constructed by the Hopewell. However, given that many settlements could have been enclosed, the general nature of the term does not allow any firm conclusions.

7 THE LORDS WHO KNOW THE SECRET

49 **Myneich dychnut, val cunin cor,**
    Monks draw together, like a pack of dogs,
50 **o gyfranc udyd ae gwidanhor.**
    from a clash with lords who know.
51 **Ae vn hynt gwynt? Ae vn dwfyr mor?**
    Is the wind of one path? Is the sea of one water?
52 **Ae vn vfel tan twrwf diachor?**
    Is the fire, an invincible tumult, of one spark?

The Clash with the 'Lords who Know'
49 Monks draw together, like a pack of dogs,
50 from a clash with lords who know.

Stanza 7 opens dramatically with a vivid scene showing the monks packing together in fear. There are interesting possible variants of this translation as Sarah Higley shows. However in all of them the monks are likened to dogs. This usage may have been a response to Gildas, who likens Maglocunus to a dog returning to his disgusting vomit. He also mocks Aurelius 'Caninus' by punning on his name, calling him 'Caninus', meaning 'dog-like' (meant in a pejorative sense), rather than his real name which was probably the Neo-Brittonic equivalent of *Cynan*, according to Kenneth Jackson. It will later be argued that Gildas' *Ruin of Britain* created a poisonous atmosphere between the kings, their bards and the military men on one side and the self-righteous monks on the other.53

Line 50 then gives one of the most important lines in the poem – 'from a clash with lords who know'. The general sense is that the monks are being threatened and their response is to pack together in fear. Marged Haycock discusses the translation of *gyfranc* as 'clash' or 'contention'.54 The essence of the line is that the lords know something important that the monks do not know and have just revealed it to them, creating the uproar. Note that it is the *lords who know*, not just the bard. Hence the issue is not concerned with the bard vaunting his superiority in learning over the monks. The secret of what the lords know is skilfully delayed by the bard as he builds suspense towards the most important line in the poem.

Building Dramatic Tension

51 Is the wind of one path? Is the sea of one water?
52 Is the fire, an invincible tumult, of one spark?

Here the bard inserts some 'filler' questions to delay the secret and help build dramatic tension. These questions would still allow him to express contempt for the monks, as they could hardly know the answers to such ill-defined questions. Indeed, they are so vaguely defined that they are not capable of being answered in the form in which they are posed. Their prime purpose is to build suspense. They clearly do not refer to events in Annwfyn, being quite general questions. In contrast, the earlier incidents of which the monks were ignorant do refer to events in Annwfyn.

8 ARTHUR'S DEATH IN ANNWFYN REVEALED

53 **Myneych dychnut, val bleidawr,**
Monks draw into a pack, like wolves,
54 **o gyfranc udyd ae gwidyanhawr.**
from a clash with lords who know.
55 **Ny wdant pan yscar deweint a gwawr;**
They know not when darkness and dawn divide;
56 **neu wynt, pwy hynt, pwy y rynnawd;**
nor wind, what path it follows, what its rushing is;
57 **py va diua, py tir a plawd.**
what place it destroys, what land it strikes.
58 **Bet sant yn diuant – a bet a llawr.**
The grave of the saint is lost/annihilated – both grave and champion.
59 **Golychaf y wledic, pendefic mawr,**
I praise the sovereign, great prince,
60 **na bwyf trist: Crist am gwadawl.**
that I not be grieving: Christ provides for me.

The 'Lords who Know' Emphasised

53 Monks draw into a pack, like wolves,
54 from a clash with lords who know.

Stanza 8 opens similarly to Stanza 7, but this time the monks pack together like wolves. This also may have been a response to Gildas who had castigated the sinful clergy as 'wolves all ready to slaughter souls'. Here Line 54 uses *gwidyanhawr* instead of *gwidanhor*, but has been translated as in the prior stanza, 'lords who know', from the comments of Marged Haycock. The virtual repetition of these two sets of lines (Lines 49-50, 53-54) emphasises their importance and builds dramatic tension.[55]

Sustaining Dramatic Tension

55 They know not when darkness and dawn divide;
56 nor wind, what path it follows, what its rushing is;
57 what place it destroys, what land it strikes.

Then follows poorly defined 'filler' statements in Lines 55-7 that represent implied questions that the monks cannot answer. Like those in the previous stanza these do not relate to the incidents in Annwfyn, but by delaying the climax they continue to build dramatic tension.

Grieving over Arthur's Death

58 The grave of the saint is lost/annihilated – both grave and champion.
59 I praise the sovereign, great prince,
60 that I not be grieving: Christ provides for me.

Finally comes Line 58, the most important line in the poem – that the grave of the saint is lost or annihilated in Annwfyn, both grave and champion. This line provides the answer to the crucial question of what the lords know – that Arthur, the Christian king, has been killed in Annwfyn and his grave and body are lost forever. The 'saint' and 'champion' in Line 58 is the 'sovereign, great prince' in the next line, about whom the bard is trying not to grieve. He sums up resignedly that Christ provides for him. Sarah Higley also gives a similar translation to Line 58, setting out various options that incorporate the above meaning.[56]

This concept of the lords knowing about the death of a great chief and 'telling the monks' is repeated in a later *Book of Taliesin* poem, where it is applied to the Irish hero, Cú Roí. This parallel theme occurs in Line 17 of *Marwnat Corroi m(ab) Dayry* (The Deathsong of Cú Roí son of Dáiri). There the poet asks whether the monks know about the death of the passionate treasure-chief. The line needs some emendments, but Haycock's analysis is persuasive.[57] Cú Roí was a mythical Irish hero who has been given some Arthurian characteristics. Line 17 in *Marwnat Corroi* appears to be derived from the *Preideu Annwfyn* lines and shows that the Taliesin 'persona' who later composed *Marwnat Corroi* did understand the meaning of Lines 49-50, 53-4 and 58-9 from *Preideu Annwfyn*.

ARTHUR AS A CHRISTIAN

Line 58 describes Arthur as a saint, which agrees with early church usage as denoting a devoted Christian (for example, Romans 1:7; 2 Corinthians 1:1). This usage is also consistent with the way Gildas applies the term in *The Ruin of Britain*. In sections 28.1, 32.2, 35.4, 65.2 and 66.4 of his book Gildas uses 'saint' simply to refer to devout Christians. There is no strict requirement for martyrdom or miracles. In Section 10.2 he also applies 'saint' to St Alban who was martyred and did perform a 'miracle' in Section 11, but this is not the general rule. A Christian martyrdom would clearly be sufficient as proof of devotion to God, but would not appear to be necessary. Gildas himself later acquired the title and he died of old age. The term came to be applied to monks,[58] and the later saints' *Lives* are full of 'miracles' but Gildas' usage simply requires devotion to God.

The presenting of Arthur as a Christian king appears in the well-known texts, the *Historia Brittonum* and *Annales Cambriae*. It also appears in a very early work, *Kadeir Teÿrnon*, probably by the same bard who composed *Preideu Annwfyn*. In *Kadeir Teÿrnon*, the opening section refers to a brave, authoritative king, later introduced as Arthur. In Line 8, Marged Haycock translates that this king had a 'reverence of scripture'.[59]

This reverence by Arthur would have probably been combined with a providential view of Christianity (as Gildas held) – that if Arthur professed Christianity then God would help him in battle. Other early kings seem to have had this view; for example, Clovis the Frankish king as described in *History of the Franks* by Gregory of Tours.[60]

THE MYSTERY OF ARTHUR'S GRAVE

Black Book of Carmarthen: Stanzas of the Graves

The death of Arthur in North America gives the answer to the longstanding mystery about Arthur's death and grave that occurs in the legends noted in Chapter 3 and in the inexplicable ending to Arthur's life given in Geoffrey of Monmouth's *History* where the dying Arthur is taken overseas to Avalon. The mystery is expressed in Stanza 44 of *Stanzas of the Graves*, as translated by Thomas Jones:[61]

> **Bet y March, bet y Guythur,**
> There is a grave for March, a grave for Gwythur,
> **bet y Gugaun Cledyfrut;**
> a grave for Gwgawn Red-sword;
> **anoeth bid bet y Arthur.**
> the world's wonder a grave for Arthur.

In essence, the stanza says that in contrast to other British heroes, Arthur's grave is a complete mystery. The important word is *anoeth*, translated here as 'wonder' by Jones but it is difficult to find an exact meaning. It occurs in *Culhwch and Olwen* where it appears to mean 'something almost impossible to achieve'. In the sense given above, it probably means 'something almost impossible to understand'.

The mystery concerning Arthur's death apparently survived in a legend in which Arthur lay wounded or dying in a distant land over the ocean. In his *History* and *Life of Merlin* Geoffrey of Monmouth elaborates this legend in naming the land Avalon and having Arthur's wounds being attended by nine priestesses who were skilled in healing, led by Morgen. This left open the possibility that if his wounds could be healed, he could be brought back to expel the Saxons. The absence of a grave allowed the belief that Arthur was not dead to develop. This belief persisted in Cornwall until at least 600 years after his death. When a party of canons from Laon in France visited Cornwall about 1113, a member of the group, Hangello, expressed the view that Arthur was dead. This created a near riot by the Cornishmen, in which bloodshed was only narrowly averted.[62] The death of Arthur in America explains the absence of a funeral and grave-site in Britain, in contrast to the other British kings recorded in the *Stanzas of the Graves*.

Camlann

In the *Annales Cambriae* it is stated that Arthur had died with Mordred at Camlann in 537/539. Unfortunately, this reference may have been inserted into the annals at a very late stage, perhaps 400 years after Arthur's death, so that it can hardly be trusted. The second problem is that our modern image of Mordred has been coloured by Geoffrey's imaginative account portraying Mordred as an arch-villain who not only usurped Arthur's throne but also committed adultery with Guinevere.

In contrast, the Welsh bards portray Mordred as a paragon of virtue and on good terms with Arthur right up to the poetry of Tudur Aled[63] who wrote in the period 1465-1525. Sadly, nothing in the early Welsh poetry mentions Camlann, making it difficult to know if any information can be extracted from the *Annales Cambriae* reference.

Rachel Bromwich does mention a late tradition that seven men survived Camlann, the very same number that survived Annwfyn. Camlann probably means 'crooked or curved riverbank', as the alternative 'crooked enclosure' seems unlikely for a battlesite. The name occurs in the Afon Gamlan and in two other places near Dolgellau in Wales. However it is unlikely that Arthur died there in a civil war as his body would probably have been recovered and buried with honour. If he did die at Camlann, it is argued that Camlann was in one of the river valleys of the Hopewell sphere in America where the river had a sharp change of direction. Perhaps the Britons fought their last battle where one of the rivers twisted sharply to form a 'crooked bank' which gave this name to the battle.[64]

ATTEMPTS TO TRUNCATE THE POEM

Praising the Great Earthly King

The opening line of the poem is translated 'I praise the sovereign, prince, king of the land'. The Welsh word *wledic* means 'sovereign' or 'lord' which can mean an earthly king ruling his subjects (for example, the British king, Maxen Wledig) or the Christian God. In Line 2 this *wledic* is the subject of: 'who has enlarged his dominion across the world's shores'. These two lines imply that it is an earthly king that *wledic* represents, not the Christian God. It seems implausible to describe God as extending his sovereignty across the world's shores – being God, he has sovereignty everywhere. Further, the poem in Lines 5-6 states that 'nobody before him went into it, into the heavy blue chain [the ocean]'. This certainly cannot refer to the Christian God. It also cannot refer to Gweir, who is only a loyal servant or loyal youth, someone too insignificant to be given credit for leading an expedition across the ocean. It must refer to the *wledic*, the great earthly king named as Arthur in Line 21, 'when we went with Arthur'.

Incorrect claims of Christian Interpolations

Despite the above, some scholars in the late 19th and early 20th centuries did form the viewpoint that the two lines referred to God. Further, in spite of very strong internal evidence to the contrary, they formed the view that the poem was 'magnificently pagan'. Having arrived at this preposterous conclusion they thus decided that the first two lines must have been an interpolation inserted by Christian monks. In similar fashion they interpret the last two lines, Lines 59 and 60, as referring exclusively to God, and hence by this perverted logic these too must be Christian interpolations. This viewpoint is espoused by John Rhŷs in his Hibbert Lectures: 'The poem opens with the usual tribute to Christianity which not infrequently begins and ends the Welsh poems most replete with heathen lore'. Charles Squire also expressed this view: 'With the exception of an obviously spurious last verse, here omitted, the poem is magnificently pagan'. D. W. Nash extended this 'editing' by removing the entire last two stanzas. He remarks at the end of Stanza 6: 'This is the end of the poem. The remaining lines consist merely of the ordinary abuse of the monks, and have evidently been added by a very inferior hand, and at a later date'.[65]

These views, while wrong in the case of *Preideu Annwfyn*, were possibly formed by the presence of later poems in the *Book of Taliesin* that do have a Christian opening; for example, *Golychaf-i Gulwyd* (I Petition God), *Kanu y Med* (Song of the Mead) and *Kanu y Byt Mawr* (Song of the Greater World). These poems are later than *Preideu Annwfyn* and have partially copied its wording but with *wledic* referring to God. In fact, *Golychaf-i Gulwyd* notes important events in Welsh tradition and has a section on *Annwfyn*, or more specifically, *kaer sidi*. However, instead of describing it as a disaster with constant tribulation, the poem adopts the paradise view of *kaer sidi*. It refers to a lack of sickness and old age, and describes three musical instruments playing (by themselves!) in front of a fireplace. Instead of the four peaks being mountains, the *banneu* (peaks) in *Golychaf-i Gulwyd* are four supports for *kaer sidi*, which are surrounded by the sea. This is imagery identical to that in *The Voyage of Bran*, with the four supports there being made of white bronze. There is also a fountain there whose drink is sweeter than white wine. Apart from this travesty, it betrays its later composition by its references to characters who appear in the much later Welsh literature: for example, Brân in the *Mabinogi*; Ceridwen in the tale of Gwion Bach.

Golychaf-i Gulwyd, *Kanu y Med* and *Kanu y Byt Mawr* are also later than *Kadeir Teÿrnon*, as they copy the reference made to Elffin in the latter, but in elaborated forms. *Golychaf-i Gulwyd* is also later than *Kat Godeu*, as it refers to that battle in Line 29. It would seem that the three Arthurian poems were so highly regarded that later bards referred to parts of them to show off their learning of important events from the past.[66]

The Bard as a Christian

The truncation of *Preideu Annwfyn* suggested above is a massive error. The opening lines introduce the great king and his expedition over the shores of the world. It creates the setting for Gweir's imprisonment in the next line which would otherwise be too abrupt and without context. Similarly, the last two lines give a perfect ending to the poem, with the bard praising the great prince whose death had been announced in the previous line. The bard's attempt to suppress his grieving by turning to Christ is consistent with other Christian references throughout the poem.

Despite the above assertions that the poem was pagan, the poem itself indicates that the bard was a Christian, but one who had a broader, more worldly view than the monks. In Line 4, the bard uses the Christian term *ebostol*. Marged Haycock translates it as 'epistle', taken as 'story'. Given that its use is not dictated by other purposes (it is not required by rhyme), this is a very Christian expression to use as a term for 'story'. Haycock notes that its usage to mean a story of the secular kind is extremely rare, with no other examples being known.[67] Secondly, in Line 8 the bard refers to Judgement Day, which is consistent with Christian theology. Thirdly, he indicates that he will always pray for Gweir, consistent with Christian practice. Finally, in Line 58 he describes Arthur as a saint, which is consistent with the view of Arthur as a Christian king in other literature.

At the end of *Preideu Annwfyn*, the bard is devastated by Arthur's death. His Line 59 is so similar in wording to Line 1 that there can be little doubt that he is referring to the same *wledic* in both lines. If it is the earthly *wledic* Arthur in Stanza 1, then it has to be the earthly *wledic* Arthur in Stanza 8. In the first half of Line 60, the bard says that he is praising Arthur as a way of preventing himself from grieving. He then turns to Christ for comfort. The emotion expressed here is raw, consistent with a composition of the poem not long after returning to Britain. It seems real and heartfelt.

THE COMPLETE POEM

1   I praise the sovereign, prince, king of the land,
who has enlarged his dominion across the world's shores.
The prison of Gweir was prepared in the mound fortress
according to the account of Pwyll and Pryderi.
Nobody before him went into it,
into the heavy blue chain – it restrained a loyal servant.
And for the sake of the spoils of Annwfyn bitterly he sang.
And till Judgement (Day) our bardic prayer shall endure.
Three fullnesses of Prydwen, we went into it.
Except seven, none returned from the mound fortress.

2   I am honoured abundantly, song was heard
in the four-peaked camp – turning (to face) the four (peaks).
My poetry, from the cauldron it was spoken.
By the breath of nine maidens it was kindled.
The cauldron of Annwfyn's chieftain: what is its form?
Dark around its rim and pearls.
It does not boil the food of a coward: it was not so destined.
The flashing sword of Lleawc was thrust into it,
and in the hand of Lleminawc it was left.
And before the door of the gate of Hell lamps burned.
And when we went with Arthur, a renowned tribulation.
Except seven, none returned from the camp of the mead-feast.

3   I am honoured abundantly, songs are heard
in the four-peaked camp, isle of the strong door.
Flowing water and jet are mingled.
Bright wine their liquor before their retinue.
Three fullnesses of Prydwen we went upon the sea.
Except seven, none returned from the camp of extreme coldness.

4   I set no value on little men, (merely) concerned with scripture.
Beyond the glass fortress they did not see Arthur's valour.
Three-score hundred men were standing on the wall:
it was difficult to speak with their watchman.
Three fullnesses of Prydwen went with Arthur.
Except seven, none returned from the camp of obstruction.

5   I set no value on little men, loose their shield straps.
They do not know who was created on which day,
what hour of the slender day the Cwy were born,
who made them who did not go to the Defwy meadows.
They do not know the brindled ox, thick his headring,

seven-score joints in his collar.
And when we went with Arthur – disastrous visit.
Except seven, none returned from the camp of God's Peak.

6   I set no value on little men, weak their resolve.
They do not know which day the chief was created,
what hour of the slender day the owner was born,
what animal they keep, with its silvery head.
When we went with Arthur – woeful conflict.
Except seven, none returned from the enclosed camp.

7   Monks draw together, like a pack of dogs,
from a clash with lords who know.
Is the wind of one path? Is the sea of one water?
Is the fire, an invincible tumult, of one spark?

8   Monks draw into a pack, like wolves,
from a clash with lords who know.
They know not when darkness and dawn divide;
nor wind, what path it follows, what its rushing is;
what place it destroys, what land it strikes.
The grave of the saint is lost/annihilated – both grave and champion.
I praise the sovereign, great prince,
that I not be grieving: Christ provides for me.

Given that the discussion above on the meaning of the poem has been lengthened by commentary, a simpler more concise summary is now given. This summary incorporates the inferences made on the interaction between the Britons and the sixth-century Native Americans.

Stanza 1

The poem begins with the bard praising a great King, later revealed to be Arthur. This king has enlarged his sovereignty across the world's shores. Nobody before him had gone into the new land, understood here as sixth-century North America. A junior member of the expedition, a loyal servant (or youth) named Gweir, had been captured and taken prisoner by the Native Americans. His imprisonment was reported by Pwyll and Pryderi, two of Arthur's men. The perspective then shifts back to Britain where the bard visualises Gweir singing sadly in his prison and states that he will pray for Gweir until Judgement Day. Apart from his literal prison, Gweir is effectively imprisoned by 'the heavy blue chain', a metaphor for the vast ocean. It is this 'heavy blue chain' that Arthur was the first to penetrate. Its vast expanse makes rescue effectively impossible.

Gweir's capture occurred at *kaer sidi*, near one of the mound complexes that had been built long ago by the Hopewell culture. During their floruit of around 650 years the Hopewell had built a huge network of such mounds. They were centred in the river valleys of southern Ohio and the neighbouring states. Only a small number survived the expedition, of which the mound fortress was one such stopping place.

Stanza 2

The bard is in Annwfyn, being praised for his poetry at the 'four-peaked' camp. This was at Montreal, with the peaks being Royal, St-Bruno, St-Hilaire and Rougemont. It was the bard who was turning to face the four peaks rather than an erroneous 'revolving fort'. He boasts about the quality of his poetry, so inspired that it was seemingly conjured by magic through nine priestesses kindling a cauldron. This imagery of the nine priestesses would have been familiar to the bard's audience. Such stories were known from at least AD 44, as shown in the work of Pomponius Mela.

The bard then relates they had captured a real cauldron that belonged to one of the chiefs of the new land. It had a dark rim which contrasted with pearl decoration. He comments that 'it does not boil the food of a coward', his respect for the bravery of its owners, the Native Americans. The flashing sword of Lleawc was thrust into it and it was left with Lleminawc, two of Arthur's men. A cauldron decorated with pearls would have been plausible for the Hopewell culture and their successors but certainly implausible for most metal cauldrons in Britain. The cauldron would have been a large clay ceremonial pot. As such, the inset holes for the pearls would have been fairly easy to create by pushing the pearls into the soft clay or by drilling into the hardened clay. In one Hopewell site alone, about 100,000 freshwater pearls were found when it was excavated.

The stanza ends with the vivid imagery of Arthur and his men about to enter Hell. Only a small number of men survived the expedition, of which the camp of the mead-feast was one such stopping place.

Stanza 3

The bard is again praised for his poetry at the four-peaked camp, but the 'strong door' is now introduced, later argued to have been the St Lawrence River. This was the Britons' entrance to the new land but its strong currents and dangerous obstacles would have allowed only a very slow and difficult upstream progress.

Then follows a vivid word-picture of part of the journey – an image of flowing water mingled with jet or jet blackness, which could have a number of meanings as discussed earlier. The camp named at the end of the stanza was one of extreme coldness. A further image of *gloyw* wine being served to the men may be related to the cold if this were like the modern *glühwein*, a wine that is served heated.

Arthur's ship *Prydwen*, possibly packed well beyond its normal loading, was leading the sea voyage. Only a small number survived the expedition, of which the camp of extreme coldness was one such place.

Stanza 4

Here the bard is one of the few survivors. Back in Britain he expresses his contempt for the monks. He has no respect for these 'little men' who are just ignorant ecclesiastical scribes. Then follows a series of striking images from the expedition, of which the monks were ignorant. First, the sailors sail past a 'glass fortress', a metaphor for a large iceberg. Similar imagery of a glass tower in the middle of the sea and a crystal pillar in the sea appears in the *Historia Brittonum* and the *Navigatio* of St Brendan. The iceberg sighting is consistent with a northern route to America as there is a zone where the icebergs drift down the east coast of Newfoundland.

Beyond the iceberg zone, on the mainland they met the Native Americans. A large number were standing on a wall, possibly one of the earthen walls that enclosed their mounds. This would have been an intimidating encounter. As their language was so radically different, it was difficult to communicate with them. It was possibly at this stage that 'Arthur's valour' was displayed, if fighting developed. Only a small number survived the journey, of which the camp of obstruction was one such stopping place.

Stanza 5

The bard again expresses his contempt for the 'little men' monks, this time delivering the ultimate insult, that they are cowards. He also shows interest in the origins of the Annwfyn inhabitants, wondering whether they were part of God's creation and whether they were created on the Sixth Day, as were the Britons. These questions on the origins of the Annwfyn people would not make sense if they were mere fictional characters who were created by the bard to entertain. It implies that they were real people. They were called the *Cwy* (pronounced as in 'we') by the Britons.

He remarks that they did not go to the *Defwy* meadows, a way of saying that they are unknown in Britain. These meadows are probably those along the River Dee which runs through Chester. It is thus possible that this was the starting point from which they sailed. His aside that the *Cwy* do not visit Britain reflects his view that they were ordinary mortals with limitations. Had they been immortals or fairies no such limitations would apply – they could visit anywhere, as shown in the Irish Otherworld stories.

Next comes an important image that suggests the new country is North America. They sight a huge animal never seen before, the 'brindled ox'. In vivid and concise poetic language the bard lists three characteristics: a huge head, a massive neck, and a coat of noteworthy colour variation. This is an excellent description of the American buffalo (bison). The Britons may have seen the buffalo in the region of densely-built earthworks, as they were seen in historical times along the Muskingum and Scioto Rivers where there is a concentration of mounds.

The stanza ends with the bard's distress: 'And when we went with Arthur – disastrous visit'. Then comes the refrain, that only a small number survived the expedition, of which the camp of God's Peak was one such stopping place.

God's Peak was probably a mountain of such superb grandeur that it would be a suitable residence for God.

Stanza 6

The bard continues to pour his contempt upon the monks, claiming they have no manly resolve. They are 'little men' who never had to face up to extreme dangers like Arthur's men in Annwfyn. He again reflects on the origins of the Native Americans and, in particular, 'the owner' (*perchen*). This reference is clarified in the next line when he states that the Native Americans keep an animal that has a 'silvery head'. This animal is the North American river otter whose lustrous coat gives a silvery appearance when wet. The poet's image probably refers to its silvery head being carried above the water when swimming. The Native Americans made carvings of the otter in their animal effigy smoking pipes. Again the stanza ends with the bard's distress: 'When we went with Arthur – woeful conflict'. Then comes the gloomy refrain, that only a small number survived the expedition, of which the enclosed camp was one such stopping place.

Stanza 7

The perspective then shifts back to Britain where the monks, likened to a pack of dogs, are drawing back in fear from a clash with the 'lords who know'. The monks have just been told the secret. The bard delays revealing the secret by posing vaguely-defined 'filler' questions that are not related to events in Annwfyn. They extend the wait and build dramatic tension.

Stanza 8

The final stanza opens with the monks, this time likened to a pack of wolves, again drawing back in fear from a clash with the 'lords who know'. The bard continues to build suspense with implied 'filler' questions that have nothing to do with the events in Annwfyn. Finally he reveals the secret in Line 58 – that the grave of Arthur, the Christian king, has been lost or annihilated in the new land overseas, and the body could not be recovered. The bard then concludes by praising Arthur (who he refers to as the sovereign, great prince) as a way of ameliorating his grieving. His Christian beliefs are evident when he states that Christ will provide for him.

6
DEATH OF ARTHUR IN AMERICA

THE ANNWFYN SECTION IN KAT GODEU

Introduction

In *Preideu Annwfyn* the bard relentlessly builds up suspense before finally announcing Arthur's death in Annwfyn with the line: 'the grave of the saint is lost/annihilated – both grave and champion'. That poem does not explicitly describe fighting between the Britons and the people of Annwfyn but does infer it through brief word pictures. Firstly, there is Gweir, captured and imprisoned at *kaer sidi*, his fate unknown, with the bard vowing to pray for him until Judgement Day. Also the confrontation between the Britons and the Native Americans massed on the wall seems to be associated with 'the valour of Arthur'. It suggests that fighting may have followed. There is also the seizure of a 'cauldron' into which Lleawc thrust his flashing sword. This cauldron prompted the poet to say that 'it does not boil the food of a coward', a comment on the bravery of the Native Americans and a clear indicator of fierce battles with them.

A second Welsh poem, *Kat Godeu* (Battle of the Trees) has a section on the expedition to Annwfyn, appearing between Lines 189 and 204. This poem explicitly refers to torrid fighting and then appears to describe Arthur's last moments alive and how he died. The bard then gives a moving tribute to his king. This section is an important supplement to *Preideu Annwfyn* and was probably composed by the same bard, as will be argued in a later chapter. The Annwfyn section in *Kat Godeu* is self-contained and therefore can be discussed independently of the rest of the poem, which will be done here. In the next chapter, a significant part of the *Kat Godeu* poem will be discussed and a speculative attempt to explain its meaning will be given.

The Kat Godeu Bard

Kat Godeu appears to have been composed by an old man who is now recounting the important events in his life. He complains that no one visits him any more except one friend, Goronwy, from the Edrywy meadows. He was formerly a bard who had sung his poems from a young age and had sung before the 'Lord of Britain'. The latter is argued here to be Arthur as Arthur is named later in the poem where the druids are asked to prophesy to him. In his usual indirect way the poet here is implying that he was Arthur's bard which agrees with his claim that he sailed on the Annwfyn expedition. He was also a fine warrior as a young man with a swift horse *Melyngan* and had killed hundreds of warriors.[1]

One of the most important events in his life was the horrific time he spent in Annwfyn. This is recounted in a sixteen-line section of *Kat Godeu*. Apart from *Preideu Annwfyn*, this section gives the only extended treatment of Annwfyn that appears in Welsh poetry. As in the latter, it describes the encounter in disastrous terms, with fierce fighting and the death of Arthur – evidence for its authenticity. The other mentions of Annwfyn in Welsh poetry are brief, the most prominent of them occurring in *Golychaf-i Gulwyd* which describes Annwfyn as a paradise with musical instruments that play by themselves, water that is sweeter than white wine, and so on.

It is argued here that the same bard composed both *Preideu Annwfyn* and *Kat Godeu*. He probably composed *Preideu Annwfyn* shortly after returning to Britain, when there was serious tension between the monks and the lords, following the publication of Gildas' *The Ruin of Britain*. He appears to have composed *Kat Godeu* many years later as an old man, when reflecting on the significant events in his life. It also appears likely that he composed a third poem, *Kadeir Teÿrnon*, which deals with events in Britain after Arthur's death and mentions a eulogy to Arthur in which Arthur was blessed. If this were composed by Arthur's bard, it may have been composed a short time after *Preideu Annwfyn*.

Synopsis of the Annwfyn Section

The Annwfyn section opens with the native inhabitants using the streams and rivers of the region to muster for battle. The bard then boasts about his own valour in heated battles, as he describes himself killing large numbers of the Annwfyn people. He remarks on the lust for battle of the Annwfyn warriors and that the fighting was so furious that every man fought with the passion of one hundred warriors.

Then comes a difficult few lines in which the bard remarks with pride that his bloodspotted sword had brought him an honour. This honour had been bestowed on him from a lord in a concealed place. The lord, referred to as 'the boar', was then killed by a meek one.

This ends the details of the fighting in Annwfyn, but the bard continues in a philosophical mood in Lines 201-2. He reflects on how transient life is, but that God is directing events and history: God makes civilisations and remakes them when they are destroyed, the process continuing again and again. On an individual level, the bard also believes that God is controlling events. In the first 23 lines of *Kat Godeu* (not shown here) the bard indicates his belief in the transmigration of the soul by listing all the states of matter, both inanimate and animate, in which his soul had dwelt. In this process, paralleling God's governance of civilisations, God makes individuals (whose souls depart at death) and makes them again (when souls reincarnate), and yet again. This implies that people, including Arthur, will have their opportunity to appear on earth again.

The bard then gives a moving tribute to the dead lord, who can only be Arthur, describing his shining name and accomplishment in leading his host of warriors. A translation of this Annwfyn section now follows, beginning at Line 189 of *Kat Godeu*.

TRANSLATION OF THE ANNWFYN SECTION

189	**Yn Annwfyn llifereint**	
	In the streams of Annwfyn	
190	**wrth urwydrin dybydant.**	
	they muster for battle.	
191	**Petwar vgeint cant**	
	Four-score hundred (men)	
192	**a gweint yr eu whant.**	
	I pierced despite their aggression.	
193	**Nyt ynt hyn, nyt ynt ieu**	
	They are not older, nor younger	
194	**no mi yn eu bareu.**	
	than me in their passions (for battle).	
195	**Aryal canhwr ageni pawb**	
	Everyone born (there) had the passion of a hundred	
196	**a naw cant oed genhyf inheu.**	
	and (the passion of) nine hundred did I have.	
197	**Yg cledyf brith gwaet**	
	My bloodspotted sword	
198	**bri am darwed,**	
	brings me honour,	
199	**o douyd o golo lle yd oed:**	
	from the lord from a concealed place where he was:	
200	**o dof yt las baed.**	
	by a meek one was the warrior killed.	
201	**Ef gwrith, ef datwrith,**	
	He (God) made, He remade,	
202	**ef gwrith ieithoed.**	
	He made peoples (again).	
203	**Llachar y enw, llawffer:**	
	Shining his name, strong of hand:	
204	**Lluch llywei nifer.**	
	Brilliantly he governed the host.	

THE FIGHTING

The Streams of Annwfyn

189 In the streams of Annwfyn
190 they muster for battle.

Here the Native Americans are using the streams of Annwfyn as a means of transportation. They are gathering in a central location in readiness for battle. What is the probable location for this gathering? In *Preideu Annwfyn*, the camp at *kaer sidi* is given prominence in the opening stanza, being the site where Gweir was captured. It was the camp probably named after the ceremonial earthen mounds that had been built by the Hopewell culture. The Hopewell's central region for complex earthworks in mid to southern Ohio, with its navigable streams and rivers, would suit this scenario very well.

The Passion for Battle

191 Four-score hundred (men)
192 I pierced despite their aggression.
193 They are not older, nor younger
194 than me in their passions (for battle).
195 Everyone born (there) had the passion of a hundred
196 and (the passion of) nine hundred did I have.

Lines 191 to 196 refer to the fierce fighting that developed. The old man is boasting about the number of warriors he killed – four-score hundred, or 8,000 warriors.[2] He did this in spite of the enemy's aggression. In Lines 193 and 194, the bard pays the enemy a compliment, saying that they are similar to him in their passion for battle. He then continues his admiration for the enemy in Line 195, stating that each of them had the passion of 100 normal warriors. But in Line 196 he then tops this by saying that he himself had the passion for battle of 900 warriors!

The comment that the Annwfyn people are not older, nor younger than the bard in their passion for battle is of interest. It suggests that he viewed the enemy as real people, not fairies or fictitious opponents. Despite the obvious differences between the Britons and the Annwfyn people, the bard viewed them as not dissimilar to himself in their passion and courage. Had they been fictitious creations of the bard, placed in the role of killing nearly all of Arthur's warriors, one would have expected the bard to have depicted them as fearsome, invincible opponents.

THE DEATH OF ARTHUR

The Honour from a Lord in a Concealed Place

197 My bloodspotted sword
198 brings me honour,
199 from the lord from a concealed place where he was.
200 By a meek one was the warrior killed.

The bard gives an account of the death of a lord, whom he calls the boar (*baed* in Line 200). Animal metaphors to describe warriors were often used. For example in *Y Gododdin*, stanza A.69, the hero Gwanar is likened to a wild boar while in stanza B1.10, the heroic Bleiddig, son of Beli, is referred to as a boar.[3] Given Arthur's tragic association with Annwfyn in *Preideu Annwfyn*, it is certain that the dead warrior-lord is Arthur. To begin, Lines 197-8 state that the bard's bloodspotted sword brings him honour.

Then two difficult lines follow, of great potential interest. In Line 199, this honour was bestowed on him 'from the lord from a concealed place, where he was'. Leading scholar Patrick Ford translates this line as: 'from a lord from his place of concealment'.[4] However, the translation of Line 199 is not really straightforward. The copying of the text seems to have been botched by the scribe, who appears to have been looking ahead to the next line, Line 200, which begins '*o dof yt*'. The scribe begins Line 199 with '*o douyd*', which does not make sense. It could mean 'from God', but it makes no sense at all to have God hiding in a place of concealment. It also makes no sense to have God in a place of burial, 'where he was', another alternative.

Further, it is difficult to see how either of these unlikely interpretations can relate to a warrior's bloodspotted sword bringing him honour.[5] It would therefore appear that Patrick Ford was correct in rendering the beginning of Line 199 as 'from a lord'.

Who was the Meek one?

200   By a meek one was the warrior killed.

This line is difficult in understanding the meaning, though the translation seems straightforward. Marged Haycock gives a similar translation, using the literal translation 'boar' instead of warrior.[6] The difficulty in this line is the word *dof*, which means meek one or tame one. It is difficult to make sense of the line under these translations. The poet has already described the great bravery and passion for battle of the inhabitants, so it seems unlikely that one of them could be the meek or tame one.

A minimalist interpretation is that Arthur had been fatally wounded in the battle and was taken away to a concealed place while the battle raged. Arthur then bestows an honour on the bard before he dies. This distinction could simply be a general acknowledgement that the bard had fought bravely. The minimalist interpretation, however, fails to explain who the 'meek' one was who killed Arthur.

A Mercy Killing and possible Beheading

A more radical interpretation is that the 'meek one' in Line 200 was the bard himself. Here 'meek' could be used in the sense that the killing was performed by a friend as an act of mercy, not as the act of an enemy. If so, then the honour could have been a request by the dying Arthur that he be killed by the bard. A further step could involve his head being taken away and protected. As the entire body would be too heavy to take away while under attack, the purpose was to ensure that the head did not fall into the hands of the enemy, where it could be mutilated or paraded as a trophy.

An alternative translation by Marged Haycock may have relevance here. To create an additional rhyme, she emends the text of Line 197 so that *brith* (spotted, stained) becomes the compound *brithwed*, and thus *gwaet* (blood) is placed at the beginning of Line 198 instead of the end of Line 197. As an alternative translation for Line 198, she offers 'blood of fame does it (the sword) spill for me'. As noted above, she also translates that the boar was slain by the meek one. This scheme also lends itself to the scenario of the bard killing Arthur. Here the 'blood of fame' could be Arthur's blood.[7]

Beheadings and Mercy Killings in Europe

If this scenario seems improbable, there are a number of examples implying the need to protect the head of a dead king. At *Haethfelth* in AD 633 the Saxon king, Edwin, was killed by the forces of Cadwallon and Penda. The great scholar, Ifor Williams, infers that Edwin's head was cut off to protect it. The Saxons then took it to York where it was placed in the Church of St Peter. His body was buried separately in the Whitby monastery.[8]

In 642, Cadwallon and Penda also killed the Saxon king, Oswald, at the battle of *Maserfelth*. They cut off his head and placed it on a stake. The hands were also cut off and displayed on stakes. A year later, the new Saxon king, Oswiu, arrived with his army to retrieve them, and then buried the head at Lindisfarne and the hands and arms at Bamburgh. These stories about the heads of Edwin and Oswald appear in Bede's *Ecclesiastical History*.[9]

A third example appears in a poem, *On Urien and the Men of the North*, by a poet who had adopted the 'persona' of the sixth-century bard, Llywarch Hen, but the poem was probably composed in the ninth or tenth century. Llywarch, a first cousin of Urien, flees the battlefield with Urien's head after having cut off the head to protect it. The grief and anguish Llywarch suffers is the theme of the poem. Later in the poem, Urien's body was recovered and buried with honour.[10]

A further example occurs in *Branwen Daughter of Llŷr*, the second tale in the Welsh collection of stories, the *Mabinogi*. It concerns the Arthur-like figure of Brân the Blessed. In this story, Brân was mortally wounded by a poisoned spear. Knowing he was about to die, he orders his comrades to cut off his head, carry it to London and bury it there.[11] The *Mabinogi* was written perhaps in the 11th or 12th centuries, as noted earlier from the research of Thomas Charles-Edwards and Patrick Sims-Williams.

Kenneth Jackson quotes classical sources that the Celts in Gaul took their enemies' heads as trophies. They cut off the heads on the battlefield, and hung them around the necks of their horses as they rode away. Some heads were also fixed on buildings to display them. The heads of their most famous opponents were embalmed and proudly kept in a chest, to be brought out and displayed to visitors.[12] As will be shown below, there is some evidence that the Hopewell may also have decapitated the heads of their enemies.

Native American Artifacts with Decapitated Heads

Similar to the Celts in Britain and Europe, there is evidence that the Native Americans practised trophy-taking behaviours in decapitating the heads of their enemies. This practice goes back to the Archaic period in Eastern North America. Christopher Schmidt and Rachel Sharkey refer to cases recently excavated in the Ohio River valley in southern Indiana (from the Middle and Late Archaic periods), where both decapitation and forearm removal have been observed.[13]

The Hopewell era was generally characterised by prosperity and regional co-operation, but some of their figurines appear to suggest decapitation. A Hopewell artifact that was excavated from the Seip Earthworks, southwest of Chillicothe, appears to show a decapitated head. It is a Hopewell effigy pipe, made of dark grey-brown soapstone. Chad Thomas, Chris Carr and Cynthia Keller view the pipe as depicting 'a dog eating a decapitated human head held between his front paws'.[14]

A second Hopewell figurine also appears to show a decapitated head. The Wray figurine, found at the bottom of a large mound of the Newark Earthworks in 1881, shows a shaman dressed in a bearskin, with the bear's head attached. The top of the shaman's head and his forehead are entirely enclosed by the bear head and cloak, giving a fearsome sight. In his lap, the shaman is holding a decapitated head. Jaimin Weets, Chris Carr, David Penney and Gary Carriveau comment in a note on the figurine: 'The association of bear with death and death rites among the Scioto Hopewell is suggested by the Wray figurine from the Newark site, which shows a man in bear costume (or wrapped by a bear spirit) with an apparently severed head on his lap and arms placed in a ritual posture'. Brad Lepper suggests that the shaman may have been transforming from a human to a bear spirit.[15] Some photos of the Wray figurine and the dog eating the human head can be found on the website of the Ohio Historical Society.

These two sites in Chillicothe and Newark were closely associated, as noted previously. Brad Lepper has argued that they were connected by a great road built by the Hopewell communities, a massive project that would have required a coordinated effort from the two sites.

Parallels between Arthur and Brân the Blessed

Brân the Blessed in the *Mabinogi* story above may be distinguished from another Bran character in the Irish Otherworld story, the *Voyage of Bran son of Febal*. The latter story is discussed in Chapter 9. They have different fathers. However, there is clearly a relationship between the two as they do associate with the similarly named figures, Manawydan fab Llŷr (for Brân the Blessed) and Manannán mac Lir (for the Irish Bran).

Brân the Blessed has very strong similarities to Arthur, the *Mabinogi* tale appearing to borrow details from the early Arthurian poems. Such stories may have a complex derivation, absorbing details from a number of sources, many untraceable, over a long period of time.

John Koch notes the similarities between Brân and the ancient Celtic chief *Brennos*, both in their names and circumstances of their death. Brennos led the Celtic army that invaded Greece in the Winter of 279-278 BC. He was wounded by a missile in the assault on the Delphi sanctuary. In their retreat, Brennos told his men to kill him and the other wounded men to reduce the burden of the journey home. They seemed to have been reluctant to do this, so Brennos drank deeply of undiluted wine and killed himself. The new chief then carried out Brennos' harsh request, killing all the wounded and ill, some 20,000 men.[16]

As can be seen from the above, Brân the Blessed may have absorbed some features from this ancient Brennos of 280 BC. However, there are so many parallels between Brân and Arthur, some very specific, that it appears that Brân was modelled on Arthur in the later story that was eventually written into the *Mabinogi*. As noted in Chapter 3, Thomas Jones thought that Brân's expedition to Ireland in the *Mabinogi* was a rationalized form of the earlier *Preideu Annwfyn* account.[17] It is difficult to avoid the conclusion that Brân was modelled on Arthur, given the arguments in this book for early dates of the Arthurian poetry, as the Brân tale in its final form did not appear until approximately 500-600 years later. These parallels include the following:

- Both had the epithet 'the Blessed' attached to their names (Arthur in the poem, *Kadeir Teÿrnon*).
- Both led their warriors overseas – Arthur to Annwfyn and Brân to Ireland.
- As a result of their absence overseas, the issue of who was minding the country was raised: for Arthur in *Kadeir Teÿrnon*; for Brân in *Branwen Daughter of Llŷr* and in Triad 13.
- Both engaged in a horrific battle while overseas.
- Both are associated with a cauldron while fighting.
- Both were killed in their battle.
- Seven people survived Arthur's battle in Annwfyn and seven people survived Brân's battle in Ireland.
- Three people, Pryderi, Manawydan and Taliesin were with Brân in Ireland and were among the seven survivors. These same three were also associated with Arthur in Annwfyn – Pryderi, explicitly, and the bard Taliesin, implicitly, in *Preideu Annwfyn* and Manawydan and Pryderi (both explicitly) in the later *Book of Taliesin* poem *Golychaf-i Gulwyd* (I Petition God).
- Brân means 'crow'. A famous line in *Y Gododdin* links Arthur with a warrior who brought down crows to feast on his dead opponents. Further, certain folkloric beliefs have Arthur's soul existing in the form of a crow, as in Cervantes' *Don Quixote*. Edmund Chambers relates that in Cornwall, his soul is thought to reside in the Cornish chough, the red-legged crow.[18]

If the viewpoint of the bard killing Arthur as an act of mercy and decapitating him is correct, then this creates a further parallel between Brân and Arthur. It prompts the question: was the author of *Branwen Daughter of Llŷr* aware of a belief that Arthur was beheaded at his death and did he thus incorporate the same incident into his later tale of Brân's death?

Morddwyd Tyllion (Pierced Thighs)

Another detail in the story of Brân's death may be relevant to the death of Arthur. John Koch refers to 'an obscure traditional utterance' by which Brân is called in relation to his fatal wound – *Morddwyd Tyllion*. It means 'pierced thighs'. The story suddenly introduces what at first appears to be a new character, Morddwyd Tyllion, but the context makes it evident that this is another name for Brân.[19] Later in the story, Brân's death is attributed to being wounded in the heel by a poisoned spear, which gives a slightly different version of his death. It is clear that the epithet *Morddwyd Tyllion* was highly valued by the Welsh as traditional knowledge from the way it is awkwardly inserted into the story.

As the mythological Brân was modelled on Arthur, it is a possibility that this is how Arthur was fatally wounded in Annwfyn, speared in the thighs by the Native American warriors. In the late twelfth century this 'pierced thighs' motif was woven into Chrétien's *Perceval* when referring to the wounded Fisher King, a further recognition of its importance.[20]

Summary

The circumstances related above concerning Arthur's death are intriguing. They seem to show a wounded Arthur concealed in a hiding place while the Britons were under attack. It may be inferred that Arthur was wounded or dying (although not explicitly stated) for if he were not, it would imply the deepest disgrace for any warrior, let alone the peerless Arthur. The bard's blood-stained sword has brought him honour, given by the concealed lord. It is possible that this honour is for his general valour in battle. However if we stop there, then it leaves the line about the warrior lord killed by the 'meek one' unexplained.

If we take the further step to infer that the meek one was the bard then the inference about beheading the king and retaining the head to protect it is not unreasonable. It could explain why the author of *Branwen Daughter of Llŷr* had the dying Brân ask his comrades to cut off his head.

A Tribute to Arthur

The ending of the Annwfyn section within *Kat Godeu* is of great interest for several reasons. Firstly, it uses the word *gwrith*, a very old form of the verb 'was made' according to John Koch.[21] This old word also appears in Line 4 and Line 146 of the poem. It is evidence for the antiquity of the poem and it is significant that it occurs in the Annwfyn section. Koch's argument suggests that the inferred word in British, **wrichto-*, probably became *gwrith* in Neo-Brittonic, which was the language spoken by Arthur.

Secondly, the poem reveals the bard's philosophy of life. We already know that he holds the ancient belief in the transmigration of souls, the soul gaining experience in non-living and living matter, experiencing different stations in life, as shown in Lines 1-23 in *Kat Godeu*. However he is also a dedicated Christian, regarding Christ's crucifixion as one of the three worst cataclysms in history (in Line 73). He has now just described another great disaster that he has experienced personally, the killing of Arthur and his comrades in Annwfyn. However the bard seeks consolation in the viewpoint that God is in control of it all. Civilisations come and go, but God is in charge, making and remaking peoples. In Lines 201-2 he states: 'He (God) made, He remade, He made peoples (again)'. In the section where he discusses the word *gwrith*, John Koch provides a translation which has a similar meaning: 'nations were made, were unmade, were made (again)'.

This process is paralleled by the rebirth of individual souls, as described by the bard for his own case at the start of the poem. Therefore Arthur was not lost forever – he may return in some other guise. The bard then moves on from God's governance of civilisations and souls to give a final tribute to Arthur in Lines 203-4, summing him up as follows:

> Shining his name, strong of hand: Brilliantly he governed the host.

7
INTERPRETING THE 'BATTLE OF THE TREES'

THE 'BATTLE OF THE TREES'

Introduction

Kat Godeu, usually translated as the 'Battle of the Trees', is a long poem with difficult allusions, which has received considerable attention from Celticists. It seems to describe a massive unspecified catastrophe for the Britons which was located in southwest Scotland, near Caer Nefenhyr. This terrifying event is likened to one of the three greatest cataclysms in the history of the world, where the Britons were drenched in blood 'up to our thighs'. After appealing to God for help, they were saved by a magically animated army of trees. The enemy who was killing the Britons is not clearly identified, so the whole poem remains mysterious.

This poem has some lengthy sections on the transmigration of the soul and Christian references, an integral part of the poem, indicating a Christian bard who retained some old druidic beliefs. A Christian would be unlikely to hold this unusual set of beliefs after AD 600, which suggests a very early date for the poem, as discussed in Chapters 9 and 13. In recounting the battle, the bard displays a humorous element as he describes how small, insignificant vegetation such as heather, clover, bracken and gorse aided the large trees as they battled the enemy.

The natural tendency is to interpret the poem solely as an imaginative fantasy. However other elements, such as the acute distress of the Britons, suggest that the poem was based on a real disaster now sufficiently distant in time so that it could be interspersed with humour and placed in a quasi-magical setting for entertainment. Although the 'Battle of the Trees' itself is not a focus of this book, a speculative attempt to explain the meaning of this difficult poem will now be given.[1]

Location

In *Kat Godeu* the catastrophe occurs in the vicinity of Caer Nefenhyr, which is remembered in Welsh tradition in the long prose tale *Culhwch and Olwen*, where it is associated with Arthur. Marged Haycock endorses the proposal of John Lloyd-Jones that 'Nefenhyr' is linguistically associated with the *Novantae*, a British tribe which occupied the Galloway region of southwest Scotland. She thinks it probably means 'the king of the Novantae tribe'.[2]

In *Culhwch and Olwen* Glewlwyd, Arthur's gatekeeper, reminisces with Arthur over the most important places they had fought at or visited. These included Caer Nefenhyr.[3] The remembering of this fort in Welsh tradition indicates that the mysterious calamity that occurred there was regarded as a significant event to the Britons.

The Trees as Allies

In the opening 23 lines of *Kat Godeu* the bard refers to the many forms of existence his soul had occupied before his present life. In the last of these forms of existence, he was a tree in a great fire. This then sets the scene for considering trees as living things that are closely related to mankind – they contain souls that may later appear in a human body. Thus if they could be animated, they would form natural allies to the Britons in their desperate struggle against the mysterious enemy.

WHO WAS THE ENEMY?

The Great Scaly Beast

Who or what was the likely opponent in this real-life disaster? The bard's indirectness has left most commentators puzzled as to the identity of the enemy. Francesco Benozzo assumes that the trees are fighting 'an army of Britons'. Caitlin Green considers the enemy to be the monstrous forces of the Lord of the Otherworld opposed by Arthur leading an army of trees animated by magic. Marged Haycock comments that 'It is disappointing that the enemy here is not identified'.[4] It is argued below that the enemy is described in the poem just prior to the start of the battle. In Lines 30-1, the bard refers to 'a great scaly beast' with a hundred heads:

> 30 **Gweint mil mawrem,**
> I pierced a great scaly beast,
>
> 31 **arnaw yd oed canpen.**
> a hundred heads on him.

See the translations by Jon Coe and Simon Young, and Marged Haycock.[5] In Lines 30-40, the poet provides considerable detail in describing this beast, which conveys the imagery of a dragon. It has a hundred heads, carries fierce battalions under the roots of its tongues, and has battalions in the napes of its many necks. It also has one hundred claws, is speckled like a snake and torments many human souls imprisoned in its skin.

Typhon

This imagery is remarkably similar to that applied to *Typhon* (also Typhoeus or Typhaon) as he battled the Greek god, Zeus. He appears in Hesiod's *Theogony*, an epic from ancient Greece, composed hundreds of years before Christ, perhaps around 700 BC. Robert Lamberton notes that the Typhon section may be a later addition to the *Theogony*. However its date is not an issue here as a version of the story was known in the fifth century AD, well before *Kat Godeu* was composed.[6] This greatly elaborated version occurs in *Dionysiaca*, which was written by Nonnos of Panopolis, a Greek who was living in Hellenized Egypt.

Both these earlier works use imagery similar to the *Kat Godeu* poet. The Hesiod descriptors below are from the translation by Hugh Evelyn-White. Hesiod states that Typhoeus had one hundred heads. They were the heads of a snake, 'like a fearful dragon'. He had dark, flickering tongues, and fire burned from his heads when he glared.[7]

The Nonnos descriptors are given in the translation by William Rouse. Nonnos describes Typhon's one hundred heads, the speckled nature of his serpents, his many necks, his legions of arms, and all the tongues of all his throats. He also states that every hair on him belched viper poison.[8]

If the bard who composed *Kat Godeu* were thinking about a Typhon-like creature, then the threat came from the skies. Nonnos, in particular, gives an extended account of how Typhon first ravaged the heavens and finally left the skies to whip up the seas.[9]

Comet Imagery

Leading British astronomers Victor Clube and William Napier link Typhon to a fireball swarm that was part of an earthly impact event. This disaster was also associated with a large comet which they argue most likely had its origins in the constellation Taurus.[10]

Some comets could inspire fear in this pre-scientific era through their strange appearances, resembling great beasts. Pliny, in the first century AD, collated drawings of the different shapes of comets that had been sighted. These are reproduced in *The Origin of Comets*, written by Bailey, Clube and Napier.[11] To the average sixth-century person such comets would probably have instilled awe and fear.

AN ENVIRONMENTAL DOWNTURN AD 540

Dendrochronology

Through the science of tree ring dating (dendrochronology), Michael Baillie has identified a period spanning AD 536-545 in which an environmental downturn occurred. After an initial downturn in 536, a partial recovery took place followed by a severe slump in 540. In this period the trees suffered, with severely restricted ring growth. The effect was noted worldwide: in Irish oak, European oak, Finland pine, USA foxtail and bristlecone, and Argentinian fitzroya.[12] This data is invaluable because the tree ring dating technique does not have large standard errors of measurement and it points to something physical that cannot easily be dismissed.

Further information comes from literature surveys that contain marked climate anomalies which affected agriculture. The year 536 was associated with a mystery cloud that dimmed the sun – a dry fog that could imply fine layers of ash and aerosols suspended in the stratosphere. Shortly afterwards, the well-documented Justinian plague, thought to be a bubonic plague, took hold in Constantinople in 541 and spread throughout Europe. It probably reached Britain a few years later.[13]

The Volcano and Comet Hypotheses

Two rival hypotheses have been suggested to account for this downturn. One could be the eruption of a large volcano throwing up sufficient acidic dust to cause widespread dimming and cooling of the atmosphere. The presence of sulphate deposits in Antarctic and Greenland ice cores indicates a dust veil around 531 to 536 which could have come from a volcano.

A second hypothesis is based on the notion that the earth may be at risk of bombardment by debris from space in certain historical periods. Clube and Napier point out that there is a broad tube of meteoric debris enveloping the Taurid meteor stream and Comet Encke. Within the Taurid stream there are between one and two hundred asteroids of more than a kilometre in diameter. They argue that this material is probably the remnants from the breakup of a giant progenitor comet. It periodically enters the Earth's orbit as shown in their book *The Cosmic Winter*. They identify a key bombardment period around 400-600, consistent with surges in meteor shower activity seen by ancient Chinese observers.[14] If the earth's orbit intersected with the broad tube of meteoric debris associated with Comet Encke, debris could rain down as meteor showers and meteorites. This material could comprise chunks of rock but also a smaller rocky 'hail', both of which could be fatal. Larger unstable material could also explode, creating massive airbursts and shockwaves. This type of catastrophe could explain the *Kat Godeu* beast (the comet) and the disasters that befell the Britons.

There are two issues here. One is to explain the general environmental downturn from AD 536 to 545. Another is to account for the specific case of *Kat Godeu*, if possible. On the first issue, either a large volcanic explosion or the impact of a cometary fragment could potentially account for the dust veil. The issue is still open. Indeed, the two approaches are not mutually exclusive. One approach is provided by Larsen et al. in *Geophysical Research Letters*. They argue that the sulphate deposits in ice cores from both Greenland and Antarctica were most likely produced by an explosive eruption from a large volcano situated near the Equator. One possibility is the crater lake, Ilopango, in El Salvador. An alternative argument is given by Emma Rigby, Melissa Symonds and Derek Ward-Thompson in research published in *Astronomy and Geophysics*. They argue that a comet or comet fragment, possibly from the Taurid stream, could have exploded high in the earth's atmosphere with the dusty debris being distributed around the globe. They estimate that a comet fragment with a radius of only about 300 metres would be sufficient to create the dust veil.[15]

The second issue, involving the *Kat Godeu* beast, could be explained by sustained local bombardment from space debris, with no worldwide effect. This may have occurred at various points within the AD 400-600 period identified by Bailey, Clube and Napier. Thus the *Kat Godeu* episode is not constrained to the 536-545 period, and if the dates for Badon and Arthur's death in the *Annales Cambriae* are nearly correct, it may have happened a few decades before the above period.

ROCKY 'HAIL' FROM SPACE

The Nature of the Poem

It is hypothesised that the *Kat Godeu* catastrophe was based on a real event, occurring decades before the poem was composed. The bard, now an old man many years removed from the horror, has placed the catastrophe in a quasi-magical setting where the trees were animated, fighting the enemy on behalf of the Britons. He has done this to entertain, and has added the touches of humour where small insignificant vegetation fought bravely alongside the huge trees. This type of poem, where contrasting types of vegetation are part of the fighting, does lend itself to incremental accretions over time. Later bards may have added lines with new types of vegetation and may themselves have added some of the humorous touches. Marged Haycock points out that Line 91, where a cherry tree joins the fighting, appears to have an Old English loan word for cherry (*siryan*) which would imply the work of a later bard.[16]

The Importance of the Tree Tops

In Line 26, the bard introduces the battle by saying:

> 26   Keint yg kat godeu bric
>   I sang in the battle of the tree tops

Haycock provides this translation for the unemended text.[17] It focuses the calamity on the tree tops. This interpretation is supported by Line 147 below that emphasises the importance of the upper branches of the huge oak trees in the battle.

> 147   An maglas blaen derw
>   The top of the oak ensnared (the enemy) for us

The translation here is given by Haycock in her 1990 paper.[18] If the beast were in the sky, as appears from the Typhon imagery, then it seems that the tree tops were helping to block a threat from above.

A Scenario of Bombardment

One possible scenario is derived from examples collected by John Lewis, a researcher on threats posed by bombardment from space. Lewis asks the question: 'is it really possible that tens of thousands of small stones should fall from the sky at the same time?'. He then gives many examples collected from all over the world from ancient to modern times.[19] It is hypothesised that space debris, associated with a comet 'beast', was raining down stones of various sizes, which would have caused a huge number of fatalities if men were caught out in the open. After entering the earth's atmosphere, other more loosely-bound material may have exploded in airbursts and created powerful shockwaves. The poem speaks of the Britons being in 'blood up to our thighs' and in Lines 69-70 refers to the event as the greatest of the three catastrophes that had ever occurred in the world. This event must have been far more significant than mere meteor showers, where the debris burns up in the atmosphere.

Trees blocking the rocky hail
It appears that the bard thought that this catastrophe was a lead-in to the Day of Judgement. In Line 74 he remarks: 'and the Day of Judgement *at hand*' (*racllaw*). It is possible that the bard and his comrades were sheltering in the forests of southern Scotland and had witnessed the bombardment, the trees shielding them from a direct aerial attack. The large trees would have taken the brunt of the onslaught, dissipating the velocity of the projectiles and giving the Britons a greater chance of survival.

This devastating scenario explains why the Britons themselves could not fight the battle, but needed the trees to fight on their behalf – it was not a conventional enemy. In a burst of bravado (in Line 30) the old bard claims that he 'pierced the great scaly beast'. But given the other examples of gross exaggeration of his fighting prowess in the poem, this can be taken lightly. All it may mean is that he was there, 'fighting' the beast, for the benefit of the audience of the poem.

ARTHUR FIGHTING A DRAGON

Prophesying to Arthur
It would appear that Arthur was based there, in southern Scotland, when the catastrophe occurred. The bard claims that he sang in the battle of the tree tops before the 'Lord of Britain' and also claims that he was in Annwfyn, as was discussed previously. This implies that he was Arthur's bard and that the Lord of Britain was Arthur, which helps to explain some rather enigmatic lines close to the end of the poem. In Lines 238-9, the druids and wise men are asked to prophesy to Arthur. If intermittent bombardment had been occurring over an extended period of time, Arthur may have consulted his wise men for their advice about what it meant and how to stop it. It is possible that the bard himself was one of these advisers, attempting a resolution through the magical arts, and in this sense was fighting the beast. Straight after this section is a repeat of the three greatest catastrophes in the history of the world, emphasising the importance of this event. If such airbursts did sporadically occur over an extended period in the 400-600 interval, then perhaps these inexplicable and uncontrollable events may have been part of the motivation for Arthur to explore new lands.

The bard concludes the poem with the knowledge that the event was now years in the past and that Judgement Day was averted after all. In the last four lines of the poem, he now appears to be confident about the future, stating at the end that he is exhilarated by the prophecy of Virgil. This appears to be a reference to the prophecy in Virgil's *Eclogue 4*, where Virgil foresees a golden age to come. There is evidence that Virgil was well known in early medieval Britain as argued by Ken Dark. He also suggests that the *Vergilius Romanus* book containing Virgil's works, illustrated by priceless coloured paintings, may have been produced in western Britain in the late fifth or early sixth century.[20]

Late Tales of Arthur Fighting Dragons

It is possible that this catastrophic event involving the 'great scaly beast' was interpreted in later centuries as Arthur fighting a dragon. Tales of such feats may then have been developed and elaborated by the storytellers, becoming common knowledge. In the twelfth century when pious monks were writing their hagiographical stories and wanted the strongest possible foil to show the saint's superiority, they chose Arthur. In their *Lives* of St Carannog and St Euflamm, they present Arthur as seeking dragons to fight but then show him as being ineffectual in this task, requiring the saint to conquer the dragon in both cases.[21]

An Example supplied by Clube and Napier

Victor Clube and William Napier have unearthed a tantalising example of a possible fireball explosion in the midlands of Britain which would have been of enormous value were it able to be investigated by archaeologists. In 1834, the London *Penny Magazine* reported on the draining of land in the Isle of Axholme, east of Doncaster. Many oak, fir and various other tree types were discovered 5 feet underground with their tree trunks aligned northwest to southeast. Further to this strange alignment, the trees had been severed by fire, not by the axe, with their ends being charred. Clube and Napier point out the striking resemblance of this scene to that presented by the trees aligned in the 1908 airburst over Tunguska in Russia.[22]

SUMMARY

Chapters 6 and 7 have concerned the enigmatic Welsh poem, *Kat Godeu*. It appears to have been composed by an old bard, reflecting on the important events he had lived through. One was his experience in Annwfyn where he fought in torrid battles and witnessed the death of Arthur. It is argued that this bard also composed *Preideu Annwfyn* not long after he and the few survivors made it back to Britain. This chapter has been concerned with the main part of *Kat Godeu* which deals with a mysterious 'Battle of the Trees'. This occurred near Caer Nefenhyr within the Galloway region of southwest Scotland. The bard claims to have been there as a young man, singing in 'the battle of the tree tops'.

In the interpretation provided here, the 'great scaly beast' (described in eleven lines just before the battle started) is the enemy, probably a fierce-looking comet that inspired fear among the Britons. It would appear that the meteoric or cometary debris, which travelled in the broad tube enveloping the comet, rained down in the earth's atmosphere. One can only speculate on what happened, but a bloodbath had occurred. It is also possible that multiple airbursts had occurred, each unleashing a hail of stones that had their energy dissipated by the dense forests, a scene witnessed by the bard. The poem itself appears to be saying that the tops of the oak trees were ensnaring the enemy for the Britons.

Ifor Williams has suggested the intriguing possibility that this event later became known as the battle of the Caledonian Forest, the *Cat Coit Celidon* of the *Historia Brittonum*.[23] If this were the case, then the mysterious physical phenomenon that terrified the Britons, recorded in *Kat Godeu*, has become mixed in with Arthur's conventional battles.

8
THE AFTERMATH OF THE VOYAGE

THE CHAIR OF THE SOVEREIGN

Kadeir Teÿrnon (traditionally translated 'Chair (throne) of the Sovereign') is another *Book of Taliesin* poem that conveys much information about Arthur in dealing with the aftermath of his death. It is argued in the next chapter that this poem was probably composed by the same bard that composed *Preideu Annwfyn* and *Kat Godeu*. The poem is difficult, particularly in the last section where foreign invaders, other than Saxons, appear to be attacking Britain. Rather than dealing with the poem as a whole, the relevant sections will be discussed to see what they can tell us about Arthur.

The unemended Welsh text and a tentative English translation are given below. The translation retains the pattern of using either 'with his' or 'and his' (*ae* in the Welsh text) to begin a series of consecutive lines, Lines 5-11. This seems to have been the intention of the poet. However this approach requires that words like *rechtur* (governor) are represented as verbal nouns (as given below) or abstract nouns. Marged Haycock tries a different approach that does not retain the pattern above.[1] Despite these difficulties in giving an exact translation, the general sense of each line is usually evident. Lines 3 to 22 refer to Arthur.

Translation of Introductory Section

1 **Areith awdyl eglur**
   The proclaiming of a clear poem
2 **awen tra messur**
   of inspiration beyond measure
3 **am gwr – deu, awdur**
   about a man – brave, authoritative
4 **o echen Aladur**
   from the family of Aladur/Mars
5 **ae ffonsa ae ffur**
   with his staff and his wise nature
6 **ae Reom rechtur**
   and his governing of Rheon
7 **ae ri rwyfyadur**
   and his royal sovereignty
8 **ae rif yscrythur**
   and his honouring of scripture
9 **ae goch gochlessur**
   and his bloody protection

10	**ae ergyr dros uur**
	and his attack across the wall
11	**ae kadeir gymessur**
	and his commensurate chair
12	**ymplith goscord nur.**
	amongst the lordly retinue.
13	**Neus duc o Gawrnur**
	He took away from Cawrnur
14	**meirch gwelw gostrodur.**
	pale horses under saddle.
15	**Teyrnon henur,**
	The venerable sovereign,
16	**heilyn, pascadur.**
	the provider, feeder.
17	**Treded dofyn doethur**
	The third profound (song) of the wise man
18	**y vendigaw Arthur.**
	(was) to bless Arthur.
19	**Arthur vendigan**
	Arthur was blessed
20	**ar gerd gyfaenat:**
	in a harmonious song:
21	**arwyneb yg kat**
	a defence in battle
22	**ar naw bystylat.**
	trampling (his enemies) nine at once.

A EULOGY TO ARTHUR

1 The proclaiming of a clear poem
2 of inspiration beyond measure

This poem begins with the bard boasting about his 'clear' poem that is based on inspiration (*awen*) beyond measure. This poem, however, is hardly 'clear' in its entirety. The last section (which will be briefly outlined but not analysed here) is particularly difficult. The bard's boasting is also a strong feature of *Preideu Annwfyn* and *Kat Godeu*, as has previously been seen in a discussion of those poems.

From Line 3 to Line 22 the subject is Arthur, though in typical fashion the bard is very indirect – he lets the audience infer that it is Arthur before finally mentioning his name in Line 18. This indirectness is also a feature of *Preideu Annwfyn* and *Kat Godeu*. In *Preideu Annwfyn*, Arthur is not mentioned by name until Line 21, although his ship Prydwen is mentioned in Line 9. In *Kat Godeu*, Arthur (who was initially called the 'Lord of Britain' in Line 27) is not mentioned by name until Line 239.

Likened to the God of War, Mars
3   about a man – brave, authoritative
4   from the family of Aladur/Mars

Here Arthur is compared to the family of the probable Celtic god, Aladur, who was apparently twinned with the Roman god of war, Mars. This is a reference to his military reputation. In the mid 1700s a silver-gilt plaque was found in Barkway, Hertfordshire showing the two names *Marti Alatori* and an image of a helmeted Mars. In addition, the names *Mar(ti) Ala(tori)* appear on the South Shields Roman altar found in 1887. The Romans had twinned the local Celtic gods with their Roman gods, a well-known example being Sūlis with the Roman Minerva.[2]

In AD 391 the emperor Theodosius I abolished official support for all the gods except the Christian god. This reference to the very obscure Celtic god, Aladur, is important given that the bard was a Christian who also believed in the transmigration of the soul and inspiration from the cauldron, as will be later discussed. This unusual mix of ancient beliefs is consistent with an early date for the poem.

Carrying a Staff
5   with his staff and his wise nature

This line is a quite difficult one. Marged Haycock tentatively emends *ffonsa* to *ffous*, thus translating it as 'famous'.[3] Here *ffonsa* is translated as 'staff', from *ffonn* meaning 'stick' or 'staff'. Arthur is portrayed carrying a staff in the c. 1400 tapestry in the Cloisters, Metropolitan Museum of Art, in New York. The original tapestry presented the Christian heroes: Arthur, Charlemagne and Godfrey de Bouillon and was part of the *Nine Worthies* set.[4]

It is possible that the imagery of Arthur holding the staff in the tapestry has also been taken from *Kadeir Teÿrnon*, an unknown translator in the past having taken *ffonsa* to mean staff. This is of course no guarantee that it is correct, but it is not implausible. The early Christian kings may have used a sceptre with a small cross at the top.

Governor over Rheon
6   and his governing of Rheon
7   and his royal sovereignty

In Line 6, Arthur is portrayed as the governor (*rechtur*) of Rheon (*Reom* is a misspelling). The semi-Latin *rechtur* is very old, thought to be Neo-Brittonic by John Koch.[5] Its Latin form *rector* was used three times by Gildas. If this poem were composed after the *Historia Brittonum* then one would expect Arthur to be depicted as the victor at Badon and there to be some mention of his *Historia* battles. However this lack is consistent with the thesis here that *Kadeir Teÿrnon* was composed before the 800s.

Rheon is a little-known location that is not mentioned in the *Historia*. It appears in Triad 1 of the Welsh Triads in the form Pen Rhionydd. William Watson and other leading scholars identify it with Loch Ryan in southwest Scotland.[6] Two other Arthurian locations, Caer Nefenhyr and Coit Celidon, are associated with southwest Scotland. The closeness of Rheon to Ireland suggests that Arthur won his Scottish reputation by protecting the Britons from the bloodthirsty Irish invaders feared by Gildas.

Arthur's 'royal sovereignty' and 'commensurate chair' are referred to in Lines 7 and 11. They concur with the view of *Preideu Annwfyn* and *Kat Godeu* that Arthur was a king, despite the doubts expressed on the nobility of his pedigree in the Vatican recension of the *Historia Brittonum*.

Respect for the Scriptures

8   and his honouring of scripture

Line 8 indicates that Arthur respected the scriptures, if *rif* is taken as praise, or honour, as Haycock does.[7] This is consistent with the other references suggesting that Arthur was a Christian king, implied by the strong influence of Christianity in *Preideu Annwfyn* and *Kat Godeu* and his bard calling him a 'saint' when announcing his death. The later *Historia Brittonum* and the *Annales Cambriae* also depict him as a Christian battle commander.

Prowess in Battle

9   and his bloody protection
10   and his attack across the wall

These lines indicate that Arthur's men spilt blood to protect and maintain order and depicts them launching an assault over a wall or rampart. It is not impossible that this reference could have been to Hadrian's Wall, given that Arthur had a northern presence in Rheon.

Arthur's Chair (Throne)

11   and his commensurate chair
12   amongst the lordly retinue.

Lines 11 and 12 offer something specific about Arthur. They indicate that he had a chair appropriate to his status; that is, a throne. This has been the traditional translation of several leading scholars.[8] However Marged Haycock argues that *kadeir* probably has the alternative meaning of 'song' rather than 'chair'. Here it is argued that 'chair' is the appropriate meaning and that the whole poem is essentially about Arthur's throne. It concerns the aftermath of Arthur's death and who will succeed him.[9] Did Dark Age kings in Britain have thrones? They did. In *The Ruin of Britain* (in Section 31.1) Gildas berates Vortipor for his transgressions. He caustically remarks that Vortipor sat 'on a throne full of guiles' (*in throno dolis pleno*).[10]

Conflict between Arthur and Caw

13 He took away from Cawrnur
14 pale horses under saddle.

These lines imply a battle between Arthur and Cawrnur, who was probably the Caw from the two *Lives* of Gildas. In the earlier Rhuys *Life* written in Brittany, Caw comes from Arecluta (Strathclyde) and is said to be the father of Gildas. In the later *Life of Gildas* by Caradoc of Llancarfan, Arthur kills the brother of Gildas, Huail. In Lines 13-14 Arthur is victorious against Caw, his spoils being pale horses carrying their saddles. It implies the death of Caw's horsemen and the capturing of their horses still under saddle.[11] As Caw was based in Strathclyde, his conflict with Arthur is another indicator that Arthur was in southwest Scotland, consistent with Arthur's links to Rheon, Caer Nefenhyr and the Celidon forest.

The Venerable Sovereign

15 The venerable sovereign,
16 the provider, feeder.

Lines 15-16 imply that Arthur was highly respected and provided for his people. It is very interesting that *Teÿrnon* (sovereign) is here being applied to Arthur. This is important given that there was a powerful king, Teÿrnon Twrf Liant, in *Pwyll Prince of Dyfed*, a later story in the *Mabinogi*. This king closely resembles Arthur. He interacts warmly with Pwyll and Pryderi who reported the capture of Gweir in Annwfyn. This *Mabinogi* story states that Teÿrnon Twrf Liant was the former overlord of Pwyll, just as Arthur was the overlord of Pwyll in *Preideu Annwfyn*. He is described as 'the best man in the world' a term applied to Arthur's men in the poem *Pa Gûr*, as translated by Patrick Sims-Williams.[12] If Teÿrnon Twrf Liant were a later character based on Arthur, then how Teÿrnon was viewed is of interest, an issue that will be discussed in Chapter 12.

The Blessing of Arthur

17 The third profound (song) of the wise man
18 (was) to bless Arthur.
19 Arthur was blessed
20 in a harmonious song:
21 a defence in battle
22 trampling (his enemies) nine at once.

Lines 17-22 refer to a song in which Arthur was blessed, sung by a wise man, one of his advisers. What was the significance of this song? In a later part of the poem the soldiers are said to be bereft at Arthur's death and the bard himself is distressed. The most probable explanation is that the song is part of a eulogy and would include a prayer for Arthur's soul. Lines 21 and 22 may include part of the song, briefly describing Arthur's valour in battle, smashing his enemies and trampling them into the ground.

AN IMPLICATION THAT ARTHUR WAS OVERSEAS

The Three Stewards who Minded the Country

Immediately after the reference to Arthur's eulogy, the bard asks: 'Who were the three stewards who minded the country?' which gives an indirect pointer to Arthur's expedition overseas to Annwfyn. The issue of 'who minded the country' appears in three literary sources: *Kadeir Teÿrnon*, Triad 13 of *Triads of the Island of Britain* and the second story of the *Mabinogi, Branwen Daughter of Llŷr*. It will be argued that it first appeared in Lines 23 and 24 of *Kadeir Teÿrnon*, given below, and that these lines were the basis for the elaborations in the other sources.

> 23   Pwy y tri chynweissat
>   Who were the three stewards
> 24   a werchetwis gwlat?
>   that minded the country?

These two lines follow directly after the Arthurian introduction in Lines 3 to 22, which implies continuity with Arthur's activities. It indicates that the king overseas was Arthur. Further, the necessity to appoint stewards to mind the country indicates that Arthur's absence was nontrivial, that he was overseas for a significant time.

There is no contextual information in the poem that serves to explain the meaning of this question. This lack suggests that the bard's audience were already aware of the context and knew that Arthur had been absent from Britain, giving another indication that the poem was of an early date. It would seem that the disastrous nature of the expedition made it inappropriate to mention it directly in a poem describing a eulogy to Arthur and lauding his achievements.

The Mabinogi Reference

As mentioned briefly in Chapter 6, this 'caretaker of Britain' theme is taken up centuries later in the tale of Brân the Blessed (a mythological character modelled on Arthur) in the second tale in the *Mabinogi*. When Brân invaded Ireland, seven caretakers were chosen to mind Britain, with Caradawg the son of Brân as the chief over them.

This story elaborates the theme given above in *Kadeir Teÿrnon*, with the caretakers being given names and being associated with seven horsemen. Rachel Bromwich argues that the author of this *Mabinogi* story increased the number of caretakers from three to seven to conform with the placename in the story, *Bryn Seith Marchawg*, which translates as the 'Hill of the Seven Horsemen'.[13]

The Triads Reference

A third reference to the theme of caretakers for Britain occurs in Triad 13 of the Welsh Triads, as recorded by Rachel Bromwich.[14]

Triad 13: Three stewards of the isle of Britain

> Caradawg son of Brân
> and Cawrdaf son of Caradawg
> and Owain son of Maxen Wledig.

This triad does not answer the question posed in *Kadeir Teÿrnon* which refers to three people put in charge while Arthur was away. The author of the triad has not addressed this *Kadeir Teÿrnon* question but he has appreciated the importance of the theme of 'minding the country'. He has thus created three separate instances where minding the country had occurred and then supplied dubious answers with a single person in charge of each.

The third line refers to Maxen Wledig (Magnus Maximus), an historical figure who left Britain with his troops to fight on the continent, where he became *Augustus* (emperor) in the west. He was executed in northern Italy in 388. Gildas refers to him in Section 13 of *The Ruin of Britain*. The triad claims that he had a son, Owain, who minded the country while Maxen was away, but there is no supporting evidence for this.

The first line names Caradawg who appears several times in the triads. His father is shown as Brân, the mythological figure based on Arthur. The second line mentions Cawrdaf, who was recorded as Caradawg's son in *Bonedd y Saint* (Lineage of the Saints).[15] Caradawg is also linked to Arthur in other triads. In Triad 1 he is Arthur's chief of elders in Celliwig in Kernyw, while in Triad 18 he is one of Arthur's most famous battle-horsemen, the precursor to the term 'knights'.[16] A variant of Triad 18 has Arthur himself sing an *englyn* (a stanza of three lines) describing Caradawg as a pillar of the Cymry (the Britons). Although Caradawg seems to have been a real person connected to Arthur, there is little evidence for him minding the country in Arthur's absence. Triad 13 and the *Mabinogi* do place him in this role, but this may have been merely an inference from his 'chief of elders' position in Triad 1. Given his association with Arthur, it is no surprise that Caradawg is linked with Brân.

It is argued in Chapter 12 that the figure of Brân replaced Arthur in later literature when a superstition arose against Arthur's name as a result of his death in Annwfyn. However it is unlikely that Caradawg was Arthur's son, as could be construed from this triad, as this relationship is never made in the literature and later works make him Arthur's first cousin.[17] Apart from Maximus, little is known about the others. The value of the triad is that it shows that the theme of 'minding the country' from *Kadeir Teÿrnon* was very important to the Britons, which prompted the author to meet this need by supplying examples, however dubious.

The Early Form of the Kadeir Teÿrnon Reference

As noted earlier, Rachel Bromwich convincingly argues that Triad 13, with only three stewards, was earlier than the *Mabinogi* reference with seven stewards. However, Triad 13 is not as early as the *Kadeir Teÿrnon* reference. In the latter, the bard raises the issue in the form of a question, but does not supply the answer. If the poem were a late work, composed after the triad, it would be pointless for the bard to ask the question in his poem – the audience could simply reply with the triad's answer. This would detract from the bard's reputation as a repository of arcane knowledge and deflate the authority he held over the audience.

The bard also asks other impenetrable questions in this poem without supplying the answers, such as 'Who were the three wise ones who guarded the portent?" (Lines 25-6) and 'What are the names of the three fortresses which now lie under flooding?' (Lines 43-4). These questions have not later become famous and have faded into obscurity.

Although *Kadeir Teÿrnon* does not directly refer to Arthur's expedition to Annwfyn, it raises the issue of 'who minded the country' which does imply that he was absent for a considerable time. Further, the Britons obviously regarded the issue as important for it to be preserved in the Welsh Triads and later in the *Mabinogi* as shown above.

THE BARD'S BELIEFS

In Lines 33-8 the bard reveals that he is a Christian, yet also holds the old beliefs in the magic of the cauldron and the transmigration of the soul.

33 **ban gwir pan disgleir**
   (it is) fine when the True One shines
34 **bannach pan lefeir**
   even finer when He speaks
35 **ban pan doeth o peir**
   (it is) fine when came from the cauldron
36 **ogyrwen awen teir.**
   the threepart inspiration.
37 **Bum mynawc mynweir**
   I was a torqued nobleman
38 **yg korn ym nedeir.**
   with my horn in my hand.

Gratitude to God

33 (it is) fine when the True One shines
34 even finer when He speaks

Here Arthur's bard is grateful to God, the True One, for His actions and pronouncements, the latter presumably the scriptures.

Praise for Inspiration from the Cauldron
35 (it is) fine when came from the cauldron
36 the threepart inspiration.

Here the bard is praising the cauldron and its role in releasing inspiration. This magical process appears to be compatible with the bard's Christianity, the inspiration itself perhaps seen as a gift from God. This exactly parallels the beliefs of the *Preideu Annwfyn* bard; namely, that his inspired poetry came from the cauldron and his turning to Christ for comfort.

Belief in the Transmigration of the Soul
37 I was a torqued nobleman
38 with my horn in my hand.

In these lines the bard recalls a previous incarnation as a nobleman wearing a torque (or torc), an ornament of honour, and holding a horn. This line is similar in form to those showing the transmigration of the soul at the start of *Kat Godeu*. It is thus evident that the transmigration of the soul, inspiration from the cauldron and belief in the Christian God are an integrated part of the bard's belief system.

A SUCCESSOR TO ARTHUR

Lines 59-67 of *Kadeir Teijrnon* briefly deal with the deep distress of Arthur's warriors and his bard at Arthur's death and the qualities needed for the king who will take his place.

59 **Kadeir Teyrnon,**
The Chair of the Sovereign,
60 **keluyd rwy katwo.**
he is a skilful one who keeps it.
61 **Keissitor ygno,**
A renowned fighter will be sought,
62 **keissitor kedic,**
an aggressive one will be sought,
63 **ketwyr colledic.**
as our warriors are bereft.
64 **Tebygafi dull dic**
I am (similarly) distressed
65 **o diua pendeuic**
from the annihilation of the prince
66 **o dull diuynnic**
with the fierce nature
67 **o Leon luryc.**
with the lorica of Lleon.

Choosing a Successor to Arthur

59   The Chair of the Sovereign,
60   he is a skilful one who keeps it.
61   A renowned fighter will be sought,
62   an aggressive one will be sought,

In Lines 59-60 the bard is referring to the Chair (Throne) of the Sovereign as the kingship. To hold on to the throne the king needed to be skilful. The next two lines suggest that the throne was now vacant and indicate the kind of successor who would be needed to occupy it, one renowned in battle or an aggressive warrior. These descriptors are consistent with the language of Gildas in Section 21.4 of *The Ruin of Britain* who referred to brutal tyrants being replaced by even more oppressive tyrants and reflect the reality that a king had to use force to retain power and protect his realm.

Arthur's Death

63   as our warriors are bereft.
64   I am (similarly) distressed
65   from the annihilation of the prince
66   with the fierce nature

These lines imply that there is a current leadership vacuum and the warriors are 'lost' or bereft, as is the bard. This distress comes from the annihilation of the prince with the fierce nature, identified as Arthur in the first 22 lines of the poem. The language used here for annihilation (*diua*) is also used in *Preideu Annwfyn* in consecutive lines, including the key line that announces Arthur's death, Line 58 in *Preideu Annwfyn*. The fact that Arthur's death in both poems is associated with annihilation appears to indicate that the body was not recovered but was lost in Annwfyn.

Arthur's Location

67   with the lorica of Lleon.

This line is important as it gives a clue to the location of Arthur. He wore the breastplate (lorica) of *Lleon*. The lorica was a tough leather breastplate that was reinforced with metal to protect the body, perfectly apt armour for a sixth-century warrior, as described by Leslie Alcock.[18]

Lleon is discussed by Marged Haycock who states that it may either refer specifically to Caer Lleon, which is Chester, or to refer to northeast Wales in general.[19] This information is consistent with *Preideu Annwfyn*, where the bard states that the inhabitants of Annwfyn did not visit the *Defwy* (Devwy) meadows which refer to Deva, the Roman name for Chester. It has been argued previously that the *Defwy* meadows refer to those along the River Dee, which runs through Chester. If these identifications are correct, then they suggest that Arthur was from northeast Wales.

WILD WEATHER CONDITIONS

If *Kadeir Teÿrnon* were composed in the sixth century, then it gives valuable information. One very intriguing section implies extensive flooding around the time of Arthur's death. Apart from Lines 43-4 which pose the question of which three fortresses are now flooded, a section comprising Lines 53-8 deals with flooding. The expert translation of Marged Haycock vividly depicts the disaster.[20] Waves are now washing over places where beaches formerly were. The slopes, sheltered spots and hills are affected. An angry wind is violently lashing the waves. One could view these lines metaphorically as an expression of disaster and misery following Arthur's death, but this view seems unlikely for several reasons.

The first is that Lines 43-4 ask which three fortresses were now flooded, a question that requires a specific answer, implying that the flooding was real. Secondly, the last line mentions an Elffin, probably the Elphin whose father Gwyddno Garanhir lived near Degannwy and had a fish weir on the shore of the Conwy, according to the late story *The Tale of Taliesin*. Gwyddno had his lands flooded in Welsh tradition. Further, directly after the flooding section, the bard refers to the 'chair' of the sovereign and says that it will take a skilful king to hold on to it. He seems to be saying that the incoming king has many problems to face, not the least of which are the flooding and violent winds.

Flooding at Lough Neagh circa 540

The poem is placing this wild weather shortly after Arthur's death. It is thus possible that the violent storms described here are manifestations of the environmental downturn that was noted by Michael Baillie. He refers to the death of trees circa AD 540 near Lough Neagh in Ireland and suggests that this may have resulted from a large rise in water level in this huge lake.[21] If the poem is describing the same catastrophe as that noted by Baillie, then it implies Arthur's death was shortly before 540. This would agree well with the *Annales Cambriae* date of 537/539.

THE POEM'S ENDING

The ending of *Kadeir Teÿrnon* is a mysterious one. It abruptly changes from dealing with Arthur's death and possible successors to a section that seems to imply an invasion of Britain by foreign peoples who have come from over the seas (Lines 74-9). These enemies are from the stock of Saraphin. Marged Haycock argues that this term probably means 'Saracen', which could mean no more to the bard than pagan outsiders.[22]

This theme is similar to that recorded by Geoffrey of Monmouth in his *History*, where he has Ireland and Britain being invaded by the mysterious Gormund, King of the Africans.[23] It also appears in the Arthurian section of the *Leges Anglorum Londoniis Collectae* that was discussed in connection with the *Northern Lands List* in Chapter 3. In the *Leges Anglorum* material,

Arthur was stated to have expelled Saracens and other enemies from the British kingdom, as discussed by Kent Hieatt.[24] None of the details in these sources can be taken as historical but the general proposition that a foreign people, referred to here as Saracens, had invaded Britain at this time is not impossible. The end of the poem gives a plea by the bard to release Elffin, apparently from these foreign invaders. As this rather unintelligible ending does not tell us any more about Arthur, it will not be further discussed in the main text.[25]

SUMMARY

Kadeir Teÿrnon has marked similarities to *Preideu Annwfyn* and *Kat Godeu*. It uses the same expression (*diua*) to describe Arthur's death as does *Preideu Annwfyn* and has the warriors and the bard himself distressed over Arthur's death, similar to the bard's grieving in *Preideu Annwfyn*. Although it does not mention Annwfyn as the other two poems do, it raises the issue of 'who was minding the country' which does imply that Arthur was absent from Britain for a significant time. There are further similarities between *Kadeir Teÿrnon* and the other two poems. All three have a Christian perspective. Further, *Kadeir Teÿrnon* shares with *Preideu Annwfyn* the theme of poetic inspiration coming from the cauldron, while it shares with *Kat Godeu* the theme of the transmigration of the soul.

Kadeir Teÿrnon is a poem that tells us a good deal about Arthur, some of it of an unusual nature. It stresses his bravery and valour in battle (Lines 3, 4, 9, 10, 13, 14, 21 and 22). However, it completely ignores the now famous battle of Badon and the other battles in the *Historia Brittonum*. The bard is more interested in Arthur's governance of Rheon, an obscure location that has been identified by scholars as the area around Loch Ryan in southwest Scotland. Gildas refers to the terrifying raids of the Irish, sailing across the Irish Sea to Britain, and at one stage capturing a large region of southern Scotland down to Hadrian's Wall. The shortest and easiest route for the northern Irish to get to Britain would have been to sail to this Loch Ryan area. Arthur's governance of the region suggests that he was there to repel the Irish and pacify the region. This perspective of *Kadeir Teÿrnon* is quite unusual compared to that of the *Historia* and later writings.

The poem also mentions Arthur fighting a Cawrnur who is probably the Caw of Arecluta in the Rhuys *Life of Gildas*. Caw was a Briton rather than a Saxon. If Arthur were protecting Rheon, then his fighting Caw, who was based in Strathclyde, would not be implausible due to the relatively close distance between the two areas. It is certainly much more plausible than Caw raiding Arthur by sailing from Scotland down to Wales.

Although attention is given to Rheon, Arthur's home base seems to have been in north Wales as the summing up after his distressing death portrays him with the lorica of Lleon. As discussed by Marged Haycock, Lleon could be the specific Caer Lleon, which is Chester, or it could refer to the general area of northeast Wales. This location is consistent with that indicated by the *Preideu Annwfyn* bard, which refers to the Defwy meadows. It has been argued that the latter are the meadows along the River Dee that runs through Chester.

Kadeir Teÿrnon describes Arthur as a Christian king, having a respect for scripture. Further, like *Preideu Annwfyn* and *Kat Godeu* it has a Christian perspective, with the bard expressing gratitude to God (the True One) for His actions in the world, and pronouncements, probably the scriptures. Arthur also appears as a Christian king in the other later works such as the *Historia Brittonum* and the *Annales Cambriae*.

The central theme of the poem is that Arthur's throne is vacant. After a lengthy introduction praising Arthur, a song is sung by a 'wise one' to bless Arthur, which appears to be part of a eulogy for the dead king. The bard refers to the vacant chair and remarks that it will take a skilful one to hold on to it. He then describes the type of king needed to fill it, a famous warrior or an aggressive one. He sadly remarks how Arthur's warriors were bereft at his death, as he is himself, and refers to it as the annihilation of the prince with the fiery nature, using the same Welsh expression as in *Preideu Annwfyn*.

It appears that shortly after Arthur's death, extreme weather conditions hit north Wales. A later section of the poem refers to violent environmental conditions, where some fortresses are flooded. The sea is now covering the beaches and slopes. Formerly safe, sheltered spots are now under threat from the waves, which are being lashed by angry winds.

These could be manifestations of the environmental downturn identified by Michael Baillie which intensified in 540. If this is correct, then Arthur's recorded death date of 537/539 in the *Annales Cambriae* may be close to his true death date. These events are all set in the aftermath of Arthur's death and the poem would appear to have been composed shortly after this time. It is not impossible that it could be a skilful, imaginative reconstruction of Arthur's death by a late 'persona' bard who is re-enacting events hundreds of years before his time, but the outlook of the poem, which ignores Badon and the *Historia* battles, tells against this.

9
DATING THE THREE POEMS

OVERVIEW OF THE DATING

Dating Preideu Annwfyn

In this chapter various methods will be used to date *Preideu Annwfyn*. Firstly, it will be dated from its historical context. It will be argued that the poem provides an eyewitness account and was composed not long after the publication of Gildas' *The Ruin of Britain*, a diatribe against his own British people: the kings, their bards, the military and clergy. It created a poisonous atmosphere that accounts for the animosity that the bard displays in *Preideu Annwfyn*. In the last five of the eight stanzas, he expresses his contempt for the monks, repeatedly calling them 'little men' and virtually accusing them of cowardice. If Gildas' work were written about 540, then *Preideu Annwfyn*, giving an emotional outburst by the bard, would have been composed not long after this when the work was being heatedly discussed.

It will also be shown that there are early works which contain elements that seem to be derived from *Preideu Annwfyn*, this being evident from their more elaborated form or through their partial misconceptions. These works are the *Historia Brittonum* and five early Irish works – *The Voyage of Bran*, *Echtrae Chonnlai*, *Dún Scáith*, *Bricriu's Feast* and the *Voyage of Mael Dúin's Boat*. A case can be made that some of these Irish works may be as early as the seventh century. This evidence by itself suggests that *Preideu Annwfyn* may date to the 600s or earlier.

Dating Kat Godeu and Kadeir Teÿrnon

The other poems *Kat Godeu* and *Kadeir Teÿrnon* are mainly dated through their sharing of features with *Preideu Annwfyn*. The commonalities between these three poems will be set out, showing pairwise comparisons of similar features, suggesting a common authorship. However *Kat Godeu* does have a link to an early Irish work, the poem *Dún Scáith*, which is to be explored below. Further, the three Arthurian poems also appear to contain language fragments that are archaic, features of the Neo-Brittonic language current at the time of Arthur, as will later be discussed.

The totality of the evidence suggests that an early dating is strongest for *Preideu Annwfyn*, but the interlocking evidence is also quite strong for *Kat Godeu*. The evidence is less strong for *Kadeir Teÿrnon*, yet this poem has an early outlook that ignores the *Historia* battles and puts Arthur in Rheon in southwest Scotland, certainly a logical location given his northern fame. In evaluating this data it may be noted that acceptance or rejection of an early dating is not of an 'all or none' nature if the arguments that a common poet composed all three are rejected.

DATING FROM HISTORICAL CONTEXT

Introduction

A feature of *Preideu Annwfyn* that has not been understood by proponents of the mythological view is the bard's persistent raging against the monks. This is not an incidental feature of the poem but is strongly evident in five of the eight stanzas. It goes far beyond the bard contending for superiority in learning with the monks but expresses contempt, bordering on hatred. He has little respect for the monks, whom he dismisses as mere scripture learners. He implies they are cowards, and describes them as having no strength of will, unable to move outside their 'soft' comfortable life. He likens them to dogs and wolves, in the most pejorative way. What could account for this rage? The most probable answer is the intemperate tirade written by the cleric Gildas who attacked his own British people so strongly that it has led some scholars to question whether *The Ruin of Britain* was actually written by a Briton.[1]

Gildas' Attack on the Five Kings

Gildas launches a blistering attack on five kings, revealing the lurid details of the vile murders they committed, their intrigues and their sex lives.[2] He also makes puns ridiculing the kings. The first is Constantine from the peninsula of Dumnonia, which Gildas apparently puns as 'Damnonia'.[3] Gildas accuses Constantine of murdering two royal youths at the holy altar of a church and of committing frequent adulteries against his wife, finally putting her aside and turning to sodomy.

The second is Aurelius 'Caninus' whose crimes are parricides, fornications and adulteries. He also wages civil wars, plundering the realms around him. His whole family were apparently bloodthirsty like this and had been killed in youthful and untimely deaths. He is now likened to a withered solitary tree in the middle of an barren field, and unlikely to live much longer given his propensity to war. Gildas mocks him by punning on his name, calling him 'Caninus', which means 'dog-like' (meant in a pejorative sense), rather than his real name which may have been the Neo-Brittonic equivalent of Cynan, as mentioned in Chapter 5.

The third king is Vortipor, tyrant of the Demetae, in southwest Wales. He is like a 'leopard' in his behaviour, spotted with wickedness. His hair was now beginning to whiten, as Gildas comments, so it appears that Gildas had seen him recently. Gildas castigates him as 'you worthless son of a good king!'. He is defiled from top to bottom by various murders and adulteries. On top of these, his soul is burdened (after the honourable death of his wife) by his incest with his shameless daughter.

Next is Cuneglasus, based in north Wales, whose name would normally be translated as 'blue hound'[4] or 'grey hound'. However, Gildas distorts the elements of this name to emphasis his brutality, preferring the lesser used meaning of 'tawny' hound. Gildas then interprets this 'hound' as one who tears apart, rendering the meaning as butcher (*lanio*), and thus translates the name as 'tawny butcher', as discussed by eminent Celtic linguist Kenneth Jackson. Michael Winterbottom gives 'red butcher' which aptly emphasises Gildas' intention.[5] Cuneglasus is a despiser of God and an oppressor of God's agents and is admonished for his anger and rage. He is accused of rejecting his own wife and turning his attentions to his wife's sister, who had promised herself to God in perpetuity.

Maglocunus, the most powerful king, is introduced as the 'dragon of the island', probably the isle of Anglesey off the northwest coast of Wales with its chief settlement in Aberffraw.[6] He is described as 'first in evil'. While he was only a youth, Maglocunus murdered his uncle and seized his uncle's throne. However his rule was unsatisfying and then he suffered remorse, resolving to abandon his former life and become a monk. After some time as a monk he unfortunately reverted to his former way of life, 'like a sick dog returning to his fearful vomit', according to Gildas. However instead of returning to his blameless first wife, he murdered her, along with his nephew, which allowed him to marry his nephew's widow. The wedding was public and its legitimacy was proclaimed by the lying tongues of his parasites. The latter were almost certainly the bards of Maglocunus.

Although the lives of these kings seem vile by our standards, it should be kept in mind that they needed to be brutal to hold onto power. Many of their murders were probably designed to remove rivals to the throne. Were these British kings any worse than kings elsewhere at the time? A reading of *The History of the Franks* by Gregory of Tours, which provides a vivid account of contemporary kings across the Channel, would soon dispel this notion.[7]

Excoriation of the Bards

Gildas' contempt of the bards is made evident in his address to Maglocunus (given below), in which he calls the bards criminals and liars and exaggerates the physical aspects of their singing to create disgust, as in the translation by Hugh Williams:[8]

> When the attention of thy ears has been caught, it is not the praises of God...that are heard, but thine own praises (which are nothing); the voice of the rascally crew yelling forth, like Bacchanalian revellers, full of lies and foaming phlegm, so as to besmear everyone near them. In this way the vessel, once prepared for the service of God, is changed into an instrument of Satan.

The translation of Michael Winterbottom is equally damning:[9]

> ...from the mouths of criminals who grate on the hearing like raving hucksters – mouths stuffed with lies and liable to bedew bystanders with their foaming phlegm.

The British Military as Cowards

Gildas also showed his contempt for the British warriors as in the following malicious comments:[10]

> They present their back, instead of their shields, to the pursuers, their necks to the sword, while a chilling terror ran through their bones: they hold forth their hands to be bound like women; so that it was spread far and wide as a proverb and a derision: the Britons are neither brave in war nor in peace faithful.

Later, in describing the British attempts to fend off the Picts and the Scots, Gildas continues his insults.

> To oppose their attacks, there was stationed on the height of the stronghold, an army, slow to fight, unwieldy for flight, incompetent by reason of its cowardice of heart, which languished day and night in its foolish watch.

There can be no greater defamation for a warrior than to be compared to a woman or called a coward. Given that Gildas and his fellow clerics never had to put their own lives at risk as warriors, these words would be galling to the bard. One may ask how these words were designed to encourage the Britons to repent of their sins and turn to God, the ostensible purpose of Gildas' work. They go far beyond a mere desire to see his people return to a godly way of life. They suggest an embittered state of mind, a theme that will be discussed in a later chapter.

THE BARD'S ANGER AT THE MONKS

The Bard's Mental State

If the thesis of this book is correct, the bard was one of the few survivors who managed to return to Britain. He had seen his comrades and his king killed in the ferocious battles in Annwfyn. In *Preideu Annwfyn* the bard reveals his devastation in the last stanza, where he states that he is praising Arthur as a way of preventing himself from grieving. He then turns to Christ for comfort. This emotion certainly seems raw and heartfelt. He also uses the present tense when praising Arthur in the first and last stanzas. It is as though Arthur is still king in the bard's mind and he is having trouble accepting the fact that Arthur is dead.

In this mental state, the bard returns to Britain to find that Gildas has trashed the things he holds important. The kings have been trashed, with Gildas exposing the lurid details of their personal lives and relationships. The bravery of the British warriors has been trashed – Gildas refers to them as ineffectual cowards and likens them to women. Finally, the British bards have been trashed in a most vile way by Gildas.

What the monks knew concerning Arthur's expedition to Annwfyn is not known. The destination may have been kept a secret or perhaps the monks were aware that they were sailing to explore a new land that had recently been discovered or was rumoured to exist. That Gildas does not mention such an expedition is of little consequence – he was selective in what he wrote, tailoring the facts to give an unduly negative view of the Britons for his purpose of portraying them as sinners. If the monks knew about the expedition, they may have been scornful of its value and made disparaging comments. Gildas had been highly critical of the administration for at least 10 years and was spurred on by the prayers of his brethren to put his complaints into writing.[11] If prior criticisms of the expedition existed, then its ignominious failure must have rankled the bard. Then on returning to Britain to be confronted with Gildas' tirade against the kings, warriors and bards, he must have seethed with anger, his emotion gaining release in his contempt for the monks in *Preideu Annwfyn*.

The Bard's Use of Gildas' Imagery

As noted earlier, Gildas mocks one of the kings by distorting his name to 'Caninus', meaning 'dog-like', a demeaning distortion. He also plays with the name of Cuneglasus, emphasising the brutality of the 'hound' part of the name by rendering it as 'butcher'. Hence he is a vicious dog who tears flesh – a 'red butcher'. He also refers to Maglocunus as a sick dog returning to his vomit, selected from Proverbs 26:11. In responding to Gildas, the bard uses similar imagery. In *Preideu Annwfyn*, he describes the monks as huddling in fear like a 'pack of dogs' from their clash with the lords who knew about Arthur's death.

Gildas uses 'wolves' to refer to sinful clerics – instead of conforming to the biblical metaphor of shepherds, they are like wolves that slaughter souls.[12] In a later section, he refers to Jesus' saying that he sends out his apostles like sheep in the midst of wolves. Gildas, however, claims that the current clergy are like wolves in the midst of sheep.[13] In *Preideu Annwfyn*, the bard also employs this imagery to refer to the monks, having them pack together like wolves.

WAS THE BARD AN EYEWITNESS?

Explicit Claims to be an Eyewitness

Chapter 5 presents the view that Arthur led an expedition over the sea to North America in the sixth century, where the men explored the country by moving from camp to camp. This story is told in poetry by Arthur's bard who explicitly claims to be an eyewitness. In the first six stanzas he says that 'we went on the sea', 'we went into it' and 'went with Arthur'. He refers to himself entertaining Arthur's retinue with his poetry at the 'four-peaked' camp and describes his turning to view all four peaks when at that camp. He is explicitly stating that he was there.

Poetic Images of an Eyewitness

The bard also presents vivid images of certain incidents that would seem to have come from an eyewitness. He describes the capture of a 'cauldron' of the native inhabitants, a ceremonial clay pot with a dark rim and decorated with pearls. These pearls would seem a highly unlikely feature for a cauldron as conventionally conceived. However, it fits well with the Native Americans of the Hopewell culture, where thousands of freshwater pearls have been found in their earthen mounds along along with pearl necklaces and animal effigy pipes with pearl insets used for eyes. On independent grounds, these Native Americans would have been the obvious choice as the people of the mounds (at *kaer sidi*), having built a network of mounds in eastern North America during their floruit between about 150 BC and AD 500. This image of the 'cauldron' seems to be the description of an eyewitness.

The bard also describes a dramatic encounter between Arthur's men and a large group of Native Americans who were standing on a wall, probably one of their earthen walls. There is an implicit sense of intimidation in this image. It was very difficult to communicate with them, a natural consequence of the radically different languages. This also appears to be an image that could only have come from someone who was there.

There are also concise descriptions of two animals which appear to be the American buffalo and North American river otter. The buffalo's description is so apt that one wonders how it could be anything else. The river otter is also captured perfectly through its 'silvery head', an image that would be seen if the otter were swimming with its head above the water's surface, its wet fur giving a glossy sheen. The bard refers to this animal as being kept or tamed. This surprising information is remarkably apt as the otter would have been very useful for catching fish, and has been trained to do this from early times by many cultures. This again fits the Hopewell, centred in a region with many rivers and streams, who carved effigy pipes in the form of the otter, some depicted holding a fish in the mouth.

The Raw Emotion Consistent with that of an Eyewitness

Preideu Annwfyn is a poem full of emotion. There is a deep sadness as the bard reflects on the capture of Gweir as he sings bitterly in his prison. He vows to pray for Gweir until Judgement Day. The bard's imagery then shifts abruptly as he describes a happier time, seemingly earlier in the expedition, when he was entertaining the men and receiving acclaim in an atmosphere of revelry. However, the general tenor of the poem is one of a gloomy, sombre mood resulting from the repeated disasters. We are reminded of this in the relentless mournful refrain in the last line of the first six stanzas. All these emotions relate to the time spent in Annwfyn and give every appearance of being genuine.

There is also the extraordinary tirade against the British monks in which the emotions of hate and contempt are mingled. This sustained attack occurs in the last five of the eight stanzas of the poem. Under the view that the poem is describing a fantasy visit to an imaginary world, it is difficult to formulate an explanation that seems adequate. Marged Haycock makes an attempt by arguing that the bard is attempting to upstage the monks in a contest for supremacy in learning.[14] Hence he continually points out the things that the monks do not know, but which he does. It is argued that while this may be partly true, it does not fully explain the emotional force of the poem. It fails to explain his virtual accusation of cowardice in the monks in Line 35 and his accusation in Line 43 that the monks are weak-willed and by implication have never faced up to the dangers that he and his companions have endured. It does not explain the sustained deriding of the monks as 'little men'. There is an element of hatred and contempt that goes far beyond that of a contest for superiority in learning.

Further, leaving aside the poorly-defined questions or implied questions in the last two stanzas (which are designed to sustain dramatic tension) the items that the monks don't know are anchored in the context of Annwfyn. They are not independent items of traditional knowledge or book learning being used by the bard to upstage the monks. There is also the secret of something the monks don't know, but which the lords do know: the death of Arthur overseas in Annwfyn. This important secret has nothing to do with a contest of learning.

Did the bard really go?
Assuming the expedition to Annwfyn were real, one could argue that the apparent eyewitness descriptions could have been relayed to the bard from someone else who had actually returned from the expedition. But if such were the case, it renders pointless the bard's railing against the monks as people who would not have the courage to undertake such an expedition. If he had not gone on the disastrous expedition himself then the distinction between the poet and the 'little men' would be greatly diminished. Yet the continued emphasis on the 'little men' over three whole stanzas ('merely concerned with scripture', 'loose their shield straps', 'weak their resolve') implies that the bard really did go. The intensity of the resentment he holds against the monks is hard to explain otherwise. If the whole story were an imaginative fantasy concocted by the bard, then it is difficult to understand why he should obtain psychological satisfaction by mentioning *fictions* as things the monks do not know. If one is going to taunt someone over their ignorance, it only has a point if the knowledge is real and important.

Linking Christ to a lie?
In the last two lines of the last stanza the bard is praising the dead king and using Christ as comfort in his sorrow at the king's death. Such an ending is somewhat unexpected. In relying on Christ as his source of comfort, the poet reveals that he is a Christian and that his faith is vital to him. It is clearly sustaining him in this tragedy. This then raises the question: could a devout Christian, who believed literally in the Last Judgement, lie about his role in

the expedition and actually link Christ to this lie as he does in the last stanza? It seems unlikely.

Consequences of Assuming an 8th-century Date

Suppose we consider the viewpoint that the poem represents a fantasy that was composed late, say 750, as a source of entertainment. Then one wonders how the poet's grief could manifest so convincingly. If it were a fiction, then the disasters would not have been real but merely the author's creation and he would be pretending to have the various emotions evident in the poem. He would be pretending to suffer as an eyewitness, pretending to be deeply worried about Gweir, pretending to be overcome with grief at Arthur's death, and pretending to use Christ as his comforter. He would also be pretending to despise the 'little men', who were merely the products of his imagination. Further, one also wonders why he would have created the strange imagery of monks shrinking in fear when receiving information from lords 'who know', an image that has the ring of truth.

The second scenario is that the poet sincerely believed that the story he conveys in the poem was based on real events, but this also seems untenable for a 750 date of composition, being over 200 years from Arthur's death date. It would be like a modern day person visibly lamenting the death of a hero like Captain James Cook, killed in Hawaii in 1779. While the remembrance of Cook's death may bring feelings of regret, the emotions are not raw and there is no emotional impact. An analogous situation would also apply had the poet created this poem 200 or more years after Arthur's death.

Consider also the nature of the message being conveyed. The message is essentially telling selected people that Arthur had been killed and his body was not retrievable. This message is only of importance if it is conveyed soon after the incident, otherwise it loses its utility. It would be odd to announce Arthur's death, in such a dramatic manner as the poem does, had Arthur died over 200 years beforehand. Moreover, the essential message of the poem (that Arthur died in Annwfyn) was hardly likely to be useful in the eighth century. At that stage, legendary material had developed about Arthur. The marvels concerning Arthur were undoubtedly circulating then, two of which appeared in the *Mirabilia* attachment to the *Historia Brittonum* of 829-30. Something written in the eighth century would more likely be a laudatory piece, praising his warlike prowess and celebrating his victories, not relating his demise and the slaughter of his men.

Summary

Under the historical view the raw emotions follow logically from the events in Annwfyn. The bard has seen his colleagues decimated and has lost his king, a man he admired and loved. This admiration is expressed at the start of the poem where he extravagantly praises Arthur in the opening line. He then refers to Arthur's achievements – he had extended his sovereignty across the shores of the world, something no one else had ever done. In the last few lines

Dating the Three Poems 137

he continues his praise as a way of preventing himself from grieving. In both *Kat Godeu* and *Kadeir Teÿrnon*, two poems probably by the same bard, there are similar tributes to Arthur.

DATING VIA HISTORIA BRITTONUM

It will now be shown that early literary works contain elements that seem to derive from *Preideu Annwfyn*, beginning with the *Historia Brittonum*.

The 'Glass Fortress' as Iceberg

In *Preideu Annwfyn* the sailors pass a 'glass fortress', argued here to be poetic imagery for a large iceberg. Moving beyond (*tra*) this object, Arthur's valour was shown. The Britons then met a large group of the inhabitants who were standing on a wall, possibly one of the earthen enclosures for their mounds, but could not understand their language, as shown in the lines below:

30 Tra chaer wydyr ny welsynt wrhyt Arthur.
    Beyond the glass fortress they did not see Arthur's valour.
31 Tri vgeint canhwr a seui ar mur:
    Three-score hundred men were standing on the wall:
32 oed anhawd ymadrawt ae gwylyadur.
    it was difficult to speak with their watchman.

A related incident appears in the *Historia Brittonum* in Section 13 where the object is described as a 'glass tower in the middle of the sea' (*turrim vitream in medio mari*). Marged Haycock draws attention to the close resemblance of these two accounts.[15] It is argued below that the *Historia* version was derived from Lines 30-2 of *Preideu Annwfyn*.

A third instance occurs in the *Navigatio* of St Brendan, where the monks meet a 'crystal pillar' in the sea. David Dumville dates the *Navigatio* to about 750-775, but cannot rule out the possibility that it was earlier, perhaps as early as the 600s.[16] In Section 23 of the *Navigatio*, Brendan and his men sail up to the crystal pillar and explore it, estimating the length of each side.[17] It would appear that the 'glass fortress', the 'glass tower in the middle of the sea' and the 'crystal pillar' in the sea were all icebergs.

The Historia Brittonum Account

The *Historia* iceberg incident is part of a myth on the founding of Ireland: that in 30 ships, people came from Spain to settle in Ireland. There they lived for a year. Then comes a diversion from the foundation myth – they set sail again (apart from one ship that had been wrecked) and meet a glass tower in the middle of the sea. They see men standing on the glass tower and ask them questions, but get no reply. This seems rather pointless, but then the account becomes absurd. For one year, they attack the tower with both women and men on board. Then upon landing on the beach that was around the glass tower they are all killed when the sea swallows them. The story then returns to the foundation myth, stating that from the people left behind (from the ship that was wrecked) Ireland was populated. This summary is based on the translation by Pamela Hopkins and John Koch.[18]

The Historia account derived from Preideu Annwfyn

It is argued here that the *Historia* account is a garbled version of the *Preideu Annwfyn* lines. The latter, as interpreted here, are coherent and contain no supernatural or cartoonish features. The *Historia* account is inane, deriving from a misunderstanding of the *Preideu Annwfyn* account. It appears to be based on many retellings of the poem's lines, with details dropping out and the meaning of lines being misinterpreted or lost.

To begin, the *Historia* author misses the significance of *beyond* the Glass Fortress and places the action on the iceberg itself. In *Preideu Annwfyn*, the iceberg is only acknowledged in passing. The Britons had to go beyond the iceberg zone to the mainland, where the conflict was actually situated. The *Historia* author has misinterpreted the location of the men on the wall and places them on the iceberg. So this absurdity becomes part of the story.

Does the *Historia* author understand that the glass tower in the sea was really an iceberg? It appears not, as it would be a rather pointless exercise to commence an attack on an iceberg. His incomprehension is shown by his adding detail to normalise the situation. So the author adds a 'beach' around the tower for the invaders to land. His lack of understanding indicates further information that has been lost.

In addition, the reason for the communication problem, that there were two groups of people who spoke radically different languages (Line 32) has been lost. The uncomprehending storyteller merely relates that the men on the glass tower would not respond to the sailors' attempts to communicate. He appears not to know why, giving no explanation, which naturally leaves the reader puzzled.

Finally, the farcical attack on the inhabitants of the iceberg, lasting a year, is probably the remnant of much earlier versions of a battle inferred from the phrase mentioning Arthur's valour. It would seem that the *Preideu Annwfyn* account has gone through many retellings over time, with details such as 'beyond', 'Arthur's valour' and the 'watchman' dropping out, so that the final *Historia* compiler seems clueless as to the meaning of the story.

It is clear from the close resemblance between the *Preideu Annwfyn* lines and the *Historia Brittonum* story (as noted by both Kenneth Jackson and Marged Haycock) that the 'glass fortress' and the 'glass tower in the middle of the sea' were considered to be the same object.

The Grafting of the Story onto the Foundation Myth

The iceberg incident from the *Historia* is irrelevant to the foundation theme: that the Spanish settlers in 30 ships came to Ireland to live. Apart from the people in the damaged ship, the 29 ships unaccountably set sail again which allows the iceberg incident to be inserted, but these people do not populate Ireland as they are all killed. The people who do populate Ireland are those from the damaged ship who remained in Ireland. Thus the iceberg incident is superfluous to the main theme and appears to have been clumsily grafted onto the foundation myth from a pre-existing source.

Conclusion

The inanity of the *Historia* material suggests that it was a garbled account derived from *Preideu Annwfyn*. It appears that the iceberg incident has been inserted into the Ireland foundation myth from pre-existing material. The *Historia* was compiled in 829-30 and it was argued that *Preideu Annwfyn* was a bardic response to Gildas and was thus composed circa 540. If the 'glass tower in the middle of the sea' story were the result of many retellings of an original based on *Preideu Annwfyn*, it would have had roughly 290 years to transform from the original to its degenerate state in the *Historia*.

DATING VIA VOYAGE OF BRAN

Some images and incidents in *Preideu Annwfyn* also appear in the early Irish literature, but in a more elaborated form in the latter. The first Irish work considered here is the *Voyage of Bran son of Febal*. As discussed in Chapter 6, this Irish Bran may be distinguished from the Welsh Brân the Blessed.

When was the Voyage of Bran Composed?

In the late 19th century, Kuno Meyer dated the *Voyage of Bran* to the 600s:[19]

> The Voyage of Bran was originally written down in the seventh century. From this original, sometime in the tenth century, a copy was made, in which the language of the poetry, protected by the laws of metre and assonance, was left almost intact.

In a 1976 paper, James Carney dates it from the late 600s to the early 700s. However, near the end of this paper he comments that it could have been composed to commemorate the death of Mongán (mentioned in the text), giving a date shortly after 629. Carney reverts to a more conservative date of around 700 in a 1983 paper. Liam Breatnach notes features of the language which could imply a later date, c. 700-750. Seámus Mac Mathúna suggests a date ranging from the late 600s to the early 700s.[20]

Overview of the Story

Prince Bran is alone when he hears sweet music behind him, which lulls him to sleep. On awakening, he is holding an apple tree branch – it is silver with white blossoms. He takes it to his royal house where all there notice a woman dressed in strange raiment. She sings quatrains about her home, the isle of women, which is a paradise. It is without grief, sorrow, sickness, debility, death or sin. Sweet music, the best of wine and treasures of every hue are enjoyed. It stands on four pillars of white bronze in the sea. Some quatrains are devoted to the coming of Christ and the last two quatrains invite Bran to go there. Then the apple tree branch springs from Bran's hand to the woman and she disappears. Bran and his crew set sail and after two days he sees a man in a chariot, riding across the waves towards him. It is Manannán son of Lir (a sea god) who is going to Ireland to father a child, Mongán. He also sings quatrains to Bran on the isle of women. In the last quatrain of his song, Bran is urged to go there.

Before approaching the isle of women, they encounter an island where the inhabitants gape at them and laugh but will not converse with them. One of Bran's men joins these islanders and becomes like this himself. The sailors address their former comrade but he does not respond.

Eventually they reach their destination where they enjoy the women for many years, but it seems only a year to them. Eventually one gets homesick and they decide to return to Ireland but are warned by the head woman not to touch the land there. But on arriving in Ireland the homesick man cannot resist and leaps onto the shore where he dissolves into ashes. They have been away for centuries. Seeing that he can no longer return without death, Bran sails off again.[21]

Four Pillars of White Bronze derived from the Four Peaks

In *Preideu Annwfyn*, there are four peaks (*banneu*) which describe a certain camp: 'the four-peaked camp, isle of the strong door', in Line 24. The simplest explanation for these is that they are four mountain peaks. They seem to have found derivatives in the *Voyage of Bran*, but as four pillars of white bronze which support the Otherworld island above a swirling sea. The woman sings about these supports to Bran in describing her island: 'A fair course against the white-swelling surge – four pillars uphold it' (Quatrain 2) and 'Pillars of white bronze under it' (Quatrain 4).[22]

This *Voyage of Bran* imagery appears in the later *Book of Taliesin* poem, *Golychaf-i Gulwyd*, in which Marged Haycock translates *banneu* as 'turrets', around which the sea swirls.[23] As noted in Chapter 5, *Golychaf-i Gulwyd* also portrays Annwfyn as a paradise. It appears that a simple feature like the four *banneu* of *Preideu Annwfyn* has been misunderstood and elaborated. The four peaks have become four pillars supporting the Otherworld island above the sea, with the further elaboration that they are made of white bronze.

The Island where the Inhabitants do not Reply

A second feature is another derivative of the 'beyond the iceberg' incident in *Preideu Annwfyn*. Instead of being located on an iceberg as in the *Historia Brittonum*, the non-responding people inhabit an Otherworld island. The *Preideu Annwfyn* scene depicting peoples with different languages being unable to communicate is again transformed into a farcical situation in the *Voyage of Bran*. No satisfactory explanation is given as to why the people do not reply to the sailors. The information has been lost. The account is also elaborated with additional details to 'explain' the strangeness, making the inhabitants gape at the sailors and burst into fits of laughter. This failure to communicate is considered as some form of abnormality caused by living on the island. When one of Bran's sailors joins the people on the island he too becomes affected and is unable to communicate with his colleagues.

DATING VIA ECHTRAE CHONNLAI

When was Echtrae Chonnlai Composed?
Echtrae Chonnlai (Connlae's Adventure) can be placed early in the Old Irish period, according to John Carey, which suggests the late 600s. In a detailed discussion of both poems, Kim McCone considers that *Echtrae Chonnlai* may have been composed a little before the *Voyage of Bran*. He suggests that the 700-750 period would be a suitable dating for both but that it would be rash to exclude the possibility that both works were from the late 600s.[24]

Overview of the Story
Prince Connlae, the son of Conn, is visited by a beautiful woman dressed in unfamiliar clothing. Only Connlae can see her but all hear her. The woman remarks that she is from 'the land of the living', where there is neither old age, nor death, nor sin, where they have everlasting feasting and harmony without strife. She lives in a great fairy mound (*síd*) and her people are called people of the *síd*. She loves Connlae and wants him to come with her to this wondrous place to be king. Conn calls for his druid, Corann, and explains that his son is being enticed away by the spells of an unseen woman. Corann then chants a spell that prevents all from hearing the woman and Connlae from seeing her, but he still hears her. As she leaves she throws an apple to him which he eats for a month, taking no other food or drink. The apple remains whole no matter how much he has eaten.

At the end of the month the woman returns – her pleas are heard by all, indicating that Corann's spell has been broken. Conn again calls for his druid. In response, the woman replies that Conn should not love druidry and that a righteous one (St Patrick) will come to destroy the druids' spells before the deceitful devil himself. She also explains that her land has only women and maidens. Finally Connlae is enticed away, leaping into the woman's glass ship to sail off with her to the land of the living.[25]

Derivatives of the Glass Fortress
This story has features in common with *Preideu Annwfyn*. Its inhabitants are called the people of the *síd*, who live in fairy mounds. In *Preideu Annwfyn*, one of the camps is *kaer sidi* which, it has been argued, refers to the large earthen mounds of the Hopewell people. Apart from the earthen mounds, *Preideu Annwfyn* and *Echtrae Chonnlai* both refer to objects made of glass or crystal, but one is a poetic metaphor while the other is taken literally. In

Preideu Annwfyn, an iceberg is poetically called a 'glass fortress'. Those who have seen Edinburgh, which had an ancient fortress on top of the massive rock where Edinburgh castle now stands can appreciate how apt this poetic imagery would be. A huge iceberg looming above the sea could very easily inspire the name 'glass fortress'.

However, in *Echtrae Chonnlai* the glass feature is a ship, which is inane. This glass ship is mentioned twice, in Lines 40 and 45. It seems that the idea of glass objects had became associated with the Otherworld and as only the *Preideu Annwfyn* account provides an obvious naturalistic explanation of the 'glass fortress', it would appear that other instances of glass objects were derived from this. Retellings of *Preideu Annwfyn* with its glass fortress may have led to other storytellers creating the glass objects in order to signify an Otherworld location.

A later poem, the *Voyage of Mael Dúin's Boat*, was probably composed in the 800s according to Liam Breatnach.[26] In visiting the various Otherworld islands, Mael Dúin explored an island with a glass bridge. As mentioned in Chapter 5, the author of *Mael Dúin* has derived other features from *Preideu Annwfyn*, in particular the revolving 'fiery' rampart and associated door of the gate of Hell.

DATING VIA DÚN SCÁITH

Dún Scáith (Fortress of Shadow) is a poem describing a raid on an overseas fort by Irish hero Cú Chulainn and his men. It is incorporated into two Irish stories. Three stanzas of it appear in *The Tragic Death of Cú Roí mac Dáiri*, and the full poem appears in *The Phantom Chariot of Cú Chulainn*.

Dating of Cú Roí and The Phantom Chariot

These stories are quite early. Thomas Cross and Clark Slover state that *The Tragic Death of Cú Roí mac Dáiri* belongs to the oldest parts of the Ulster cycle of stories, which could date it to the 700s or earlier. *Cú Roí* itself refers to the other story (*Phantom Chariot*) when it reproduces the three stanzas. Patrick Sims-Williams regards *Cú Roí* as being at least as old as the eighth century, which probably puts both tales and the embedded *Dún Scáith* poem in the 700s or possibly earlier.[27]

Overview of the Story

The *Phantom Chariot* containing the full *Dún Scáith* poem begins with King Lóegaire telling St Patrick that he will not believe in God unless St Patrick demonstrates God's power by conjuring up the dead hero Cú Chulainn. St Patrick does this and Cú Chulainn recalls his heroic exploits, one of which was his raid on the overseas Fortress of Shadow, as told in the *Dún Scáith* poem. It has doors of iron on each side but these are smashed down by Cú Chulainn who kicks them into fragments. The raiding party is then attacked by monsters bursting forth from a pit in the fortress: serpents, toads, and dragon-like monsters. After defeating the monsters, Cú Chulainn seeks out a cauldron filled with gold and silver. This cauldron has the magical property that three cows can fill it with the milk of thirty cows. The men then escape by swimming away from the fortress, accompanied by the three swimming cows, with loads of gold upon the cows' necks. A storm wrecks their boat so that Cú Chulainn supports his men while swimming away – nine men on each hand, thirty on his head and eight upon the sides of his body, eventually reaching a harbour in Ireland safely.[28]

The Strong Door

Dún Scáith shares features in common with *Preideu Annwfyn* that appear to be derived from the latter. Line 24 of *Preideu Annwfyn* refers to the 'strong door'. As interpreted here, the 'strong door' was a poetic way of saying how difficult it was to make progress. In Chapter 10 it was argued that it refers to the St Lawrence River, which was the Britons' entrance to the new land. Its powerful currents and very dangerous obstacles would have made upstream sailing very difficult.

The 'strong door' of the poem was not literally a door that was very strong. Marged Haycock also treats it as a poetic expression with her 'stout defence of the island'. However, the *Dún Scáith* poet has taken the *Preideu Annwfyn* term literally as he has the Fortress of Shadow protected by 'Doors of iron on each side'. So a poetic expression 'isle of the strong door' has become a literal 'isle of iron doors' for the Otherworld island.[29]

The Cauldron as Spoils of a Raid

Preideu Annwfyn refers to a cauldron of the chief of Annwfyn, apparently captured as the spoils of a raid. It is interpreted here as a large ceremonial pot and is described as having a dark rim and pearl decoration. The unusual and unexpected detail of the pearls is perfectly consistent with what is known about the Hopewell culture of sixth-century America and their successors, as previously discussed. Lleawc thrust his sword into it and it was left in the hand of Lleminawc, possibly the same person. There is nothing outlandish or cartoonish about this incident.

In contrast the incident about the cauldron in *Dún Scáith* is cartoonish in the extreme. There are three cows in *Dún Scáith* that fill the cauldron with their milk. But the cauldron has the magical property that allows the three cows to fill it with the milk of thirty cows. Then it somehow becomes filled with gold and silver which makes it desirable to carry away. This leads to the comical scene of the three cows, loaded with gold, swimming away from the fortress with Cú Chulainn supporting his men on his body while swimming. Both cauldron incidents are in the context of warriors sailing to a mysterious land over the ocean with a 'strong door' (or iron doors) and ferocious fighting. If the *Dún Scáith* cauldron raid is related to the raid in *Preideu Annwfyn*, then its cartoonish, elaborated features would suggest that it was derived from the latter.

A Metaphor for Hell made into a Literal Hell

Preideu Annwfyn describes a disastrous expedition in which most of the men were killed, where there was 'woeful conflict' in Line 47 and where the men are pictured as standing 'before the door of the gate of Hell' in Line 20. The latter expression is a superb poetic metaphor for the disasters that eventually engulfed the expedition.

In contrast, the author of the *Dún Scáith* poem has taken the metaphor literally and created his tale with literal Hell-like features. The very name 'Fortress of Shadow' implies a dark location, like the Biblical Hell. Inside the fortress is a pit containing monstrous creatures, a strong feature of Hell as depicted by the bottomless pit in the Book of Revelation from which horrific beasts emerge (Revelation 9:2-10 and 11:7). It would appear that the *Dún Scáith* composer has misinterpreted the metaphor from *Preideu Annwfyn* as denoting a literal Hell and has created a similar tale elaborated with features of Hell from the Bible.

DATING VIA BRICRIU'S FEAST

Bricriu's Feast (Fled Bricrenn) is a long Irish story, a part of the Ulster cycle, which survives in several versions. The original was probably composed in the 700s according to Thomas Cross and Clark Slover. It is of interest here because it provides a very early example of the 'revolving fort' as discussed in Chapter 5. The Irish hero, Cú Roí, had a revolving fort and chanted a spell over it every night so that it turned as quickly as a mill-stone.[30]

In *Preideu Annwfyn*, the second half of Line 12 can be translated 'turning to face the four peaks' which interprets the 'turning' as performed by the bard, not the fortress. The bard is talking about himself in Line 11 ('I am honoured abundantly, song was heard') and also about himself in Line 13 ('My poetry, from the cauldron it was spoken'). It is thus quite reasonable to conclude that the bard is also talking about himself in Line 12 when he uses the expression 'turning to face the four peaks'. It seems that after mentioning the camp's name, the four-peaked camp, he decided to continue with an expression that partially explained it, remembering how he turned to view all four peaks while in the camp. If this explanation is correct, then the camp or fort is not revolving and the instances of the magical revolving fort in other literature are based on a misconception.

The 'revolving fort' also appears in the Irish tale, *Voyage of Mael Dúin's Boat,* probably composed in the 800s. Here the 'revolving fort' is further elaborated. The composer of *Mael Dúin* has not only taken the erroneous 'revolving fort' from *Preideu Annwfyn* but has also borrowed the metaphor 'And before the door of the gate of Hell lamps burned' from Line 20 of *Preideu Annwfyn*. He then combines the two borrowings by describing an island enclosed by a fiery, revolving rampart with a door in it. The hellish nature of the door and the rampart is shown by the word 'fiery' to indicate the flames of Hell. A translation is given by Whitley Stokes.[31]

It would appear that an understandable misconception in translating Line 12 of *Preideu Annwfyn* has created the concept of the 'revolving fort' which has been adopted into the Irish literature. This would indicate that *Preideu Annwfyn* preceded both *Bricriu's Feast* and the *Voyage of Mael Dúin's Boat* and is indicative of an early dating.

COMPARING KAT GODEU TO DÚN SCÁITH

In another comparison of interest, the composer of *Dún Scáith* appears to have been familiar with *Kat Godeu*. He seems to have copied the nature of the horrific creatures emerging from the pit of Hell from *Kat Godeu*, as will be discussed below.

Comparison with Kat Godeu

There is a strong relationship between Lines 30-40 in *Kat Godeu* and stanzas 4-7 in *Dún Scáith*. In the latter, there is a pit in the fortress from which burst forth three types of monsters – serpents, toads, and dragon-like monsters. The toads had sharp beaks which bit the noses of the Irish warriors, but Cú Chulainn pulverised them between his fists and palms.

In *Kat Godeu*, the monster from the skies (argued in Chapter 7 to be a comet) is described similarly in terms of the same three creatures – a great scaly beast resembling a dragon, a black forked toad, and a great speckled snake tormenting souls in its skin. In this book, it is interpreted as the one great beast having characteristics of all three creatures. In her introduction to *Kat Godeu*, Marged Haycock regards them as three separate beasts which provides a parallelism with *Dún Scáith*.[32] It has already been argued that the great scaly beast in the sky resembles the *Typhon* of Greek mythology, in the tales of Hesiod and Nonnos of Panopolis. However in those accounts, the toad-like nature of the beast is absent, but it is shared in the *Kat Godeu* and *Dún Scáith* accounts.

It is difficult to avoid the conclusion that the *Dún Scáith* stanzas are related to *Kat Godeu*. It would appear that *Kat Godeu* is the earlier, as a case can be made that the beast represented a real object that killed many of the Britons. The powerless Britons prayed to God for relief. It was so serious that the Britons thought it a lead-in to Judgement Day and some were drenched in 'blood up to our thighs'.

In *Dún Scáith*, the attack is an obvious fantasy. The cauldron holds the milk of three cows but has the magical property that allows them to fill it with the milk of thirty cows. It also is conveniently filled with gold and silver. The beasts emerge from a pit in the fortress, a cartoonish feature depicting the place as a Hell. The toads bite the nose of Cú Chulainn and cling to his snout. However they are no real threat – Cú Chulainn is quite equal to the task and smashes them to bits with his fists. In *Kat Godeu* the beast is portrayed as a real threat which terrifies the Britons whereas in *Dún Scáith* the beasts are merely a vehicle to show off the heroism of Cú Chulainn.

Summary

A summary of the literary comparisons is given in Table 9.1 below with very approximate estimated datings.

Table 9.1 Features Derived from Preideu Annwfyn and Kat Godeu

Preideu Annwfyn		Historia Brittonum (829-30)
People on wall (on land)	→	People standing on iceberg
Peoples with different languages	→	People don't reply to questions
Arthur's valour	→	For one year, the iceberg is attacked with men and women on board
		Voyage of Bran (early 700s)
Four peaks (*banneu*)	→	Four pillars of white bronze holding up the island above the sea
Peoples with different languages	→	People don't reply but instead gape and laugh at Bran's men
		Echtrae Chonnlai (c. 700), and Mael Dúin (800s)
Iceberg metaphor 'glass fortress'	→	Literal Otherworld glass objects (glass ship, glass bridge)
		Dún Scáith (c. 700)
Metaphor 'isle of strong door'	→	Literal 'doors of iron' smashed to pieces by the hero
Metaphor 'door of gate of Hell'	→	Literal hellish features: dark place, pit from which beasts emerge
'Cauldron' decorated with pearls	→	Magical cauldron – three cows fill it with milk of thirty cows
		Bricriu's Feast (c. 750)
Bard turns to view four peaks	→	'Revolving fort'
		Mael Dúin (800s)
Metaphor 'door of gate of Hell'	→	Revolving fiery rampart with door
Kat Godeu		**Dún Scáith (c. 700)**
Beast like dragon/toad/snake	→	Three beasts: dragon, toad and snake emerging from pit of Hell. Toads bite the hero's snout

Concluding Comments

It has been argued that *Preideu Annwfyn* was partly an emotional response by Arthur's bard to Gildas' *The Ruin of Britain* and was composed shortly after that work became widely known in about 540. To test whether a case could be made for such an early date, the poem was compared to the *Historia Brittonum* (829-30) and the five Irish works of varying dates, some of which could be as early as the 600s. It is suggested that features of *Preideu Annwfyn* appear in these other works in a way that indicates that the source is *Preideu Annwfyn*. The copied features are either taken literally, or misunderstood, or elaborated, often in a cartoonish manner. Further, a case can also be made that the beasts emerging from the pit of Hell in *Dún Scáith* are derived from the *Kat Godeu* poem.

COMPARISON OF THE THREE POEMS

In this section, pairwise comparisons of features with common content are made between *Preideu Annwfyn, Kat Godeu* and *Kadeir Teÿrnon*, which could indicate a common authorship. A discussion of these features requires a great deal of space and so is presented in the Notes, but summaries of the commonalities are provided below. This evidence is weaker than that given previously in this chapter as a skilful poet who adopted the 'Taliesin persona' could have written poems that imitate an earlier genuine poem by Arthur's bard. However each of the three poems is in the voice of Arthur's bard and there is enough commonality to suggest that the hypothesis of a common poet is not unreasonable, as summarized below.

Commonalities between Preideu Annwfyn and Kat Godeu
- The only two portrayals of the Otherworld that present it as a terrible conflict with many deaths, rather than a paradise
- Christian beliefs
- A mention of Judgement Day
- Portraying Arthur as a king
- A deep respect for Arthur
- The use of the unusual word *muchyd*
- Fighting with the Annwfyn people
- Noting the bravery of the Annwfyn people
- Distress at the death of Arthur
- A statement about Arthur's death in Annwfyn
- An interest in the numbers 3, 9 and their multiples.

An extended discussion of these points, giving the details from the poems, is given in the Notes appendix.[33]

Commonalities between Preideu Annwfyn and Kadeir Teÿrnon
- An implication that Arthur had been away from Britain
- The locating of Arthur in northeast Wales
- Christian beliefs
- Portraying Arthur as a king
- A deep respect for Arthur
- The use of questions
- Inspiration from the cauldron
- Distress at the death of Arthur
- Use of same word *diua* for the death of Arthur
- An interest in the numbers 3, 9 and their multiples.

An extended discussion of these points is given in the Notes Appendix, where examples from each poem are provided.[34]

Commonalities between Kat Godeu and Kadeir Teÿrnon

Many of the commonalities between these two poems are shared with *Preideu Annwfyn* and have already been given. To summarise these: the implication that Arthur was absent overseas, Christian beliefs, Arthur shown as a king, a deep respect for Arthur, distress at the death of Arthur and the use of the numbers 3, 9 and their multiples. There are three features, however, that are unique to these two poems.

The first is the bard's unusual integration of beliefs, both in Christianity and the transmigration of the soul. In *Kat Godeu*, the belief in Christianity is shown in the calling on God to save the Britons and the claim that Christ's crucifixion was one of the three greatest cataclysms in the history of the world. Belief in transmigration is shown in the first 23 lines of *Kat Godeu* which lists the previous states of matter the bard's soul had inhabited. In *Kadeir Teÿrnon*, his Christian beliefs are shown in the bard's approval of Arthur's reverence for scripture and in his praise for the existence of the 'True One' (God) and His pronouncements. His belief in transmigration appears in Lines 37-8 where he lists a previous incarnation as a nobleman.

The second is the use of the word *ieithoed* to mean 'peoples'. It appears in *Kat Godeu* in Line 202 and in *Kadeir Teÿrnon* in Line 74. This usage does not occur in any of the other *Book of Taliesin* poems classified as legendary by Marged Haycock.

The third commonality is that both poems refer to Arthur as being in the same area – in the Galloway region of southwest Scotland. In *Kat Godeu* the mysterious battle takes place at Caer Nefenhyr (Line 41), derived from the ancient British tribe that lived there, the Novantae. In *Kadeir Teÿrnon* the place is Rheon (Line 6), probably the area around Loch Ryan. Both places are highly valued in Welsh tradition, with Nefenhyr being mentioned by Arthur's gatekeeper in *Culhwch and Olwen* and Pen Rhionydd (Rheon) being referred to in the very first triad of the Welsh Triads as Arthur's northern court. Further, one of Arthur's battles, *Cat Coit Celidon*, also appears to be in this region, seemingly being within an easy reach of both Glasgow and Carlisle according to Kenneth Jackson.[35]

ARCHAIC LANGUAGE REMNANTS

Each of the three poems seems to contain elements of archaic language (pre-Old Welsh) which could be indicative of an early date. These will be briefly outlined below.

Preideu Annwfyn

In a number of papers, John Koch has drawn attention to archaic language remnants in *Preideu Annwfyn*. Firstly, he notes what he considers to be three instances of archaic third person plural deponent verbs, which he states were inherited from the very early Proto-Celtic, but which were otherwise obsolete in the surviving records of Brittonic.[36]

Secondly, one of these verbs, written *glywanawr*, needs an 'or' ending to rhyme with the following lines. The 'or' ending occurred in older forms of the verb. It would appear that a scribe was copying an old manuscript in which the word appeared as something like 'cliuant(h)or' according to John Koch, which the scribe then incorrectly read as 'cliuant(h)ōr', having the longer 'ō' sound.[37] The scribe then modernised 'ōr' to 'awr', a language change noted by Kenneth Jackson who established that this diphthongization of 'ō' to 'au' or 'aw' would have occurred sometime in the 700s.[38]

The above suggests that the old manuscript could have been written in the eighth century. Koch remarks that a date in the 700s is defensible.[39] His arguments suggest no impediment to the poem having being composed in the Neo-Brittonic period (which begins not long after about AD 500) if other considerations pointed to such a dating. More recently, Koch states that a language similar enough to Welsh already existed in the 6th century to enable poetry composed then to survive the language modernization into Old Welsh and Middle Welsh.[40]

Kat Godeu

There are several possible remnants of archaic language in *Kat Godeu*. One possibility is the verb *gwrith*, an archaic form of the verb 'was made'. John Koch argues that the word *gwrith* was derived from the inferred word in the British language, **wrichto-*.[41] The word occurs in Line 4: *credaf pan writh*; Line 146: *an datwrith datedw*; and Lines 201-2: *ef gwrith, ef datwrith, ef gwrith ieithoed*, the latter occurring in the Annwfyn section of the poem. The form *gwrith* may have been used in Arthur's time as part of the Neo-Brittonic language. In the much later *Book of Taliesin* poem, *Mabgyfreu Taliessin* (Juvenilia of Taliessin), it occurs as *gwnaeth* (Line 80). However, it is unclear how long the old form *gwrith* may have persisted in later poetry.

Secondly, Koch[42] refers to examples of possible archaic initial *uu-*, which were misunderstood as a variant of the old *ou-*, and were modernized by the scribes to *eu-*. He notes possible cases in *Kat Godeu* in Lines 167-8: *o Eurwys o Euron, o Euron o Vodron*. He also thinks that this could imply an exemplar older than circa 625 if the poem were composed in Wales. However, see the contrary comments of Marged Haycock.[43]

Further, Marged Haycock points out the unusually high frequency of some archaic absolute verbal forms in the poem – *eithyt, gwneithyt, seinyssit, gwiscyssit, bernissit, ffynyessit, glessyssit*. Finally, Haycock notes the 'subject + verb' word-order: *ffuonwyd eithyt* (Line 9), *auanwyd gwneithyt* (Line 11), and *onn goreu ardyrched* (Line 26), another archaic feature. However, while noting these archaic features, she is cautious about inferring that the poem is old, as they could be taken from older poetry and used in *Kat Godeu* to 'strike a deliberately archaic note'.[44]

Kadeir Teÿrnon

This poem uses the archaic Brittonic word *rechtur*, which appears in a long rhyming sequence that includes the words *rechtur* (Line 6), *rwyfyadur* (Line 7) and *uur* (Line 10). These same three words appear contiguously, in the same order, in the poem *Y Gododdin*. They occur in stanza B1.14, Line 760 and in the parallel line in stanza B2.36, Line 772. John Koch considers the latter stanza was probably composed before the defeat of Edinburgh in 638 and lists *rector* (as it occurs in B2.36) as a pre-Old Welsh feature.[45] In his Neo-Brittonic reconstruction, he writes the word as *rechtur*. He also suggests that what the bards actually sang was the semi-Latin *rechtur*.[46]

The use of the same three words (in the same order) in *Kadeir Teÿrnon* and *Y Gododdin* could imply a relationship where one is derived from the other. If the usage in *Y Gododdin* were based on *Kadeir Teÿrnon*, then this could imply a very early date for *Kadeir Teÿrnon*. However, the direction of the relationship cannot presently be established. It is also possible that the three words became stock rhyme words. If the latter, then perhaps the very old word *rechtur* continued to be used in later periods due to its usefulness as a rhyming word. Koch notes that old features can persist: 'Old features will coexist with younger in natural discourse, and this is especially true of the super-standard language of poets'.[47]

SUMMARY

This chapter has argued that the three poems, *Preideu Annwfyn*, *Kat Godeu* and *Kadeir Teÿrnon*, could have been composed in the sixth century and that all were probably composed by Arthur's bard. The key poem is *Preideu Annwfyn*, which through its emotional content seems to have been composed in the aftermath of Gildas' publication of *The Ruin of Britain*. In speculating on the dates of composition, *Preideu Annwfyn* was probably composed first (around 540) and then *Kadeir Teÿrnon* shortly after. There was probably a gap of several decades to *Kat Godeu* which was composed when the bard was old and the horrors that he had endured had receded.

Evidence has been provided that a single bard could have composed all three poems. A series of pairwise comparisons between content features in the three poems was conducted. The commonality of the features suggests that the hypothesis of a single poet for all three poems is not unreasonable. However, it is possible that skilful poets who adopted the 'Taliesin persona' could imitate features of earlier poems.

It has been argued that dating *Preideu Annwfyn* as a partial response to Gildas' biased tirade is the only satisfactory explanation of the bard's anger and contempt for the monks, which occupies the last five of the eight stanzas of the poem. The important items that the monks do not know refer solely to incidents or events occurring in Annwfyn. They are not independent items of knowledge that the bard would use to engage in a contest of learning with the monks. The bard would only obtain psychological satisfaction in stating that the monks were ignorant of these items if the items represented true and important information. Given the bard's anger at the monks, the idea that the depicted journey was an imaginative fantasy (composed by the bard only to entertain) is extremely implausible as the bard would gain little emotional release by claiming that the monks do not know fictional items he invented from an imaginary Annwfyn.

Further, it seems likely that the bard was an eyewitness who did go on the expedition. His vivid descriptions appear to be those of an eyewitness whose horrific experiences in Annwfyn contrasted sharply with the soft life of the monks. This contrast fuelled his anger and contempt for the monks, prompting him to call them cowards and 'little men' who did not have the resolve to endure the hardships that he had suffered.

As the composition of *Preideu Annwfyn* closely fits the context of *The Ruin of Britain*, this would date it to about 540 or a little after. To determine whether this early date is plausible, features from the poem are compared to seemingly derivative features from other early literature. These are listed in Table 9.1 and indicate that some of the *Preideu Annwfyn* items have been either misunderstood or are elaborated, sometimes in a cartoonish fashion, in the other literature. From this material a case can be made that *Preideu Annwfyn* was composed in the 600s or earlier. In addition, *Kat Godeu* has one item listed in Table 9.1 which could also suggest a similar dating. Further, all three poems seem to contain remnants of archaic language, which would support the other arguments given above for early datings.

10
AN ATTEMPT TO RECONSTRUCT THE VOYAGE

EARLY VOYAGES IN THE NORTH ATLANTIC

Introduction

The central thesis of this book is that King Arthur led an expedition to North America in the sixth century. Although difficult to date, it may have set out in the mid 530s at about the time that Gildas was pondering whether to write *The Ruin of Britain*. From the detail in *Preideu Annwfyn* and the issue of 'who was minding the country' in *Kadeir Teÿrnon*, it would appear that the expedition was away for at least a year and perhaps several years. Eventually the few survivors (including Arthur's bard) made it back to Britain only to be confronted by the devastating criticism of Gildas, which prompted the bard's outrage against the monks in *Preideu Annwfyn*.

In this chapter a speculative attempt to reconstruct the route is made. While it may appear to be an overly ambitious task, the clues in the poems seem to indicate a northern route across the Atlantic. It is likely that they explored the Gulf of St Lawrence and located the St Lawrence River. They seem to have sailed partway up this river, camping at the site of Montreal, the 'four-peaked' camp. The Lachine Rapids may have prevented their main ships getting any further but they appear to have followed the St Lawrence River, perhaps using a combination of sailing and portage in smaller skin-covered boats, making their way across (or past) Lakes Ontario and Erie. Moving southwest beyond the lakes, they probably entered the Ohio Eastern Woodlands where the Hopewell had built their extensive network of mounds. There they encountered a woeful conflict and their progress appears to finish. It may be objected that this procedure builds an itinerary on such slender foundations that no certain knowledge can be obtained. While this point is acknowledged, it is of interest to speculate about what might have happened, on a probabilistic basis, using the clues in the poems.

Before examining Arthur's voyage, other early voyages which provide a context will be outlined. It is now well known that the Norse sailed to North America in around AD 1000, roughly 500 years before Columbus' famous discovery. They appear to have reached Iceland by c. 870, colonised Greenland by c. 985 and reached Canada under Leif Eiríksson around 1000 as summarised by Robert Park.[1] A Norse settlement was discovered in Canada at L'Anse aux Meadows near the northern tip of Newfoundland. It was found in 1960 by Helge Ingstad who made several archaeological expeditions to the site between 1961 and 1968. His wife, Anne Stine Ingstad, directed these archaeological works.[2] The Norse sagas had described visits to a place called Vinland and these had influenced Ingstad's search.[3] Well before the Norse settlement, there were prior journeys into the Atlantic that suggest an early knowledge of the important 'stepping stones' that could have been used for Arthur's voyage to North America. These are briefly discussed below.

Pytheas to Thule (Iceland)

Around 320 BC, Pytheas of Massilia (modern Marseilles) voyaged to Thule. While his writings have not survived, his journey can be partly reconstructed from the writings of others, the fullest accounts of which are critical of him. He made his way from Massilia to Britain which he explored with a scientific interest and estimated its perimeter.

From the north of Britain he was taken or guided to Thule, an island reached by sailing for six days. It was the extreme limit of the known world. Near Thule was a strange phenomenon resembling a 'sea-lung', which one could neither walk nor sail upon, probably a combination of slush ice and sea fog. North of Thule, he noted a frozen sea after a day's sailing. In Summer on Thule the sun barely retreated at night, disappearing for only a few hours before appearing again. Most scholars identify Thule with Iceland although some other places have been proposed, the main one being Norway. Barry Cunliffe believes the arguments in favour of Iceland are 'unassailable' and provides a succinct account of the evidence.[4]

St Brendan

The *Navigatio* of St Brendan suggests geographical knowledge of the islands in the northwest around the time of Arthur. As mentioned earlier, several writers have argued that Brendan may have reached America.[5] Given that he sailed in a curragh, it is difficult to believe he made it all the way there and back again, despite the intrepid expedition of Tim Severin who sailed from Ireland to Newfoundland in a leather curragh. Of course, Severin had the great advantages of modern geographical knowledge, safety equipment and communication devices.

However even the rigorous Samuel Morison thinks that there is truth in the *Navigatio*. He regards Brendan as a real person whose historical voyages into the Atlantic were enhanced by Celtic imagination. He remarks: 'We are not straining the evidence to conclude that Brendan sailed for several trips, if not for seven years, on the circuit Hebrides-Shetlands-Faroes-Iceland, possibly as far as the Azores'.[6]

Gwyn Jones also thought that Brendan could have reached Iceland and could have witnessed an eruption of a volcano there.[7] He suggests that the volcano could have been either Hekla or Katla, or another crater in Öraefi. Geoffrey Ashe in his *Land to the West* book gives similar views, unsure of whether Brendan reached America himself, but suggesting that his voyages may have been augmented with the knowledge of other voyages into the Atlantic. Brendan's death date is AD 575 from the *Annals of Tigernach* and *Chronicum Scotorum*, while Arthur's is 537/539 from the *Annales Cambriae*. It would suggest that Arthur's voyage was made before Brendan's, perhaps about 20 years earlier.

Cormac and Báetán

Brendan was a contemporary of Cormac and Báetán, all three appearing in the *Life of St Columba* by Adomnán. Báetán sailed for 'many miles' over the seas but was unable to find a suitable place of retreat. Cormac also sought such a place, without success, in three voyages into the Atlantic.[8] In one he reached Orkney and in the last may have sailed as far as the Arctic Circle according to Simon Young.[9]

Christian Crosses carved into Rock in Iceland

Kristján Ahronson discusses Christian cross carvings which are associated with St Columba's monastery in Iona, Scotland. A *simple cross*, comprising perpendicular straight lines that cross, is an early form. If found in Britain, this simple form would be associated with the late sixth or seventh centuries. The crosses that are linked with St Columba in Argyll are more complex, being described as *expanded terminal crosses*. In this form, the four end points of the crosses are elaborated, being drawn out into little triangular-shaped tips. Ahronson remarks that it is reasonable to associate this style of cross with that of the Columban monastic houses of the seventh and eighth centuries. This cross form appears in Ireland, western Scotland, and the Western and Northern Isles.[10]

In southern Iceland there is also a body of expanded terminal crosses, five of which have been examined by Ahronson. Three of these five crosses were found on the Westman Islands (off the southern coast of Iceland) in sheltered alcoves on an exposed cliff. The other two crosses were cut into a sandstone wall in a cave on the mainland of southern Iceland. Carvings of an expanded terminal cross and a barred terminal cross were also found in the Shetland Islands and dated to c. 750 and c. 700 respectively. Ahronson's quite reasonable hypothesis is that the clerics associated with the Columban family of monasteries had spread north to other islands including Iceland. As noted above, Cormac made three journeys into the Atlantic seeking a remote place to worship God. A similar picture is provided by the Dicuil account (to be discussed below), Bede and the later Norse literature of the *Landnámabók* and *Íslendingabók*.

The expanded terminal cross carvings suggest that Columban clerics may have visited Iceland as early as the 600s or 700s. Further, in the Iceland cave containing the two expanded terminal crosses, Ahronson found two *simple cross* form carvings. If found in Britain these would be associated with the late 500s or 600s, as noted earlier.

Roman Coins found in Iceland

One puzzling occurrence is the find of four *antoniniani* (low-value Roman coins) in southeast Iceland. Two were found at Bragðavellir in 1905 and 1933, issued under the emperors Probus and Aurelian respectively. A third coin was found at nearby Hvaldsur in 1923, issued under Diocletian. These three coins were discussed by Kristján Eldjárn. More recently, a fourth coin issued under emperor Tacitus was found in 1966 at Hvitarholt.[11] How these coins arrived in Iceland is far from clear. An interesting feature of the coins is the narrow date range in which they were issued, as shown by the reigns of the emperors given below:

- Aurelian   (AD 270–275)
- Tacitus   (AD 275–276)
- Probus   (AD 276–282)
- Diocletian (AD 284–305).

From the above we note that the beginning of Aurelian's reign to the end of Diocletian's is a mere 35 years. Eldjárn suggests that a Roman ship could have taken the coins to Iceland in the 300s. As Britain had Roman coinage under the centuries of Roman occupation, the Britons could have brought the coins to Iceland according to Alonso-Núñez.[12] The Norse did not colonise Iceland until about AD 870. It is not impossible that they brought these coins, but it would need to be explained why they brought such low-value coins having such a narrow date range – coins that would have been nearly 600 years old. The early dates and the very narrow date range would suggest early visitors to Iceland.

Dicuil's Account of Clerics in Iceland

Dicuil was an Irish scholar who wrote a geographical work, *Liber de Mensura Orbis Terrae* (Book on the Measurement of the Earth) about AD 825. He was probably writing from Aachen. He cites Isidore of Seville in stating that Thule is the furthest island in the ocean, lying between north and west of Britain. Isidore clearly equates Thule with Iceland.

Dicuil states that about thirty years previously, clerics living on Thule told him about the nightly conditions around midsummer where the sun appears to hide as though behind a small hill, such that there is no darkness. The men could act as though it were day, and even pick out lice from their shirts. Dicuil also confirms the information from Pytheas that, after sailing north for one day, men would find the sea frozen over. Given that the clerics' account was thirty years previously, then clerics had been living there from 795 or before.[13] Dicuil's account is supported by the Norse sagas. The *Íslendingabók* (Book of the Icelanders) states that when the Norse arrived they found it was already occupied by Irish Christians, as shown from the following excerpt from the text of Gwyn Jones:[14]

> There were Christian men here then whom the Norsemen call 'papar'. But later they went away because they were not prepared to live here in company with heathen men. They left behind Irish books, bells, and croziers, from which it could be seen that they were Irishmen.

Bede in his *Thirty Questions on the Book of Kings* also states that it was light at night in midsummer on Thule as people visiting from there (in his own age) 'abundantly attest'. Paul Meyvaert dates this to about 715, implying visits to Iceland in the early 700s, if Iceland were Thule.[15]

Dicuil also mentions a group of islands with many sheep and sea-birds, which appears to be the Faroes, and relates that it had been inhabited by Irish hermits for nearly 100 years. As he wrote in about 825, this would give circa 730 as a date for occupation.[16]

Conclusion

This section outlines the case for early explorations of the islands north and west of Britain. From a northern Britain starting point, these islands could form a convenient set of 'stepping stones' on the way to North America. They are the Orkney islands, visible from the very north of Scotland; the Hebrides on the western side of Scotland; the Faroes, northwest of Scotland, and then Iceland, further to the northwest.

Iceland was known at a very early date, about 860 years before Arthur, if Cunliffe is correct in identifying Thule with Iceland. There is also a strong probability that the Britons knew about Iceland and actually guided Pytheas there.[17] Other data suggests that Christians could have been on Iceland as early as the late 500s (if the simple crosses are a guide) and the 600s-700s, from the expanded terminal crosses associated with the Columban family of monasteries. It would appear that not long after the time of Arthur, British Christians were sailing in small seaworthy boats to these islands, seeking places to worship God in solitary locations. The Columban monasteries in Argyll were very active in this voyaging. St Columba referred to three such voyages of Cormac, including one to the far north.

The sixth-century Brendan may have voyaged in the north, possibly visiting Iceland, as discussed by Samuel Morison, Geoffrey Ashe and Gwyn Jones. Other evidence from Dicuil and Bede (also supported by the Norse sources) suggests that Christians were on Iceland in the 700s. The above discussion has presented data suggesting a very early knowledge of the islands north of Britain. It is not inconsistent with Arthur having knowledge of such regions and leading an expedition himself.

CELTIC SHIPS

We have no direct knowledge of the type of ships that a sixth-century British ruler such as Arthur would have used for such a journey. However, there is no reason to doubt that sufficient ship-building expertise would have been available to him. The Britons were in contact with the people of Brittany both at the time of Julius Caesar and at the time of Arthur, and presumably for much of the intervening period. Caesar in his *Gallic War* (Book 3, in Sections 9-16) describes the large impressive ships sailed by the Veneti, a people of Brittany, in 56 BC.

He also states that in the leadup to the sea-battle between the Veneti and the Romans, the Veneti summoned assistance from the Britons, who thus were probably present at the battle. Given that the Britons were providing assistance to the Veneti, it is not unreasonable to assume that the Britons had a good knowledge of the Veneti ships and that their own shipbuilders could construct similar ships for ocean travel.[18]

The Veneti Ships

Caesar provides a detailed description of these Veneti ships. They had flatter hulls than the Roman ships, which allowed them to more easily handle the ebb tides and shallow water around a coastline and were very strongly built, made of oak, which enabled them to withstand rough weather. Large cross timbers a foot thick supported the decks, secured with iron bolts as thick as a man's thumb. The ships had high prows and sterns which could resist strong waves and foul weather. Instead of linen sails, they had sails of skins or thinly stretched leather, which would have enabled them to more easily withstand the storms and powerful winds of the ocean. He also noted that the Roman ships were unable to harm the Veneti ships through ramming, as the latter were so strongly built.

About 220 Veneti ships fought the Roman fleet. The Romans eventually won the battle by using long poles with sharpened hooks to cut the rigging of the Veneti ships, thus disabling their sails. Although the Veneti had lost the battle because of the Romans' tactics, Caesar's admiration of the hardiness and utility of their ships for travel on the ocean and for safely exploring along a coastline in shallow waters is strongly evident.

Frequent contact between the Britons and the Bretons was also occurring in the years leading up to Arthur's time. The Britons had been migrating to Brittany during the 400s and the rate of this migration probably increased due to the Saxon onslaught in Britain, as Gildas relates. There is no reason to assume that shipbuilding skills in both Brittany and the seafaring areas of Wales had been lost between the times of Caesar and Arthur.

Romano-Celtic Ships

Maritime archaeology expert Seán McGrail describes a group of vessels with common features called 'Romano-Celtic'. Some of their features echo the ships of the Veneti described by Caesar. McGrail thinks it probable that the Veneti ships were the forerunners of the Romano-Celtic group. An excellent example is the Barland's Farm ship which was excavated in south Wales in 1993. It was built in oak and was located on the northern shore of the Severn Estuary. Other examples were found in the Thames estuary, near the Channel island of Guernsey, and from a wide region stretching from the Swiss Lakes and down the Rhine River to the Netherlands.[19]

Two types of vessels were found, river barges and seagoing vessels. The barges were of an elongated box shape and were used on canals and rivers where they were either towed or sailed if the winds were suitable. The three seagoing vessels were the Barland's Farm ship found in south Wales, dated to about AD 300, the Guernsey ship, dated to about AD 275, and one of the Thames ships, dated to about AD 150.

McGrail relates that a distinctive characteristic of these ships is that they were constructed by building the frame first. To give the hull its shape, the framing was first fastened to the plank-keel and posts to define the hull's shape. Later, the planking was then attached to this framing by large iron nails. These were clenched by hooking the nail tips into the inside faces of the boards of the framing.

He contrasts this interesting approach with that used in contemporary Mediterranean and Nordic ships. In the latter, the vessels were built 'plank-first', where the planking was first shaped and fastened together to form the shape of the hull. After this was done, the frame was added. McGrail notes the innovative nature of the Romano-Celtic approach:[20]

> The Celtic innovative, frame-first sequence was subsequently used one thousand years later to build the ships of the fifteenth- and sixteenth-century explorers such as Dias, Vasco da Gama, Columbus and Magellan.

Isidore of Seville

A valuable summary of shipping knowledge was made by Isidore of Seville in his *Etymologies*. Although the date when it was completely finished is not clear, there is a dedication to King Sisebut which was written before AD 621. This dedication was the preface to an early draft and was written just over 80 years after Arthur's death.

The summary appears in Book XIX and is well organised into four parts: (i) Ships, (ii) Parts of the ship and its equipment, (iii) Sails, and (iv) Ropes, with each part comprising a number of subparts. For example, it describes six kinds of sails as follows. The *acation* was the largest sail and was raised in the middle of the ship. The *epidromos* was the next largest sail and was raised in the stern. The *dolo* was a small sail fixed to the prow. The *artemo* was a sail more for directing the ship than for gaining speed. The *siparum* was a topsail useful when the winds eased. A reading of this source gives a good appreciation of the variety of ships, sails and equipment possible and dispels any notion that the ships of that time were necessarily primitive.[21]

SPECULATION ON ARTHUR'S ROUTE

Although we cannot be certain, Arthur's expedition most probably took the 'stepping stones' route to America. A speculative route is shown below in Figure 10.1. It is based on a likely knowledge of Iceland in the sixth century, the fact that a large iceberg was observed, the stay at a freezing cold camp, the desirability of staying close to land, and that the currents were operating similarly to those of modern times.

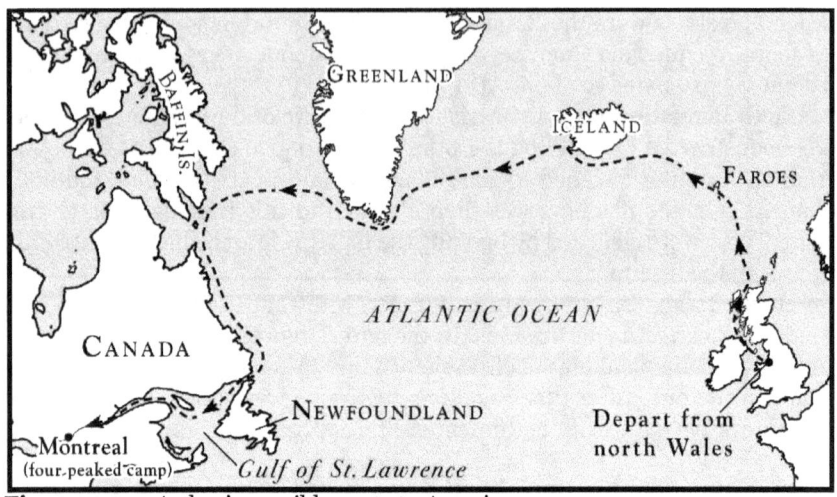

Figure 10.1 Arthur's possible route to America
(Map: Sarah Dunning Park)

From Britain to Iceland

Arthur's starting point may have been the north Wales coast, possibly from the mouth of the River Dee as suggested in Chapter 5. They may have sailed past the Isle of Man to the Rheon area in southwest Scotland, an area which was associated with Arthur in *Kadeir Teÿrnon*. From there, they may have sailed through The Minch channel to the isle of Lewis, where they probably made a stop at what is now Stornoway. If there is any truth in the *Gestae Arthuri* story that they wintered in the northern isles, then Stornoway would have provided a safe anchorage.

Alternatively they may have sailed across the north of Scotland to winter in the Orkneys, if such wintering did occur. From their departure point in the isles of Scotland, they could have sailed to the Faroes, and then on to Iceland. This route was probably familiar to them and would have provided them with opportunities to stop at these intermediate points, where necessary, to take on fresh food and water.

The assumption that the Britons sailed on a northern route is based on several considerations, some from the Welsh poetry and others which are independent of it. To consider the latter first, it has already been argued that Britons of that time may have known how to get to Iceland from the northern isles of Britain. This route involved relatively short distances of ocean before reaching the next safe harbour. It is unlikely that they would have sailed straight across the Atlantic at an approximately constant latitude as Jacques Cartier did in his voyages in the 1130s. Given the great uncertainties regarding their destination and the more primitive ships, to attempt such a route without the crew being reassured by regular land sightings may have been regarded as madness.

The Welsh poetry also suggests a northern route as implied by Arthur's crewmen seeing a huge iceberg and by their stopping at a camp of extreme coldness. In *Preideu Annwfyn*, they saw a 'glass fortress', considered here to be a poetic metaphor for a large iceberg. This metaphor is a concise picture of what an iceberg must have appeared like to the crewmen. It may have resembled the ancient British fortresses in Scotland perched on top of the massive rock formations at Dumbarton, Stirling and Edinburgh. The most likely place that the men would have seen a large fortress-like iceberg would have been within the iceberg zone off Labrador and Newfoundland, as will be later discussed.

From Iceland to Greenland

The catalyst for Arthur's expedition may have been reports of other lands west of Iceland that had been discovered either by accident when ships had been blown way off course, or as the result of further explorations west of Iceland. Pytheas from Massilia was assisted by the Britons to get to Thule. He reports that after sailing north of Thule for a day one would be stopped by ice. If Thule were Iceland, then it would seem that the Britons felt able to sail to Iceland and explore the nearby regions some 860 years before the time of Arthur. Over this long time interval it is surely not unreasonable to assume that people visiting Iceland or living there may have gained knowledge of the existence of Greenland.

Extended visibility in the Arctic

In fact, under certain optical conditions, Greenland is visible from Iceland. Vilhjálmur Stefánsson makes this very clear: 'you cannot go far off shore from northwestern Iceland without being able to see both countries...You cannot climb the mountains of northwestern Iceland on many different days without catching a glimpse of the [Greenland] coast [22]

From northwest Iceland the shortest distance to Greenland is about 285 kilometers. In general, an object this distant would not be visible, it being beyond the horizon because of the earth's curvature. However, the cold arctic seas can produce air temperature inversions that enable light to be refracted so that an observer can see beyond the horizon.

Waldemar Lehn has shown that the Norse in Iceland may have used these effects to discover Greenland and that the images of Gunnbjörn's Skerries seen by the Norse may have been only an optical effect created by Greenland's mountains. The cold ocean can create an air temperature inversion, where the temperature *increases* with altitude within the inversion layer, before decreasing with altitude. This temperature increase causes the air density to decrease sharply with altitude, enhancing the refractive capability of the air. Lehn discusses several models including optical ducting and the *Hillinger* effect. He argues convincingly that Eirik the Red may have gained knowledge of the Greenland coast from people who had seen Gunnbjörn's Skerries, most probably from optical ducting [23]

To Cape Farewell

After heading west from Iceland the Britons would have then encountered the favourable polar easterly winds and the south-westward pulling currents which would have carried them down the east coast of Greenland to the southern tip near Cape Farewell. These currents also take the icebergs (which break off the glaciers in eastern Greenland) in a south-westerly direction along this coast.

Cape Farewell to America

After passing Cape Farewell, the relatively warm current of west Greenland runs strongly north Here the Britons may have been pulled north in the direction of Nuuk where the Norsemen established their Western Settlement. Although the current continues to travel north into Baffin Bay, there are westward current branches that would have enabled the ships to cross the Davis Strait [25] The seamen may have been grateful to take advantage of these to avoid being pulled too far north and may have emerged in the vicinity of southern Baffin Island or northern Labrador. If there is any truth in the *Gestae Arthuri* account, an exploratory party may have entered the Hudson Strait and observed its strong indrawing currents and magnetic disturbances as mentioned in Chapter 3. Eventually, however, the expedition would have used the cold currents on the west of the Davis Strait to travel south down the coast of Labrador to escape the cold.

The Iceberg Zone

The icebergs off Newfoundland are formed when the glaciers of Greenland creep towards the sea. Once there, they break off, forming the icebergs which are composed of fresh water. The glaciers of east Greenland are one source, the southerly currents carrying the icebergs down to Cape Farewell, the southern tip of Greenland. From there the warm west Greenland current pulls most of them north up the west coast. Many are dissipated before reaching Disco Bay, while some drift westwards across the Davis Strait towards the coasts of Baffin Island and Labrador where they join other icebergs travelling south. The surviving east Greenland icebergs that continue travelling north are then joined by the main source of icebergs from the glaciers of west Greenland (from Disco Bay northwards). This combined group of icebergs travel north in an anticlockwise loop around Baffin Bay. They are further joined by icebergs from Ellesmere Island and then travel south past Baffin Island and Labrador.

If the winds are from the east or northeast, some of the icebergs drift into the shallows and inlets of Labrador and Newfoundland where they are grounded and eventually disintegrate.[26] Some pass into the Strait of Belle Isle, entering the Gulf of St Lawrence. The majority continue down the east coast of Newfoundland, eventually meeting the waters of the Gulf Stream where they melt and carve under the warm currents and wave action. Both Deborah Diemand and John Marko give diagrams of the iceberg paths.[27]

Approximately 85% of the icebergs off Newfoundland are from the west of Greenland, about 10% are from the east of Greenland, and about 5% are from Ellesmere Island.[28]

The waters off southeastern Newfoundland are relatively shallow due to the vast underwater plateaux known as the Grand Banks of Newfoundland. The region on the eastern edge of the banks from about 43° - 48°N latitude is called 'iceberg alley' and is a focus of much attention. In 1912, the Titanic sank from colliding with an iceberg that had drifted past the east coast of Newfoundland. This resulted in the creation of the International Ice Patrol (IIP). From 1914 the IIP began patrolling the Grand Banks.[29] It compiles many detailed statistics on iceberg movements and locations, including the number of icebergs drifting south of the 48°N latitude.

Speculation on where the Bard saw the Iceberg

Where is the most likely place for the bard to have seen a large fortress-like iceberg? A simple answer is probably north of the 48°N parallel that is the focus of the IIP. This parallel of latitude passes through the middle of east Newfoundland. This simple answer requires qualification. The IIP records give some large variations in the frequency of icebergs passing latitude 48°N. Further, there is a tendency for a pattern to persist over a few years: large numbers tend to occur in groups of three to four years, and low numbers in groups of four to nine years.[30]

The number of icebergs sighted declines with latitude, with more seen at higher northerly latitudes and declining in an approximately linear manner moving south. Curtis Ebbesmeyer and his colleagues provide a graph where a least squares straight line is fitted to the data from latitude 67°N to 48°N. This graph shows that one would expect to see roughly three times as many icebergs at the latitude of the Strait of Belle Isle than at the Grand Banks of Newfoundland.[31] They refer to this decline as a loss rate of approximately two icebergs for each kilometre moving south. In addition, the average size of the icebergs is reduced in the more southerly latitudes from melting, carving and splitting due to wave action and warmer waters, as expertly discussed by Deborah Diemand.[32]

John Marko and his co-authors provide IIP data giving iceberg numbers drifting south of latitude 48°N for each month.[33] The largest numbers occur in the months April and May and reduce in June (the month giving the third largest number). It seems likely that Arthur's expedition would not have left Britain until some time in May at the earliest, when the weather was suitable, and thus probably did not approach the iceberg zone until late June or even early July depending on the number and duration of their stopovers. They may have reached the zone when the number of icebergs crossing latitude 48°N was declining. In summary, taking the above points into consideration it suggests that Arthur's bard saw the large fortress-like iceberg in a location north of latitude 48°N, although the large variance in the iceberg data does not give certainty.

AMERICA

The Gulf of St Lawrence

Strait of Belle Isle

If Arthur sailed via Iceland, the ocean currents would have favoured a route where he passed Cape Farewell and was then carried north by the warmer current on the west coast of Greenland. Eventually he would have reached the westward currents that would have enabled him to cross the Davis Strait. He could then have followed the cold southward currents off the coast of Labrador. It is assumed that it would have been desirable for the ships to keep the coastline in sight as far as possible. This would have been a dangerous area and one where an iceberg sighting would have been likely. Barring some unpredictable course caused by a storm, Arthur's expedition probably sailed into the Gulf of St Lawrence.

The first opportunity would have been at the Strait of Belle Isle between Labrador and Newfoundland. This strait is crowded by ice for much of the year but may have become navigable by the time of year that Arthur arrived, assuming that conditions in the sixth century were either similar to or more benevolent than today's conditions. The Canadian Ice Service disseminates detailed charts showing that the ice in the strait tends to clear around mid June or July, which would probably have been around the time that Arthur approached.

If Arthur were tracking the coast of Labrador, it is not unlikely that he would have entered the Strait of Belle Isle. If he did, it is possible that he followed the treacherous northern shore, passing north of Anticosti Island, eventually reaching the mouth of the St Lawrence River. This would have been the most direct route to the interior of North America. In his second voyage of 1535, Jacques Cartier entered the Strait of Belle Isle in the month of June, reaching Blanc Sablon on the 29th, and was not much affected by icebergs.[34] Cartier took a fairly direct route along the north coast of the Gulf to the St Lawrence River. However, he had benefited from his thorough exploration of the Gulf in his 1534 voyage and he also had on board two young Native Americans to guide him.

Entering the Gulf via southern Newfoundland

If Arthur missed the Strait of Belle Isle, he may have followed the currents down the east Newfoundland coast, reaching the Grand Banks. Here they would have found a plentiful supply of fish to replenish their stores. If he continued to track along the coastline, he may have entered the Gulf of St Lawrence via the Cabot Strait.

This route may have occupied much time and increased the potential for mishaps. The Gulf is a very large area and may have required an extensive exploration and many anchorages. Looking for suitable land, he may have explored the southern areas of the Gulf, including Prince Edward Island and the mainland of New Brunswick.

A prior expedition?
It is possible that some unknown explorer had made the initial discovery of the Gulf before Arthur's expedition and had conducted a reconnaissance. It is highly doubtful that Arthur would have committed a large expedition to such a distant country unless he had a reliable and detailed report on what had already been found. The *Preideu Annwfyn* poem gives an impression that the expedition was quite large by its mournful contrast that only a small number made it back to Britain. Further, if the 'three fullnesses' of Prydwen could be taken as an sign of crowding in the ships, it may also suggest a large number. Prior knowledge of the Gulf would have been a great advantage in locating the most suitable areas to explore.

Up the St Lawrence River to Quebec

If Arthur spent some time exploring the Gulf (which would have been a very pleasant place in Summer and Autumn) it is likely that he would have found the St Lawrence River. This river would have served as the entrance to the interior of North America. The Britons may have attempted to sail up it for several reasons:

- it provided an exploratory pathway that allowed them the certainty of being able to retrace their route;
- the river and its environment would be a sure source of fish and game;
- they could transport materials more easily, and
- they could stay within the safety of their ships in a potentially hostile environment.

If the 'four-peaked' camp were Montreal (as argued in the next section), it would appear that Arthur, like Jacques Cartier, did sail partway up the St Lawrence. Cartier found it hard going. The powerful downstream currents made progress difficult at times with stops required to wait for the flood tide from the Gulf to counteract the strong St Lawrence currents.

Samuel Morison points out some of the hazards and difficulties. The section of the river near Pointe des Monts on the north side and Cap Chat on the Gaspe side is extremely dangerous when incoming tides from the Gulf meet the strong river current. A strong cross current develops, running south across the river, which can pull ships onto the Gaspe shore. Another very dangerous section occurs where the Saguenay River meets the St Lawrence River.[35] Further upstream at Hare Island, the St Lawrence river current was so strong that Cartier could make no progress at all. He had to anchor and wait for the flood tide. Finally Cartier made it to the site of Quebec City but only after a hard struggle upstream with the crew of all ships manning their oars.[36] It is probable that Arthur would have experienced many of the same problems as Cartier and it would not be surprising if he lost some ships on this leg of the journey.

THE FOUR-PEAKED CAMP – MONTREAL

In Stanzas 2 and 3, *Preideu Annwfyn* alludes to the 'four-peaked' camp in the context of the bard singing his poetry and an atmosphere of mead-carousal revelry. This would probably indicate that the camp was early in the journey well before the expedition was overwhelmed with disasters, suggesting that it was before the Britons had entered the Ohio Eastern Woodlands. The name of the camp seems to derive from the four striking mountain peaks that were nearby. Further, the poem indicates that from near the campsite one would have to turn to see all four peaks.

Approaching Montreal

A plausible identification for the four-peaked camp would be Montreal. The site is further upstream along the St Lawrence river than Quebec and is an enforced stopping place as ships cannot continue sailing past it because of the Lachine Rapids to the south. When sailing upstream on the approach to Montreal an unusual huge flat hill appears on the right bank side. From the top of this hill spectacular views of the surrounding countryside are obtained. This is Mont Royal, 231m above sea level. In the middle of the St Lawrence at this point is the island, Île Ste-Hélène (St Helen's Island). Although this general port area has been artificially altered in modern times, in the sixth century the most desirable anchoring place would probably have been near the Old Port on the right bank.

After their camp had been set up, it would be natural for Arthur's men to climb Mont Royal to study the progress of the river and the surrounds, just as Cartier did in 1535. From the top of Mont Royal, Cartier was dismayed to see the Lachine Rapids which would have blocked any further progress on the river.[37] Arthur's men may have had the same reaction, wondering how they could get their ships past the rapids.

The View from Mont Royal

Looking east across the St Lawrence River from Mont Royal, Arthur's men would have seen three other unusual flat hills similar to Mont Royal. These are Mont St-Bruno, Mont St-Hilaire and Mont Rougemont. These huge hills are particularly striking as the area on the eastern side of the river is a flat plain. Mont St-Bruno is the closest, but is the lowest at 218m. Mont St-Hilaire appears partly behind it but is higher at 415m and stretches to the right of St-Bruno. Further to the right is Mont Rougemont at 384m. These heights are from sea level.[38] From Mont Royal, they appear as huge flat hills, each one stretching for several kilometres in a north-south alignment.

In the present day, the view is partly interrupted by the tall modern buildings of Montreal. However, in Arthur's time they would have dominated the level plain, as shown by the photos in Figures 10.2 and 10.3 below. Through a study of Figure 10.3 one can imagine what the view would have been like without the Montreal buildings.

Figure 10.2 Mont Royal behind Montreal, the first of the Four Peaks (Photo: R. MacCann)

Figure 10.3 Mont St-Bruno, Mont St-Hilaire and Mont Rougement (L to R) across the St Lawrence River, viewed from Mont Royal (Photo: R. MacCann)

All four hills are part of a chain named the Monteregian Hills. These are the remains of intrusive igneous rock that have resisted weathering. There are other members of this chain but they are either too far away to be normally seen or are obscured. Mont Yamaska is further out and is hidden from view behind Mont Rougemont when the panorama is viewed from Mont Royal. Mont St-Gregoire appears as a little spike further to the right of the others but is insignificant compared to the other three.

'Turning to Face the Four Peaks'

If Arthur made a camp near the Old Port area of Montreal, it would be a near certainty that some members of his expedition would have climbed Mont Royal. It appears that his bard did and became aware of the other three peaks. To name the camp the 'four-peaked' camp after Royal, Bruno, Hilaire and Rougemont would have been an apt piece of naming.

One can envisage the bard trudging up the rising ground from the Old Port area towards Mont Royal. He is looking ahead and towards the summit of Mont Royal. At some point in his climb, he turns 180 degrees and sees the other three similar peaks across the St Lawrence river and is stunned by the magnificent view. In *Preideu Annwfyn* he remembers this moment, recorded in Line 12.

EXPLORING NORTH AMERICA

The Strong Door

If Montreal were the four-peaked camp, then there is a ready explanation for the 'strong door' in *Preideu Annwfyn*, 'isle of the strong door' (Line 24). The isle here could refer to a prominent island in the St Lawrence River, such as Île Ste-Hélène, but it is much more likely to refer to the new country in its entirety, conceived as an island. A 'door' would have been a good metaphor for the St Lawrence, providing a valuable entry passage to the new land. The 'strong' aspect probably refers to the immense difficulties posed by the river in reaching the camp. Some of these have been briefly described in sailing upstream to Quebec. Great dangers were lurking at various places and the relentless downstream currents would have allowed the ships only a slow progress. The leg from Quebec to Montreal is even more difficult, as noted by Samuel Morison, who refers to it as the most difficult part of Cartier's entire voyage of 1535.[39]

From Quebec to Montreal

The first major danger would have been from the Richelieu Rapids where the navigable area narrows to a channel less than a quarter of a mile wide. At the Gulf ebb tide, the downstream current runs through this channel at 5½ knots. Outside this channel the river is littered with banks of shale covered with boulders. A short distance after, this area is followed by one broken into five channels, but fortunately with weaker currents. Arthur would have had to wait for the flood tide to get through all these obstacles and would have needed to carefully plan his approach.

A further dangerous area would have been at Lac St-Pierre, where the St Lawrence widens into a lake. Here the effect of the Gulf tides ceases. This area is very shallow, of average depth about 3 metres. Some of Arthur's men may have proceeded ahead in smaller skin-covered boats, taking depth readings with a pole or a lead-line to help determine a safe course across the lake. Finally, after crossing the lake, there is a maze of islands through which the St Lawrence flows into Lac St-Pierre. Which channel should the mariners take to progress safely? This may have taken a good deal of exploration to find the right course for the ships. In Cartier's 1535 expedition, a friendly group of Native Americans indicated the best channel to take and that it would take three more days to get to Montreal.

The Advantage of Small, Manoeuvrable Ships

We have no direct knowledge of Arthur's ships, but they were likely to have been considerably smaller than Cartier's main ships. If so, they would have been more suitable for such delicate navigation in shallow water than larger ships. They may have used sweep oar rowing (like Cartier's ships), with each man having an oar being partnered with another man controlling an oar on the other side of the ship.

When Cartier sailed from Quebec to Montreal, he did so in his smaller pinnace, *L'Emerillo,* in which he crossed Lac St-Pierre, leaving it anchored at the western end. He then used longboats to reach Montreal. Both Cartier and Columbus greatly appreciated the capabilities of such smaller vessels, being much more suitable for coastal exploration but equally capable of crossing the ocean.[40] As suggested earlier, the Britons may also have used the smaller skin-covered boats to explore ahead and take depth readings. Barry Cunliffe refers to the skin-covered boats of the Inuit and suggests that similar boats could have taken Pytheas to Thule. He states that they were typically 10 to 15m long and could carry between ten and thirty people, but were so light that they could be carried by two men.[41]

Through a combination of careful planning, exploring ahead in smaller boats where necessary, awaiting favourable winds, and spells of rowing, it would have been possible to get to Montreal by ship. The great difficulties in reaching the four-peaked camp would have fully justified the use of the term, 'the strong door'.

The Frigid Camp

Preideu Annwfyn mentions a stay at a 'camp of extreme coldness' (Line 28). This would be consistent with an approach to America from a northern route, as assumed above, and being unable to travel far enough south to reach warmer regions before Winter set in. This fate also befell Cartier in his 1535 voyage. After reaching Quebec and then briefly visiting Montreal it was too late in the season to attempt to sail home across the Atlantic to St Malo. He was forced to spend Winter in Quebec, from mid-November to mid-April. His men were shocked at the cold. The St Lawrence turned to ice over 12 feet thick while the snow ashore was four feet deep. The drinks in their wooden casks froze. On board their anchored ships, the deck and even below hatches were covered in ice which was four fingers' breadth thick.[42]

In *Preideu Annwfyn* the 'camp of extreme coldness' is mentioned four lines after the four-peaked camp, both occurring in Stanza 3. If these two camps were the same (as possibly implied by their proximity in the stanza) then Montreal would also be the camp of extreme coldness. This would be a good fit as the Winter in Montreal is similar to that in Quebec. The sixth-century Britons may have been just as surprised by the severity of the Winter as the sixteenth-century Frenchmen.

God's Peak

In Line 42 of *Preideu Annwfyn* the 'camp of God's Peak' is mentioned. This is here interpreted as a large majestic mountain peak. Given that the St Lawrence river runs between the Laurentian and the Appalachian mountain chains, there is no shortage of candidates. One possibility could be Mount Katahdin in Maine, perhaps reached from an overland journey east from near Quebec. Alternatively, they may have spent some time in the good lands in New Brunswick, perhaps in Miramichi Bay or the Bay of Chaleurs. They may have reached Mount Katahdin after exploring southwest through New Brunswick. Another possibility could be Mount Marcy in New York state, perhaps located after an exploration around Lake Champlain when the expedition was exploring south from Montreal. However, with so many possibilities and the lack of a precise route it is too difficult to suggest any particular peak with confidence.

Exploring South of Montreal

For Arthur's main ships, Montreal may have been the end of the line. The Lachine Rapids would probably have prevented their ships getting past Montreal. The account given above has Arthur's ships struggling up the St Lawrence to reach Montreal. It is important to keep in mind that this is speculation on what could have happened rather than what is known to have happened. Clearly, it is not known that they actually did this. They may have attempted to sail from Quebec to Montreal in their ships and given up due to the difficult sailing conditions, the 'strong door'. Perhaps they set up their base camp lower down the river, possibly at Quebec as Cartier did. Or perhaps they did the Quebec to Montreal leg in their skin-covered boats. Whatever their means of progress, it appears that they did reach Montreal one way or another as the four huge hills there do seem to be a good fit for the four-peaked camp.

From Montreal, the expedition travelled broadly southwest towards the Ohio Eastern Woodlands, where the Hopewell had built a vast array of earthworks. It is possible that they followed the St Lawrence River by using their smaller skin-covered boats, carrying these boats on land when the sailing conditions were too difficult. Certainly, these boats would have been useful for crossing Lake Ontario and Lake Erie.

ENTERING THE OHIO EASTERN WOODLANDS

Eventually the Britons reached the Eastern Woodlands of Ohio and nearby states. The broad route can be seen from Figure 4.1, showing the St Lawrence River, Montreal, the Great Lakes and the distribution of Hopewell mounds. When the Britons met the Native Americans, some of their observations were recorded in their poetry. Apart from the fighting that developed, the five elements below are among those recorded in the ancient Welsh poems *Preideu Annwfyn* and *Kat Godeu*:

- Earthen mounds
- The use of pearls
- The American bison (buffalo)
- The North American river otter tamed by the inhabitants
- An abundance of rivers and streams giving easy transportation.

An Attempt to Reconstruct the Voyage 171

It will be shown below how these elements were closely associated with the Native Americans of central and southern Ohio.

The Mounds

Preideu Annwfyn introduces the camp associated with the mounds (*kaer sidi*) in the opening stanza, signifying its importance. This was where Gweir was imprisoned by the Native Americans – the bard was deeply worried about Gweir's fate, declaring that he would pray for him until Judgement Day. Given the importance of the mounds to the Hopewell and their successors, any intrusion of a foreign group would signal danger. The Britons with their strange iron weapons would have been perceived as a formidable threat. It seems almost inevitable that violence would have developed.

The densest and most complex earthworks were located along the Scioto and Muskingum river valleys from central to southern Ohio. In Chapter 4 three important Hopewell earthworks were briefly described: the Newark Earthworks, the Hopewell Earthworks and Mound City. The density of such structures over a small area may be seen from the map in Plate II of Squier and Davis.[43] This plate shows just a section of the earthworks along the Scioto River near Chillicothe. The Hopewell mounds were enclosed by earthen walls of a remarkable variety of shapes and combinations. Most of the mounds were dome shaped, some were loaf (or elliptical) shaped and some were like pyramids with truncated tops that formed platforms, with sloping ramps giving access to the tops.[44]

The walls which enclosed the mounds were often circles and squares, but other shapes include the rectangle, octagon, rhombus and ellipse. They often had ditches following the perimeter wall, sometimes on the inside, sometimes on the outside. It would appear that some of these ditches were filled with water, serving a ritual purpose.[45] The joining of the enclosures include the following interesting examples: a square and circle touching in a tangent, a rectangle and circle intersecting to form a chord, and a vertex of a square just touching the circumference of a circle. Often two shapes were joined by a short avenue of parallel straight walls. Sometimes there was a geometrical relationship between sets of earthworks that were many miles apart, an example being the Octagon earthworks at Newark and the High Bank earthworks near Chillicothe.[46] The density of the mound building in the south of Ohio and the great complexity of the earthworks may have created a sense of wonder in the Britons.

The Native Americans' use of Pearls

In *Preideu Annwfyn* the Britons captured a cooking vessel of the Native Americans, described in Line 16 as 'dark around its rim and pearls'. This description is certainly consistent with what we know of the Hopewell who produced fine pottery and used pearls extensively for decoration. Olaf Prufer points out the Hopewell's use of freshwater pearls, remarking that 'they were literally heaped into some of the mounds'. He refers to the Hopewell site west of Chillicothe which yielded around 100,000 pearls and the Turner site in Hamilton County yielding around 48,000 pearls). Brad Lepper also remarks that about 18,000 freshwater pearls were found at the Seip-Pricer mound, about 17 miles west of Chillicothe.[47]

These pearls were employed in simple necklaces and in more elaborate decoration, with strands over the chests of high-status males. In addition, the Hopewell made many animal effigy pipes with the bowl being carved in the shapes of animals, birds and aquatic creatures. Holes were made for the 'eyes' and these were frequently filled with pearls.

Bears' teeth were also highly prized by the Native Americans, often being strung together onto a necklace. Olaf Prufer notes that the canine teeth of grizzly bears were often inlaid with freshwater pearls. To do this, they were able to drill a precise circular hole into the tooth, select a pearl of appropriate size and then glue the pearl into the hole. Examples of both the animal effigy pipes and the bears' teeth, showing the holes for pearls, can be viewed on the Ohio Historical Society website.

The Hopewell also made superb pottery, some of which may have been made for special purposes. Brad Lepper reproduces a beautiful example of a large pot with stylized images of waterfowl.[48] From the quality of this fine workmanship, it is clear that the Native Americans took great care to produce such well-made ceremonial pots.

Pearl decoration in ceremonial pottery

Given their great artistic skill and their extensive use of pearls elsewhere, it seems likely that the Hopewell and their successors would have used pearls in the decoration of their ceremonial pottery. A possible example of this is given by Olaf Prufer in his *Scientific American* paper.[49] He provides a photograph of some Hopewell artifacts from the McGraw site, with a bear's tooth placed alongside a piece of pottery. The bear's tooth has two circular holes drilled into it, typical of the holes that held freshwater pearls.

The pottery piece has two identical circular holes which look to have held pearls. Below the rim, the pot is decorated by a series of intersecting lines which form a pattern of diamond shapes on a dark background. This pattern is terminated by a horizontal line of dashed incisions. The first circular hole is on this line. Below this line is a plain band that is lighter in colour than the band comprising the diamond patterns. The second circular hole is directly under the first, where the plain band finishes and a new diamond-like pattern begins. Like the bears' teeth holes, the pottery holes give the appearance of having held pearls.

In *Preideu Annwfyn*, the light colour of pearls appears to be contrasted with a dark colour around the rim of the pot. It appears that the Hopewell culture had an artistic liking for contrasting material of different colours. For example, Michael Spence and Brian Fryer remark that the Hopewell probably juxtaposed silver and copper in their artistic creations because they enjoyed the striking visual contrast.[50]

The American Bison (Buffalo)

As the Britons moved into the Ohio heartland they had opportunities to see the American bison. There are two groups, the plains bison and wood bison. As discussed briefly below, Arthur's men would have seen the plains bison. The bison have been hunted to near extinction following European settlement but how many would there have been in Arthur's time? Although it is difficult to answer this with any precision, Thomas McHugh estimates that the carrying capacity of the land may have supported around 30 million. Dale Lott suggests a little less, perhaps 24 to 27 million.[51]

The wide distribution of bison in prehistoric times

The bison were distributed widely across America as indicated by the maps provided by Dale Lott and by Hal Reynolds, C. Cormack Gates and Randal Glaholt.[52] Both maps place the wood bison to the far northwest, well out of the reach of Arthur's expedition. For the plains bison, Lott's map shows the most densely occupied area to be west of the Mississippi River and east of the Rocky Mountains, running from northern Texas well into Canada. The east of the Mississippi was more sparsely occupied for periods of typical climate. Hal Reynolds and his colleagues make the important statement that the far eastern limit for buffalo was the Allegheny Mountains, which run southwest through eastern North America.

The fact that the *Preideu Annwfyn* bard saw the American bison implies that the expedition moved inland west of the Allegheny Mountains and did not just sail along the coastal areas of North America. As will be discussed below, opportunities for seeing the bison would have occurred in the main region where the earthworks were densely distributed.

Bison observed in the Ohio heartland

In referring to the Hopewell earthworks, Olaf Prufer remarks: 'Perhaps the most striking assemblage of these works is located in southern Ohio in the valleys of the Muskingum, Scioto and Miami rivers'.[53] The first two of these locations exactly match where the 18th-century missionary David Zeisberger, who lived among the Native Americans in Ohio, noted the appearance of the buffalo. His writings were translated from German into English by Archer Hulbert and William Schwarze. They state that buffalo had once appeared in great numbers along the Muskingum River but at the time of writing had shifted to near its mouth. In addition, there had been reports of buffalo observed along 'the banks of the Scioto River and further south ... in herds numbering hundreds'.[54]

The bison's appearance

The plains bison fits the description of the 'brindled ox' of *Preideu Annwfyn* more than the wood bison. It has a 'massive, heavy head' which seems to be carried low because of its high shoulder hump and massive forequarters, according to Reynolds, Gates and Glaholt. The bard concisely refers to this as 'thick his headring'. Reynolds et al. also refer to its 'short, thick neck and a high shoulder hump' which the bard describes poetically as having 'seven score joints in his collar'; that is, a huge number of joints would be needed to hypothetically fit around his neck.[55]

Reynolds and his colleagues note that the huge head, the massive neck and strong shoulders give the impression that the forequarters are out of proportion to the much smaller hindquarters. The plains bison also has an unusual distribution of fur which had prompted the bard's poetic use of the term brindled (*brych*). It has a yellowy-brown 'robe' or 'cape' around the shoulders, the hump and back. There are two annual molts, in Spring and Autumn, which give it a patchy, uneven appearance.[56] It differs sharply in texture and colour from adjoining regions. The photo in Figure 10.4 below shows the dark shaggy hair of the head, the contrasting yellow-ochre fur of the cape and the shorter hair of the body.

Figure 10.4 The 'Brindled Ox'
(Photo: Jack Dykinga, Agricultural Research Service, USDA)

It is worthwhile to reflect and consider whether any rival hypotheses can satisfactorily explain the enigmatic 'brindled ox'. To date, there has been no explanation in the literature as to what the brindled ox was or why it was chosen. If this story were a late fiction, designed to entertain and show the bard's superiority in learning over the monks, then it would be implausible for the bard to choose the image of a British ox to taunt the monks about their ignorance.

The ox as a working animal was such a common sight in early medieval Britain that no one (including the monks) could possibly be ignorant about its characteristics.[57] There had to be something special about the 'brindled ox' in Annwfyn to distinguish it from the ordinary ox that was well known to all. These distinguishing features are stated in the poem: a huge head and neck that seem so large as to be out of proportion to the rest of the body and the unusual fur on the 'cape'. Arthur's bard could be certain that the monks had never seen the 'brindled ox' and knew nothing about it because it was not located in Britain, but in Annwfyn.

The North American River Otter

In line 45 of *Preideu Annwfyn* the bard refers to an owner (*perchen*) and then clarifies this in the following line by referring to an animal with a silvery head that is 'kept' by the Native Americans. This animal is to be identified with the North American river otter whose lustrous coat develops a silvery sheen when wet. The poet's image of the 'silvery head' could refer to the otter's head being carried above the water when swimming, a fact about the otter noted by Serge Larivière and Lyle Walton.[58]

The fact that the Britons saw that the river otter was kept or tamed by the Native Americans would seem to indicate that initially relations between the two groups were friendly. If relations had always been hostile it is difficult to see how the Britons could have gotten close enough to their camp to observe this unexpected occurrence without being attacked.

The North American river otter was present in great numbers in the Eastern Woodlands in mid and southern Ohio. This region has numerous rivers and streams in which the river otter would have flourished. Mound City, north of Chillicothe, is a major site containing about 23 earthen mounds, these being enclosed by an earthen wall in the shape of a square. An effigy pipe in the form of an otter was found at Mound City and is on display in the Visitor Center there.

A second effigy pipe in the form of an otter is on display in the British Museum and a photograph of the pipe is on the Museum website. This pipe was also found at Mound City. Of the eight otter effigy pipes identified in this book, five were carved carrying a fish in their mouths. The otter is perfectly adapted to catching fish and it is well known that they can be trained, as is done in some zoos. It is not difficult to believe that the Native Americans were able to train the otter to assist them in catching fish, as implied by the *Preideu Annwfyn* line that the animal was 'kept'.

The photo below indicates that when the fur is wet the otter's head could give a silvery appearance to an observer watching it swim.

Figure 10.5 North American river otter – tamed animal with 'silvery head' (Photo: Dimitry Azovtsev)

Bradley Lepper provides photographs of animal effigy pipes found in the Tremper Mound, a Hopewell site five miles north of Portsmouth.[59] These remarkable pipes are notable for their realistic portrayals and attention to detail. One shows an otter standing upright with its head raised (so that the nostrils are above the eyes) holding a fish in its mouth. While it could be inferring too much from the image, the raising of the otter's head makes it look as though the otter is offering the fish. A second view of this otter pipe, taken from the side, is provided below in Figure 10.6, courtesy of the Ohio Historical Society. Regardless of one's interpretation of this image, Eugene Gudger has shown how humans in different parts of the world have trained the otter to help them catch fish by various methods for well over a thousand years.[60] In China, he traces this training back to before AD 600 and provides photos of otters resting in the Chinese fishing boats of their masters in more modern times.

Figure 10.6 Hopewell carving – river otter with fish
(Photo: Courtesy of Ohio Historical Society)

The Streams of Annwfyn

In the *Kat Godeu*, poem, lines 189-90 tell us that the inhabitants of Annwfyn mustered for battle by means of the streams. A good candidate for these are the rivers of Ohio where the densest cluster of large earthworks are found, according to Olaf Prufer. The mustering for battle via the streams would be an odd statement to make if the warriors were in Britain where one would expect them to gather for battle by marching or on horseback. However, it would certainly have been appropriate for the Native Americans of Ohio who had an extensive network of river systems on which to navigate, as shown in Figure 10.7 below.

Apart from the Ohio River itself, three major river systems give access to large areas of this territory – those associated with the Scioto, Muskingum and Miami Rivers, as shown in Figure 10.7. Given the density of Hopewell earthworks along the Scioto River, this could have been where the Britons encountered the mounds at *kaer sidi*. Tribes from all along the Scioto and nearby could have canoed down the river and its tributaries to reach a meeting place for battle.

The streams of Annwfyn may also have helped the Britons to explore the new country. If they travelled by land, passing to the east of Lake Erie, they may have found the Allegheny River. This river would have allowed them to explore in their skin-covered boats, camping along the river when night fell. The Allegheny joins the Ohio River which would have provided an efficient way to travel south and then west until the Falls of the Ohio were reached.

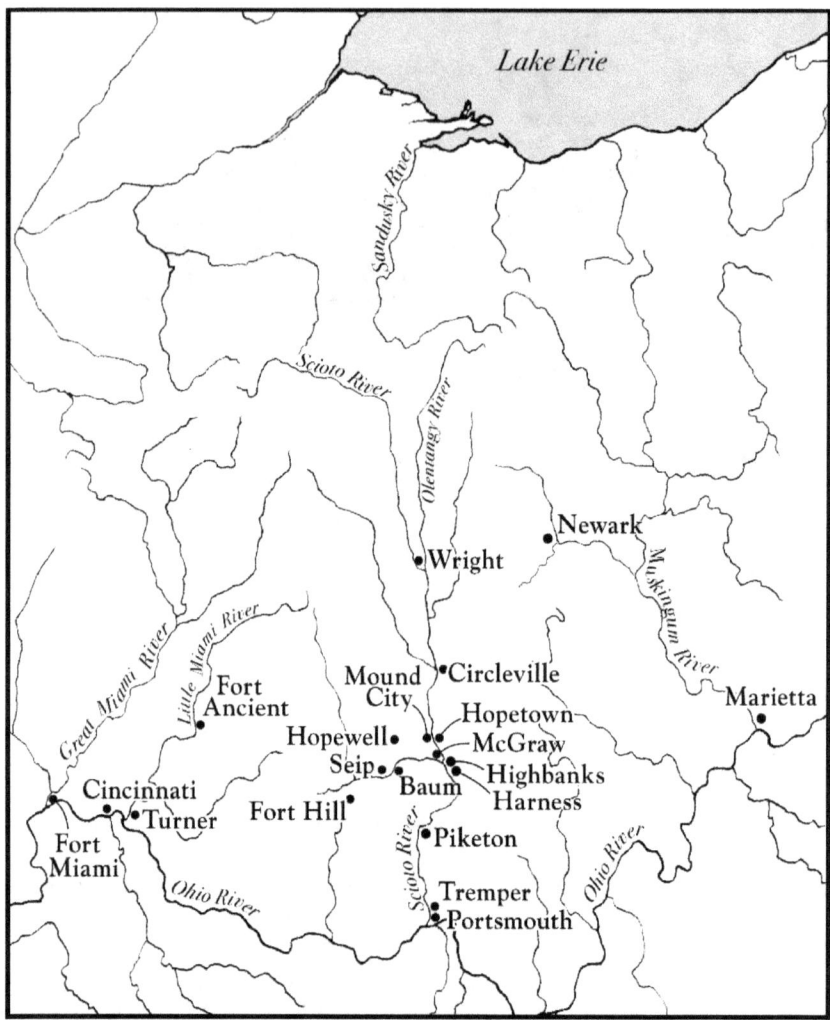

Figure 10.7 The rivers of Ohio showing important Hopewell earthworks
(Map: Sarah Dunning Park)

Another possibility is that the Britons used skin-covered boats to cross the Great Lakes associated with the St Lawrence River. In crossing Lake Erie, they may have explored Sandusky Bay and established a camp there. From there, the Sandusky River and its tributaries would have taken them to within a short distance of the Scioto River system and access to the dense cluster of earthworks. This route would also allow them to join the Ohio River. These comments are merely speculation on possible routes and do not exclude the neighbouring states which also had Hopewell mounds. They could have explored parts of Pennsylvania, Indiana, West Virginia, Kentucky and other nearby states.

CONCLUSION

It is argued that Arthur's expedition took a northern sailing route, probably via Iceland, and sighted a massive iceberg before reaching North America. Given this northern route, they probably entered the Gulf of St Lawrence and explored it during Summer and Autumn. It would appear that they found the St Lawrence River and sailed upstream as far as the conditions allowed, apparently enduring a freezing Winter at one of their camps. They appear to have reached the site of present day Montreal (the four-peaked camp), the peaks being Royal, Bruno, Hilaire and Rougemont. From there, continuing southwest past Lakes Ontario and Erie would have brought them to the heart of the Hopewell territory.

In the Eastern Woodlands it seems that bitter fighting occurred at *kaer sidi*. Their earthworks were sacred to the Native Americans and must have appeared to be under threat from these strange invaders with their powerful iron weapons. The *Kat Godeu* bard in typical bardic exaggeration refers to the thousands of inhabitants that he had killed, remarking that each man had the passion for battle of 100 normal fighters. The *Preideu Annwfyn* bard also surprisingly comments on the bravery of the owners of the pearl-decorated 'cauldron' – that it did not boil the food of a coward.

Kaer sidi may have been the place where the Britons met the inhabitants standing on a wall and found it almost impossible to communicate with them (*Preideu Annwfyn*, lines 30-2). The valour of Arthur is referred to in this stanza, suggesting fighting developed. It was also at the mounds that Gweir was captured and could not be rescued by the Britons. The bard is deeply apprehensive as to Gweir's fate and vows to pray for him until Judgement Day. The central region containing the complex earthworks seems to mark the end of any further progress made by Arthur's expedition and may have been the place where they were decimated, with only a remnant escaping.

11
A REAPPRAISAL OF THE TRADITIONAL ARTHURIAN EVIDENCE

THE TRADITIONAL EVIDENCE FOR ARTHUR

The previous chapters have provided new evidence that Arthur's influence was far greater than previously thought. Apart from his well known exploits as a warrior and battle commander, he led an expedition which explored sixth-century America. This evidence has been derived from the three *Book of Taliesin* poems *Preideu Annwfyn*, *Kat Godeu* and *Kadeir Teÿrnon*, poems that are generally not considered relevant to the historical Arthur.

However there is other well-known material that has been studied by many scholars in search of the historical Arthur, although this has often been viewed negatively or dismissed as providing little information. In particular, the analytical techniques that are employed may treat each bit of evidence separately, emphasise its shortcomings, and then conclude that the piece of evidence is not sufficient to reach a 'safe' conclusion on Arthur's historicity. Then the next piece of evidence is analysed similarly, independently of the previous material. This corrosive treatment of each independent piece tends to give a 'false negative' result.

Further, the analysis of the evidence may be considered in relation to a preconceived theoretical model which attempts to 'shoehorn' straightforward statements about Arthur into agreement with the model. In Arthur's case the result is that a genuine historical king who made an indelible impression on his countrymen has been relegated to a legendary figure, a Celtic god, a myth, or a folkloric figure – a massive 'false negative' error.

In this chapter the traditional material is examined in detail and gives a consistent picture. When considered jointly, the totality of all the evidence suggests that Arthur was viewed as an historical person, a peerless military figure. In addition, it will be argued here that the sceptical treatment often applied to the Arthurian reference in the poem *Y Gododdin* is likely to be without foundation and that the Arthurian stanza was probably composed in the sixth century, perhaps only a decade or two after Arthur's death. The material to be considered includes:

- Four men named after Arthur
- Arthur in the poem *Y Gododdin* (The Gododdin)
- Arthur in the poem *Marwnad Cynddylan* (Deathsong of Cynddylan)
- Arthur in the poem *Geraint son of Erbin*
- Arthur in the *Historia Brittonum*.

MEN NAMED AFTER ARTHUR

An early piece of evidence for Arthur's historicity comes from men who were apparently named after him. In the period c. 560-600, we know of four men born in Britain or Ireland called Arthur, or variants of this name. What caused this cluster of names to appear? Hector and Nora Chadwick state that by the sixth century the name Arthur was familiar throughout all the Celtic regions of Britain. Yet before this time they state that the 'Arthur' name was 'practically unknown'.[1]

It seems that a famous person called Arthur had emerged in the early sixth century, creating such an impression that fathers later in that century named their sons after this person. It was also a society that esteemed the heroism of the warrior, suggesting that the famous person was renowned for these qualities.[2] The four men and very approximate estimates of their birthdates are as follows:

- Artur, son of King Aedán of Dalriada   c. 560
- Artuir, son of Bicoir the Briton   c. 590
- Artur, grandfather of Feradach   c. 600
- Arthur, son of Petr   c. 575

Artur, son of King Aedán of Dalriada

Aedán, the Scottish king of Dalriada, was a powerful and warlike ruler. He seems to have formed an alliance with the northern Britons in an ambitious attempt to drive the Saxons out of Northumbria.[3] Aedán and his son Artur appear in the *Life of Columba* written by Adomnán of Iona, probably in the late 600s. At the Battle of Miathi in about 590, Prince Artur and his brother were killed, a high cost for Aedán's victory.[4]

Aedán died in about 609, an old man, after renouncing his kingship and retiring to a monastery in Kintyre. It seems that he was born about the time of Arthur's death, circa 535. As Prince Artur died in battle about 590, he was possibly born about 560. As a young man, Aedán may have heard stories of Arthur's valour and, given his alliance with the Britons, it may have inclined him to name his son after the peerless warrior.

Artuir, son of Bicoir the Briton

The *Annals of Tigernach* record the killing of Mongán mac Fiachna by Artuir, son of Bicoir the Briton. Mongán's estimated death date varies between 620 and 626 in the Irish annals (*Four Masters*, 620; *Ulster*, 625; *Chronicum Scotorum*, 625; *Iona*, 626).[5] This Artuir was British but his killing of Mongán occurred in Kintyre, a part of Dalriada. It suggests that Artuir lived in the north, if not in Dalriada then perhaps in the neighbouring British territory of Strathclyde around Dumbarton. Regardless of Artuir's exact location, here is another person apparently named after Arthur, born perhaps around 590, and associated with northwest Britain.

Artur, grandfather of Feradach

In 697 a council met at Birr in County Offaly (in Ireland) to enact the Law of Adomnán which aimed to give women, children and ecclesiastics protection against acts of violence. Adomnán was abbot of the monastery on the island of Iona in Dalriada and head of the group of monasteries which had been formerly administered by Columba.

The penalties for breaking this law are given in *Cáin Adamnáin*, which was translated and edited by Kuno Meyer. The law had a wide coverage in Ireland, Dalriada and other parts of Scotland. A group of forty ecclesiastics and fifty-one laymen was formed to act as guarantors and on this list was a 'Feradach grandson of Artur'.[6] Assuming around 30 years per generation, this would give a birthdate for Artur of roughly 600.

Arthur, son of Petr

This Arthur appears in genealogies from two documents that confirm each other, as they are seemingly independent. The first segment below is from the Dyfed genealogy in the Harleian Genealogies, MS 3859, British Library. The second genealogy segment is from the *Expulsion of the Déisi*, an Irish work dating from the 700s but surviving in manuscripts from the twelfth century and later.[7]

Guortepir	→ Cincar	→ Petr	→ Arthur
Gartbuir	→ Congair	→ Retheoir	→ Artuir

These extracts are equivalent. Guortepir and Gartbuir are the same person (the great grandfather of Arthur/Artuir) and he can probably be identified with the Vortipor who was berated by Gildas in *The Ruin of Britain*. If so, we can estimate the year of birth of this Arthur. If Gildas wrote about 540 when Vortipor was around 55 (his hair was whitening according to Gildas), then assuming 30 years to a generation gives a birth year of approximately 575 for this Arthur.

It is of interest that the Arthur son of Petr appears in a genealogy from Dyfed in southwest Wales. However, the region had been settled by the Irish Déisi tribe from circa AD 350. The dynasty is of Irish origin, as noted above from its appearance in the *Expulsion of the Déisi*. He therefore shares this characteristic of being of Irish descent, or being closely associated with the Irish, with the three previous Arthurs discussed above.

These Arthurs were of sufficient importance to be historically recorded in a time for which written records are scarce, so they may represent a small fraction of such people. They appear at just the right time in the historical record to have been named after a great military figure who died in the first half of the sixth century. According to the *Annales Cambriae* Arthur died in circa 537/539. Although some scholars have contested this date, it fits in well with the environmental calamity of AD 540 that occurred not long after his death, according to *Kadeir Teÿrnon* in Chapter 8.

Arthur's Association with Southwest Scotland

In *Kadeir Teÿrnon* Arthur is associated with a region in north Britain called Rheon. In Triad 1 of *Triads of the Island of Britain* it is called Pen Rhionydd. This region is identified with Loch Ryan, in Galloway (southwest Scotland) by a number of scholars.[8] The presence of Arthur in Galloway and his fame as a military figure could explain why the nearby Aedán of Dalriada named his son after Arthur.

This probably also explains why Arthur is mentioned as the epitome of heroism in the early northern poem *Y Gododdin*, composed in the mountain court of Eidin, modern Edinburgh. The Britons in Edinburgh and Strathclyde would have been able to maintain regular contact due to the short distance between the two centres. When Edinburgh fell to the Angles in AD 638, the Gododdin stanzas were probably preserved in Strathclyde.[9] In placing Arthur in Rheon, it is not meant to imply that this was his permanent base, although this is not impossible. Triad 1 informs us that Rheon was Arthur's northern sphere of influence and names two others in the south. Where his home territory was located is a difficult problem which will be discussed in detail in Chapter 12, based on information from the Welsh poems.

ARTHUR IN Y GODODDIN

The Arthurian Reference

In *Y Gododdin*, the Arthurian reference occurs in an eight-line stanza that praises Gorddur, a British warrior. Gorddur is said to have brought down black crows to the front of the wall of the fortress. This reference to crows was a standard way of praising a warrior, meaning that the hero killed so many of the enemy that their dead bodies enticed crows down to feed on their flesh. Although Gorddur was indeed such a hero, the next line notes as an aside 'though he was not Arthur'. This negative type of comparison would usually be considered an insult, but that is not intended here. Arthur's fame as a warrior was such that no current fighter had reached this standard and no shame could be attached to the comparison – the very fact that Gorddur was being compared to the peerless Arthur was an honour.

The Gododdin

Y Gododdin is attributed to Aneirin, the north British bard mentioned with Taliesin and others in the *Historia Brittonum*. The Gododdin were a British tribe, known as the Votadini in pre-Roman and Roman times. Their capital was the mountain court at what is now Edinburgh. Their large territory, also known as Gododdin, stretched southward into northern England, probably bounded by the River Tees. The poem commemorates the men who feasted at their lord's stronghold at Edinburgh for a year before riding south to fight the Angles at Catraeth, probably modern-day Catterick, near Richmond. Some Angles had been settled there from c. 450, according to Leslie Alcock but the majority of the Anglian material comes from the sixth century.[10] The poem laments that the Gododdin warriors were defeated by a larger force and virtually all 300 of the Britons were killed.

This battle probably took place in the middle to late sixth century.[11] Many of the stanzas may have been composed in Edinburgh after the battle. It is thought that when Edinburgh finally fell in 638 these stanzas were brought to Strathclyde where at some period they were preserved in a written form. Other stanzas appear to have been added in Strathclyde. For example, the one on the death of Domnall Brecc at the battle of Strathcarron in 642 was added there, probably not long after the battle.

The Gododdin Text – A, B1 and B2

The text of *Y Gododdin* appears in the *Book of Aneirin* of which the earliest manuscript (MS Cardiff 2.81, Central Library) dates from c. 1265, around 700 years after the purported time of composition. This script was written by two persons, 'A' and 'B' who appear to have been using different sources. Part A consists of 88 stanzas in a Middle Welsh spelling while Part B provides a partially modernised Middle Welsh spelling (from Old Welsh) for the first 23 stanzas (denoted B1). Part B then abruptly changes to a more consistent Old Welsh spelling for the last 19 stanzas (denoted B2). Further, some stanzas are repeated across the different parts – 29 stanzas in Part B appear in Part A, in varying degrees of closeness.

The B2 text in general contains the densest concentration of linguistic archaisms earlier than Old Welsh according to John Koch.[12] These are a part of Neo-Brittonic, the language Arthur would have spoken. The Arthurian stanza is one of these B2 stanzas, denoted B2.38.

A Comparison of Two Stanzas

Was B2.38 composed in the sixth century? John Koch considers that it was probably archaic material composed before AD 638.[13] In the discussion below, the Arthurian stanza will be compared to another *Y Gododdin* stanza (B2.28), honouring the hero, Yrfai. The latter stanza will be argued to be sixth century on content grounds. These two stanzas share four distinctive stylistic features which suggests that they were probably composed by the same poet. If so, this would then date the Arthurian stanza to the sixth century. The four stylistic features are:

- a negative comparison in a parenthetical clause,
- the use of enjambment (explained below),
- the emphatic appearance of the hero's name at the very end,
- using the same expression to begin successive lines.

The translations below are approximate but are based on those in the 1997 *Y Gododdin* text of John Koch, while the Welsh text has been taken from the 1908 edition of J. Gwenogvrn Evans. The names in the translation are given in modernised Welsh spelling.[14]

B2.38 GORDDUR

1. **Ef guant tra tri gant echassaf.**
   More than three hundred of the finest were killed.
2. **Ef ladhei a uet ac eithaf.**
   He cut down at both the centre and the flanks.
3. **Oid guiu e mlaen llu llarahaf.**
   The generous man was splendid before the noblemen.
4. **Go dolei o heit meirch e gayaf.**
   He used to give horses from the herd in Winter.
5. **Go chore brein du ar uur | caer**
   He used to entice down black crows in front of the fortress wall
6. **(ceni bei ef Arthur).**
   (though he was not Arthur).
7. **Rug ciuin uerthi ig clisur,**
   Among warriors mighty in deeds,
8. **ig kynnor guernor – Guaurdur.**
   before the barrier of alder wood – Gorddur.

B2.28 YRFAI

1. **Gnaut i ar fisciolin amdiffin Gododin,**
   It was usual for him on a frisky horse to fight for Gododdin,
2. **im blain trin terhid rei.**
   in the frontline of men eager for battle.
3. **Gnaut i lluru alan buan bithei.**
   It was usual for him to be swift like a deer.
4. **Gnaut rac teulu Deor em discinhei.**
   It was usual for him to attack the warband of Deira.
5. **Gnaut mab Golistan (cen nei bei | guledic i tat)**
   It was usual for Wolstan's son (though his father was no prince)
6. **indeuit a lauarei.**
   that what he said was heeded.
7. **Gnaut ar les minidauc scuitaur trei,**
   It was usual, for the mountain court, that shields be shattered,
8. **guaurud rac Ut Eidin – Uruei.**
   bloodied before the Lord of Eidin – Yrfai.

A negative comparison in a parenthetical clause

In the stanzas above, the English translations of both parenthetical clauses are shown in parentheses. In B2.38, Line 6, the famous clause is 'though he was not Arthur', a clause whose authenticity has been strongly debated. In B2.28, Line 5, the corresponding clause is the relatively little known 'though his father was no prince'. Of all the Gododdin stanzas, these are the only two which have this type of negative aside.

Enjambment
Enjambment occurs when the rhyming part of a line does not occur at its very end – further text is needed after the rhyming word to complete the meaning expressed. Consider only the Welsh text. In B2.38 line 5, the rhyming part (*uur*) is not the end of the line. The end word is *caer* which in the B2.38 stanza above is displayed to the right of a vertical line. Similarly in B2.28, line 5, the rhyming part (*bei*) is not the end of the line. The end text is *guledic i tat* which is also displayed to the right of a vertical line.

The emphatic use of the hero's name at the end
In B2.38, line 8, the hero's name appears only once in the stanza at the very end – Gorddur. Similarly in B2.28, line 8, the hero's name occurs only once at the very end – Yrfai. It appears that the poet would have pronounced each name emphatically to end the stanza in a climax.

Using the same expression to begin successive lines
In B2.38, Lines 4 and 5 are linked by the compound verbs *Go dolei*...(He used to give...) and *Go chore*...(He used to entice down...). In B2.28, Lines 3-5 are linked by the expression *Gnaut*... (It was usual for...), which is also employed to begin other lines in the stanza.

The Early Date of both Stanzas
The use of all four of these distinctive features strongly suggests that the same poet composed both stanzas. If this is true, it has an important implication for dating the Arthurian stanza. There are two features about the Yrfai stanza that suggest it was composed before the fall of Edinburgh in 638. Koch argues convincingly that Golistan, the name of Yrfai's father, can be identified with the Saxon name Wolstan, which is a variant of the very common Wulfstan (also Ulfstan). It implies that Yrfai's father was an Anglo-Saxon; that is, he was English.[15] This fully explains the negative parenthetical clause that his father was no prince. Despite this handicap in his pedigree, it seems that Yrfai's natural talent allowed him to reach a dominant position as indicated by his title 'Lord of Eidin'. This surprising feature indicates that the stanza was composed early, probably around 550. It is highly unlikely to have been composed after the Gododdin people had lost all their lands and their capital, Edinburgh, to the hated Saxons.

Further, B2.28 contains another feature suggesting an early date. The enemy of the Gododdin is given as the Deira (*Deor*), Saxons who settled on the east side of England, south of the River Tees. The Gododdin held the large territory in northern Britain, from around the Firth of Forth and extending southwards to the River Tees. When the Saxons moved north into Gododdin territory this encroachment resulted in conflict. Eventually they took over the Gododdin lands and captured Edinburgh in 638, their conquered territory being called Bernicia. It seems that Saxon Bernicia did not yet exist (or was insignificant) when the poet composed the stanza, as the enemy was the more distant Deira. This would date B2.28 to before 638 and probably to the mid-sixth century. If the same poet did compose the Arthurian stanza, then it may be only a decade or two after Arthur's death when his deeds were fresh in the memory of the Britons.[16]

Is the Arthurian Reference an Interpolation?

Thomas Charles-Edwards presents a criterion for a probable early dating of *Y Gododdin* stanzas.[17] As noted earlier, there are A and B versions of some of the stanzas, with the B version divided into B1 and B2. He states that it is only when a stanza appears in both the A and the B versions that one can have any confidence that it goes back before the ninth or tenth century.

In discussing B2.38, Caitlin Green misinterprets the work of Charles-Edwards when she states: 'Charles-Edwards suggests that it [stanza B2.38] should consequently be considered an interpolation into the text, probably belonging to the ninth or tenth century'.[18] However, Charles-Edwards has not said or suggested any such thing, neither in his 1978 paper nor in his 1991 paper. Borrowing some terms from mathematics, Charles-Edwards' criterion may be a *sufficient* condition for a stanza to be regarded as probably early, but it is certainly not a *necessary* one. The Yrfai stanza (B2.28) appears to be very early, as argued above, but it does not appear in the A stanzas. If a stanza is not in both Part A and Part B, its status as a possible early stanza should be considered as open, not inferred to be an interpolation. Scholars may then examine the stanzas, especially the B2 ones, to determine whether they are early on the basis of features of the language and content.

John Koch has identified one possible pre-Old Welsh feature in B2.38 and he thus classifies it as probably having been composed before the 638 fall of Edinburgh.[19] As discussed above, it has been argued on the basis of stylistic features that B2.38 and B2.28 were probably composed by the same poet and that both were probably sixth century.

A second suggestion is that the Arthurian clause itself (Line 6) may be an interpolation into the stanza, either through inserting it or the overwriting original material, as suggested by Alfred Jarman.[20] He provides no evidence to support his scepticism, but merely lists the interpolation as a possibility. However as argued above, this negative parenthetical clause is part of a set of distinctive features that suggests a common authorship, implying that it did exist in the original of B2.38.

A third suggestion is that the name 'Arthur' itself may not have been in the original clause but possibly that of another warrior. Richard Barber states that Arthur's name was often substituted for earlier heroes.[21] This possibility is discussed below.

'Arthur' substituted for another name?

Consider the hypothetical case where the name 'Arthur' was substituted for that of another warrior, X, in the parenthetical clause. As 'Arthur' rhymes with the surrounding lines, X would need to rhyme and preferably maintain the same rhythm. However, apart from Arthur and Gorddur, two-syllable men's names ending in 'ur' are uncommon. In addition, even if one could be found, he would have needed to be a very famous warrior so that the negative comparison made sense. Indeed, even in the improbable case that another superlative warrior with a rare name ending in 'ur' did exist, then the line would probably be perceived as an insult, which would defeat the purpose of praising the hero. It would therefore seem extremely unlikely that the name Arthur has been substituted for that of another warrior.

Summary

The Arthurian stanza (B2.38) honouring Gorddur shares four distinctive stylistic features with the Yrfai stanza (B2.28) suggesting that the same poet composed both. Stanza B2.28 appears to have been composed not long after the Catraeth battle. Its sixth-century dating is implied by the fact that Yrfai's father was English, giving him an undesirable pedigree. This would make it virtually impossible that he would be lauded as a hero after the English had taken Edinburgh in AD 638 and dispossessed the Gododdin Britons of all their lands. In addition, the enemy was the quite distant Deira, suggesting that the nearer Saxon Bernicia did not yet exist or was insignificant when the poem was composed. Both features suggest a dating in the sixth century well before Edinburgh fell to the Anglo-Saxons. Additional arguments are also given which imply that it is unlikely that the Arthurian line (or stanza) was a late interpolation.[22]

ARTHUR IN MARWNAD CYNDDYLAN

Marwnad Cynddylan (Deathsong of Cynddylan) is an elegy for a British chief from the old kingdom of Powys. Cynddylan was allied to Penda of Mercia, who was king of the powerful Anglo-Saxon kingdom in central England. In 655, both Cynddylan and Penda and were killed by Oswiu of Northumbria in the battle of Winwaed, near Leeds. Jenny Rowland argues that this defeat was the historical context for the elegy to Cynddylan.[23]

The oldest surviving copy, dated to about 1631-34, appears in MS 4973 in the National Library of Wales. However despite the very late dating of this manuscript, the poem does seem to be an authentic seventh-century poem similar in style, metre and phraseology to *Y Gododdin* according to Rachel Bromwich.[24] It may possibly have been composed soon after the battle, as discussed by Caitlin Green.[25] If so, it would have been about 120 years after the death of Arthur, when he was viewed as a warrior hero of the past, but before the fables and marvels about him were fully formed. The Arthurian reference in Line 46 reflects this sense of a great warrior of the past.[26]

> 46 canawon artir wras, dinas degyn
>   whelps of stout Arthur, a mighty fortress

In the *previous* line of the poem (which is not shown above), the poet had referred to the British warriors as his brothers-in-arms. In Line 46 above, these men are described as whelps (*canawon*) of Arthur; that is, descendants in the sense of being courageous warriors. Arthur is also given the metaphor of a 'mighty fortress', conventional praise imagery.

This Arthurian reference is similar to that in *Y Gododdin* but no one has argued that it is an interpolation. Both are mere mentions, comparing fallen warriors in the eulogies with the heroism of Arthur and his men. The main difference is that the *Y Gododdin* stanzas about Catraeth were composed in the north (probably in Edinburgh) while the elegy to *Cynddylan* may have been composed in what is now Shropshire. Arthur's reputation as a peerless battle leader was widespread at this early stage – evident in both the north and south of Britain.[27]

ARTHUR IN GERAINT SON OF ERBIN

The Arthurian Stanza

A third poetic reference to Arthur is given in an elegy to Geraint the son of Erbin (*Gereint fab Erbin*). This poem is in the englyn metre in which each stanza has three rhyming lines. It appears in *The Red Book of Hergest*, *The Black Book of Carmarthen* and also in a fragment from *The White Book of Rhydderch*, with differing stanzas and stanza orders. Jenny Rowland gives a composite reconstruction, based on the fuller *Red Book of Hergest* order, noting variants from the other texts. Arthur appears in Stanza 15 of the *Red Book* as shown below.[28]

1   **Yn Llongborth llas y Arthur**
    In Llongborth were slain to Arthur
2   **gwyr dewr kymynynt a dur**
    brave men who hewed with steel
3   **amherawdyr, llywyawdyr llauur.**
    emperor, director of the toil (of battle).

This interpretation has Arthur's brave men being slain, as Arthur directs the battle. However the *Black Book* version (Stanza 8) differs in Line 1, as shown below, with little difference in the other two lines.

1   **En Llogborth y gueleise y Arthur**
    In Llongborth I saw (belonging) to Arthur

In this line the poet *saw* Arthur's brave men who hewed with steel, a quite different meaning. Apart from this difference, the preposition 'y' preceding Arthur in the *Black Book* Line 1 is problematic. This is discussed by Patrick Sims-Williams who argues that the *Red Book* interpretation where Arthur's brave men are being slain is the more probable.[29]

In the corresponding Geraint stanza (which is not shown here), it is the brave men of Geraint who were also being slain. In both versions, Arthur is called 'emperor', director of the toil of battle.

A Possible Historical Context

The most direct interpretation of Arthur's appearance in this poem is that the poet believed that Arthur had actually fought at Llongborth. In favour of this view is the fact that Arthur and his soldiers are not being directly compared in valour to the men in the poem, as occurs in *Y Gododdin* and *Marwnad Cynddylan*. They are just portrayed as fighting bravely with Geraint, while taking heavy losses. If so, this may be a historical battle of Arthur's that is not recorded in the *Historia Brittonum*.

A second interpretation is that Arthur's appearance was unhistorical and the poet simply included an englyn on Arthur to enhance Geraint's heroism, without using an explicit comparison, a view held by Green.[30]

However if this were the case, it is odd that both Arthur's brave men and Geraint's brave men were being killed. Could this be a real battle that Arthur lost? This outlook seems incompatible with the battle list of Arthur in the *Historia Brittonum* of 829-30, and later literature, where he is portrayed as virtually invincible. Geraint appears to be a not uncommon sixth-century name.[31] If this were a genuine historical battle in which Arthur fought, what are the possibilities?

Location of Llongborth

Llongborth means 'ship harbour' or 'sea port' and John Morris has suggested Portsmouth as its location, but this has received little support.[32] Langport in Somerset is also a possibility. One location that seemingly links the names Llongborth, Geraint and a real battle site is the harbour at Penbryn Beach in Ceredigion. Peter Bartrum reproduces a valuable statement made in 1740 by Theophilus Evans that Llongborth was probably Llanborth in the parish of Penbryn in Ceredigion:[33]

> There is a place near there commonly called *Maesglas*, but the old name was *Maes-y-llas* ('The Field of the killing') or *Maes Galanas* ('The Field of Massacre').

This region contains the fifth-century burial stone of a Corbalengus, an Irish name, but he had been settled there long enough to gain acceptance as an Ordovician, as indicated by the stone's inscription.[34] The Ordovician port at Penbryn Beach was probably in use in the sixth-century. Over the centuries, the 'Llong' part of Llongborth could have been displaced by 'Llan' (enclosure). Several miles inland from the beach is a site called *Bedd Geraint* – the grave of Geraint. Although the poem only mentions his brave men being slain, the very fact that the poem was honouring Geraint's memory in association with Llongborth suggests that he did die there.

The 'Emperor' Descriptor

An interesting feature of the poem is that Arthur is described as *amherawdyr* or *ameraudur* (emperor), a title that may seem unusual for a sixth-century king. However the Latin *imperator* (emperor) was also used by Adomnán in his *Life of Columba* to refer to Oswald when he defeated Cadwallon.[35] In this context, it probably means overall commander. That battle took place about AD 634 at Heavenfield, north of Hexham, near Hadrian's Wall. Adomnán probably wrote the *Life* just before 700.[36]

It is noteworthy that this Roman title could be used then to describe kings in Britain, even though it was nearly 300 years since the Romans had left. Jenny Rowland dates the poem in the range from c. 850 to the late 800s. However John Koch thinks that the poem could have its beginnings in the 700s, as is possibly suggested by Adomnán's use of the 'emperor' descriptor around 700.[37] The emphasis on the slaying of Arthur's men may also suggest a 700s dating, a time before Arthur was portrayed as virtually invincible in the *Historia Brittonum* of 829-830.

The most natural interpretation of the poem is that Arthur was present at the battle and his men were taking heavy losses. If the battle were historical and at Penbryn Beach, then the opponents may have been Irish invaders. If Arthur were not present at the battle, being inserted into the poem to enhance the heroism of Geraint, the reference is similar to that in *Y Gododdin* and *Marwnad Cynddylan*. In either case, this would give another heroic view of Arthur at a relatively early date.[38]

THE HISTORIA BRITTONUM

The Arthurian battle list in the *Historia Brittonum* was discussed in Chapter 2 where it was argued that it was derived from an underlying Welsh poem. This list again places Arthur in an historical setting as a warrior and battle commander. Although it is not explicitly stated that he was a king, he was commander of the armies of a coalition of kings, a role aptly described by the term *ameraudur*. The picture here is consistent with those obtained from *Y Gododdin*, *Marwnad Cynddylan* and *Geraint son of Erbin*.

However, the historical validity of the battles has been attacked. One line of criticism is that battle lists appearing in early Welsh poetry were simply a haphazard collection of famous battles that were recycled among the heroes of the Britons. Rachel Bromwich suggests that this applied to the Dark Age heroes in general, not just to Arthur: 'that names of famous battles became transferred from one hero to another in early bardic poetry'. This idea also occurs in the works of several other authors.[39]

Peter Field has exposed the flimsiness of the case for this proposition.[40] If this were true it would indicate that the composition of such poems was not contemporaneous with the kings being honoured, as a bard is hardly going to sing to his king about haphazard battles that the king did not fight. Moreover, it would imply that the poems had to be composed many years after the king's lifetime, well beyond the memories of the king's offspring and retinue. It could also imply that the *Book of Taliesin* battle-listing poems dedicated to Cynan, Urien and Gwallawg (thought by Ifor Williams to be composed by the historical Taliesin) were created many years after their deaths and were not composed by Taliesin.

An analysis of Arthur's battles casts doubt on the hypothesis that they are all a haphazard collection of famous battles. The four battles in Lincoln are very plausible ones, at a place where one would expect Arthur to have fought with the Angles. There is no account of any other British king fighting the Angles in this location whose battles could have been transferred to Arthur. It is also doubtful that a poet could shift the very famous battle of Badon to Arthur if the victor were someone else. The battle at the river Tribruit is attributed to Arthur in other poetry, suggesting that it really was his battle. The battle at Chester is also a very plausible one for Arthur, given his north Wales location, to be argued in the next chapter. Further, there is consistent literary evidence that Arthur did fight in southwest Scotland which makes a battle there at the Caledonian Forest not implausible.

While the above notion is far from proven, it is possible that some of the battles that are assigned to Arthur may not be his. A bard singing his praises many years after his death may have 'improved' Arthur's exploits by adding other battles. However this is unproven. It is also possible that other battles Arthur fought did not find their way into the battle listing poem. For example, the Llongborth battle where Arthur's men suffered heavy losses is missing. Camlann, the notorious battle where he was killed, is also missing from the list. Probably the most important point to be derived from the battle list is the picture painted of Arthur – that he was a peerless battle leader who had command of the armies of a coalition of kings. It is this picture that generated the poem underlying the battle list, a poem that preceded the compilation of the *Historia Brittonum*.

THE ANNALES CAMBRIAE

There is a further Arthurian source that has been commonly used to justify Arthur's historicity. As noted in Chapter 2, Arthur is mentioned in two entries in the *Annales Cambriae*. These are his victory at the battle of Badon hill in 516/518 and his death with Medraut at Camlann in 537/539. However most scholars now believe that the Badon entry in the *Annales* is not independent of the battle list in the *Historia Brittonum*.

It is also possible that the Badon entry could have been added to the *Annales* up to 400 years after Arthur's reputed death date. Apart from the 516/518 date, the *Annales* give no other useful detail additional to that of the *Historia*. The second entry concerning Arthur's death at Camlann used to be regarded by scholars as important evidence for Arthur's historicity, but now tends to be regarded sceptically. These references will be considered in more detail below.

The Arthurian Entries
The entries below are in Latin, followed by an English translation.[41]

516/518
Bellum Badonis in quo Arthur portauit crucem Domini Nostri Iesu Christi tribus diebus et tribus noctibus in humeros suos et Brittones uictores fuerunt.

The Battle of Badon in which Arthur carried the cross of our Lord Jesus Christ for three days and three nights on his shoulders and the Britons were the victors.

537/539
Gueith Cam lann in qua Arthur et Medraut corruerunt.

The Battle of Camlann in which Arthur and Medraut fell.

Current View of the Arthurian Annales Entries
In the 516/518 entry, there is an obvious embellishment concerning Arthur carrying a cross for three days and three nights which may have been added much later to modify the original entry. Initially it was thought by Leslie Alcock that the original entries had been recorded year by year in Easter Annals so that they were contemporaneous with events.[42] However Kathleen Hughes has convincingly argued that the *Annales* were based on a Welsh chronicle, starting in the year 796, and kept at St Davids in southwest Wales. To this chronicle, two additional sources were added to extend the chronicle entries back before 796: a set of Irish annals that ran from 453 to 613 and a northern British source that began in 624. The Arthurian entries mentioned above were not in any of these three sources. It would appear that at some time after 796, the Irish and north British sources were added to the Welsh chronicle to give the complete annal list and it is thought that this is when the Arthurian (and the other British entries) may have been added. It is quite possible that this compilation (and hence the Arthurian entries) could be late, perhaps as late as the mid-tenth century.[43]

The 'Shield' and 'Shoulder' Confusion
Both the *Historia Brittonum* and *Annales Cambriae* refer to Arthur carrying an object on his shoulders into battle. In the *Historia* the object is an image of the Virgin Mary but in the *Annales* it is a cross. Carrying an object on the shoulders into battle seems unlikely in both cases. It was argued long ago that *scuid* 'shoulder' had incorrectly replaced *scuit* 'shield', suggesting that the references were to an image on Arthur's shield.[44]

Images on shields were used in the Roman armies and may have been adopted by the Romanised Britons. The *Diptych of Stilicho* is an ivory carving retained in the treasury of Monza Cathedral that shows the Roman general, Stilicho, posing with his wife and child. On Stilicho's shield is a cartouche which shows two figures of slightly differing heights, probably the Emperor Theodosius I and his empress, dating to the late fourth century. In addition, an illustrated muster roll of late Roman army units, the *Notitia Dignitatum*, shows a variety of images on shields.[45] If *scuid* did replace *scuit*, it is unlikely that the same mistake should have happened twice, suggesting that the two accounts were not independent. That is, one account was derived from the other or both were derived from a previous account where the mistake was made. This confusion will be discussed below.

Historia: Mary's image on Arthur's shoulders at Guinnion fort
In the *Historia*, Arthur carries an image of the Virgin Mary on his shoulders at *Castell Guinnion*. As noted earlier, if the image were on a shield (*scuit*), this would give a rhyme with the battle at *Tribruit*. Secondly, any such image was probably not of the Virgin Mary. The veneration of Mary was probably not practised, or was rare, in the Welsh Christianity of the early sixth century according to Richard Barber.[46] Geoffrey Ashe claims that the veneration of Mary was practised in Italy at an early stage and also makes a case for one possible instance in Dumnonia, but he considers this to be rare or possibly unique.[47] If the image on the shield were not of Mary, it was probably a cross. The Christian Emperor, Constantine, bore a cross on his shield so it is not implausible that the Christian Arthur also did so.

Annales Cambriae: Cross on Arthur's shoulders at Badon
In the *Annales* reference to Badon, Arthur carries a cross on his shoulders for three days and three nights. This could parallel the story of the Saxon king Oswald, about a century after Arthur's time, who held a wooden cross upright on the battlefield at Heavenfield while his men heaped earth around it (Bede's *Ecclesiastical History*, Bk.3, Ch.2). However setting up a cross on the battlefield is quite different to carrying a cross on the shoulders for the battle's duration. An explanation of the origin of this improbable scenario is given in the next section.

Explanation of the 'Shield/Shoulder' Confusion
The explanation below gives primacy to the battle-listing poem underlying the *Historia* account. At the fortress of Guinnion, the poem referred to a cross on Arthur's shield (*scuit*), which gave a rhyme with the battle at *Tribruit*. At a second stage in transmission, from a written source, *scuit* (shield) was then misread as *scuid* (shoulders) which created the scenario of Arthur carrying the cross on his shoulders at fortress Guinnion. At a third stage, a pious monk who venerated Mary may have replaced the cross by an image of the Virgin Mary, and added a lengthy elaboration to produce the final version given in the *Historia* battle list.

The *Annales* account may derive from the *second stage* above – with the cross on Arthur's shoulders at the fortress of Guinnion. Later, an *Annales* compiler transferred the image of Arthur's carrying the cross to the more famous battle, Badon. Thus the Badon reference in the *Annales Cambriae* can now be explained as a derivation from the *Historia Brittonum* battle list. Under this argument, the *Annales* reference adds nothing to our knowledge of Badon beyond the date given for the battle.

Note that this does not disprove the idea that Arthur may have been listed as the victor of Badon in early material. It is conceivable that such material from an early record was merged at a later stage with the 'shoulder' material above which resulted in its final elaborated form in the *Annales*. Maglocunus, a contemporary of Arthur, was associated with the Degannwy hillfort only 3 miles from Dinarth. He is listed in the *Annales* as dying in 547/9 of the plague, called the Yellow Pestilence in the *Life of St Teilo*. If one accepts that accurate material for Maglocunus survived to appear in the *Annales*, then one should admit the possibility that the Arthurian reference could have been based on similar early material that was later elaborated with the 'shoulder' confusion.

Arthur and Medraut dying at Camlann

The second reference in the *Annales Cambriae* lists Arthur and Medraut as dying at Camlann, which means 'crooked river bank'. Unfortunately, there is no early supporting evidence for this. Other late Welsh references to Medraut present him as a paragon of virtue so he could have been on Arthur's side rather than Arthur's opponent. Perceptions of Medraut have been heavily distorted by Geoffrey of Monmouth's pseudo-history in which he invents a role for Medraut as Arthur's treacherous nephew who seized the crown and lived in adultery with Guinevere. Given Geoffrey's tendency to literary fiction, one would be entitled to completely ignore this fanciful scenario. If Arthur did die at Camlann, then it has been argued previously that the 'crooked bank' where Arthur died was at one of the rivers in Hopewell territory in eastern North America, perhaps along the Ohio or Scioto rivers.

This *Annales* reference gives Arthur's death date as 537/539, which is close to the time of Gildas writing *The Ruin of Britain*. Without relying on the *Annales* date, it has been argued that Arthur died in America and the few survivors of Arthur's expedition arrived back in Britain not long after the publication of Gildas' book at about 540. This argument is independent of the *Annales* date for Arthur's death, but it gives a similar answer.

SUMMARY OF THE TRADITIONAL EVIDENCE

The evidence considered in this chapter suggests that Arthur had a massive reputation as a military commander at a time not inconsistent with the dates ascribed to him in the *Annales Cambriae*. The apparent naming of people after Arthur (a name that was 'practically unknown' previously) is important as it circumvents the doubts raised concerning written documents that any Arthurian reference could be a late interpolation. This naming occurs at just the right time for it to be based on a famous historical figure from the early sixth century. The evidence discussed for Arthur's historicity is given below in chronological order. The dates given are very approximate and are based on the arguments given in the text.

Circa 550 'though he was not Arthur' in Y Gododdin
It has been argued that the Arthurian stanza (B2.38) shares four distinctive stylistic features with another *Y Gododdin* stanza (B2.28), which honours the hero Yrfai, and was therefore composed by the same poet. The Yrfai stanza appears to be sixth century due to its content, suggesting that the Arthurian stanza was also sixth century. The latter honours Gorddur, a great warrior, though he was not Arthur. It implies that Arthur was revered as a military figure, the benchmark to whom others could aspire.

Circa 560-600 Four Men Named after Arthur
Approximately two decades after Arthur's death, the first person named after Arthur was born c. 560: Artur the son of Aedán of Dalriada. This was followed by Arthur son of Petr, Artuir son of Bicoir and Artur grandfather of Feradach from about 560 to 600. Three of these Arthurs were associated with what is now southwest Scotland which, combined with the Edinburgh reference in *Y Gododdin*, implies that Arthur fought in the north. This is supported by references to a region called Rheon in *Kadeir Teÿrnon* and Pen Rhionydd in Triad 1 of the Welsh Triads, which was probably the Loch Ryan area of southwest Scotland where Arthur fought.

Circa 655 Arthur in Marwnad Cynddylan
In 655 a battle took place in Winwaed, near modern Leeds. The forces of Penda (the Mercian king) and Cynddylan (who was supporting him) were defeated by those of Oswiu of Northumbria. It appears that shortly after the battle, a poem was composed to commemorate the death of Cynddylan. His bard refers to the defeated warriors as his 'brothers-in-arms' and refers to them as descendants of stout Arthur (descendants in the sense of being brave warriors, like Arthur's men). Arthur is described as 'a mighty fortress'. This reference is very similar to that of *Y Gododdin*, remembering Arthur for his valour as a warrior.

Circa 750-800 Arthur in Geraint son of Erbin
A natural interpretation of this poem has Arthur directing the toil of battle at Llongborth alongside Geraint and his men, while sustaining heavy losses. Arthur is described as 'emperor', a title used elsewhere in a seventh-century context. Adomnán in his *Life of Columba* referred to Oswald as 'emperor' when he defeated Cadwallon at Heavenfield. Adomnán's *Life* was written in the late 600s. This weighty title is not to be equated with that of the Roman emperors but it gives a view of Arthur as a military commander who was in charge of a coalition of British armies, a role which is explicitly stated in the *Historia Brittonum*.

829-30 Arthur in the Historia Brittonum

This battle list, presumably based on a poem in Welsh, gives a list of battles purportedly all won by Arthur. Even if one adopts a sceptical view that the battles may not all be Arthur's, the existence of the poem implies a heroic view of Arthur before the compilation of the *Historia Brittonum*. This view is totally consistent with that expressed in all the texts above – that Arthur was a peerless warrior and supreme military commander.

The two references to Arthur in the *Annales Cambriae* are not given here as their inclusion in that document may have occurred at quite a late stage. Further, one reference appears to be not independent of the *Historia* while the other is not corroborated by any independent sources. Nevertheless, the sources which are given above are quite consistent in depicting Arthur as a renowned warrior and battle commander.

As indicated in Chapter 1, by the time of the *Historia Brittonum* legends about Arthur were developing, as shown by the two marvels appearing in the *Mirabilia* of the *Historia*. Similarly, legends were accruing about Ambrosius, the Romano-British gentleman whom Gildas greatly respected. The *Historia* depicts Ambrosius, the military commander, as a boy wizard, born of a virgin mother, who confounded the magicians of Vortigern and prophesied that the Britons would eventually drive out the Anglo-Saxons. Geoffrey of Monmouth later adapted this tale from the *Historia* and transformed Ambrosius into the fictional Merlin. The totality of the evidence reviewed above indicates that it is far more probable that Arthur was a historical figure who later developed legendary aspects, rather than a myth, legendary figure, folkloric figure or Celtic god who later became historicized.

12
WHO WAS ARTHUR?

AN OVERKING IN GILDAS

Introduction

This chapter will seek to determine where Arthur fits into the sixth-century context – who he was, his geographical location and his general sphere of activities. The various 'solutions' offered for these very difficult problems have resulted in a wide range of different localities across Britain.[1] There have also been efforts to identify Arthur with known historical figures but none of these have received general acceptance.[2] In this chapter a tentative attempt will be made to investigate these issues.

This analysis will be based primarily on *The Ruin of Britain* by Gildas and the two sixth-century Welsh poems *Preideu Annwfyn* and *Kadeir Teÿrnon*. It will be argued that there is information in Gildas that has not been entirely understood, that implies an unnamed overking in the background who is a good fit for Arthur. Gildas states that the five sinful kings he is criticising are part of the retinue of a Pharaoh, where he is using a metaphor from the Old Testament story of the Exodus.

Further, the two Welsh poems indicate that Arthur's home territory was in north Wales. In particular, he appears to have had a centre of power at the Dinarth hillfort in Colwyn Bay, east of Llandudno. This in turn leads to an identification of Arthur's woodland region in Kernyw and, in the following chapter, a possible identification of Arthur's bard.

Moreover, it will be argued that Arthur was a seafarer who must have spent considerable time in in southwest Scotland, around Loch Ryan. A home territory in north Wales would have allowed him to readily sail to the Isle of Man, the Solway Firth and harbours in Galloway, and allow him to control the waters between Britain and Ireland. The theories put forward here are speculative, but it is worthwhile to make the attempt so that their merits can be evaluated.

A number of references in *The Ruin of Britain* point to a figure fitting the role attributed to Arthur in Welsh tradition. They suggest the existence of an overking with whom Gildas was familiar, but to whom his animosity was evident. He refers to this figure using two terms, 'the Bear' and 'Pharaoh'. As will be shown below, the embittered Gildas suppressed the names of certain military men, including the powerful British king, Vortigern. 'The Bear' is *Arth* in the Britons' sixth-century Neo-Brittonic language. It was suggested as a possible reference to Arthur in the scholarly literature by Alan Anderson in the early twentieth century and more recently by Bernard Bachrach. 'The Bear' was also argued to be Arthur by Graham Phillips and Martin Keatman in the popular literature.[3]

Gildas' Suppression of Names

In *The Age of Arthur*, historian John Morris comments on how few Britons were actually named by Gildas. For the fifth century, the best manuscript of *The Ruin of Britain* refers to only the the Romano-Briton, Ambrosius, whom Gildas greatly admired. Gildas provides considerable detail that praises the aristocratic Roman family background of Ambrosius, seemingly to highlight these characteristics against those of the sinful Britons.[4]

In contrast, Gildas suppresses the name of the overking called Vortigern who had invited Saxon mercenaries to come to Britain. The great scholar, Theodor Mommsen, thought that the best manuscript was that written at St Augustine's, Canterbury in the 900s (Cotton MS Vitellius A. vi, BL). In this manuscript Vortigern is never mentioned by name. Gildas refers to him on three occasions, but each time speaking in code. The first time he calls him 'arrogant tyrant'. In the second, Gildas calls him 'Pharaoh', after the Pharaoh whose chariot drivers were destroyed by the returning waves in the Exodus from Egypt. In the third, he calls him 'ill-fated tyrant'. However Vortigern's identity is hardly in doubt as Bede later calls him *Uertigernus*, an old form of the name, in 725 and *Uurtigern(us)*, a primitive Old English form, in 731. His name is also given in later manuscripts of *The Ruin of Britain*, the Avranches and Cambridge manuscripts.[5]

Given the notoriety of Vortigern, it is quite certain that Gildas knew his name. Why would Gildas not name him? He answers this in Section 27 in which he refers to the bloody military men 'who should have been rooted out vigorously, name and all': he hated the military so much that he wanted all their names to be obliterated.[6] The Saxon priest, Bede, appears to have approved of Gildas' statement as he also adopted this attitude regarding evil kings. He remarks: 'the name and memory of those apostates ought to be utterly blotted out from the list of Christian kings and that no year should be assigned to their reign'.[7] This issue will be discussed later in this chapter where it is argued that Gildas was a very embittered man because his brother Huail had been executed by Arthur.

Cuneglasus and 'The Bear'

Cuneglasus is one of five kings whom Gildas berates. In Section 32, Gildas addresses him as '(you) bear' and describes him as 'driver of the chariot of the Bear's Stronghold', as given by Michael Winterbottom.[8] It is extremely doubtful that the Bear's Stronghold was named after a group of animals, real bears, who had lived there.

Rather, it seems to refer to a powerful military figure as Winterbottom's punctuation appears to indicate. This prompts the questions: Who was 'the Bear'? Where was his 'Stronghold'? The obvious candidate for the Bear is Arthur, given that 'Bear' in Neo-Brittonic (the language of the Britons at the time of Gildas and Arthur) was *Arth*, as shown by John Koch.[9] It would seem that Gildas was continuing his trend of punning on kings' names and relating them to animals.

This observation about the aptness of the pun is not intended to explain the etymology of the name Arthur – it may have been ultimately derived from the rare Latin name *Artorius*, which would become 'Arthur' when it was adopted into Welsh.[10] The key concept here is the 'Bear's Stronghold', written in Latin by Gildas as *receptaculi ursi* using the genitive singular for 'Bear'. It is this reference that enables Gildas to refer to Cuneglasus as '(you) bear' as the meaning of Cuneglasus has simply no relationship to 'bear' and there is nothing else that connects him to a bear. As noted earlier, Gildas produced a contrived translation that enabled him to render Cuneglasus' name as 'red butcher', although a more straightforward translation would give 'blue (or grey) hound'.

'The Bear' and 'Pharaoh'
Cuneglasus is 'driver of the chariot of the Bear's Stronghold' but given that chariot usage in warfare had long ceased by the sixth century, what can it mean? Here Gildas is using Biblical imagery of the Pharaoh's men driving their chariots to destruction in the Red Sea, an event he refers to repeatedly (Sections 1.3, 11.1, 23.2 and 37.2). Cuneglasus is being likened to one of the Pharaoh's chariot drivers. He is subordinate to a powerful figure called 'the Bear'. In Section 37, Gildas then makes this subordinate role explicit when he describes Cuneglasus and the other kings as being part of the retinue of a Pharaoh, but through their sinful behaviour contributing to the ruin of the Pharaoh's kingdom.[11] Thus Cuneglasus is subordinate to 'the Bear' (Section 32) and also subordinate to 'Pharaoh' (Section 37). This suggests that 'the Bear' and 'Pharaoh' were the same person, an overking above the five kings. Gildas is here treating Arthur the same way he treated Vortigern – speaking in code. He refers to Vortigern as 'arrogant tyrant' and 'Pharaoh' and Arthur as 'the Bear' and 'Pharaoh'.

Apart from the chariot driver imagery, the language of Gildas suggests that 'the Bear' was a distinct person to Cuneglasus. In referring to the latter as '(you) bear' and as 'driver of the chariot of the Bear's Stronghold', Gildas is indicating two 'bears'. He refers to Cuneglasus in the second person with '(you) bear', and then refers to 'the Bear's Stronghold' in the third person. If Gildas had meant only one 'bear' this would be a jarring and misleading use of language, something a scholar of his learning and mastery of Latin would be unlikely to make. Michael Lapidge comments on the high level of polish and sophistication of his Latin.[12] If he did intend only one bear, it would have been easy for Gildas to have said 'driver of the chariot of *your* stronghold' or some similar expression.

The result of combining both the imagery of the Pharaoh's subordinate chariot driver and Gildas' use of the second and third persons implies that 'the Bear' was someone distinct from and superior to Cuneglasus. It seems that Cuneglasus had a major role in leading the warriors under 'the Bear'. He is described as making war against men with arms 'special to himself', the meaning of which is unknown, but it does reveal his prowess in warfare and probably contributed to Arthur's great military reputation. Gildas translates Cuneglasus' name as 'red butcher', remarkably similar to the Welsh Triads' reference to Arthur as 'red reaper.'[13]

The Bear's location

The 'Bear's Stronghold' is probably the Bryn Euryn hillfort at Llandrillo-yn-Rhos.[14] From this imposing site, wide-ranging views are found, which would have given an early warning of approaching threats. Kenneth Jackson argues that 'Bear's Stronghold' was equivalent to *Din Eirth* in the British language which had retained the genitive case. In the 1200s, *Dineirth* was the name of the township coterminous with Llandrillo-yn-Rhos. It later became Dinarth in Modern Welsh and was called this until around 1875 according to David Longley and Lloyd Laing.[15] The Bryn Euryn name has been used since the late 19th century. In this book, the older Dinarth name is used as it reflects the meaning in Gildas – 'stronghold of the Bear'.

A King More Powerful than Maglocunus

It is evident that Gildas regards Maglocunus as the most powerful of the five kings that he lambasts. He remarks of Constantine that he knows that he is still alive, hardly an endorsement of power. He remarks of Vortipor that the end of his life is gradually drawing near. Aurelius 'Caninus' is still relatively young, but has lost all his family in plundering raids and Gildas doubts that he will live too much longer. Cuneglasus is a brutal butcher who could be a rival for his first cousin, Maglocunus. However it is only to Maglocunus that Gildas applies the statement that he is driving kings (of unspecified identity) from their lands and killing them to achieve his ends.

Gildas provides further support for a powerful figure such as 'the Bear' with some fascinating comments when he addresses Maglocunus. Given the power of Maglocunus, it is surprising that Gildas twice implies that he is not the most powerful British king at that time. In Hugh Williams' translation, Gildas describes Maglocunus as follows:[16]

- 'exceeding many in power'
- 'superior to almost all the kings of Britain, both in kingdom and in the form of thy stature'

The above points indicate that there was a British king more powerful than Maglocunus, a conclusion also reached by Kenneth Dark, who remarks that Gildas was 'implying the existence of a 'greater king' in Britain'.[17] He would certainly not have included Saxon leaders in this comparison. There has been no identification of any other contemporary British king who was thought to be more powerful than Maglocunus. Welsh tradition produces only the one candidate – Arthur. As will be suggested by the argument below, it is probable that this king was located in one of the areas that Gildas knew best, Wales and the Devon/Cornwall peninsula.

The Probable Limits of Gildas' knowledge

From Gregory of Tours' account of near contemporary Frankish kings, the latter were not dissimilar to the five British kings in their sexual behaviour, murders and intrigues, as shown in Lewis Thorpe's translation.[18] While the sins of the five British kings are horrific by our modern standards, it would be implausible to assume that these kings were any more wicked than the worst of the British kings in the north of Britain or elsewhere. Unpalatable as they may seem, many of the murders were attempts to secure the throne through the 'elimination of collaterals': the political assassination of family members having a claim on the kingship.[19]

In Section 14 of *The Ruin of Britain*, Gildas refers to the Picts as being in the north of Britain while in Section 21 he mentions the Picts as being in the far end of the island. Given that the Saxons largely controlled the east, these two statements suggest that Gildas was based in the southwest. This conclusion is supported by the fact that he supplies extensive personal data on the five kings from this region. In Section 31, Gildas also mentions that Vortipor's hair was already whitening, which suggests that he had recently seen him, probably in Demetia in southwest Wales. It would seem that Gildas' indepth knowledge of the kings was restricted to the southwest of Britain.

If it can be assumed that the five kings were no worse than the kings in other areas of Britain, it would suggest that Gildas selected them because they were noteworthy in the circumscribed area about which he knew. That is, he had in depth information about the kings in Wales and from across the Bristol Channel in Devon and Cornwall but appeared to know little about kings in the north of Britain and other areas. If this were so, then it appears that there was at least one king in this area known to Gildas who was more powerful than Maglocunus.

The Pharaohs

Vortigern as Pharaoh

In *The Ruin of Britain* Gildas refers to an overking, identified as Vortigern by Bede, who foolishly invited the Saxon mercenaries to come to Britain in the fifth century. Using a metaphor from the account of the Exodus in the Old Testament, Gildas refers to the overking as 'Pharaoh', and he describes the advisers of Vortigern as follows:[20]

> Foolish princes of Zoan, as it is said, giving unwise counsel to Pharaoh.

The sixth-century Pharaoh

In Section 37 Gildas surprises the reader by using the Pharaoh metaphor again. He refers to the five wicked kings he has just denounced and implies that there is an overking above them whom he calls 'Pharaoh'. These five kings are shown in a subordinate role to the overking but their appalling behaviour and brutality are destroying his kingdom. They are likened to five mad chariot horses that are pulling the Pharaoh's army to destruction into the Red Sea. In the Michael Winterbottom translation:[21]

> ...these five mad and debauched horses from the retinue of Pharaoh which actively lure his army to its ruin in the Red Sea...

The obvious reading here is that there was a 'Pharaoh' or overking above the five kings, an interpretation independently made by Fabio Barbieri and Chris Gidlow.[22] Who was this 'Pharaoh' who had Cuneglasus, Maglocunus and the other three kings as part of his retinue? As Cuneglasus was called the chariot driver of 'the Bear', it seems to indicate that 'the Bear' and 'Pharaoh' were the same overking, a strong military leader who had control of north Wales from his hillfort at Dinarth.

There are also the statements, given in two places, that imply there was at least one king superior even to the powerful Maglocunus. The most plausible location for this powerful king would be in the area which Gildas knew, Wales and Dumnonia. Dinarth is in a strategic position in this area. In Section 56 of the *Historia Brittonum*, Arthur is placed in this role. Arthur fought alongside the kings of Britain but he was the overall commander of the combined forces in their battles.

The Situation at the Time of Gildas' Writing

At the time Gildas was writing *The Ruin of Britain* (c. 540) it would seem that Arthur was overseas in Annwfyn if his death date of 537/539 in the *Annales Cambriae* is approximately correct. He may have already been killed, but the news had not yet reached Britain. If it had, Gildas would quickly have known about it. From the intimate details he gives of the five kings, it is clear that he had a network who kept him very well informed. Arthur's bard describes a dramatic scene in *Preideu Annwfyn* where the lords are informing the monks about Arthur's death and the monks are drawing back in fear, indicating the poisonous relationship between the two groups.

It appears that while Arthur was overseas in Annwfyn, Maglocunus was increasing his power, taking over the lands of other kings and depriving some of their lives (see *The Ruin of Britain*, beginning of Section 33). In the later literature Maglocunus is associated with Degannwy near Llandudno. Gildas makes no reference to Maglocunus occupying Degannwy, but refers to him as the 'island dragon' (*insularis draco*). The island here is unlikely to be Britain as a whole since the Saxons controlled a large part of it. It probably referred to Anglesey, the island off northwest Wales, with its capital at Aberffraw.[23] Later, it seems that Maglocunus moved east from Aberffraw to Degannwy, to the east of the River Conwy, as suggested by Geraint Gruffydd.[24] It is argued here that this occurred after Arthur's death. It is not clear what this move would have meant for Cuneglasus. He may have been one of the kings killed by Maglocunus, or he may have accepted Maglocunus, who was his cousin, as an overlord.

Summary

It is argued above that there are several sections in Gildas which suggest an overking more powerful than Maglocunus. This king apparently resided in the general region from which Gildas obtained most of his information on the kings, probably Wales. The best candidate for this overking would be 'the Bear' who had the brutal Cuneglasus as his 'chariot driver', one of his chief commanders. The fact that 'bear' in the Neo-Brittonic language at the time of Gildas was *Arth* suggests that Arthur was 'the Bear' and that Gildas was thus continuing his trend of punning on names.

GILDAS' HATRED OF THE MILITARY

Gildas made extremely disparaging remarks about the British military men, likening them to women and implying that they were cowards, as discussed in Chapter 9. These remarks are extraordinary as Gildas despairs of their civil wars and plundering raids against their own people. In those endeavours, the military men could hardly be likened to women and cowards. Secondly Gildas, as a cleric, would never have to put his own life on the line in battle, so his hypocrisy is breathtaking.

Further, he appears to derive pleasure from asserting that the Britons' cowardice in war and faithlessness in peace had became a mocking proverb, spread far and wide (*The Ruin of Britain*, Section 6). It is doubtful that such a proverb had ever existed but Gildas obtained malicious satisfaction from making it a part of his account. These remarks suggest that Gildas was a very embittered man.

Arthur and Gildas' Brother, Huail

A possible reason for Gildas' embittered state of mind is that Arthur may have killed Huail, brother of Gildas. The Rhuys *Life of Gildas*, written in Brittany, was probably composed in the 800s, but was based on older traditions. This *Life* relates that Gildas was the son of Caunus, Cau-us, or Caw-us, according to Hugh Williams. In Winterbottom's book, Cauuos is given. In other texts he is known as Caw (in Triad 21 and in *Culhwch and Olwen*) and Cawrnur (in *Kadeir Teÿrnon*).[25]

The *Life* states that Caw was from the district of Arecluta (*Arecluta regio*). The expert Celtic linguist Kenneth Jackson states that the language *Arecluta regio* was archaic and belonged to the sixth century. He points out that such language is of equal value to that in *The Ruin of Britain* as it could only have come from a contemporary manuscript.[26] This suggests that we should take seriously the claim that Gildas was the son of Caw. This *Life* also states that Caw had a son called Cuillum (Welsh variants being Hueil and Huail) who was active in warfare and became king after his father's death.

A later *Life of Gildas* was written by Caradoc of Llancarfan in the twelfth century. In this *Life*, Arthur eventually had Huail captured on the Isle of Man and killed.[27] In the late 1100s, Gerald of Wales in *Description of Wales* (ii, 2) wrote that Gildas had refused to acknowledge Arthur because Arthur had executed his brother.[28] Arthur may have brought Huail to north Wales for beheading as there is a large stone on display in Ruthin, a town in north Wales, that is said to be the stone on which Huail was executed. This area has strong associations with Arthur: only 5 miles north of Ruthin is the hillfort Moel Arthur, part of the Clwydian Range.

In spite of the learned statements of Jackson on the archaic language in the Rhuys *Life*, some scholars are sceptical as to whether Gildas was the son of Caw and brother of Huail. It is not improbable, but these hagiographical tales hardly inspire confidence. They may contain a few grains of truth and it is possible that Arthur's killing of Huail was one of them. If Arthur did kill Gildas' brother, it could explain Gildas' hatred of the British military, and in particular, his hatred of Arthur. If the above *Lives of Gildas* are discounted entirely it leaves the extravagant comments of Gildas, that liken the military to women and cowards (despite their brutal civil wars), as totally lacking an explanation.

The Military Men: '...and their names forgotten'

In Section 27 of *The Ruin of Britain*, Gildas provides an introduction before his denunciation of the five kings. There, he refers to wicked tyrants exalting their military companions, who were bloody, murderous, proud, adulterers and enemies of God. Gildas states that rather than being exalted, such foul military men should not only be destroyed but have their names obliterated or forgotten. In the John Giles translation:[29]

> ...enemies of God, who ought to be utterly destroyed and their names forgotten.

In the Hugh Williams translation:[30]

> ...enemies of God, if chance so offers, who ought, together with their very name, to be assiduously destroyed.

Here Gildas is expressing his hatred of the military men and appears to be implying that the suppression of their names in *The Ruin of Britain* was a deliberate action on his part. As noted earlier, Bede who followed Gildas, also held this view on suppressing names. This attitude could certainly account for Gildas' failure to name the overking whom he refers to as 'the Bear' and 'Pharaoh', who is argued in this book to be Arthur.

It could also account for his failure to name the victor of the Battle of Badon – it would have been anathema for him to have named Arthur as the victor if Arthur were not only the leading military man but also the killer of his brother. The photos given below were taken in the north Wales town of Ruthin where the stone on which Huail was said to have been beheaded by Arthur stands in the town square.

Stone of Huail at Ruthin (Photos: R. MacCann)

Figure 12.1 Nameplate for the Stone of Huail

Figure 12.2 The stone on which Huail was said to have been beheaded

EVIDENCE FOR A NORTH WALES LOCATION

Dinarth

If Arthur were 'the Bear' of Gildas then his home territory would have been north Wales. He seems to have had a major stronghold at the Dinarth (Bryn Euryn) hillfort at Colwyn Bay, just east of Llandudno. The late tale of Arthur capturing Huail on the Isle of Man and Huail's claimed beheading stone in Ruthin are also consistent with a north Wales location, if these can be trusted. A general north Wales location is also suggested by the two poems *Preideu Annwfyn* and *Kadeir Teÿrnon* as will be argued below.

As can be seen from the photos in Figures 12.3 to 12.7 below, Dinarth was perfectly positioned to give an early warning of seaborne invaders, due to its expansive views along the coastline.

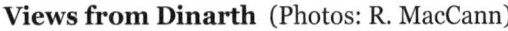
Views from Dinarth (Photos: R. MacCann)

Figure 12.3 Dinarth: looking east

Figure 12.4 Dinarth: looking north

Figure 12.5 Dinarth: looking northwest towards Little Ormes Head

Figure 12.6 Dinarth: looking west; Anglesey and Puffin Island in the distance

Figure 12.7 Dinarth: looking southeast

The Defwy Meadows

Further evidence of a north Wales location comes from *Preideu Annwfyn*. In Line 38 Arthur's bard relates that the inhabitants of Annwfyn did not go to the Defwy Meadows. This suggests that the Defwy Meadows were in the bard's, and hence Arthur's, home territory. The name is pronounced *Devwy*, with the 'f' pronounced as a 'v'. The Roman name for Chester was *Deva*, and this town sits on a major river, the Dee. North Wales has a number of names ending in 'wy', the ending derived from *gwy*, meaning 'a flow' (of water). It appears that the Defwy meadows were the meadows along the Dee. If so, then the bard may be implying from the fact that the Annwfyn people do not visit there, that it was the place from which the expedition was launched, from the mouth of the River Dee.

Support for this translation comes from the poem *Yspeil Taliessin* (Spoils of Taliesin) thought to be sixth century by Ifor Williams. In this poem John Koch tentatively translates *Deuwy* as 'Dee' in the line 'It is very pleasing at the Dee as the war-band arrives'.[31] Another name for the Dee appears in the Harleian 3859 manuscript, on the lands held in Wales by the sons of Cunedda Wledig. There, a Latin note refers to the river Dee as *Dubr Duiu*, or in Welsh *Dyfrdwy* ('water of the Dee'), a name used today. But this is centuries later than the *Preideu Annwfyn* reference. If the translation of Koch is correct then the *Preideu Annwfyn* translation should also be rendered 'Dee'. This would link Arthur to the River Dee, which passes through Llyn Tegid (Bala Lake) and flows approximately east and then north through Chester to the Dee estuary. Llyn Tegid was the site of the Roman fort, later called *Caer Gai*, which was linked by legend to Cai, Arthur's supposed foster brother, who features in the late Welsh poem *Pa Gûr* and later became the Sir Kay in the Arthurian romances.

The 'Lorica of Lleon'

In *Kadeir Teÿrnon* (Chair of the Sovereign) there is a section that refers to a beloved king with a fiery nature, whose men were bereft at his death. He wore the lorica (breastplate) of Lleon. It has been argued in Chapter 8 that this king was Arthur and that the title of the poem refers to Arthur's vacant throne after his death in Annwfyn. If Arthur wore the lorica of Lleon then he would be linked with northeast Wales. Lleon (which refers to a Roman legion) could be the town Caer Lleon, which was Chester itself, or it could also refer to the general area of northeast Wales of which Chester was a part, as discussed by Marged Haycock.

Caerleon in southeast Wales (also a Roman legion city) was sometimes confused with Chester and was often distinguished from the latter by calling it Caerleon-on-Usk to denote the river on which it was located. It is possible that Geoffrey of Monmouth made this mistake in basing Arthur at Caerleon-on-Usk in his pseudo-history, possibly suggesting a familiarity with *Kadeir Teÿrnon*. Haycock indicates that later court poets used the term Lleon as a touchstone of valour.[32]

The Battle at Chester

Another link to north Wales is Arthur's battle at Chester from the *Historia* battle list. The Chester location is one of the most probable identifications in the list according to Kenneth Jackson.[33] If Arthur were based in north Wales then a battle at Chester would not be implausible, but this battle has been doubted by several scholars as no Anglo-Saxons were settled there in Arthur's time. Thus it has been argued that a much later battle, the Battle of Chester in circa 613-615, has been attributed to Arthur.[34] This is quite implausible, even bizarre, as this battle was about 100 years after Arthur's time and was infamous as a defeat for the Britons, not a victory. Solomon, son of Cynan, (presumably the British king) was killed at the battle. It became notorious for the slaughter of 1200 unarmed monks who were praying for the Britons and were massacred by the forces of Aethelfrith. In 731, Bede vividly related the incident in his *Ecclesiastical History* (Book 2, Chapter 2).

Although the Anglo-Saxons were not settled near Chester in Arthur's time, Gildas describes them as raiding from the east coast until they reached the sea at the west coast and that all the *coloniae* (main cities) were destroyed. David Dumville observes for the case of Chester, York and London that 'it is by no means incredible that these are what Gildas meant'.[35] It is thus quite conceivable that Arthur could have had a battle at Chester against a raiding party of Saxons.

Further, it is quite unnecessary to assume that the battle was against the Saxons. It may have been a plundering raid from another British chieftain, the sort of raid to which Gildas attests. It could even have been an attack from the Irish raiders, sailing into the mouth of the Dee. The *Historia Brittonum* of 829-30 indicates that the Irish had previously been in north Wales before being subjugated by Cunedda and his sons.

The Location of Garwen and her father Hennin

Two pieces of obscure data support the view that Arthur was 'the Bear' of Dinarth. The first piece comes from the Welsh Triads, in which Triad 57 lists Arthur's three mistresses, one being Garwen the daughter of Hennin.[36] The second is that data on where Garwen and Hennin were buried is preserved in the *Stanzas of the Graves* from the *Black Book of Carmarthen*, as translated and discussed by Thomas Jones. In Stanza 70, the burial places of the major north Wales figures are listed. These include Garwen, who was buried on the morfa. This is the long beach at Llandudno called the *Morfa Rhianedd* (Seastrand of the Maidens), that stretches between the Great and Little Orme headlands.[37] This beach is close to Dinarth.

The family of Maglocunus (Maelgwn Gwynedd) were also buried there – his wife, Sanant, and son, Rhun. Sanant is listed as his wife in the *De Situ Brecheniauc* genealogies.[38] If Maelgwn did move to Degannwy after Arthur's death then the burial of Sanant and Rhun nearby makes perfect sense. That Arthur's mistress, Garwen, was buried so close to Dinarth is consistent with Arthur being 'the Bear' of Dinarth.

Further, Garwen's father, Hennin, was buried only 9 miles to the east of Dinarth at the Dinorben hillfort, as recorded in Stanza 71. Thomas Jones has argued that his grave may be the cromlech noted by Willoughby Gardner when he surveyed Dinorben between 1912 and 1922. The Dinorben hillfort will be further discussed later in this chapter.[39]

A Possible Location for Arthur's Kernyw

In the pre-Galfridian Welsh literature, Arthur is associated with a place called Celliwig, Gelliwig or Kelli Wic, which was in the region of Kernyw. This place appears in Triad 1 of the Welsh Triads, and briefly in the Welsh poem *Pa Gûr*, and also five times in *Culhwch and Olwen*, a Welsh prose story.[40] Celliwig means 'woodland, forest' according to Rachel Bromwich or 'forest grove' according to Oliver Padel.[41] It suggests that Arthur enjoyed living for periods in a woodland setting where he could hunt and fish with the trusted members of his retinue.

The second placename, Kernyw, is usually translated as Cornwall, the prominent peninsula in southwest Britain. Did this specific identity hold in the sixth century? Gildas, writing circa 540, addressed king Constantine who was probably located in Cornwall, perhaps at the major sixth-century centre of Tintagel. However, Gildas did not employ the term Kernyw but instead used Dumnonia (which he seemingly punned as 'Damnonia') to refer to the entire Devon/Cornwall peninsula. Thus, it is not clear whether Kernyw was used in Arthur's time to refer to what is currently Cornwall.

A Kernyw near Dinarth

If Arthur were 'the Bear' of Dinarth, then one would ideally expect to find Kernyw or Celliwig in the near vicinity. Thus it is of considerable interest that the placename Kernyw is preserved in the name of the village of Llangernyw, located about 8 miles inland (as the crow flies) from the hillfort at Dinarth. The name Llangernyw consists of the two elements 'Llan' meaning 'sacred enclosure' (for a religious centre) and the placename, Kernyw.

As for the Gelliwig name, a river called Afon Gell is close by, joining the River Elwy barely a mile north of Llangernyw. There is also a place called Gell nearby, about 2 miles northwest of Llangernyw, which could be a remnant of the Gelliwig name, possibly the shortening of this name over many centuries. However, as there are many wooded places throughout Wales containing Gell in the name, this placename is only significant because of its close location to Llangernyw and Dinarth. It is suggested that Arthur's Gelliwig in Kernyw may have been in the wooded region just inland from the hillfort at Dinarth, where Gildas locates 'the Bear'. To summarise, within an 8 mile span inland from Dinarth, the following placenames are found – Afon Gell (the river), Gell and Llangernyw.

Why does the *kernyw* placename occur at this north Wales site? Scholars have derived this name from an old word in the British language, *corn*, which means 'horn'. The eminent scholar William Watson argued that the ancient

British tribes known as the *Cornovii* were called this because they lived on 'horns' of land; for example, the tribes living in Cornwall and on the Wirrall peninsula.[42] Ptolemy (circa AD 150) linked the Wirrall Cornovii with Deva (Chester). The Llangernyw site does seem to be too far west to be linked with this Cornovii tribe, although it is not impossible.

However perhaps the peninsula that is bounded on the west by Degannwy and on the east by Llandrillo-yn-Rhos was perceived as having two 'horns', the Great Orme and Little Orme, which gave rise to the *kernyw* placename. In the time of Arthur, the *kernyw* name may have been used to refer to the area comprising these 'horns' and a broad region around it, including the area in which Llangernyw is sited.[43]

Arthur's Son by Eleirch

In *Bonedd y Arwyr* (Lineage of the Heroes), Part 2 concerns the children of Iaen. It states that Eleirch the daughter of Iaen was the mother of Cydfan, the son of Arthur.[44] In *Culhwch and Olwen*, the sons of Iaen were said to be 'related to Arthur on his father's side'. This expression is thought by Rachel Bromwich and D. Simon Evans to be derived from the belief that the sons of Iaen were 'in-laws' to Arthur through Eleirch and that it really means 'related to Arthur on *their* father's side'.[45]

The sons of Iaen were also 'men of Caer Dathl'. This fort is mentioned in the *Mabinogi* story, *Math son of Mathonwy*, where there was a court at Caer Dathl in Arfon.[46] Arfon was an old territory in northwest Wales, facing the Menai Strait and Caernarfon Bay, which gave its name to Caernarfon. It is not known whether Eleirch had been a wife of Arthur or another mistress. If Eleirch were located in Arfon with her brothers, it may indicate that Arthur periodically visited the place to see her and his son, Cydfan. This is additional evidence linking Arthur to north Wales and could imply that the territory of Arfon was part of his kingdom.

ARTHUR'S NORTH WALES KINGDOM

It has been argued that Arthur was probably a Christian overking in north Wales, but able to draw on manpower from a wide area when needed. Like most of Wales in the sixth century, north Wales was heavily Christianised. Kenneth Dark provides a brief outline of the evidence for the presence of Christianity in north Wales in the fifth and sixth centuries.[47]

Arthur and his supporters probably controlled the major strategic points in the region. His domain had no Roman villas or towns, except perhaps Chester, which shows evidence of continued occupation, according to Chris Snyder.[48] There were probably agricultural estates, with the high status ones protected by earthen or wooden enclosures. Inside these, the dwellings were built of wood or drystone walls. Lower status farms were unenclosed. Royal and elite families probably reoccupied the hillforts of the region, many of which were constructed during the Iron Age.

North Wales Hillforts

Both Kenneth Dark and David Longley identify the sites of early medieval date that could have had elite settlement.[49] In north Wales, these sites include Bryn Euryn, Degannwy, Pen-y-Corddyn, Dinorben, Bwrdd Arthur and Dinas Emrys. These and a few others argued here to be in Arthur's domain will now be briefly considered.

Dinarth (Bryn Euryn)

Dinarth, 'the fortress of the Bear', was probably a main residence of Arthur. It has been investigated by David Longley and Lloyd Laing. The summit had a citadel which had commanding views in all directions. The approach from the south and southwest is broken by scarps, some precipitous. One such scarp on the south side creates a terrace below the summit citadel. Longley and Laing state that 'the summit defences must once have been substantial and impressive'.[50]

This citadel was safeguarded by its rampart, faced with a huge defensive stone wall that was well-constructed, being built of large quarried limestone blocks. The wall was about 14 degrees from the vertical and underpinned to stabilise the structure on the slope of the hill. Behind the facing blocks were other limestone blocks that were set in a random concentration. Above and behind these, the bulk of the rampart consisted of smaller limestone rubble. The rampart was an impressive 3.7 metres thick. The back of the rampart was also faced with limestone blocks.

It was a 'hierarchically organized' fort according to Lloyd Laing. Such forts had a major central focus, the 'citadel', and outer 'wards' created by sections of walling often joining natural rocky outcrops.[51] The citadel would have been occupied by the king and the high-status members of his retinue. These forts are typically situated on craggy outcrops. The majority of such forts occur in Scotland, with Dunadd and Dundurn being major examples. They do not resemble forts of Iron Age origin. With its extensive views in every direction, steep sides and impressive rampart for the citadel, Dinarth was sited and built to enhance security.[52]

Other important hillforts near the coast

The twin-peaked Degannwy site lies only 3 miles to the west of Dinarth, in a commanding position overlooking the Conwy estuary. Between 1961-66 it was excavated by Leslie Alcock.[53] It was a high-status site where imported Mediterranean pottery of possible sixth-century date was excavated. Welsh tradition links it to Maglocunus, who probably moved there after Arthur's death. Signals from Degannwy were probably visible from Dinarth.

The hillforts of Pen-y-Corddyn and Dinorben were a few miles to the east of Dinarth. The former was originally large, about 24 acres with an annex of 13 acres. It is less than half a mile from the Roman road running west from Chester. Kenneth Dark notes the finds of late Roman coins, a belt buckle, and a brooch dating from the AD 400-700 period.[54]

The Dinorben hillfort has been destroyed by quarrying, but excavation reports on work done from 1912 to 1969 were written by Willoughby Gardner and Hubert Savory. Many Roman coins were found, suggesting it prospered economically. Possible sixth-century items include Anglo-Saxon metalwork and a blue glass bead with white and yellow inset decoration. The fort was originally Bronze Age but seems to have been reoccupied in the sixth century, as indicated by the radiocarbon dating of animal bone. It has an interesting association with Hennin, the father of Garwen.[55]

Bwrdd Arthur (Arthur's Table) is an imposing hillfort of 13 acres on the northeast coast of Anglesey. It faces the Irish Sea with views to the west of Red Wharf Bay, and to the east, Puffin Island and across Conwy Bay to the Great Orme. The remains of walls built from large limestone blocks are still visible. It has not been excavated but Gardner and Savory report finds of brooches, many silver and copper coins, red pottery, rings, keys, buckles and copper clasps. Kenneth Dark classifies it as a probable high-status site, the residence of an elite family.[56]

Inland Hillforts

Dinas Emrys is a high-status hillfort that overlooks the major Snowdonian valley, Nant Gwynant. It provided the setting for the *Historia Brittonum* tale about the boy wizard Ambrosius and the fighting dragons. Dinas Emrys means 'the fort of Ambrosius'. Hubert Savory excavated it between 1954 and 1956. The finds included imported Mediterranean pottery, Phoenician red-slip dishes, gilt ornaments and jewellery. A sixth-century roundel with an inscribed Christian Chi-Rho symbol was also found there.[57]

Another hillfort with links to Arthur is Dinas Brân, 'the fort of Brân', overlooking Llangollen on the River Dee. Brân was the mythological figure modelled on Arthur. Ken Dark notes that the remains of a strong bivallate hillfort predated the medieval castle. Rectangular structures, some terraced into the hilltop, seem to be linked with the hillfort, which may have had a sixth-century occupation.[58] The 'Hill of the Seven Horsemen' (*Bryn Seith Marchawg*) lies only 10 miles to the northwest. One may remember the seven horsemen who were associated with the stewards 'minding the country' while Brân was absent overseas, which paralleled the question of 'who minded the country' while Arthur was overseas.

Steve Blake and Scott Lloyd note Guinevere's links with this area, her name appearing in *Groes Gwenhwyfar* (Guinevere's Cross) near Llangollen, as shown in 1697 by Edward Lhuyd.[59] The question of whether Guinevere was a real person is difficult to resolve. It is unclear whether she was historical or was merely a mythological creation who had become part of the Arthurian legends, there being an Irish counterpart to Guinevere called Findabair from the Ulster tales. This interesting relationship could reflect a borrowing either way or a derivation from a common source.

The eastern side of Arthur's domain contains a string of six hillforts in the Clwydian Range. Of these six, Kenneth Dark identifies three as possibilities for his 'early sites which had an elite occupation' classification: Moel-y-Gaer (Bodfari), Moel Arthur and Foel Fenlli. In addition to Moel Arthur, Arthur has been linked to Foel Fenlli, about 4 miles southeast. In his poetry Bleddyn Fardd, the 13th-century bard, used Arthur's valour when fighting at Foel Fenlli as yet another exemplar – 'like Arthur at Caer Fenlli' (*ual Arthur wrth Gaer Uenlli*).[60]

Speculation on Arthur's Kingdom

Margaret Nieke and Holly Duncan present a model that describes reciprocal relations between people of different social stations. A king could probably offer protection and perhaps livestock in return for labour and agricultural produce. His royal status was partly determined by his capacity to maintain numerous clients and this would be enhanced if his tribute was seen to be collected and consumed.[61] An efficient way of doing this would be to create a series of centres which the king would visit.

David Longley refers to the formalisation of these relationships in the later Welsh law books, where two townships were set aside in each *cwmwd* (commote) for the king's use. One of these, the *maerdref*, contained the land and hamlets of the bond tenants who worked the land. Within the *maerdref*, the *llys* (court) comprised the buildings, eating hall, stables and so on for the king's use. It allowed the king to conduct business, meet with his people, dispense justice and be visibly supported.[62] In the early sixth century this model undoubtedly existed, probably in a simpler form. In this role, Arthur may have visited some of the hillforts noted above and the other centres in north Wales under his direct control.

If Arthur were the unnamed 'Pharaoh' in Gildas' text then the five kings would be expected to give Arthur their support. To maintain such relations he probably visited places under the control of these kings, perhaps Dinas Powys near Cardiff, or Tintagel in Cornwall, outside his normal domain. In these cases, the visits would be aimed at cementing alliances and reciprocal visits with lavish gift giving may have occurred.

If Maglocunus were reigning only in Anglesey in Arthur's lifetime then Arthur's domain may have stretched from Chester in the east to the Menai Strait in the west and possibly the Llŷn peninsula. His southern boundary may have been roughly aligned with the River Dee, from Llyn Tegid east to Dinas Brân and following the Dee to Chester. This is of course speculation based on the use of major rivers as natural boundaries.

If Arthur were a seafarer, as suggested by *Preideu Annwfyn*, he may have berthed his ships along the Dee, near Chester. As mentioned earlier, Chris Snyder notes the evidence suggesting that Chester was still occupied by the Britons in the sixth century, with the port in operation. Geraint Gruffydd also refers to the efficient Roman road system passing through Chester, just south of the major hillfort at Dinorben, and beyond. Using these Roman roads, the west of north Wales would have been easily reached, including Arfon and regions further south.[63]

The Mobility of Dark Age Kings

It can be shown through historical examples that widely distributed battles were fought by Dark Age kings in Britain. Aethelfrith, who murdered the monks at Chester in circa 613-615, was based in far-away Northumbria. Kenneth Jackson discusses the widely distributed battles of the British king Cadwallon: at Priestholm (now Puffin Island off Anglesey), near Doncaster, at York, in Northumbria, and finally dying in battle near Hexham close to Hadrian's Wall.[64] It is not unreasonable to expect that Arthur too fought over widely dispersed areas. He could have fought the Saxons around Lincoln by travelling east from north Wales. If Badon were fought around the eastern Welsh border region, Arthur could have called on men over a wide area to meet at a suitable place before riding to engage with the Saxons. If he were the Pharaoh in Gildas, he may have been able to call on military assistance from kings throughout Wales and even as far as Dumnonia.

However, the notion that Arthur was the king of the whole of Britain is unrealistic. Archaeological evidence shows that the Saxons occupied much of southeast Britain in circa 540. Gildas claims that the Saxon encroachment prevented the Britons from visiting the shrines of St Alban of Verulamium (in Hertfordshire) and Saints Aaron and Julius of the City of the Legion.[65] It is difficult to see how the latter could refer to Chester. If it were Caerleon (on Usk) then it suggests that Britons travelling by land from Somerset, and further south, to Caerleon may have been impeded by Saxon raids. It seems that the Saxons had moved far to the west at the time of Gildas' writing. This encroachment is shown by the distribution of Anglo-Saxon cemeteries in the sixth century. While Arthur may have won key battles against the Saxons (for example, Badon and the Lincoln battles), the notion that he largely cleared the Saxons from the island, from the *Life of St Goeznovius,* seems to have been a later medieval inflation of his achievements.

SPECULATION ON ARTHUR'S FAMILY

In the Vatican recension of the *Historia* doubt is cast upon Arthur's nobility. Although he was the overall battle commander of the armies of the kings of Britain, 'there were many more noble than himself'. The little that is known about his pedigree will be surveyed below.

Uthyr Pendragon

Marwnat Vthyr Pen (The Deathsong of Uthyr the Chief), a poem from the *Book of Taliesin,* suggests that at some point Uthyr Pendragon was seen as Arthur's father. However, the poem appears to contain late elements, ninth century or later, and could have been composed 300 years after Arthur's time.[66] In the late Welsh pedigrees, Arthur appears as the son of Uthyr in Mostyn MS 117, no. 5 and in *Bonedd yr Arwyr* (Lineage of the Heroes), nos. 30a and 30b.[67] The poem is probably earlier than the pedigrees, and pre-Galfridian, but its validity is doubtful. Unfortunately, this information has no historical value, with Uthyr being unable to be currently linked to any dynasty or historical figure.

Eigyr

On the maternal side, Arthur's mother is given as Eigyr in *Bonedd yr Arwyr*. Pedigree 31 shows his mother as Eigyr, the daughter of Gwen, the daughter of Cunedda Wledig, as reproduced by Peter Bartrum. Geoffrey of Monmouth gives her name as Ygerna. She is not named in early Welsh literature, so this evidence is rather tenuous. This pedigree makes Cunedda Wledig the great grandfather of Arthur on his mother's side. The two wicked kings from north Wales named in *The Ruin of Britain*, Cuneglasus and Maglocunus, also have Cunedda Wledig as their great grandfather according to the pedigrees in the Harleian 3859 manuscript.[68] In summary:

Cunedda	→	Gwen	→	Eigyr	→	Arthur
Cunedda	→	Einion Yrth	→	Owain Ddantgwyn	→	Cuneglasus
Cunedda	→	Einion Yrth	→	Cadwallon Llawhir	→	Maglocunus

If all these pedigrees were correct, Arthur would have been a contemporary of Cuneglasus and Maglocunus. This fits well with Arthur's identification as 'the Bear', who had Cuneglasus as his 'chariot driver' in Gildas. It also puts all three persons into the leading family of north Wales. However the Arthur pedigree cannot be trusted. It may have been made up long after Arthur's lifetime to fit Arthur into Cunedda's family. There is also doubt about the other two pedigrees. David Dumville notes that the *Historia Brittonum* gives Cunedda as the *atavus* of Maglocunus which he argues strictly means the fifth ancestor, not the third. However the *Historia* may not be trustworthy here. Further, Geraint Gruffydd argues that there are other instances where such kinship terms are used more loosely.[69]

A Speculative Scenario

The following is one attempt to place Arthur in relation to Cuneglasus and Maglocunus and should be regarded as very tentative. From Gildas, it has been argued that the 'Bear's Stronghold' was a reference to Arthur's hillfort (*Dinarth*) as the 'Bear' (*Arth*) was Gildas' pun on Arthur's name. In addition, Cuneglasus was called the chariot driver of the 'Bear's Stronghold', which suggests a subordinate position, similar to Pharaoh's chariot drivers in the Exodus, an event to which Gildas repeatedly refers. In one metaphor, the five sinful kings whom Gildas castigates are referred to as the 'five mad and debauched horses from the retinue of Pharaoh' which suggests that 'the Bear' and 'Pharaoh' were one, an overking identified with Arthur. Placing Arthur at Dinarth locates him in the cantref of Rhos, a region associated with the lineage of Cuneglasus.[70]

The Vatican recension of the *Historia Brittonum* relates that there were many more noble than Arthur, and given this, it would have been easier for

Arthur to come to power in Rhos if he did have some relationship to the family of Cunedda. As noted above, a late pedigree has him descend from Cunedda via his mother and grandmother.

To explain his rise to power, suppose that Arthur was a minor member of the families connected to Cunedda. Gildas describes Maglocunus killing his uncle, probably Owain Ddantgwyn, and taking his throne while in 'the first years of his youth'. Maglocunus may have been about 16, Arthur in his 20s and Cuneglasus a baby. Maglocunus probably killed any older brothers of Cuneglasus and other main claimants to the throne. Arthur's nondescript bloodlines may have kept him in the background and accepting of the new rule of Maglocunus, while Cuneglasus as a baby was spared.

Maglocunus found the kingship not to his liking and instead vowed to become a monk but there was now a shortage of contenders for the throne as he had killed them all in the coup. By this stage, Arthur's qualities as a 'strong man' with popular support may have become evident, a leader who could ensure stability. Maglocunus, about to become a monk, may have endorsed the Christian Arthur, with Cuneglasus still only a boy. This route to the throne was not uncommon. While one route was through a royal pedigree, another was through popular support. Gildas refers to kings who had been anointed, then killed and replaced with others who were crueller (section 21.4). In his eyes, Arthur was probably one of these 'tyrants'.

Maglocunus then studied to become a monk but developed doubts and eventually abandoned his vows. A catalyst for this may have been the death of his father, Cadwallon Llawhir, ruler of Anglesey and based at Aberffraw. Maglocunus assumed his father's throne and became 'dragon' of that island. Molly Miller suggests a period of c. 534-49 for his reign.[71] Arthur as 'the Bear' may have expanded his domain beyond Rhos while the younger Cuneglasus eventually became a major battle leader under Arthur. When Arthur died in Annwfyn, Cuneglasus took over the throne of Rhos, restoring the royal lineage. Late sources have Maglocunus moving to Degannwy, only 3 miles from Dinarth. This may have resulted in the demise of Cuneglasus or perhaps followed his death. No claim is being made that this is exactly what happened but to suggest what could have happened. The purpose is to show how a minor member of Cunedda's family could have gained power in the framework established by the narrative of Gildas.

THE SUPERSTITION SURROUNDING ARTHUR'S NAME

Several researchers agree that Arthur's name attracted a superstition against its use. Peter Bartrum comments that the name 'Arthur' became extremely rare among Welshmen in Wales. In the sixth century in Wales, it appears in only the Irish pedigree which contains 'Arthur son of Petr' but in no Welsh pedigree. Bartrum could find no occurrences of the name up to the end of the sixteenth century. Henry VII did name his eldest son Arthur, but his son's early death at age 15 may have reinforced the superstition. Oliver Padel also remarks on this absence of the Arthur name amongst Welshmen and suggests the name may have been regarded with exceptional awe, but links it with a folkloric interpretation. Caitlin Green also studies the superstition, adopting a similar line to Padel, and links it to Arthur's journey to the Celtic Otherworld and other mythical events.[72]

Arthur's Death in Annwfyn

It is argued here that the superstition emerged as a result of Arthur's tragic death in Annwfyn. In his lifetime, Arthur had made a huge impression as an invincible warrior, the paragon to whom the other warriors could aspire. His voyage to America was a voyage to a real country with human inhabitants but it may not have been viewed this way after some years had passed. America was a distant, unknown place and the strange inhabitants there, with their extraordinary mounds, must have excited the imaginations of the people who caught snippets of information about the voyage.

How could the great Arthur, who was nearly invincible in Britain, have been killed and his men decimated? Surely his opponents must have been supernatural. So the poem *Preideu Annwfyn*, depicting a historical voyage to a real place, an unknown land, became interpreted as a voyage to a mystical Otherworld, inhabited by supernatural beings who had the power to defeat Arthur. The inhabitants of this Otherworld appear to have been regarded as immortals or fairy-like beings with magical powers, as fairies were associated with earthen mounds.

The mystery that the Britons were unable to retrieve Arthur's body must also have played on the imaginations of the people. Perhaps Arthur was not dead after all. Over the centuries, various interpretations were made of this state of affairs, becoming solidified in the Geoffrey of Monmouth version of Arthur recovering from his wounds in Avalon.

The Environmental Downturn

A second factor may have played a part in the superstition if the death date of Arthur of 537/539 is approximately correct. As discussed in Chapter 7, a major environmental downturn occurred in Britain from about 540 to 545 which was identified by markedly reduced growth rings or no growth rings in the trees sampled.[73] This could have had a major effect on agriculture but its impact is uncertain and may have varied across Britain.

Apart from crop failures, there may have been extreme weather events. The early poem *Kadeir Teÿrnon*, which purports to have been composed by Arthur's bard shortly after his death, refers to powerful winds and flooding of the coastline. This would indicate that the north Wales coast may have been badly affected. Apart from these environmental factors which would have affected the trees, the plague may have arrived. The Justinian Plague (a bubonic plague) probably reached Britain a few years after it appeared in Constantinople in 541. In addition, some parts of Britain suffered from the Yellow Pestilence, a mysterious disease said to have devastated north Wales and killed the great king Maglocunus (Maelgwn Gwynedd). This appears in the *Lives* of St Teilo and St Oudoceus in *The Book of Llandaff*, as translated by William Rees.[74]

If this downturn did significantly affect Wales, then it may have been associated with Arthur's death. At that time, there was a general belief that attributed the prosperity of a country to the personal success of its ruler. Arthur's demise in the Otherworld and the severe environmental downturn may have become linked in the minds of the people, who associated both events with supernatural causes. This may have created the superstition in which Arthur's name was avoided.

Arthur's Absence from the North Wales Pedigrees

Apart from the late pedigree in *Bonedd yr Arwyr*, Arthur does not appear in the north Wales pedigrees. It is quite consistent with the notion that Arthur had a nondescript pedigree or may even have been illegitimate. However a second factor may be relevant – the superstition concerning his mysterious death in the Otherworld and the climatic problems affecting north Wales. Even though he rose to eminence in this region, the superstition against his name probably prevented attempts to capitalise on his fame by constructing pedigree lines that included him.[75]

Later Arthur-like Characters
Teÿrnon Twrf Liant

It appears that the superstition concerning Arthur's name caused him to be represented by other characters in the Welsh literature. Two stories in the *Mabinogi* contain figures that have Arthur-like characteristics. The first tale, *Pwyll Prince of Dyfed*, concerns the father and son combination, Pwyll and Pryderi, associating with the Arthur-like figure of Teÿrnon Twrf Liant. In the *Preideu Annwfyn* poem, Pwyll and Pryderi were two of Arthur's men who sailed with him to Annwfyn, where they reported the capture of Gweir. In *Pwyll Prince of Dyfed* they interact very positively with Teÿrnon Twrf Liant, as shown below in a partial synopsis of the story.

Outline of Pwyll Prince of Dyfed

While hunting in the forest, Pwyll accidentally enters the Otherworld and meets Arawn, the king of Annwfyn. Arawn changes his shape to look like Pwyll, and vice versa, so that each can administer the other's lands. While in Annwfyn, Pwyll kills Arawn's enemy, Hafgan. After a year they swap back to their own territories and become firm friends. Pwyll then becomes known as Pwyll, Head of Annwfyn.[76]

Later in the story Pwyll's wife, Rhiannon, gives birth to a boy who then magically vanishes while she is sleeping. She receives the full blame and is punished by having to carry visitors to the court on her back (an association of Rhiannon with the Celtic horse goddess, Epona). Later, her missing boy magically reappears in the home of the king, Teÿrnon Twrf Liant. He and his wife raise the child, whom they call Gwri Golden-Hair. Teÿrnon had been Pwyll's former overlord and, as the child grows, he notes Gwri's resemblance to Pwyll. They return the boy to Pwyll and there is rejoicing as Rhiannon declares that she has been delivered of her anxiety (*pryder*). So they rename him *Pryderi*. Pwyll is indebted to Teÿrnon and he swears to uphold Teÿrnon's lands, and states that if Pryderi survives, it would be even more fitting for Pryderi to uphold Teÿrnon.

Teÿrnon Twrf Liant modelled on Arthur

This *Mabinogi* story was composed late, about 500-600 years after Arthur's time, where Teÿrnon Twrf Liant appears to be modelled on Arthur. Note that Arthur was also referred to as Teÿrnon in the poem describing the aftermath of his death, *Kadeir Teÿrnon*, as discussed in Chapter 8. Teÿrnon Twrf Liant was described as 'the best man in the world' in *Pwyll Prince of Dyfed*, as translated by Patrick Ford. In comparison, Arthur's men were also called 'the best men in the world' in the *Pa Gûr* poem, as translated by Patrick Sims-Williams. Further, Pwyll was said to have formerly subordinate to Teÿrnon Twrf Liant in *Pwyll Prince of Dyfed*, which was identical to his role as one of Arthur's men in *Preideu Annwfyn*. This loyalty to Teÿrnon Twrf Liant was lavishly reaffirmed at the end of *Pwyll Prince of Dyfed*, as noted above. This seems to be an instance where the superstition on Arthur's name has resulted in Arthurian characteristics being transferred to another character. If this is accepted, then the epithet Twrf Liant may tell us something about how Arthur was remembered. John Rhŷs translates 'Twrf Liant' as 'noise of the waves', a very appropriate epithet if Arthur were remembered as a seafarer.[77]

Brân

Another character based on Arthur is Brân the Blessed (*Bendigeidfran*). His remarkable parallels with Arthur have already been discussed in Chapter 6 in the context of a possible mercy killing and beheading for Arthur in Annwfyn. A further parallel now presents itself, if one is prepared to accept the seafarer epithet as belonging to Arthur. Brân's father is given as Llŷr which is the Welsh form of the word for 'sea', as stated by Patrick Ford.[78] Thus Brân is the son of 'the sea', while Arthur's association with the sea is evident from his epithet, 'noise of the waves'.

EVIDENCE POINTING TO SOUTHWEST SCOTLAND

It is argued below that much of Arthur's great reputation may have been forged in southern Scotland. Caradoc's *Life of Gildas* has Arthur capturing Huail on the Isle of Man. There is also evidence that Arthur was active in southwest Scotland from several sources. As noted earlier, three of the four people named after Arthur appear to be connected with the Dalriada region of Scotland, suggesting that Arthur was famous in the Irish community in that region.

Who was Arthur?

There is also the *Y Gododdin* stanza that praises a brave warrior but adds 'though he was not Arthur'. As discussed earlier, John Koch regards this stanza as having been composed in Edinburgh before it fell to the Angles in 638. It is probable that there was regular contact between the Britons in Strathclyde and the Britons around Edinburgh which would have allowed Arthur's fame to travel. As shown below, there are several other references that link Arthur to southern Scotland.

Rheon in Kadeir Teÿrnon

The poem *Kadeir Teÿrnon* (Chair of the Sovereign) appears to have been composed shortly after Arthur's death and outlines his achievements in the opening series of lines. In Line 6 he is depicted as the governor (*rechtur*) of Rheon, raising the question as to the location of this region. A number of prominent scholars that include William Watson, O. G. S. Crawford, Mike McCarthy and Marged Haycock discuss the view that Rheon was associated with Loch Ryan in Galloway, close to northern Ireland.[79] Stranraer is at the southern end of the loch.

Pen Rhionydd in the Welsh Triads

The Rheon region is also associated with Arthur in Triad 1 of *Triads of the Island of Britain*. The Triads were a collection of sayings (comprising three lines for easy recall) that preserved and transmitted knowledge important to the Welsh. In the first Triad, Arthur is described as 'chief of princes in Pen Rhionydd in the North'. Rhionydd refers to Rheon as noted by both Rachel Bromwich and Marged Haycock.[80]

The use of 'pen' (head) as a descriptor suggests a headland which would well suit the Loch Ryan area. The Triads are potentially an ancient source, probably transmitted orally for many years before being written down, so that it is near impossible to date the Rheon part of this one. Unfortunately, over many years of transmission triads have been altered or elaborated to suit various ends or reflect later beliefs. This triad comprises three parts with much of the detail given being dubious. However, it would seem that no obvious political gain is evident by associating Arthur with Rheon and the other references to Arthur with this area would suggest that this element is a genuine tradition.

Nefenhyr in Kat Godeu and Culhwch and Olwen

Another association of Arthur with southern Scotland occurs in the poem *Kat Godeu* where a massive catastrophe occurs near Caer Nefenhyr. Marged Haycock argues persuasively that Caer Nefenhyr was in southwest Scotland in a region once controlled by the Novantae people.[81] This region includes the much smaller area of Rheon (around Loch Ryan), of which Arthur was 'governor' in *Kadeir Teÿrnon*. Further, in *Culhwch and Olwen* Arthur's gatekeeper, Glewlwyd, reminds Arthur about places where they had been, one of which was Caer Nefenhyr.

The Caledonian Forest in Historia Brittonum

Finally, in Arthur's *Historia Brittonum* battle list, one of the battles is in the Caledonian Forest (*Cat Coit Celidon*). This battle is thought to have occurred in southern Scotland in a forest that was probably far more extensive in Arthur's time. Kenneth Jackson cites the legend of Lailoken to deduce that the forest was thought to be within a reasonable range of both Strathclyde and Carlisle, the legend being independent of Geoffrey of Monmouth. This requirement would be satisfied by a forest in the Galloway region.[82]

THE NOVANTAE REGION

Caer Nefenhyr is a fort in a broad region of southwest Scotland relating to the Novantae tribe and is associated with Arthur in *Kat Godeu* and *Culhwch and Olwen*. The Novantae region appears in Ptolemy's *Geographia*, written AD 140-150, which refers to the *Novantarum peninsula* and the *Novantarum promontory* (in Book 2: 3.1). This is the peninsula west of Loch Ryan, shaped like a hammerhead, called the Rhinns of Galloway. The Novantae tribe had controlled the lands from this peninsula in the far west to an uncertain boundary in the east, possibly bounded by the River Nith.

Rheon, linked to Arthur in *Kadeir Teÿrnon* and Triad 1, was probably a smaller area around Loch Ryan. Ptolemy refers to two Novantan cities, one being *Rerigonium*, which means 'very royal place'.[83] He also refers to the *Rerigonius sinus* which suggests the curved Loch Ryan shore. Where was this royal city located? Mike McCarthy thinks it was at Innermessan, about 2 miles northeast of Stranraer. A local tradition suggests that *Rerigonium* was at Innermessan and there was a Roman road which passed through Dunragit and Drumflower that terminated near Innermessan.[84]

Rheon was strategically important, giving easy access to the Solway Firth, the Isle of Man and Ireland. A powerful king there may have been able to control the Irish seaways. McCarthy notes that Luce Bay and Loch Ryan offer good conditions for beaching flat-bottomed boats and that Portpatrick Bay could accommodate keeled vessels with a deeper draft. The peninsula is a sunny site with fertile soils, abundant rainfall, good grazing land and a long growing season, a suitable area for a royal family to control. Lloyd Laing and David Longley note the dense line of defensive coastal forts on the west of the Rhinns, facing Ireland.[85]

Anchorages around Rheon

An important anchorage around Rheon would have been the sandy beach at Luce Bay, near *Dunragit*, which means the 'fort of Rheged', according to William Watson. This may have been an important site in the sixth century. Mike McCarthy argues that Rheged, the domain of the British king, Urien, was centred there, with its core including the Rhinns, Dunragit, and possibly terminating at the River Crees. This is a smaller area than the *Book of Taliesin* poems would suggest, as indicated by Laing and Longley who also included

Carlisle, the Lake District and further south. Dunragit may also have been a significant fort earlier in the sixth century, in Arthur's time.[86]

A second useful anchorage would have been Portpatrick Bay which is on the west of the Rhinns, facing Ireland. Commanding views of the Irish Sea are obtained from the clifftops. Indeed, the northern Irish coast can sometimes be seen from Portpatrick, being only 21 miles away. It is also close to Cairn Pat, an enclosed hilltop site with earthwork defences. The old name for Portpatrick was Portree, from *port ríg*, meaning the 'king's port'.[87]

The third key anchorage would have been within Loch Ryan itself. The Rhinns peninsula gives shelter from the strong ocean currents, providing safe, calm conditions for boats in Loch Ryan. The site of the former royal city of *Rerigonium* could lie at the southeast edge of the loch while Stranraer lies at the southern edge.

Hillforts

Trusty's Hill, at Gatehouse of Fleet, is one of the most important hillforts in the region according to Ronan Toolis and Chris Bowles.[88] It consists of a 'citadel' on the top of a craggy hill along with a number of lesser 'wards' on lower lying terraces, resembling Dinarth (Bryn Euryn) and Scottish hillforts such as Dunadd.

Although originally Iron Age, it appears to have had an elite occupation in the fifth and sixth centuries. It had access to luxury imported goods from the continent during the period 500-650. There is evidence of metalworking in the form of moulds and some crucibles with high-status metalwork being found, along with imported E-ware pottery. Close to the hillfort entrance, a group of Pictish symbols are cut into a rock outcrop, a somewhat surprising sign of a Pictish influence in the region if they are genuine. However some scholars are sceptical and the cautionary comments of both Craig Cessford and Kenneth Dark should be noted.[89]

Further east is a large hillfort at The Moyle, to the south of Dalbeattie. This hillfort is very close to a British jeweller's court at the Mote of Mark, a small 'fort' near the Urr estuary. Lloyd Laing and David Longley argue that the latter was occupied by the Britons in the 500s and 600s. Pottery was found dating from the early to the mid 500s. Later sixth-century activity included metalworking, as indicated by the presence of slag and furnace or hearth lining. Imported E-ware ceramics and continental glass were present before a rampart was constructed, probably in the second half of the sixth century.[90] It suggests that that much of the material could have been made for the king controlling The Moyle.

About 7 miles to the northeast of The Moyle lies Loch Arthur, a small lake, and a probable indicator of Arthur's influence in the region. The Loch Arthur name is old, appearing in 1185-6 in the registers of the Cumberland Abbey of Holm Cultram as 'Loch-artur'.[91] This naming is sufficiently close in time to the publication of Geoffrey's *History* to suggest its independence of that work and probable prior existence.

Further east, close to the Nith estuary, lies the hillfort of Ward Law, a strategic location that would allow a king to control upstream access to the River Nith. Further inland are other notable hillforts. To the northwest of Dumfries lies the substantial hillfort at Tynron Doon, giving wide-ranging views over the Nith river valley. It may have been occupied in the fifth and sixth centuries. Near Lockerbie, there exists a massive hillfort, Burnswark, covering about 6 hectares, which dominates the Annandale area. Further northeast, the Castle O'er hillfort in the Esk Valley has numerous boundary earthworks, perhaps used for raising cattle. Radiocarbon dating could imply an occupation in the fifth or sixth centuries.[92] Some of these ancient forts could have been reoccupied by Arthur's men, as early warning systems for enemy approaches and for storing valuable items and supplies.

Summary

There is consistent literary evidence that places Arthur in the area formerly occupied by the Novantae. Five literary sources put Arthur in this region by naming places where he was present, as indicated below:

Source	Place
Kadeir Teÿrnon	Rheon
Triad 1	Pen Rhionydd
Kat Godeu and *Culhwch and Olwen*	Caer Nefenhyr
Historia Brittonum	Coit Celidon

Of these, Rheon and Pen Rhionydd have been identified as the same place, closely connected to the modern day Loch Ryan area. Caer Nefenhyr would seem to be a specific fort lying somewhere in the Novantae region. The term 'Nefenhyr' probably means 'the king of the Novantae tribe'. Coit Celidon, the Caledonian wood or forest, has long been traditionally linked to a forest in Scotland. Kenneth Jackson thought that it was readily accessible from both Carlisle and Strathclyde. The Novantae territory contains a forest that fulfils this condition which is now called the Galloway Forest Park.[93]

There may be another link between Caer Nefenhyr and Coit Celidon. In *Kat Godeu*, the 'Battle of the Trees' took place near Caer Nefenhyr. As noted earlier, Ifor Williams wondered whether the 'Battle of the Trees' could be equated with Cat Coit Celidon, the battle of the Caledonian Forest. If so, then Caer Nefenhyr was at or near Coit Celidon.

ARTHUR'S NORTHERN ACHIEVEMENTS

Repelling the Irish

Why would Arthur have been present in the Loch Ryan area of southwest Scotland? It is extremely doubtful that in the early sixth century the enemy here could be the Saxons. It would probably also be too far southwest for the enemy here to be the Picts, although it is possible that the Pictish symbols at

Trusty's Hill could have been made by a victorious raiding party. Even so, it would seem that such a raid there would have been an infrequent event. The most probable answer appears to be supplied by Gildas, who refers to the terrifying raids of the Irish (Section 19.1). He refers to them crossing the sea valleys in their small craft, with a greed for bloodshed and (with the Picts) seizing northern Britain down to Hadrian's Wall.

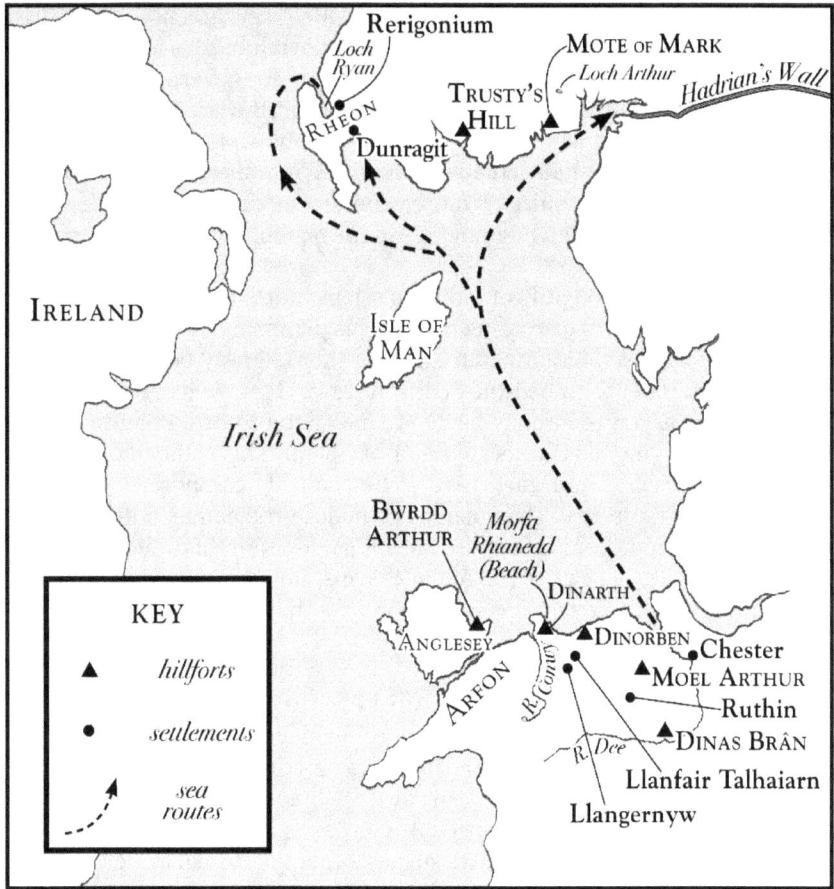

Figure 12.8 Sea routes from north Wales to Rheon and Hadrian's Wall
(Map: Sarah Dunning Park)

It is highly significant that the most direct route from northern Ireland to southern Scotland is to cross to the Galloway peninsula at Loch Ryan, as can be seen from Figure 12.8 above. For clarity, the map uses a mixture of ancient and modern names from Latin, Welsh and English and makes no attempt to render the placenames as they would have appeared in Arthur's time. The aim is to clearly show the location of important places that are mentioned in the text. It can be seen that there are many placenames in north Wales that relate to Arthur in addition to the key location, Dinarth (Bear's Stronghold), provided by Gildas. It also shows that the Rheon area in Galloway was within easy reach of his ships.

Given the favourable opinion expressed of Arthur in the northern poem *Y Gododdin* and his description as 'governor', his takeover of Rheon appears to have been well received, not viewed as a hostile operation. He may even have responded to an appeal from the British leaders there for assistance against the Irish raiders. The exact term in *Kadeir Teÿrnon* used to describe Arthur's role in Rheon is *rechtur*, which John Koch indicates is a word in the Neo-Brittonic language (a pre-Old Welsh feature) for governor. It is used in Gildas' *The Ruin of Britain* in the Latin form *rector*, the late Roman technical term for governor, in which it appears in Sections 1.14, 6.1 and 14.1. Koch suggests that the bards had actually pronounced it as the semi-Latin *rechtur*. Although it may have acquired a more general meaning such as 'ruler', even this broader use implies an ongoing role in the region, not just some transient raiding on Arthur's part.[94]

If the Scotti were a significant force in seizing north Britain up to the Wall, then they may have been crossing over to this peninsula on a regular basis if unimpeded. By then stationing an army on the Galloway peninsula, Arthur may have effectively stopped the Scotti influx on that route. A large part of Arthur's fame as a warrior may be due to his taking control of and pacifying Galloway, justifying his title as governor of Rheon. This is the outlook of the poem *Kadeir Teÿrnon*, argued here to be probably composed by Arthur's bard in the sixth century. The poem has a major problematic outlook (if it is assumed to be composed late by a Taliesin persona) in that it does not even mention any battles against the Anglo-Saxons, nor the battle of Badon, but apparently puts his governance of Rheon as a major achievement (Line 6) just after introducing him.

Defending against Raids from the North

Kenneth Dark has provided archaeological evidence that from roughly the mid-fifth to the mid-sixth century there was a concerted effort to refortify Hadrian's Wall. This suggests a central British authority to coordinate the operations. It would also appear that Anglo-Saxon mercenaries were used to supplement the British forces. Dark suggests that the British leader in charge of rebuilding may have held a post-Roman form of the command of the *Dux Britanniarum*. The new wall defences were north facing, defending against an attack from the north. This evidence is not universally accepted. It is heavily criticised by Mike McCarthy who describes the wall as only a 'curtain' from the beginning of the fifth century.[95]

If Dark is correct and the Britons were fortifying the wall from the south, then who was the enemy in the north? One possibility is supplied by Gildas, who refers to the terrifying raids of the Picts and the Irish. He refers to them being alike in their thirst for bloodshed and their seizing of northern Britain down to Hadrian's Wall. In Section 20, Gildas describes a letter sent from the

Britons to Aëtius, who was thrice consul, appealing for help against these barbarians. The mention of 'thrice consul' in the letter would date it to the range 446-54. If the barbarians were the Irish and the Picts, as suggested by the narrative of Gildas, then they appear to have been raiding around 450 and later, as the appeal to Aëtius was unsuccessful. It is uncertain how long these raids continued.

The data here is solely archaeological, there being no literary account of a strengthening of Hadrian's Wall at this time. Although there is no direct evidence to link Arthur to this defence, it would appear to have required the leadership of an overking. The *Historia Brittonum* lists an Arthurian battle at the former Roman fort at Bremenium (High Rochester), about 20 miles north of Hadrian's Wall. There is also the literary evidence that Arthur was providing a governing role to the west in Galloway, as discussed above. It is not impossible that he was also involved in defending Hadrian's Wall.

Concluding Comments

It would not have taken long for Arthur to get to southwest Scotland by sailing from the mouth of the Dee. His landing place may have been Luce Bay or he could have continued north to Loch Ryan and occupied strategic positions around the loch, including *Rerigonium*. To combat the Irish (Scotti) who were already based in Scotland, and the Picts, he may have sailed to a suitable harbour around the Solway Firth and moved inland to the east to defend Hadrian's Wall. The map in Figure 12.8 shows the sea routes Arthur may have taken to reach Rheon and Hadrian's Wall.

From the above, it can now be seen why Arthur developed such a great reputation in Scotland, being regarded as the paragon of valour in the poem *Y Gododdin* and having the nearby king Aedán of Dalriada (who formed a military alliance with the Britons) name his son after Arthur. It is possible that Arthur's military reputation was mainly won in southwest Scotland, a region he protected against the Irish. That seems to be the outlook of the poet who composed *Kadeir Teÿrnon*.

13
WHO WAS ARTHUR'S BARD?

THE BOOK OF TALIESIN POEMS

Introduction

This book has argued that three Welsh poems, *Preideu Annwfyn*, *Kat Godeu* and *Kadeir Teÿrnon* were probably composed by the same poet, who was Arthur's bard. Although the data at hand here is slender, in this chapter the identity of this poet will be explored. The three poems are preserved in the *Book of Taliesin*, held in the National Library of Wales at Aberystwyth (MS Peniarth 2). This manuscript has been dated to about 1300-1350 by Daniel Huws.[1] It consists of a diverse collection of about 60 poems, all ostensibly under the authorship of Taliesin. There is a nucleus of about twelve poems thought to have been composed by the historical Taliesin, a bard mentioned with other sixth-century bards in the *Historia Brittonum*. However the vast majority of *Book of Taliesin* poems are not by Taliesin but were composed much later, at different times by different authors.

The Legendary Taliesin

In contrast to the historical poems, an important subset of the poems has certain distinctive features: an interest in the transmigration of the soul, an interest in prophecy, boasting about arcane knowledge, and the frequent use of questions (to which no answers are given). The various poets using this style are said to have adopted the persona of the *legendary* Taliesin. These legendary poems are very uneven in quality and have been composed by a number of authors over different time periods. *Preideu Annwfyn*, *Kat Godeu* and *Kadeir Teÿrnon* are poems placed in the legendary category by Marged Haycock in her classic text. They are usually thought to have been composed centuries after the time of Arthur and are currently viewed as providing no worthwhile historical information about the sixth century. Other poems which do not fit into the historical category or this legendary category also appear in the *Book of Taliesin*.

If Arthur were a figure of mythology or an obscure Celtic god that was historicised, then the problem of the authorship of the three Arthurian poems would be of little importance. The authorship could be attributed to various poets adopting the Taliesin persona (from perhaps the ninth to the eleventh centuries) who created these stories simply to entertain. However it has been argued earlier that these are genuine sixth-century poems by Arthur's bard who purports to be an eyewitness to many of the events. Under this claim, they were composed in oral form and transmitted in this form for an unknown period before being written down and progressively modernised as the language changed over time.

The Status of the Three Arthurian Poems

It is argued here that the three Arthurian poems have historical content and do not belong in the legendary category but because of their distinctive features they served as the prototype on which poems in that category were modelled. When freed from the implausible view that the poem is a fantasy concerning Arthur sailing to an Otherworld fairyland, *Preideu Annwfyn* may be shown to contain important historical content.

It describes a sea voyage to a distant unknown land. The bard states that Arthur was the first to explore it. On the voyage the crew marvel at a large iceberg ('glass fortress'). When they reach Annwfyn, the expedition passes through a series of camps which are named after various features of the landscape. Among these are the camp of 'extreme coldness', the camp of 'God's Peak' (a mountain of such grandeur that it would be suitable for God to reside there) and the 'four-peaked camp'. The latter is argued to be at the site of modern Montreal with the four peaks being Royal, St-Bruno, St-Hilaire and Rougemont. Eventually they reached *kaer sidi*, the 'mound fortress' in the Eastern Woodlands, one of the earthwork complexes that had been built by the Hopewell. The Britons could not understand their language. While there, they observed the buffalo, pearl decoration in the pottery and the North American river otter, the latter having been tamed by the Native Americans. Near the mound fortress camp, a conflict arose and Gweir was captured by the inhabitants. The voyage became a disaster, with most of the Britons being killed, including Arthur, whose body and grave were now lost according to the bard. This interpretation gives a straightforward naturalistic explanation of a poem which is otherwise considered baffling.

The Annwfyn section in *Kat Godeu* provides additional details on the disastrous expedition, revealing that the enemy gathered for battle via the rivers or streams of the region, features evident in the Hopewell centre of power in the Eastern Woodlands. It mentions torrid fighting and again the death of Arthur, finally giving a moving farewell to the great king. In *Kadeir Teÿrnon* the poet's perspective shifts back to Britain in relating the aftermath of Arthur's death. It provides a tribute to the dead Arthur in the opening lines and then Arthur is blessed. The main theme of this poem is Arthur's Chair (Throne) and who would be sought to replace him.

It is true that this bard is interested in the transmigration of souls, the mysteries of the cauldron and prophecy. He is a Christian but with many beliefs characteristic of the druids. He boasts of incidents or events he has seen of which the monks are totally ignorant. However, these boasts are not about isolated pieces of book learning but things he has seen in Annwfyn. His poetic style is to ask questions, emphasising his own authority, and to draw attention to important points. He also asks implied questions about events in Annwfyn by stating that the monks do not know of interesting features or important events that happened there. In Chapter 9 it is argued from the historical context and through comparisons with other early texts that all three poems were composed by Arthur's bard in the sixth century. Given that their distinctive elements were copied in much later poems, it appears that these poems were highly esteemed. They served as a partial model for later poems in the style of the legendary Taliesin. However the later poems are very much inferior, sometimes producing reams of rather pointless questions: for example, 'why is a greenfinch green?; why are rosehips red?'[2]

It has been argued that the three Arthurian poems were composed by Arthur's bard and contain important historical content. All three poems are in the *Book of Taliesin* so their ostensible author is Taliesin. However, what little is known about the historical Taliesin makes it difficult to conceive of him as Arthur's bard as will be discussed below.

The Twelve Historical Poems attributed to Taliesin

Ifor Williams identified twelve historical poems from the *Book of Taliesin* that he thought were composed by the real sixth-century Taliesin. Of these, one containing archaic language praises Cynan Garwyn, son of Brochfael, from the old kingdom of Powys, who plundered the regions around him. Nine of the poems praise Urien of Rheged or his son Owain from northern Britain. The remaining two poems praise Gwallawg who ruled further south in Elmet, around Leeds. Gwallawg was depicted as Urien's ally in their fight against the Angles in the *Historia Brittonum*.

Taliesin's authorship of some of the twelve historical poems has been doubted. The poem to Cynan Garwyn has been viewed with scepticism by both John Koch and Saunders Lewis.[3] Koch comments that the poem lacks a Christian outlook (unlike the northern poems) and its higher frequency of retained old spelling features sets it apart from the others. If Taliesin were the author, it would require that he sang to Cynan while residing in Powys and later moved north to sing to Urien and Owain. While in the north he may have sung to other kings, according to the conjecture of Ifor Williams.[4] This conjecture is based on Poem 9, *Dadolwch Vryen* (The Conciliation of Urien), which suggests a rift between Taliesin and Urien and the fact that Poems 11 and 12 were sung to Gwallawg. The scenario of Taliesin serving as Cynan's bard and then moving north to serve Urien and Owain is not impossible but implies a mobile Taliesin. It would probably be chronologically possible but strong doubts still remain as to whether Taliesin was the author of the poem to Cynan Garwyn.

In addition, Graham Isaac casts doubt on the poem addressed to Urien, *Gweith Gwen Ystrat* (Battle of the White or Blessed Valley), arguing from features of the language that the poem was eleventh century or later.[5] David Dumville also expresses doubt over several poems on historical grounds.[6] Under the above criticisms, the number of historical poems attributed to Taliesin may now have decreased to ten or less.

This situation has seen John Koch call for a thorough linguistic, literary and historical re-examination of the poetry of the Taliesin corpus.[7] At the moment, the consensus view seems to be that the historical Taliesin was probably the composer of a reduced set of poems, that were addressed to

Urien, Owain and Gwallawg, kings whose lands spanned a large area from Leeds to southern Scotland.

If Taliesin did compose the poems to Urien, Owain and Gwallawg, then it is highly unlikely he could have been Arthur's bard. These kings almost certainly reigned in the second half of the sixth century, well after Arthur's estimated death date of 537/539. From the *Historia Brittonum*, Urien and his sons fight against the Anglo-Saxon king, Theodoric. According to the *Moore Memoranda*, Theodoric reigned from about 572 to 579, as discussed by Ifor Williams.[8] If Taliesin were Arthur's bard in north Wales, it would require a young Taliesin serving Arthur and then moving northwards after Arthur's death to serve these northern kings in his old age. This would be stretching a chronological framework to its outer limits.

Comparing the Historical and Arthurian Poems

An equally strong objection concerns the nature of the two sets of poems. The historical poems addressed to the northern kings are well composed, but they are rather pedestrian and formulaic. They are practical poems that praise the bravery and strength of each king, his generosity to the bard and to his people, his illustrious forebears and so on.

The three poems relating to Arthur are entirely different. They reveal an intellectual outlook with Christian beliefs which have been integrated with the old belief system of the transmigration of the soul. This bard composes many poetic lines describing his previous earthly states in both animate and inanimate matter. He delights in mysteries and often expresses information indirectly which must have left some of his audience wondering what he had meant. Further, he relishes challenging his audience with questions which demonstrate his authority, and which emphasise his extensive knowledge. He also appears to engage in prophesying the future.

In addition, there is a strong difference in the role of the two bards. The poems relating to Arthur are composed by a bard who claims to have been a warrior. In Annwfyn he killed many of the inhabitants in battle. He recalls that in his younger days he had a fast horse Melyngan, as swift as a seagull, and was a valiant warrior. The bard of the northern kings, however, does not have the outlook of a warrior. In one of his poems, entitled from the first few words, *Ar vn blyned* ('In the space of one year') he is anxiously waiting at Urien's home base, wondering whether Urien will survive the battle or be brought back dead on a bier. When Urien returns in triumph, the bard's relief is evident.[9] It does not seem plausible that the two sets of poems could have been composed by the same person. If the historical Taliesin composed the northern poems, then it appears extremely unlikely that he could have been Arthur's bard.

Finally, probably the strongest objection is that Taliesin does not name Arthur in the poems to Urien, Owain and Gwallawg. If Taliesin had been Arthur's bard before he served under Urien, then one would have expected him to proclaim that Urien shared Arthur's valour, the highest compliment one could give. The fact that he does not mention Arthur suggests that he did not know him personally.

THE BARD'S MIXTURE OF BELIEFS

The bard exhibits a curious mixture of beliefs, some of which appear to be derived from the druids, while having a genuine belief in the Christian god. Literary sources indicate that early medieval kings were assisted by sages or magicians not dissimilar to Arthur's bard. The *Historia Brittonum* describes the fifth-century king, Vortigern, as being advised by sorcerers (*magi*). They advise Vortigern where to build his fortress, and when difficulties transpire with the building material, tell him to sacrifice a fatherless boy and sprinkle his blood on the site (Section 40). A similar picture comes from the Irish work *Echtrae Chonnlai*, composed perhaps circa 700, but set before the time of St Patrick. Here the king, Connlae's father, relies on his druid Corann to cast spells to protect his son from the Otherworld woman.[10]

In *Kat Godeu* the druids and wise men are asked to prophesy to Arthur. The bard appears to be one of these sages in addition to his role as a poet but he also shows strong evidence of Christian belief. As noted in Chapter 12, Christianity was widely practised in sixth-century north Wales. The above very unusual combination of beliefs would seem incongruous if belonging to a figure of the 700s or later, but would seem more likely to have belonged to a person of the fifth or sixth centuries, as will be argued below.

The Bard's Belief in Christianity

It is clear that the bard was a Christian who gained great comfort from his beliefs. In *Kat Godeu*, he twice mentions the three greatest cataclysms in the history of the world. It is noteworthy that all three are from the Bible – the Flood, Christ's Crucifixion, and the Day of Judgement that is yet to come. In addition, for the catastrophe at Caer Nefenhyr the bard has Gwydion the enchanter call on Christ, the omnipotent one, to save the Britons. Further, in reflecting on the Annwfyn disaster the bard takes comfort in the fact that God is in control of earthly events – he makes civilisations, remakes them and makes them again and again. These are not Christian interpolations by later monks as they form a natural part of the poetic sequence, contributing in a convincing way to the meaning of the poems.

In *Kadeir Teyrnon*, the bard notes Arthur's reverence for scripture which implies that he approved, as the context is a long list of praiseworthy items. There is also a moving section on things which are pleasing, one of which is a gratitude to God, expressed in his statement that it is fine when the True One shines, even finer when He pronounces.

In *Preideu Annwfyn*, the bard indicates his belief in Judgement Day, he prays for Gweir, and refers to Arthur as a 'saint', a term used in the early church for a Christian. He also employs the term *ebostol*, taken by Marged Haycock to mean 'epistle' and hence 'story', a very Christian term. The bard is also trying to suppress his grief at Arthur's death at the conclusion of the poem and states that Christ is comforting him.

The Bard's Beliefs influenced by Druidism

Alongside Christian beliefs, the poems show beliefs influenced by druidism. In *Kat Godeu*, the bard's belief in the transmigration of the soul is evident, an ancient belief more general than reincarnation as it includes the soul residing in inanimate objects. In Lines 1-23 he lists states of matter that his soul has inhabited, many of them inanimate. These states include a mottled sword, a word in writing, the light of a lantern, a bubble in a drink, a bridge, a raindrop, a shield in battle, a string in a harp, and so on. This dwelling of souls in inanimate objects seems to be a manifestation of the ancient belief which Gildas called 'pernicious', in which the Britons worshipped mountains, hills and rivers (Section 4.3). The bard continues to give examples of the transmigration theme in *Kat Godeu*, Lines 207-10 and 231-7. He looks at his long and slender fingers in his current life and remarks that he has not been a herdsman for a long time now.

The bard makes it clear that he believes in the pre-existence of the soul, a belief that was declared anathema at the Synod at Constantinople in AD 543. This may be inferred from his many passages on the transmigration of the soul but he further states it explicitly in Lines 174-7 of *Kat Godeu*, where he mysteriously declares that the wisdom of sages had fashioned him before the world was made.

In his current life he prophesies the future. In Lines 211-4 he dresses in a chasuble and prepares his bowl so that it would give off four-score clouds of smoke. He also recounts how the druids and the wise men (which probably included himself) are asked to prophesy to Arthur, perhaps to tell him how the great scaly beast that is killing the Britons can be defeated.

In *Kadeir Teÿrnon*, the bard lists one previous life where he was a torqued nobleman holding a horn in his hand. He also holds a mystical view of the cauldron, and appreciates the inspiration that can be released from it. In the 'pleasing things' section the bard lists the triune inspiration (*awen*) that can be produced from a cauldron.

Preideu Annwfyn gives a similar view of the cauldron to *Kadeir Teÿrnon*. In Line 13, the bard regards his inspired poetry as coming from a cauldron. As discussed in an earlier chapter, it is unclear whether the bard is saying that his poetry is so good that it was seemingly produced by magic, or whether he really did use a cauldron in some way as an aid to poetic inspiration. The bard describes the cauldron as being kindled by the breath of nine maidens, imagery similar to that in the earlier book of Pomponius Mela which refers to nine maidens skilled in magic.

When could a Person hold such a Mixture of Beliefs?

Early Christianity encompassed a mixture of beliefs before the inevitable standardization of doctrine occurred. A belief in reincarnation was held by a number of eminent Christians such as Basilides, Valentinus, Clement of Alexandria, Gregory of Nyssa and possibly Origen, who made statements that appeared to support reincarnation and also to contradict it.[11] In 543, the Emperor Justinian issued an edict against Origen in 10 items, believers in these to be anathematised. The first concerned the pre-existence of human souls, while the sixth concerned beliefs that the sun, moon, stars, and so on have souls. The tenth anathematised Origen himself and any who believe in his teachings. A Synod at Constantinople was held later in 543, resulting in 15 anathematisms on Origen, two of which parallel the first and sixth on the earlier list of 10 items.

In 553 the Fifth Ecumenical Council of the Church took place, also held at Constantinople. It produced 14 anathematisms, three of which specifically anathematised Theodore of Mopsuestia, Theodoret, and a letter of Ibas of Edessa. However our interest here concerns the anathematism of Origen (and others) in the eleventh item. The inclusion of Origen in this item was not an interpolation according to Charles Hefele.[12] These decisions against Origen made the holding of a openly stated belief in reincarnation or transmigration untenable for an orthodox Christian.

When Augustine came to Britain in 597 there were some variations in practice between the British and Roman churches, including calculating the date of Easter and differences in the the baptismal rite. From the late 620s there was also controversy over the different style of the British tonsure, as discussed in detail by Caitlin Corning.[13] However, no doctrinal differences are mentioned which suggest that the orthodoxies imposed above probably also prevailed in Britain.

The bard was both a sage and a strong Christian, an intelligent man who was very well informed, being familiar with Virgil and the Greek tales about Typhon. However, in his poetry he refers to his belief in reincarnation and in the more primitive idea of his soul having previously dwelt in inanimate objects. He also refers to his inspiration from the cauldron and partakes in prophesying the future. An appendix to the 553 Ecumenical Council shows that laymen could also be anathematised if they held contrary beliefs.[14] It is difficult to see how the bard's unusual combination of beliefs could have been held by a dedicated Christian who lived after about 700, or even after 600. It suggests that the bard lived at an earlier date, a conclusion consistent with a sixth-century dating for these poems.

TALHAEARN AS ARTHUR'S BARD?

The Sixth-Century Bards in the Historia Brittonum

In Section 62, the *Historia Brittonum* refers to a cluster of five bards who were prominent in sixth-century Britain. These were Talhaearn 'Tad Awen', (A)neirin, Taliesin, Bluchbard and Cian who was called Guenith Guaut.[15] Unfortunately, poetry from only two of these bards survives, Taliesin and Aneirin. The whole *Book of Taliesin* is attributed to Taliesin, but only a few poems in it may be his. Aneirin is credited with poems in the *Book of Aneirin*, namely stanzas in *Y Gododdin*, and some other poems called *gorchanau*. The way this list is presented could suggest that Talhaearn was the leading bard. He is not only named first but is given the epithet *Tad Awen*, meaning 'father of inspiration'. He is also singled out as having 'achieved renown in poetry'. The other bards are then introduced as a group and 'were at the same time, famous in Brittonic poetry'.

This passage may imply that Talhaearn was slightly earlier in time than the others. John Morris-Jones (with the support of Ifor Williams) thought that Talhaearn was the earliest of the Welsh poets and then compared him with John Dryden's view of Chaucer as 'the father of English poetry' with the comment:[16]

> ...the one [Talhaearn] is the earliest Welsh poet, the other the earliest English.

Talhaearn's Location and Kernyw

In the previous chapter, evidence was presented that Arthur was probably located in north Wales, primarily at Dinarth. It was further suggested that Arthur enjoyed hunting in the wooded area of Kernyw and that the village of Llangernyw, only eight miles from Dinarth, is a reminder of its ancient name. It is therefore of great interest that the village of Llanfair Talhaiarn (based on Talhaearn's name) is close by, only four miles northeast of Llangernyw, both being on the River Elwy.

Importantly, Geraint Gruffydd has identified four placenames in north Wales relating to Talhaearn – Caer Talhaearn, Tre Talhaearn (his name for Llanfair Talhaiarn), Gweirglodd Talhaearn and Llechtalhaearn. He allows himself to speculate as to whether Talhaearn was a bard for Maglocunus or his forebears.[17] If the analysis here on Arthur's location is correct, then it is quite possible that Talhaearn was Arthur's bard.

Some Attributes of Talhaearn

Despite Talhaearn's eminence, no poetry survives that is credited to him. What has been said about him? He is mentioned twice in the *Book of Taliesin* poem, *Angar Kyfundawt*, in lines 71 and 165. This poem is obviously not by Taliesin, despite claiming to be in Line 53, but by a later Taliesin persona. However, it does say some interesting things about Talhaearn.

In Lines 70-2, it attributes to Talhaearn the thought that God was the True Judge of the worth of the world. This would agree with the strong Christian outlook of Arthur's bard. The saying is also reminiscent of Lines 33-4 in *Kadeir Teÿrnon* in which Arthur's bard expresses gratitude to God: 'It is fine when the True One shines; even finer when He speaks', as discussed earlier in Chapter 8. Further, Lines 165-6 of *Angar Kyfundawt* state that Talhaearn was the greatest sage. This role as a sage is a perfect fit for how the author of the Arthurian poems portrays himself.

A further point of interest is the meaning of Talhaearn's name: it means 'brow (forehead) of iron' as discussed by Kenneth Jackson.[18] This rugged-sounding name is not inconsistent with the claim of Arthur's bard that he was a warrior.

The Misplacement of Talhaearn's Poems?

The closeness of Tre Talhaearn (Llanfair Talhaiarn) to Arthur's woodland location in Kernyw may suggest that Talhaearn was his bard, the poet who composed *Preideu Annwfyn*, *Kat Godeu* and *Kadeir Teÿrnon*. The passage in the *Historia Brittonum* seems to imply that he was the leading bard as suggested by his title 'father of inspiration'. Yet none of his poetry appears under his own name. One possibility is that some of Talhaearn's poems were misclassified as Taliesin's, whether unintentionally or deliberately, and thus appear in the *Book of Taliesin* along with a small group of genuine Taliesin poems. Perhaps a compiler found the three anonymous Arthurian poems (Talhaearn's) and added them to Taliesin's, the latter being a poet whose reputation increased rapidly in the medieval period. In this hypothesis, other later poems that imitated the style of the Arthurian poems were also added, giving rise to the 'Taliesin persona'. From the arguments presented earlier, it seems highly improbable that Taliesin could be Arthur's bard if the theory is correct that Taliesin composed the praise poems to the northern kings, Urien, Owain and Gwallawg.

Conclusion

Although the evidence is slight, a speculative argument has been made that Talhaearn may have been Arthur's bard. This argument is based on the four points given below.

The first point is that the *Historia Brittonum* names him first and calls him 'father of inspiration'. This implies that his poetry was of an exceptional standard yet it apparently does not survive. At the same time, a poem which is a masterpiece, *Preideu Annwfyn*, has been given an ostensible authorship which is highly unlikely. *Kat Godeu* and *Kadeir Teÿrnon* are also high-quality poems that are left without a convincing authorship. The author of these Arthurian poems refers to 'inspiration' (*awen*) twice in *Kadeir Teÿrnon* and to his inspiration coming from the cauldron in both *Kadeir Teÿrnon* and *Preideu Annwfyn*, which could explain why Talhaearn was called 'father of inspiration' if he were their author.

Secondly, a later poem indicates how Talhaearn was remembered – that he was a devout Christian, as was the author of the three Arthurian poems, and that he was the greatest sage, a descriptor that perfectly suits the author of the three Arthurian poems.

Thirdly, Llanfair Talhaiarn, based on Talhaearn's name, is just four miles from Llangernyw, which may preserve an instance of the name of Arthur's ancient region of Kernyw. Other placenames relating to Talhaearn are also in the north Wales region.

Fourthly, the *Historia Brittonum* seems to imply that Talhaearn was earlier in time than the other four bards (which include Taliesin), naming him first and separately from the others, the latter said to have been famous 'at the same time'. If Taliesin sang to Urien in the second half of the sixth century then perhaps Talhaearn sang in the first half of that century. This was the time of Arthur, as argued earlier. Talhaearn appears to have lived in the same region and at the same time as Arthur and had the skill to produce the poetic masterpiece, *Preideu Annwfyn*.

14
REVIEW OF THE CLAIMS

REVIEW OF THE EVIDENCE USUALLY CONSIDERED

Apart from *The Ruin of Britain* by Gildas, which is not free from bias, there is little trustworthy material available to shed light on sixth-century Britain. Before reviewing the new evidence for Arthur which has been presented in this book, the fragments of early Arthurian evidence usually considered by scholars will be briefly summarised. This material gives a consistent picture of Arthur as a supreme military figure before the accretion of the legends.

References to Arthur in Early Poetry

An early reference to Arthur occurs in *Y Gododdin* in stanza B2.38, in which Gorddur the hero of the stanza is highly praised. However the poet notes that despite Gorddur's valour 'he was not Arthur'. This reference portrays Arthur as an exemplar of the valiant warrior – although Gorddur was not equal to Arthur, the very fact that he was being compared to him was an honour. It was once valued highly as evidence for Arthur's historicity but it is currently fashionable to consider it sceptically as a possible interpolation.[1] In contrast to this scepticism, this book presents a new argument for an early dating of the reference which is outlined below.

In Chapter 11 it was shown that B2.38 shares four distinctive features with B2.28: (i) a negative parenthetical clause, (ii) enjambment, (iii) the hero's name is emphasized at the very end, and (iv) it uses the same expression to begin successive lines. It suggests that the two stanzas were composed by the same poet. Furthermore, the content of stanza B2.28 indicates that it was composed in the sixth century, which would then imply a sixth-century date for the Arthurian stanza, B2.38.

What are the features of B2.28 that imply such an early date? The hero of this stanza is Yrfai whose father Golistan was described in a derogatory way as being 'no sovereign lord'. John Koch shows that Golistan was an Anglo-Saxon name, equivalent to Wolstan and the well known Wulfstan.[2] That is, Yrfai's father was English. It is therefore unlikely that Yrfai could have been honoured in poetry after AD 638 when the Gododdin had not only lost their capital, Edinburgh, but all their lands to the hated Saxons. Further, stanza B2.28 appears to have been composed before the Anglo-Saxon territory of Bernicia existed, or had become significant, as the enemy in the poem was the more distant Deira. This is additional evidence for a sixth-century dating. The above implies that the Arthurian stanza, if composed by the same poet, was also sixth century. Finally, the negative parenthetical clause ('though he was not Arthur') is one of the four distinctive features shared with stanza B2.28, suggesting that it was not an interpolation.

A second early mention of Arthur in Welsh poetry occurs in *Marwnad Cynddylan*, probably composed shortly after the battle of Winwaed in about AD 655. The warriors there are so heroic that they are metaphorically called 'whelps of stout Arthur, a mighty fortress'. This reference is similar to that in *Y Gododdin* – Arthur is used as the great exemplar from the past but is not present at the battle.

Another mention of Arthur occurs in the poem *Geraint son of Erbin*. John Koch suggests that this poem could have had its origins in the 700s.[3] Here Arthur is portrayed as directing the battle at Llongborth where his men are suffering heavy losses. He is described as 'emperor' which probably means an overall commander of armies. The 'emperor' term was also employed by Adomnán in his *Life of Columba* in referring to Oswald defeating Cadwallon at Heavenfield in about AD 634.

The Cluster of Babies named Arthur

Between about 560-600, four men were born who were named 'Arthur', a name that was hitherto 'practically unknown' according to Hector and Nora Chadwick.[4] Given the dearth of information surviving from this time, this fact is significant. It seems that this naming reflected the appearance of a hero named 'Arthur' earlier in the sixth century, consistent with the key dates given to Arthur in the *Annales Cambriae*. Further, one of these Arthurs was the son of the aggressive Aedán, the powerful king of Dalriada who formed an alliance with the Britons. Aedán's domain was not far from the Loch Ryan territory where Arthur governed, according to *Kadeir Teÿrnon*, and where Triad 1 gives Arthur a northern court.

The Arthurian Battle List

A similar picture of Arthur emerges from the *Historia Brittonum* of 829-30 which contains the Arthurian battle-listing section. Arthur fought alongside the other kings but he was the overall commander of the armies. The battles appear to have come from an earlier Welsh poem whose rhyming scheme was based partly on the names of the battles.[5] This battle list has been regarded sceptically by some scholars as most of the battles cannot be independently corroborated. Many of the battles cannot be identified. It is also possible that some battles in the list were not Arthur's while some of Arthur's battles may not have been included in the list.

However, the important point is the general view of Arthur presented, that he was a great military figure and battle commander, a picture that generated the poem which preceded the battle list. The rhyming scheme of the poem suggests that Arthur was regarded as the victor of the key battle of Badon Hill before the *Historia Brittonum* was compiled.

The above Arthurian references in the three Welsh poems, the cluster of 'Arthur' babies, and the Latin *Historia* battle list provide the early evidence traditionally considered for Arthur's historicity. The evidence is consistent –

that Arthur was revered as a military figure and was the exemplar to whom other warriors could aspire.

NEW EVIDENCE CONCERNING ARTHUR

Preideu Annwfyn and *Kadeir Teÿrnon* provide clues suggesting that Arthur was located in north Wales. These clues are consistent with Gildas' mention of 'the Bear's Stronghold' (*Dinarth*), this being his pun on Arthur's name, as *Arth* meant 'bear' in their Neo-Brittonic language. Dinarth survives today under the name Bryn Euryn, in Colwyn Bay just to the east of Llandudno. In support of this location, one of Arthur's mistresses, Garwen, was buried on the nearby 'Beach of the Maidens' (*Morfa Rhianedd*) at Llandudno while her father, Hennin, was buried several miles to the east of Dinarth at Dinorben. This stretch of coastline appears to have been a centre of power in the early sixth century as Maglocunus later moved to Degannwy, another hillfort only 3 miles from Dinarth. His wife, Sanant, and son, Rhun, were also buried on the *Morfa Rhianedd* according to the *Stanzas of the Graves*. The evidence for Arthur as an overking in north Wales is summarised below.

An Overking in North Wales

In Chapter 12 it was shown that Gildas displayed a vehement hatred of the military as indicated by his statement that they should be utterly destroyed and their names forgotten. He suppresses the name of the notorious fifth-century king who invited the Saxons into Britain by calling him 'arrogant tyrant', 'Pharaoh' and 'ill-fated tyrant' but never mentions his name, even though it is certain that he knew it. The name, Vortigern, is given by Bede writing 200 years later and in later manuscripts.

Did Gildas similarly suppress Arthur's name? Arguments are given that identify Arthur with an overking mentioned by Gildas, referred to as both 'the Bear' and 'Pharaoh'. In Section 32 Gildas addresses Cuneglasus as '(you) bear' and the 'driver of the chariot of the Bear's Stronghold'. This grammatical shift from second person to third person makes it unlikely that 'the Bear' of the stronghold was Cuneglasus. It implies that Cuneglasus was subordinate to an important figure known as 'the Bear'. It is also highly unlikely that the fort was named after bear animals who had previously lived there. Gildas, writing in Latin, uses the genitive *singular*. These points suggest that the stronghold belonged to a major figure whose name allowed a punster like Gildas to call him 'the Bear'.

In describing Cuneglasus as 'driver of the chariot' Gildas is clearly using Biblical imagery of Pharaoh's soldiers driving their chariots to destruction in the Red Sea, an incident he refers to on four occasions. Here Cuneglasus is being likened to one of the Pharaoh's chariot drivers. In Section 37 this subordinate role is made explicit when Gildas states that there is a Pharaoh above Cuneglasus and the other four kings. He refers to the five kings as the 'five mad and debauched horses of the retinue of Pharaoh' who are contributing to the ruin of Pharaoh's kingdom. These considerations imply that Cuneglasus was subordinate to a figure called both 'Pharaoh' and 'the Bear'. Given his dates in the *Annales Cambriae* and his peerless reputation as a military figure, the most likely candidate for 'the Bear' is Arthur as *Arth* meant 'bear' in the Britons' sixth-century language.

There is additional evidence of an overking in the background of Gildas' account. This king was even more powerful than Maglocunus, who was the strongest of the five kings that are castigated. Gildas states that Maglocunus is mightier than many (but not all) in power and is superior to *almost* all the kings in Britain in his kingdom. Gildas' knowledge of the kings appears to be confined to southwest Britain as all five kings are located in this region and there is no mention of any king elsewhere. It is therefore probable that a king mightier in power and kingdom than Maglocunus was located in this region of southwest Britain. These considerations would certainly make 'the Bear' a prime candidate for the overking as 'the Bear's Stronghold' (Dinarth) was a commanding hillfort in north Wales in a strategic position. It survives today as 'Bryn Euryn' in Colwyn Bay, just east of Llandudno.

The Bias of Gildas

Gildas' account is so anti-British that it has led some scholars to advance theories that it could not have been written by a Briton and was possibly a forgery by an Anglo-Saxon.[6] His berating of the five kings, his malicious descriptions of the bards, and his insulting portrayal of the military as being cowards and 'like women' so enraged Arthur's bard that he responded in kind in the last five stanzas of *Preideu Annwfyn*. Gildas had provided all the ammunition required by the Saxon historian Bede to discredit the Britons in his *Ecclesiastical History*. John Koch describes Gildas as providing 'the bias of the one-dimensional misanthrope'.[7] Despite the doubts of scholars in the nineteenth century, it is now believed that Gildas was a Briton himself, but he appears to have been an embittered one.

In the Rhuys *Life of Gildas*, his father is stated to have been Cauuos, a latinization of the Welsh name Caw, and his brother is given as the warrior Huail. Kenneth Jackson has commented on the importance of the sixth-century language which described where Cauuos lived.[8] In the Caradoc *Life of Gildas* written in the twelfth century, Arthur is said to have killed Huail, the brother of Gildas. Today a large stone stands in the north Wales town of Ruthin, said to be the stone on which Huail was beheaded. If true, this story could explain Gildas' embittered state. The twelfth-century medieval writer Gerald of Wales believed that Gildas hated Arthur for his killing of Huail and for this reason did not mention him.

If Arthur were the Pharaoh as argued above, then it is clear that Gildas detested him, as the 'mad' and 'debauched' kings were his agents. Gildas' silence on the real name of 'the Bear'/'Pharaoh' and the victor of Badon could be explained by his deliberate suppression of names. As noted earlier, in referring to the British military men he states that they should be utterly destroyed and their names forgotten, an attitude also adopted by Bede who closely followed Gildas.

Support for a North Wales Location

Both *Preideu Annwfyn* and *Kadeir Teÿrnon* support a north Wales location for Arthur. In *Preideu Annwfyn*, the bard comments that the inhabitants of Annwfyn do not visit the Defwy meadows. The Defwy would therefore seem to be a major river with which the bard was familiar. It is even possible that the bard was implying that Arthur's expedition had sailed from the Defwy. The word is pronounced 'Devwy', suggesting that it derives from Deva (the Roman name for Chester) in which case it is probably the River Dee that runs through Chester. Nearby north Wales has a number of names ending in 'wy' (Degannwy, Conwy, Elwy), the ending derived from *gwy*, meaning 'a flow' (of water). The Defwy name also appears in the *Spoils of Taliesin* poem in which John Koch tentatively translates it as 'Dee'.[9] If this translation is correct, it links Arthur to northeast Wales and suggests that his battle at Chester from the *Historia Brittonum* could be a real battle of his.

Kadeir Teÿrnon also supports a north Wales location for Arthur. There is a section of the poem that refers to Arthur's men grieving over his death and concludes with the information that he wore the lorica (battle vest) of *Lleon*. Chester was known as Caer Lleon and, as discussed by Marged Haycock, it could be either a specific reference to Chester or a more general reference to the region of northeast Wales.

The location at Dinarth is also supported by the burial sites of Arthur's mistress, Garwen, and her father, Hennin. Garwen was buried on the *Morfa Rhianedd* (Beach of the Maidens), the long beach at Llandudno. This beach is close to Dinarth. Hennin was buried at Dinorben, a notable hillfort a few miles to the east of Dinarth. A north Wales location is also suggested by the location of Eleirch, who was the mother of Arthur's son, Cydfan. Eleirch was a daughter of Iaen and lived with her father and brothers in Arfon, an old region that faced the Menai Strait and Caernarfon Bay. This also supports a north Wales location for Arthur and suggests that he may have periodically visited Arfon as overking.

To speculate on Arthur's domain, it would seem that he had a principal stronghold at Dinarth (the hillfort Bryn Euryn) and controlled the north coast of Wales. His eastern boundary was perhaps Chester, bordered by the Dee, while his western boundary probably extended to the Menai Strait and possibly the Llŷn Peninsula. His lands may have included the hillfort, Dinas Emrys, that was occupied by an elite or royal family in the sixth century. The Dee, running through Llyn Tegid and past Dinas Brân, may have been his southern boundary. This speculation is based on the use of major rivers as natural boundaries.

North Wales contained a high-quality Roman road system that would have provided an efficient route from Chester to near Dinarth and further west to Arfon. Arthur's ships could have been anchored in the mouth of the

Dee, near Chester. When Maglocunus returned to his kingship (after his attempt to become a monk) he probably ruled his father's lands in Anglesey, based at Aberffraw. After Arthur's death, he apparently moved to Degannwy, a location only 3 miles west of Dinarth.

Kernyw

In Triad 1 of the Welsh Triads, a court of Arthur is reported to be Celliwig or Gelliwig in Kernyw. Gelliwig means 'woodland, or forest', while in later times, Kernyw was translated as Cornwall. However Gildas does not use this term, referring to this southwest peninsula as Dumnonia, which he punned as 'Damnonia'. If Arthur were an overking, having Constantine of Dumnonia as one his supporters, then it is not impossible that he had a court in Cornwall. But there may be a nearer and more plausible location. About 8 miles inland from Arthur's fort at Dinarth, *kernyw* is preserved in the name of the village of Llangernyw. Earlier it was noted that several scholars derive *kernyw* from the British word *corn*, meaning 'horn'. The peninsula from Degannwy in the west and Dinarth in the east juts out into the Irish Sea with the Great Orme and Little Orme resembling two horns. It is suggested that this whole area, including further inland, may have been referred to as Kernyw in Arthur's time. As for Gelliwig, the area south of Dinarth is in a woodland setting with a Gell located nearby, while the Afon Gell runs into the River Elwy only a mile north of Llangernyw.

Checking the Influx of Irish

Arthur's battle list in the *Historia Brittonum* is introduced in the context of Arthur fighting the Saxons, who were growing in numbers and power in Britain. These battles are extremely difficult to identify and some appear to be in locations where other opponents are more plausible. For example, the battle in the forest of Celidon appears to be sited in southwest Scotland, a most unlikely location for Saxons. Gildas had made the battle at Badon Hill against the Saxons famous in his writing, as it was the only battle he ever named. This battle is attributed to Arthur in the Welsh poem that probably underlies the *Historia* battle list.

However, the poem *Kadeir Teÿrnon*, probably by Arthur's bard, provides a different perspective. After introducing Arthur as a brave, authoritative man with a warlike nature, it lists his first achievement in Line 6 – that he was the 'governor' (*rechtur*) of Rheon. This is a surprising statement, both in the location given and the way Arthur is described. A number of scholars argue that Rheon is the Loch Ryan area in southwest Scotland, referred to by Ptolemy in the second century, as discussed previously. The 'very royal city' of the Novantae, *Rerigonium*, was situated there, probably on the site of Innermessan. Loch Ryan is very close to Ireland, with ferries today running from Cairnryan on the eastern side of the loch to Northern Ireland.

The term *rechtur* was ancient according to John Koch, being an early Neo-Brittonic word from the sixth century when Arthur lived, and was used several times by Gildas in the Latin form, *rector*. It is possible that *rechtur* developed the broader meaning of 'ruler', but even if that were the sense here, it does suggest a continuity of control. It would seem that Arthur's activities in the area were not 'one-off' raids or battles.

Arthur probably maintained a force in Rheon for some time to pacify the area. Gildas had described the bloodthirsty Irish sailing over the sea valleys to Britain, and with the Picts, capturing the northern part of Britain right down to Hadrian's Wall (*The Ruin of Britain*, Section 19.1). The Loch Ryan peninsula is only 21 miles from Ireland. It appears that Arthur's activities there were to control the influx of Irish – to block their shortest route. These achievements earned Arthur an enormous reputation in Scotland as reflected in the *Y Gododdin* stanza which portrays him as a heroic paragon. Although the honorand of the stanza, Gorddur, was indeed a courageous warrior, a parenthetical aside states 'though he was not Arthur', implying that merely being compared to Arthur was an honour.

The *Kadeir Teÿrnon* poet does not even mention Badon. If Arthur had won Badon, the poet did not consider it (being only a single battle) as notable as protecting the northern Britons over an extended period of time. This outlook is entirely incompatible with anything written after 829-30 when Badon was certainly celebrated as his most important battle in the *Historia Brittonum*. It suggests that *Kadeir Teÿrnon* was a very early work.

So what is Arthur's status with respect to Badon? Given the Welsh poem behind the *Historia* battle list, it is probable that he was the victor. But this judgement is hardly secure. Unfortunately, the embittered Gildas cannot be relied upon to give an unbiased account. To him, the victor was probably a military tyrant, unless of course it were Ambrosius, in which case he would have certainly expanded his account to enlarge his hero's accomplishments. For Arthur not to have been the victor would imply that while the Britons did remember details about other sixth-century figures they forgot who won the famous battle named by Gildas, allowing Arthur to displace the anonymous victor. This seems improbable.

Arthur's Bard

If the north Wales location for Arthur is accepted, then it may also suggest an identity for Arthur's bard, the poet who composed *Preideu Annwfyn*, *Kat Godeu* and *Kadeir Teÿrnon*. Although the poems are ostensibly attributed to Taliesin, it seems unlikely that he could have composed them if he were the bard of Urien Rheged, a northern British king whose floruit was the second half of the sixth century. However, there is another possibility. Only four miles northeast of Llangernyw, also lying on the River Elwy, is the village of Llanfair Talhaiarn, apparently named after the major sixth-century bard, Talhaearn (meaning 'Iron Brow'). The eminent scholar, Geraint Gruffydd, identifies four Talhaearn placenames (one of which is Llanfair Talhaiarn) in north Wales. He wonders whether Talhaearn was the bard of Maglocunus or one of his forebears.[10]

Talhaearn is named in a group of five famous bards (including Taliesin) who lived in the sixth century. He seems to have been the leading bard, as he was called 'father of inspiration' and was named first. He was also separated slightly in time from the other four who were famous 'at the same time'. These points could imply that Talhaearn was somewhat earlier. If Taliesin sang to Urien in the second half of the sixth century then perhaps Talhaearn sang in the first half, making him contemporaneous with Arthur.

Later poetry presents Talhaearn as a great sage and having a Christian outlook, features which appear in *Preideu Annwfyn*, *Kadeir Teÿrnon* and *Kat Godeu*, while this theme of 'inspiration' is prominent in two of these poems. Although it cannot be proven that 'Iron Brow' was Arthur's bard, he seems to be an excellent candidate, appearing in the right place, at the right time, with the requisite skill and beliefs.

EVIDENCE FOR A VOYAGE TO AMERICA

This book puts forward new ideas concerning the poems *Preideu Annwfyn*, *Kat Godeu* and *Kadeir Teÿrnon* which are currently considered to contain only legendary or mythological material. It is argued that the three poems were by Arthur's bard and hence were eyewitness accounts from the sixth century. When these poems are analysed from this historical perspective, a coherent picture emerges. The key poem is *Preideu Annwfyn*, a masterpiece of building tension, which gives vivid images of what is here interpreted as a journey to North America after the conclusion of the Hopewell period. However unlike a modern narrative it does not give an ordered sequence of events. Rather, the bard presents a series of word pictures of the parts of the journey that were of interest to him. The following references to events in the poem have been ordered in the temporal sequence in which they probably occurred rather than the poetic sequence.

The Preideu Annwfyn Account
Arthur's voyage
This poem commences by praising the great king who has now extended his sovereignty over the shores of the world. Later it is stated that 'nobody before him went into it'. In Line 21, this king is identified as Arthur. From these statements it is quite evident that a new and important journey had been undertaken. These are not the sort of statements one would associate with a mythical visit to a kind of fairyland.

Passing a large iceberg
There are lines implying that it was a long sea voyage and in a later stanza it is stated that they passed a 'glass fortress'. This incident is closely related to a brief story in the *Historia Brittonum* as is well known to scholars.[11] In the *Historia*, the 'glass fortress' is described as a 'glass tower in the middle of the sea'. Both representations would suggest an iceberg. This sighting may have

occurred at the iceberg zone off the coasts of Labrador and Newfoundland. Sailing beyond the icebergs (as indicated in the poem), it would appear that they reached some part of North America. The iceberg sighting indicates that a northern route was taken, probably using the island stepping stones – the Hebrides or Orkneys, the Faroes, Iceland, and then possibly the west coast of Greenland. This northern route suggests that the Britons would have entered the Gulf of St Lawrence, either through the Strait of Belle Isle or via the Cabot Strait south of Newfoundland.

The 'four-peaked' camp

After entering the Gulf of St Lawrence, they appear to have sailed partway up the St Lawrence River. They also endured a camp of 'extreme coldness', possibly somewhere along the St Lawrence, just as Jacques Cartier did in the Winter of 1535-36 when he camped at Quebec. They also stopped at the 'four-peaked' camp, an important camp that is mentioned in two stanzas. This was early in the new land and the men seemed to be in good spirits, with the bard singing his poetry and receiving acclaim.

The 'four-peaked' camp appears to have been at Montreal, with its four interesting and unusual peaks: Royal, St-Bruno, St-Hilaire and Rougemont. In exploring the area the Britons probably climbed the nearby Mont Royal to get a view of the surrounding terrain and the way ahead. From the top of Mont Royal, the similar long flat peaks of Bruno, Hilaire and Rougemont would have been prominent in the otherwise level plain across the river. The Lachine Rapids probably prevented the expedition from getting their main ships past Montreal. Nevertheless, the Britons appear to have followed the St Lawrence, continuing southwest, past or across the Great Lakes and finally entering the Eastern Woodlands of North America.

Kaer Sidi (Mound Fortress)

When in the Eastern Woodlands the Britons camped in the most significant region of the journey at a place they called *kaer sidi*. Sarah Higley translates it 'mound fortress' and recognizes its central importance by suggesting that it would have made an appropriate title to the poem.[12] In the fantasy viewpoint, these would have been fairy mounds and the Britons would have been fighting the fairy-like creatures who lived in them. For example, Kenneth Jackson and John Bollard translate *kaer sidi* as the 'Faery City' and the 'fairy fortress' respectively.[13]

This reference to mounds represents a serious predictive test for the North America hypothesis, as one can imagine a survey of what is known of sixth-century North America yielding no mention of mounds. However this test is passed with flying colours. Well before Arthur's expedition, Eastern North America had been dominated by the rich culture of the Hopewell, 'the moundbuilders'. Their ceremonial earthen mounds had been built centuries earlier and were widely distributed across eastern North America and densely distributed along the river systems of southern Ohio. These earthworks were of religious importance to the Native Americans, which would have inevitably led to conflict with any strangers who entered the region.

Different languages
There is an interesting incident in *Preideu Annwfyn* when the Britons met the Native Americans. It is a word picture of intimidation – a large number of them had massed and were standing on a wall above the Britons. Although one cannot be sure where this scene occurred, it would suit the Hopewell central region where earthworks were abundant. The large number suggests that they had gathered together from the neighbouring areas to present a formidable front to the Britons. It would also have been highly appropriate for them to have been standing on one of the earthen walls which enclosed their ceremonial mounds. They were making sure that the mounds and their treasures were not desecrated. The British interpreter could not understand the language of the inhabitants, a situation consistent with two peoples with entirely different languages who had never met before.

Contrast the above view with the fairyland interpretation. The image of a large number of fairy creatures standing on a wall, as a show of strength, is absurd. As depicted in the literature, fairies do not need to mass together as a show of strength to achieve their ends. Rather, they work through magic and trickery. Also, the notion of fairies not being understood by the Britons is inconsistent with the accounts depicting their easy communication with humans in the Irish Otherworld stories. The fact that the Annwfyn people had to muster in large numbers to show their strength suggests they were being portrayed as human beings, not fairies.

Gweir imprisoned
Gweir, a person well known to the bard, is introduced near the start of the poem. He has been captured and imprisoned at *kaer sidi*. From the bard's positive statements about Gweir it is clear that his imprisonment is at the hands of the inhabitants rather than a punishment administered by Arthur's men. The bard seems to be terrified as to what will happen to Gweir which indicates something about the fierceness of the inhabitants – he states that he will pray for Gweir until Judgement Day.

Gweir could not be rescued as the British expedition was almost totally destroyed, with only a few escaping. The bard, now back in Britain and reflecting on Gweir's plight, gives the metaphor of Arthur sailing into the 'heavy blue chain' which imprisons Gweir over and above his literal prison – a metaphor for the vast expanse of ocean. Gweir's capture was reported by two of Arthur's men, Pwyll and Pryderi, who are father and son in the *Mabinogi* tales. In the 19th-century theories of John Rhŷs these two are claimed to be a pair of 'dark divinities' – a complete nonsense.[14]

The bard's extended and sympathetic treatment of Gweir suggests that the interpretation of the poem as a fantasy is implausible. If it were only a fantasy in which virtually all the fictional people were killed, then the deep concern over one additional fictional person does not make sense. It would make sense, however, if the character were a real person known to the bard. If Gweir were merely a character created by the bard, then why the deeply felt anxiety about him and the vow to pray for him until Judgement Day? Why devote the opening stanza to Gweir if he were simply a fiction? These would be odd and incongruous actions by the bard for the sake of a mere fictional character of low rank, only a loyal servant or loyal youth.

The 'cauldron' decorated with pearls

In the conflict with the Annwfyn warriors the Britons took a 'cauldron' as spoils of a raid, a ceremonial clay pot with dark rim and pearl decoration. The Hopewell used pearls extensively – Olaf Prufer refers to one Hopewell site which alone yielded around 100,000 freshwater pearls.[15] The bard notes the bravery of the inhabitants, saying of the cauldron's owners that 'it does not boil the food of a coward'. This implies that they were viewed as mortals, with human weaknesses, who could be wounded or killed. Again, the inhabitants are not being depicted as fairies. It would seem bizarre to compliment fairy beings, possessed with magical powers, on their courage in fighting.

The American buffalo

The bard also notes that the inhabitants have limitations on where they can travel – they do not visit the Defwy meadows in Britain. This again implies they were seen as people, not fairies, as fairies have no limitations on where they can visit. He then refers to an animal that clearly identifies the country as North America – the buffalo. He calls it the 'brindled ox' and describes its huge head and shoulders, so large that they seem out of proportion to the rest of the body. The term 'brindled' probably refers to the patchy yellow-brown cape on the shoulders and back.

The buffalo grazed along the rivers in the central Hopewell territory near the mounds, including the Scioto and Muskingum rivers. The leading scholar Olaf Prufer writes: 'the most striking assemblage of these works [the mounds] is located in…the valleys of the Muskingum, Scioto and Miami rivers'. In the late 1700s David Zeisberger, who was a missionary to the Native Americans in Ohio, reported in his writings that buffalo had been plentiful along the Muskingum and Scioto rivers.[16]

The tamed animal with the silvery head

The poet states that the Annwfyn inhabitants had tamed an animal with a silvery head. The identity of this animal may be inferred from the animal effigy carvings on the Hopewell smoking pipes. Among these are carvings of the North American river otter, often carrying a fish in its mouth. A lifelike carving shows an otter standing, a fish in its mouth, with its head raised so that the nostrils are higher than the eyes – it appears as though the otter is presenting the fish. See the photo in Figure 10.6 and this carving viewed from a different angle in the book of Bradley Lepper.[17]

It is well known that the highly intelligent otter has been trained to catch fish by many societies throughout the world, going back for well over a millennium, as discussed in detail by Eugene Gudger. The otter is perfectly at home in its aquatic environment, diving under the water to catch fish. The 'silvery head' image probably refers to the poet viewing the otter swimming on the surface, where it keeps its head above water. When its glossy fur is wet it presents a silvery sheen which the poet has accurately described.

Conflict with the Native Americans
It appears that the Britons' movement through North America terminated in the Eastern Woodlands, possibly in Ohio or nearby states where there was an abundance of Hopewell earthworks. They were decimated as a result of the 'woeful conflict' mentioned in *Preideu Annwfyn*.

Are there indications of conflict from the American perspective? Indeed there are – the Native Americans were under threat at this time. Olaf Prufer, asks 'What was the nature of the danger?' and remarks that 'Unrest of some kind appears to have been afoot throughout eastern North America'. Prufer also states that until around AD 550, the Native Americans felt secure in themselves and did not take any steps to guard their treasures from raiders.[18] Prufer's paper was published in 1964 and his dating may need to be revised to an earlier period, possibly 50 years earlier. However, given the large errors of measurement typical of such dating, Prufer's date for the conflict is close to the estimated date for Arthur's expedition in the 530s, that was obtained independently. Furthermore, the Hopewell era was usually one of peace and prosperity for at least half a millennium. It was at the close of their culture and afterwards that the Native Americans were under threat.

The climax of the poem
From Stanza 4 onwards, the perspective of the poem shifts back to Britain as the bard ferociously attacks the monks, an overflow of rage in response to Gildas' malicious slandering of the British kings, their bards, and the military in *The Ruin of Britain*. In Stanza 7, the bard depicts a vivid scene where the monks are shrinking back in fear (like a pack of dogs) from a clash with lords 'who know'. The importance of this scene is established when it is virtually repeated in Stanza 8, where this time the monks are likened to wolves packing together.

The vital question is: what do the lords know that the monks do not? This secret is skilfully delayed until nearly the end of the poem. Throughout the poem there has been the relentless repetition of the line 'except seven, none returned from ...' where various camps are named. Given this and the bard's other expressions of distress such as 'disastrous visit' and 'woeful conflict', one wonders whether Arthur himself survived.

Finally in the climax in Line 58, the bard announces what the lords know: that the grave of 'the saint' has been lost or annihilated, and that his body was not retrievable – Arthur, the Christian king, has been killed in Annwfyn.

Annwfyn in Kat Godeu

Further information on Arthur's time in America is given in the mysterious poem *Kat Godeu* (Battle of the Trees). It was composed by a old man who laments that no-one visits him anymore except one particular friend. He states that he was a former bard who sang before the Lord of Britain and was also a warrior who slew many of the enemy. He seems to be reviewing the important events of his life, one of which was his time in Annwfyn. As both this bard and Arthur were in Annwfyn, the bard is identifying himself as Arthur's bard and Arthur as the Lord of Britain. The Annwfyn section is given in Lines 189 to 204 of *Kat Godeu*.

Mustering for battle via the streams

It commences with a description of the inhabitants of Annwfyn using the streams of the region to muster for battle. This feature appears to be that of an eyewitness as one would not expect an enemy army in Britain or in Europe to gather for battle by means of the streams – they would probably arrive on horseback or by marching.

Concerning the fairyland view, it is implausible to have the fairies arriving by boats in the streams. As fairies, they could simply fly there or materialize to any location they wish. The gathering by streams, however, would have been perfectly appropriate for the Native Americans. Their elaborate earthworks were most dense along the rivers and streams of southern Ohio which formed a network of navigable pathways on which they could travel freely in their canoes.

An honour bestowed by a dying lord

The bard then describes the torrid fighting in the typical exaggeration of bardic poetry – he slew 'four-score hundred'. He remarks that the people there had a similar lust for battle as he did and notes their passion, saying that each had the passion of a hundred normal warriors. Then follows an intriguing incident of great interest. The bard's bloodspotted sword brings him an honour that is bestowed by a lord from a concealed place. This is interpreted here as the dying Arthur, who is hidden away from the fighting, presenting an honour to the bard.

Then follows a line with a clear translation but an enigmatic meaning – by a meek one was the warrior killed. It is argued that this honour may have been a request by the wounded Arthur to be killed by the bard. That is, the 'meek one' was a friend performing the necessary task as an act of mercy. It is possible that this also included a beheading so that the head could be taken away to prevent mutilation by the enemy.

As noted in Chapter 6 this would be yet another element in the striking parallels between Arthur and the later character modelled on him, Brân. In the second *Mabinogi* story (written about 500-600 years after Arthur's time), when Brân was mortally wounded he asked his men to kill him and cut off his head. The *Mabinogi* composer may have included this incident because he interpreted the *Kat Godeu* lines in the same way as above or had heard another tradition of Arthur's beheading and copied it for Brân.

A second incident in the *Mabinogi* story may also reveal how Arthur was wounded. Brân is called by the name *Morddwyd Tyllion* (Pierced Thighs), an obscure traditional epithet introduced into the narrative. This odd title is so awkwardly introduced that initially the reader may think it refers to a new character. If Brân were modelled on Arthur, as the many parallels imply, then it suggests that Arthur may have been wounded this same way in Annwfyn, pierced in the thighs by poisoned spears.

Aftermath of the Voyage
Caretakers for Britain

Kadeir Teÿrnon (Chair of the Sovereign) is the third poem considered here to have been composed by Arthur's bard. The setting is in Britain soon after Arthur's death and the initial section refers to a eulogy to Arthur. Although the poem does not mention his expedition to Annwfyn directly, it does imply that he was absent from Britain for a significant time. Immediately after the initial section, implying continuity with it, the bard asks 'Who were the three stewards that minded the country?' There is little or no material provided in the poem to explain this extraordinary question so it would appear that the bard's audience knew about Arthur's absence overseas and thus could make sense of the question.

Similarly, Brân in the *Mabinogi* had seven caretakers appointed to mind Britain while he invaded Ireland. As noted earlier, Rachel Bromwich argues that the Brân author increased the caretaker number from the original three to seven. The appointment of caretakers for Brân's absence is one of the many parallels between Arthur and Brân.

An absence of several years

The notion of caretakers for Britain, when considered in conjunction with material from the other poems, suggests that Arthur's expedition was away for a considerable time. It is highly likely that they would have left Britain as soon as good weather prevailed, in Spring or early Summer. Exploring the Gulf of St Lawrence and finding the St Lawrence River may have pretty much exhausted the fine weather before Winter arrived. Somewhere on their northern route they endured a 'camp of extreme coldness', spending Winter there. They reached Montreal, the 'four-peaked' camp, but probably would not have been able to travel any further in their main ships because of the Lachine Rapids. Somehow they continued south, possibly tracking the St Lawrence and passing the Great Lakes. They may have used smaller skin-covered boats for part of this journey, carrying them on land when the river conditions were too difficult.

Eventually they entered the Eastern Woodlands where there was an abundance of earthworks. While there they observed the buffalo grazing and noted that the Native Americans had tamed the otter to assist in fishing. At some point they became involved in the 'woeful conflict'. It appears that the Britons would have spent at least another Winter in North America, probably in the Eastern Woodlands. Overall given the above sequence of events it appears that they would have been away for at least two years, and possibly longer. If this reconstruction is correct, then they travelled a considerable way inland. This was certainly not a single-season voyage in which they crossed the Atlantic and briefly sailed along the coast before returning home.

INADEQUACY OF THE NON-HISTORICAL INTERPRETATIONS

It is argued here that the current non-historical interpretations of *Preideu Annwfyn* are manifestly inadequate. The 'Annwfyn as fairyland' view fails on many counts. There is the 'glass fortress' interpreted literally as such, a kind of glass fairy castle – an absurdity. This view is still held despite the closely related story in the *Historia* calling it as 'a glass tower in the middle of the sea' and the *Navigatio* of St Brendan describing a 'crystal pillar' in the sea. It implies that the 'glass fortress' was a metaphor for a large iceberg.

The Otherworld is a Celtic paradise where everything is perfect – death, sin, decay, sickness are unknown and happiness prevails. Yet Arthur's men had encountered terrible conditions and were almost entirely destroyed in 'woeful conflict'. The Otherworld 'people of the síd'/fairies are immortals, yet many of the Annwfyn people were killed in the fighting, as stated by the *Kat Godeu* bard. Further, the Otherworld fairies are able to travel anywhere and easily understand the humans yet the Annwfyn inhabitants did not visit Britain and could not understand the Britons. In summary, the Annwfyn in *Preideu Annwfyn* and *Kat Godeu* bears no resemblance to portrayals of the Otherworld in the extant literature of this type.

Another non-historical view does not address the issue of the identity of the Annwfyn people at all but regards the *Preideu Annwfyn* bard as trying to upstage the monks in a kind of contest for supremacy in learning. Thus the bard is frequently pointing out things that the monks do not know but which the bard does. This explanation has some truth but there is a wider context explaining why the bard is ridiculing the monks. The knowledge of which the monks were ignorant concerns incidents in Annwfyn, not items of book learning or traditional knowledge. In addition, some of the implied questions are merely fillers that were designed to increase dramatic tension by delaying the climax of the poem. The climax itself, the announcement of Arthur's death, occurs when the lords break the news to the monks in a contentious meeting where the monks are shrinking back in fear. Clearly this scene has nothing to do with a contest for superiority in learning.

Furthermore, the desire to expose the monks' ignorance was fuelled by an anger caused by Gildas' malicious slandering of the British kings, bards and military. The fact that this anger was so inflamed, occupying the last five of the total of eight stanzas, suggests that *The Ruin of Britain* had been recently disseminated and that the slanders therein were being widely discussed. The bard, having endured terrible conditions in Annwfyn and the death of his comrades and king, must have been rankled by the failure of the expedition. His statements implying that the monks were cowards and weak in resolve go far beyond a contest of learning.

Neither the 'fairyland' interpretation nor the 'contest of learning' view is adequate. They do not address the issues that the bard treats the Annwfyn inhabitants as real people with human limitations who could be wounded or killed, who mustered to confront the Britons by means of the rivers, and who could not understand the Britons' language. These interpretations also do not explain all the details of *Preideu Annwfyn*. They do not adequately explain the 'glass fortress', the 'four-peaked' camp, the 'mound fortress', the pearl-decorated cauldron, the Defwy meadows, the communication failure, the brindled ox, the tamed animal with the silvery head, the clash with the lords 'who know', the grave of the saint being lost/annihilated, and so on. These events all have a natural interpretation when viewed from a historical perspective as discussed in the preceding chapters.

Rival Explanations for the 'Glass Fortress'

In science, when trying to determine which of two hypotheses is the more probable, one seeks to design an experiment that will clearly separate the rival alternatives. Although this obviously cannot be achieved with a poem, there is an incident in *Preideu Annwfyn* that does help to distinguish two radically different viewpoints, as will now be discussed.

In the poem, Arthur is said to have extended his sovereignty over the shores of the world, which suggests a long sea voyage. On the journey the sailors passed a 'glass fortress' beyond which the monks 'did not see the valour of Arthur'. How this glass fortress is viewed gives a clear separation of alternative models. In this book, the glass fortress is viewed as a large iceberg. In the mythological view the glass fortress is a kind of glass fairy castle, a fantasy, and therefore its glass composition is not thought to be problematic. Towers of glass or crystal in the sea also appear in the *Historia Brittonum* and the *Navigatio* of St Brendan. It would not be unreasonable to infer that the same type of object is being referred to in all three texts. It is doubtful that a scholar would say, for example, that the object represents an iceberg in one instance but a glass fairy castle in another. Therefore it would not be an unreasonable inference to consider all three as three representations of the same object.

In the *Historia Brittonum* the ships sail up to a glass tower in the middle of the sea (*turrim vitream in medio mari*). This phrase suggests an iceberg is intended as no island is mentioned. Most scholars would agree that this account is closely related to certain lines in *Preideu Annwfyn*. It has been argued in Chapter 9 that the final rendering of the *Historia* account is a garbled version of *Preideu Annwfyn*, the latter preceding it by centuries. The silly details about the men standing on the glass tower who would not speak to the sailors and the subsequent attack appear to be based on lines 30-2 of the poem. It is clear from the close relationship between the texts that it was originally understood that the 'glass fortress' in *Preideu Annwfyn* was the same object as the 'glass tower in the middle of the sea'.

In the *Navigatio* of St Brendan the setting is not Otherworldly. There are wonders but these are there to show the power of God and the glories of God's dominion. The monks navigate in their small curragh and observe a 'crystal pillar' in the sea ahead. The size of the pillar takes them by surprise – after first seeing it, it takes them three days to sail up to it. When they sail alongside the pillar it is so tall that they cannot see the top of it. The sea in that region was clear, allowing the monks to discern that the pillar extended underneath the water. This feature suggests that the pillar was not built on land. The monks are amazed at this object, describing it as a wonder shown to them by Christ. It is represented as inert and uninhabited and the monks do not view it as a fairy castle. No fairies or Otherworld creatures come forth to interact with the monks. They spend four days there sailing around it and estimating the length of its sides. Although their description of the crystal pillar is elaborated with various wondrous details, there seems to be little doubt that it represents an iceberg.

From the perspective argued above, the lack of interest in interpreting the 'glass fortress' as an iceberg is interesting. Roger Loomis spent much space in discussing it but only gave the 'glass fairy castle' interpretation.[19] Other scholars continue this trend: not one mentions the possibility in their various commentaries that it could represent an iceberg. It would appear that the mythological model that these scholars have adopted is preventing them from seeing something that is starkly obvious – that the three instances of 'glass fortress', 'glass tower in the middle of the sea' and the 'crystal pillar' in the sea are all icebergs.[20] When this latter mindset is adopted, the fantasy view starts to unravel and the view that the poem is describing a real voyage comes into focus.

CONCLUSION

The above has given an outline of the new evidence for Arthur. If *Preideu Annwfyn* were composed by Arthur's bard, then its date of composition would be around 540, probably making it older than stanza B2.38 of the northern poem *Y Gododdin* which may have been composed a decade or two later. The *Kat Godeu* poem, composed by Arthur's bard in his old age, would also have been decades later. If *Kadeir Teÿrnon* were also by Arthur's bard, then it may have been composed shortly after *Preideu Annwfyn*. These statements are surmises based on the arguments presented earlier.

Preideu Annwfyn is the key poem considered in this book. The ancient Britons initially recognised its importance and understood its allusions. It was valued so highly that incidents in this poem became elaborated and incorporated into other literature, as was noted in Chapter 9. However over time, misunderstandings took place in this borrowing. Events described by metaphors were taken literally and details in a scene were misinterpreted. Further, incidents were elaborated in the other literature (as shown in Table 9.1) which tended to disguise the original meaning in the source. Over the centuries, knowledge of the poem's meaning has been lost, resulting in the current situation where the poem is largely opaque. *Kat Godeu* also has an important Annwfyn section giving supplementary information but this data has lain dormant. It is buried in the middle of a long poem whose main theme ostensibly seems to be an imaginative fantasy.

Arthur as the North Wales Overking

The new evidence on Arthur's roles in north Wales and southwest Scotland can be considered independently from that concerning his expedition to America. One could in theory accept the first and reject the second, or vice versa. The view taken here is that the evidence for the American expedition is stronger than the evidence that Arthur was from north Wales. However, the latter is very plausible. There is persuasive evidence for the existence of an overking in Gildas. The king he called both 'the Bear' and 'Pharaoh' was a powerful figure who had the warlike tyrant Cuneglasus as his subordinate 'chariot driver'. Arthur's name was perfect for the punster Gildas to call him 'the Bear', which was *Arth* in Neo-Brittonic. The fact that Gildas later refers to the five kings (Cuneglasus amongst them) as being part of the retinue of 'Pharaoh' confirms the notion of an overking.

The north Wales location implied by the stronghold at Dinarth could easily have been contradicted by the independent poetic sources considered earlier. However, far from contradicting it, they confirm it. *Preideu Annwfyn* suggests that the meadows along the River Dee were in Arthur's domain and *Kadeir Teÿrnon* states that Arthur wore the lorica of Lleon, which implies a Chester or a northeast Wales location. Arthur's battle at Chester listed in the *Historia Brittonum* is also consistent with the above.

With a north Wales location, other elements fall into place. Just eight miles inland from Dinarth the placename *Kernyw* is preserved in the village name of Llangernyw, indicating a place associated with Arthur in Triad 1 of the Welsh Triads. Further, Geraint Gruffydd notes the four placenames in the area associated with Talhaearn, a leading sixth-century bard called 'father of inspiration'. None of Talhaearn's poetry survives in his name, but it is argued here that 'Iron Brow' may have been Arthur's bard, the composer of *Preideu Annwfyn*, *Kat Godeu* and *Kadeir Teÿrnon*.

Arthur's north Wales base gave him a central location from which to operate. He was well placed to fight Badon if it were in the southeast Wales border locations where speculation often places it. He could easily have moved east to strike the Anglo-Saxons in Lindsey if his four battles in that area (and possibly a fifth) from the *Historia Brittonum* were genuine. As Arthur was a seaman, his ships would not have taken long to get his warriors to harbours around the Solway Firth or the Loch Ryan region in Galloway. In his governance of Rheon, Arthur could have landed his ships in Luce Bay and marched to any suitable destination around Loch Ryan. Or he could have sailed into Loch Ryan itself. He appears to have achieved a formidable reputation for checking the influx of Irish who were launching terrifying raids on the Britons and at one stage controlled northern Britain down to Hadrian's Wall according to Gildas.

This book has argued that Arthur was a powerful historical figure whose great achievements left such an indelible impression that legends developed around him. Arthur was not a petty Dark Age warlord, barely distinguishable from the other local chieftains, who somehow inexplicably became the focus of legends, as some would suggest.[21] The legends were based on the Britons' admiration of his achievements.

The launching of an expedition to what is now North America comes as a massive surprise. However, it does explain the mystery of Arthur's death in the *Stanzas of the Graves* and the legends that subsequently developed that Arthur was recovering from his wounds in a mysterious overseas location. In each of the three poems *Preideu Annwfyn*, *Kat Godeu* and *Kadeir Teÿrnon*, the bard indicates the deep respect that both he and Arthur's men held for Arthur, a respect which goes beyond conventional praise imagery. The *Kat Godeu* tribute sums it up succinctly:

> *Shining his name,*
> *Strong of hand,*
> *Brilliantly he governed the host.*

NOTES

Preface
[1] Dumville (1977: 188).
[2] Neyman and Pearson (1967: 190).
[3] Rhŷs (1891); Chambers (1927: 206).
[4] Dumville (1977: 187).
[5] Winterbottom (1978: 36).
[6] Williams (1899: 77).
[7] Winterbottom (1978: 31).
[8] Williams (1899: 67).
[9] McClure and Collins (1994: 124).
[10] For Dinarth, see Longley and Laing (1997: 90). The river *Devwy* appears in *Preideu Annwfyn;* Koch and Carey (2003: 365) suggest *Deuwy* could be the 'Dee'. Haycock (2007: 309) links *Lleon* with north Wales. Bromwich (2006: 164) gives Arthur's mistresses. Jones (1967: 114-5) gives the burial places.
[11] See Haycock (2007: 167-239; 293-311; 433-51) for the three poems.
[12] Jackson (1959b: 16); Bollard (1994: 20).
[13] Rhŷs (1891: 282); Jackson (1959b: 17).
[14] Nash (1858: 214); Rhŷs (1888: 248); Squire (1905: 318).
[15] Haycock (2007: 433-4).
[16] Williams (1899: 21, 45); Winterbottom (1978: 29-36).
[17] Haycock (2007: 446); Koch and Carey (2003: 291); O'Meara (2002: 53-4).

Chapter 1   Overview of Arthur
[1] *Preideu Annwfyn* is pronounced approximately as 'Prythee Annoovyn'. The 'd' in *Preideu* functions as the Welsh 'dd', pronounced 'th', so that the word is pronounced approximately 'Prythee'. The 'w' in Annwfyn is pronounced 'oo', while the 'f' is pronounced as a 'v', as in 'of'. Annwfyn has long been identified with the Celtic Otherworld.
[2] Higley (1996: 45).
[3] Prufer (1964: 93).
[4] Hulbert and Schwarze (1910: 59).
[5] Barney et al. (2006: 373-6).
[6] Hammond (1996: 60-3).
[7] Jackson (1953: 116); Charles-Edwards (1991: 29).
[8] As discussed in the Preface, assigning a person to the 'legendary' category is not necessarily safe and could result in a Type 2 error.
[9] Myres (1986: 16); Morris (1973); Dumville (1977).
[10] Padel (1994); Green (2007a).
[11] Chadwick and Chadwick (1932: 161).
[12] Bromwich (1991); Williams (1991).
[13] There is a *Mirabilia* (Marvels) appendix to the *Historia Brittonum* which lists 'marvels' associated with various sites in Britain. These include a hot pool that adjusts its temperature to that which the bather desires; an altar held up in the air by the will of God; a log associated with a well that always returns to the well when removed; a tomb that stretches or contracts to be the same length as

any man that lies down beside it; a hill that rotates in a circle three times a year; a stone which at night time walks over a particular valley, and so on.

By the early 800s, the marvels about Arthur had started to develop, two of which are included in the *Mirabilia*. One concerns Arthur killing his son *Amr* and burying him. The marvel is that when men come to measure the grave, it is sometimes six feet, sometimes nine feet and sometimes fifteen feet. That is, whatever you measure it at one time, the next time it will be a different length. The historicity of Amr is doubtful, as no early Welsh literature mentions him.

A second marvel concerns Arthur's dog leaving a footprint impression on a stone when Arthur was hunting a giant boar. The marvel is that when the stone is removed from on top of a pile, it reappears there the next day. The boar, known as *Twrch Trwyd* (or *Twrch Trwyth*), also appears in a poem *Gorchan Cynfelyn* from the *Book of Aneirin*, where the hero's valour is compared to that of the boar, but Arthur is not mentioned in this poem (Jarman, 1989-90: 24). The theme of heroes hunting a great boar is ancient, having been told centuries before Christ in ancient Greece, where the tale is a prelude to the story of the Trojan War. There a giant boar was sent by Artemis to destroy the region of Calydon in Aetolia. A later account of the story appears in *Metamorphoses* by the Roman poet Ovid, who lived during the time of Christ.

The boar hunt tales then arrived in Britain to appear first in *Gorchan Cynfelyn* (without Arthur), then in the *Historia Mirabilia* and later in *Culhwch and Olwen*. Arthur's prowess as a warrior was now such that human antagonists were no longer formidable enough or interesting enough opponents, so that the giant boar was pressed into service as an adversary.

[14] Koch and Carey (2003: 296-7). Ambrosius confounds the magicians at the court of Vortigern, revealing the existence of two snakes (dragons) beneath the foundations of his fort. The dragons fight, and after initial dominance by the white dragon, the red dragon drives the white dragon away. Ambrosius gives the interpretation that the Britons (the red dragon) would drive out the Saxons (the white dragon) and regain their lands. Ambrosius claims that his father was a Roman consul, a reference to Gildas' statement that his parents had 'worn the purple' (Winterbottom, 1978: 28).

[15] In her folkloric view of Arthur, Green (2007a) argues that the texts which portray Arthur as fighting exotic creatures suggest that Arthur was seen by the Britons as mythical himself. She assigns the titles *Protector of Britain* and *Hero Protector* to Arthur, titles which in reality are only hypothetical constructs that are designed to portray Arthur in a certain way. Arthur is thus constructed as a *Hero Protector* that protects the Britons from such supernatural threats. What are these threats? Green (2007a: 122) lists them as follows: 'Arthur protected the Britons from – dog-heads, cat-monsters, giants, dragons, witches, shape-shifters and divine boars'.

Is there any evidence that Britons in the sixth century regarded themselves as being under threat from these exotic creatures? Our only detailed sixth-century source on Britain was written by Gildas. He extensively discusses the threats that were worrying the Britons in his *Ruin of Britain*. However, there is no mention of the exotic threats that Green names. To Gildas the threats were raids from the Irish, the Picts and the Saxons and possible chastisement and testing from God, as evidenced by disasters such as famines. A similar situation existed in the near contemporary Frankish kingdoms where Gregory of Tours detailed the lives of prominent people and their power struggles, an account where such supernatural creatures are never mentioned.

Although credulous people doubtless existed in the sixth century and others may have jested about legendary creatures (as they do today), there is nothing to indicate that the average person in Britain was concerned about cat monsters, dogheads, giants, dragons, witches, shape-shifters or even divine boars. There is simply no contemporary evidence that such legendary creatures had any impact on daily life and hence no need for a hypothesised *Hero Protector* figure to safeguard the people of Britain from such non-existent threats.

If there is no sixth-century evidence that Britons were concerned about supernatural creatures, then where has the above list of exotic creatures come from? A survey of Green's (2007a) book gives the sources, reproduced in the table below, along with their approximate dating. From this table, it can be seen that the data about Arthur's supernatural opponents comes from very late sources. Sims-Williams (1991a: 39) is the source of the *Pa Gûr* dating, while Rodway (2005: 43) dates *Culhwch and Olwen*.

Supernatural creatures: their sources and dating

Opponent	Text	Date composed
Dogheads	Pa Gûr	c. 1100
Cat monsters	Pa Gûr	c. 1100
	Romanz des Franceis	c. 1190
Giants	Culhwch and Olwen	c. 1160
	Geoffrey of Monmouth	c. 1138
Dragons	Life of St Euflamm	c. 1110
	Life of St Carannog	c. 1150
Witches	Pa Gûr	c. 1100
	Culhwch and Olwen	c. 1160
Shape-shifters	Pa Gûr	c. 1100
	Culhwch and Olwen	c. 1160
Giant boars	Mirabilia	829-30
	Culhwch and Olwen	c. 1160

It is invalid to infer that any hero depicted in miraculous events in these stories was necessarily mythical. These sources are biased to the exotic and the weird to entertain. There is burlesque and farce (Roberts, 1991: 77), parody, concern with sanctifying the saints and providing them with a foil (Arthur), and the desire to entertain by creating unusual and formidable opponents.

In the *Lives* above, both Euflamm and Carannog defeat a terrifying dragon, but these saints are considered to be historical, as are St Illtud and King Meurig who appear in the *Mirabilia*. Apart from the biased nature of these sources, it is invalid to infer what people thought about Arthur in the sixth century from sources which are many centuries later. Any inference drawn from this data which

implies that Arthur was seen as fighting mythical creatures in the sixth century and so was mythical himself is worthless.
[16] See Piggott (1941); Tatlock (1950); Parry and Caldwell (1959); Wright (1982; 1984; 1986).
[17] The *Life of Merlin* is dated to circa 1150 by Parry (1925: 14-15). Merlin was a composite character, being the creation of Geoffrey of Monmouth. His portrayal of Merlin uses the following three elements:

- The placename Caerfyrddin (Carmarthen) resulted in the creation of a phantom character, Myrddin, to (incorrectly) explain how the town received its name.
- This Carmarthen Myrddin was later fused with Lailoken, the north-British wildman of the woods, associated with the battle of Arfderydd of AD 573. Lailoken's name was largely replaced by Myrddin's.
- Geoffrey took the *Historia Brittonum* portrait of the boy wizard, born of a virgin mother (based on the historical Ambrosius in Gildas) and fused him with Myrddin. In doing this, he latinized the Myrddin name to Merlinus, calling his boy wizard both Merlinus and Ambrosius.

Merlin was a composite figure, the fusion of three elements. It is unclear whether Geoffrey did the merging of Lailoken with the Myrddin of Carmarthen, or whether this merging of legends had already occurred before his time. These issues are considered in Jarman (1991) and Padel (2006).
[18] Thorpe (1966: 229).
[19] White (1962); Seaby and Woodfield (1980); Rowland (1995).
[20] Nickel (1983; 1991); Alcock (1971: 360).
[21] Thorpe (1978: 117-8).
[22] In the time of Henry VIII, Geoffrey's history came under attack from an Italian living in England, Polydore Virgil, in his *Anglica Historia*, which was eventually published in 1534. He wrote that Geoffrey's Arthur was taken from the fables of the Britons and was also embroidered by Geoffrey who then passed it off as an honest history. This prompted a fierce reaction from British scholars, particularly John Leland, that was hard fought and long sustained but Geoffrey's authority never recovered (Kendrick, 1950).
[23] Biddle (2000).
[24] Lacy (1991: xxxiv).
[25] In *Erec and Enide*, Lancelot is ranked third in the list of knights at the Round Table; in *Cliges* he fights in a tournament near Oxford (Frappier, 1959).
[26] Owen (1987: 185).
[27] Raffel (1999: 101-7; 112-4, 147-8); Le Gentil (1959: 251-2).
[28] Raffel (1999: 186).
[29] Micha (1959: 319-21).
[30] For example, Ashe (1962).
[31] Taylor (1956).
[32] Enterline (2002: 65).
[33] MacMillan and Abeles (2004: 7, 46).
[34] Muir (1968: 255).

[35] Thorpe (1966: 248).
[36] The ostensible author of the poems, Taliesin, is mentioned in the *Historia Brittonum* along with four others as notable sixth-century poets. A distinction is made between the 10-12 poems attributed to the historical Taliesin and many other poems by the 'mythological Taliesin', a persona adopted by poets who composed in a particular style emphasising the bard's far-reaching knowledge, boasting, and staccato bursts of questions. The historical Taliesin is linked with the northern chieftains (Urien, his son Owain and Gwallawg) in the later sixth century and would appear to be too late to be Arthur's bard, but the author of *Preideu Annwfyn* purports to be Arthur's bard and thus its ostensible attribution to Taliesin is problematic. This problem will be fully discussed in Chapter 13.
[37] Koch (1984; 1985-6; 1988; 1991; 1996) and Haycock (1990; 2007).

Chapter 2 Historical Context for Arthur

[1] Snyder (2003: 75-6).
[2] For a variety of recent views about the origins of the Celts see Cunliffe and Koch (2010). Sims-Williams (2012) examines whether medieval Celtic speakers in Britain and Ireland inherited more than just their languages from the ancient Celtic speakers but cannot establish a link other than language.
[3] Lewis (1976: 22).
[4] Jackson(1973: 114, 116).
[5] Chambers (1927: 14-15); Alcock (1971: 39).
[6] For example, Dumville (1984c).
[7] For translations, see Winterbottom (1978); Williams (1899).
[8] John Morris in Winterbottom (1978: 1); Dumville (1984a: 84), Baillie (1999).
[9] If Gildas wrote at age 44 and died in AD 570, but lived less than 74 years, then his time of writing would be after 540. However, the *Annales* death date of 570 is uncertain (Sims-Williams, 1983: 3). It may have been several years earlier, which could still allow a pre-540 date of writing if Gildas lived less than 74 years. Stancliffe (1997: 180) employs a similar argument based on the 570 date. This simple analysis puts weight on 570 as Gildas' death date, a date originally from the so-called 'Chronicle of Ireland'. Gildas had became well known in the church, which could suggest that 570 was not too far removed from the correct value. See Sims-Williams (1983: 3-5) for a discussion of the difficulties. Gildas' account of some fifth-century events is vague, indicating that he wrote in the sixth century. In around 600, Columbanus refers to *The Ruin of Britain*, which thus provides an upper limit.
[10] Sims-Williams (1983: 3).
[11] Dumville (1977); Gruffydd (1989-90).
[12] Jackson (1982: 36).
[13] Winterbottom (1978: 26).
[14] For example, Brett (2011: 48-9).
[15] The main manuscript from the 900s, Cotton MS Vitellius A vi (called manuscript C by Mommsen), was badly damaged by fire in 1731. Two early editions by Polydore Virgil of 1525 and John Josselin of 1568 were used to supplement the damaged manuscript. It named only Ambrosius from the fifth century. However the two later manuscripts, the Avranches (A) and the Cambridge (X) do name

Ambrosius and also the king who invited the Saxons into Britain, calling him *Vortigerno* in the Avranches and *Gurthigerno* (in an Old Welsh guise) in the Cambridge.
[16] Koch (1985-6: 63).
[17] Hines (1990: 35-6) and Dark (2000:98).
[18] One important question concerns the time at which the Saxons arrived in Britain in significant numbers. It would appear from other indications that the Saxons were a significant force in Britain from the early 400s. Given this, what is the significance of Vortigern inviting Saxon mercenaries to come over from the continent and when did this happen?

When did Vortigern invite the Saxon mercenaries?

A rough estimate of the date of Vortigern's invitation can be obtained from a letter written by the Britons to a Roman commander called Aëtius (*The Ruin of Britain*, in Section 20). Aëtius is described as 'thrice consul', which dates the letter to between 446 and 454. The Britons complain that the barbarians are pushing them into the sea, so that they face either being drowned or slaughtered. Who were these barbarians – the Picts and Irish, or the Saxons? In *The Ruin of Britain*, the Saxons are not invited into the island until Section 23, so it seems that Gildas intended the barbarians here to be the Picts and the Irish. After this fruitless appeal, Gildas describes a series of 'historical' events before he arrives at the point when Vortigern invited in the Saxons.

By estimating the likely duration of these events and taking a date for the appeal as circa 450, the date of the Saxon invitation can be estimated. Dumville (1984a: 83) attempts this and obtains a date range of about 480 to 490, seemingly rather late. He remarks that Gildas' credibility is severely strained if it is intended that this is the first Saxon arrival into Britain.

Attempts have been made to address this difficulty. Higham (1993) suggests that Gildas may have received his information about the letter to Aëtius orally. Hence the 'thrice consul' information (which implies the c. 450 starting date) may have been added by Gildas from his general knowledge of Aëtius. That is, it was not part of the letter. Therefore the letter could have been written to Aëtius much earlier in his career, which would then result in an earlier date for Vortigern's invitation to the Saxons.

Another way out of the difficulty is given by Stevens (1941), who highlights the errors made by Gildas in dating the Hadrian and Antonine Walls centuries too late, and in the wrong order. Stevens believes that Gildas' reconstruction of the fifth-century events is incorrect and that the barbarians mentioned in the letter to Aëtius were the *Saxons*, rather than the Picts and Irish. He considers that Vortigern's invitation and the Saxon arrival to have occurred in the early 440s as indicated by the *Gallic Chronicles* (see the section on this below). In this scenario, the Britons appealed to Aëtius in about 446 for help against the Saxon barbarians (Stevens, 1941: 362-3).

In his *Ecclesiastical History*, written in 731, Bede gives a date of 449 for the invitation by Vortigern and the Saxon arrival (Book 1, Chapter 15). He aligns the arrival with the time that Marcian was emperor in the east and Valentinian was emperor in the west (McClure and Collins, 1994: 26-7). Bede is out by a year, as the emperors did not begin their joint rule until 450. In other parts of the *History*, Bede gives approximate estimates: about 445 (Book 1, Chapter 23), about 447 (Book 2, Chapter 14) and about 446 (Book 5, Chapter 23).

When did the Saxons settle in Britain?
Archaeological estimates
Archaeological work indicates that Saxons were in Britain in the late Roman period. Myres (1969) describes discoveries of Anglo-Saxon pottery from the early 400s. Pryor (2004) discusses the Anglo-Saxon type houses with distinctive sunken floors, found at Mucking and West Heslerton, dating approximately to a period spanning the late 300s to early 400s. However Hines (1990) has argued for later dates, more in keeping with the mid 400s. The notion of inviting in the Germanic fighters to contain the Picts and the Irish, employed by Vortigern, was not the first time this strategy had been employed, as German mercenaries were in Britain during the Roman occupation (Hawkes, 1989; Dark, 1992) with archaeological evidence of their being stationed along Hadrian's Wall from the third century (Alcock, 1971: 94).

Zosimus
The history by Zosimus, probably written in Constantinople in the early sixth century, gives a very early date for Saxon incursions. In Book 6, Section 5 of his *Historia Nova* (New History), Zosimus relates how the Saxons attempted to take over Britain in 409. With the British troops engaged in Gaul and Spain under Constantine and Gerontius, the Saxons then 'launch a large-scale invasion of the island' according to Thompson (1977: 309).

This attack prompted the Britons in 409 to rebel against the remaining Roman administration and take up arms to organise their own defences against the Saxons. They succeeded in repelling the Saxons, freeing their cities from the barbarians. This served as an example for the Armoricans in northwest Gaul, who similarly freed themselves from their Roman officials. If accurate, this work implies significant Saxon raiding from around the time that the Romans were leaving Britain.

The Gallic Chronicles
Two important chronicles from Gaul, the *Gallic Chronicle to 452* and the *Gallic Chronicle to 511*, imply an early date for the Saxons' arrival that is compatible with the early archaeological datings. The first chronicle states that the British provinces, after suffering various defeats and calamities, were reduced to Saxon rule (for the date c. 441).

The second chronicle gives a similar account, stating that Britain, being abandoned by the Romans, passed into the power of the Saxons (for the date c. 440). If parts of Britain were under Saxon rule by 441, then the Saxon arrival must have been several decades earlier.

The Gallic Chronicles have been carefully studied by scholars, in particular, Miller (1978), Muhlberger (1983), Jones and Casey (1988) and Burgess (1990). While Jones and Casey (1988) believe that a significant Saxon takeover took place in c. 441, Burgess (1990: 192) denies that such an accurate date can be obtained from the chronicles but he does state: 'That this date is an accurate reflection of contemporary Gallic beliefs can hardly be doubted'. But the question is whether the people in Gaul at this time really did have accurate information on what was happening in Britain.

Concluding Comments
The Saxons were launching devastating raids against Britain from at least the third century. It was to help defend against these raids that the Saxon Shore forts were erected in the late third century (Burgess, 1990: 191). It would appear that the Saxons were arriving to settle from around the time of the end of Roman rule and may have been a significant force by the 440s. Unfortunately, it is still quite unclear as to when Vortigern hired his Saxon mercenaries. We have a wide range of estimates for this date: about 442-3 from Stevens (1941), about 450 from Bede and around 480-90, a date estimated from events in Gildas' *The Ruin of Britain* (Dumville, 1984a).

How did the Saxon Takeover Occur?
It is far from clear how the Saxon takeover occurred. A brief outline of the various viewpoints is given below.

The Traditional View
The picture derived from Gildas is one where the Saxons ruthlessly attacked the Britons, depriving them of their lands and freedom. The Britons were either killed, taken as slaves, pushed west into what is now Wales, or they fled overseas to Brittany or Ireland. The viewpoint of Gildas, of fierce battles being fought between the Britons and the Saxons, is supported by the ancient Welsh poetry. The 'historical' poems from the *Book of Taliesin* describe the battles between the northern Britons, Urien and his son Owain, against the Angles. An early Welsh poem, *Y Gododdin*, describes how a British force was destroyed by the Angles in an heroic attempt to take Catraeth (possibly modern Catterick). The poetry presents this time as one of frequent battles and raiding parties. This traditional view, of a mass migration over time by the Anglo-Saxons with the slaughter and displacement of the Britons is reflected in the works of Stenton (1947), Hunter-Blair (1963) and Welch (1992).

The Archaeological View
This violent picture has been disputed by archaeologists, who can find little evidence of the large-scale massacres implied by Gildas. There is no conclusive evidence for the destruction of any British city by military means in this period and no recognisable burnt debris that would be expected from the Gildasian account (Alcock, 1971; Russo, 1998).

The viewpoint that there was a massive influx of Saxons in the fifth and sixth centuries has also been challenged by many archaeologists (e.g. see Jones, 1996; also Dark, 2000). With an emphasis on population continuity, Pryor (2004: 241) states: 'we should discard the simplistic idea that invasions or mass migrations were the cause of the major changes we see in the archaeological and historical record'.

Small-Scale Models
Some scholars are sceptical of the notion of mass migration (e.g. Hodges, 1989; Higham, 1992; Hills, 2003). The size of this migration is extremely difficult to estimate. Jones (1996: 11-12, 67) attempts a rough estimate, suggesting as few as 10,000 to 20,000. He sums up this non traditional viewpoint: 'some scholars shrink the numbers of the Anglo-Saxon invaders to a small, potent elite of only a few thousand immigrants'.

Higham (1992, Chapter 8) sets out such a model as a hypothesis. Under this model, the Britons lacked the cohesiveness to organise a united defence and could not resist the relatively small groups of marauding Germanic warriors. These warriors had a near monopoly of arms and experience in war and hence were able to brutally seize the estates and land units of the British aristocracies. In spite of the Britons' numerical advantage, the Saxon takeover was effected through the intimidated Britons adopting the language, material culture and the traditions of the Anglo-Saxon elite. This adoption was undertaken by 'large numbers of the local people seeking to improve their status within the social structure, and undertaking for this purpose rigorous acculturation' (p.229). He proposes that by the sixth century, the Anglo-Saxon part of Britain comprised people with far more British than Germanic genes but the majority spoke Anglo-Saxon and Germanic culture predominated. (p.234).

Genetic Studies
Topf et al. (2006) have studied ancient migration to Britain by women. They compared mitochondrial DNA from Britons who lived between about AD 300-1000 with 3549 modern mitochondrial DNA database genotypes from England, Europe and the Middle East. This suggested shared ancestry between early British sites (predating Viking invasions) with modern populations across the north of Europe from Norway to Estonia. They suggest that this could reflect common ancestors dating back to the last glacial epoch when a land bridge, Doggerland, linked Britain to the Continent. However, they interpret their Norwich site data as possibly explained by Saxon immigration.

Other studies have compared Y-chromosome distributions from samples in England to those from samples in northern Germany and Denmark, where the Anglo-Saxons originated. Studies by Weale et al. (2002) and Capelli et al. (2003) would seem to indicate a very large migration of Anglo-Saxon men into central England. From these studies, Thomas, Stumpf and Harke (2006: 2653) make the very strong statement: 'We consider 50% to be a conservative estimate of the proportion of Y-chromosomes in the present-day English gene pool that originate among Anglo-Saxon migrants in the fifth century', and 'Explaining such a high proportion of Continental genetic material with immigration alone would require migration on a massive scale (approx. 500,000+), well above documented population movements' (p.2651).

To address this issue they construct a mathematical model which assumes a reproductive advantage to the Saxons (as the dominant class) with limited intermarriage (an 'apartheid-like' social structure) and test it via computer simulation. This allows them to use smaller migration numbers to account for the proportion of Saxon Y-chromosomes in the British population. With such limited intermarriage and having the dominant military, economic and social position, the Saxons outbred the Britons under this model, their advantage accumulating over the generations. This paper has been criticised by Pattison (2008), followed by a rejoinder in Thomas, Stumpf and Harke (2008).

Replacement of the British Language in England
Any model of the Saxon takeover should seek to account for the disappearance of the ancient British language throughout what is now England. Sims-Williams (2006) confirms that in the Roman period, the density of Celtic placenames in what became a Saxon heartland (between London and The Wash) was greater than that in ancient Wales. This British language was completely supplanted by the Germanic language that eventually developed into English. The British language survived in Wales, where it later developed into Welsh, the Cornwall peninsula, where it became Cornish, and Brittany in northwest France, where it became Breton (Williams, 1972). Linguistic perspectives are offered by Coates (2007) and Padel (2007) who note the lack of borrowing of the British language into the Germanic language. This seems best explained by a large scale displacement of the Britons by slaughter or evacuation or by the remaining Britons being effectively enslaved. Our main sixth-century source, Gildas, does refer to the enslavement of Britons by the Saxons.

Comments on Saxon Takeover Models
John Koch (1997: xliv) gives two polar extremes for explaining the eventual Saxon takeover, one being the 'ethnic cleansing' perspective of Gildas. In the other extreme, peasant Britons lived in bilingual contact with their Saxon neighbours. Over a period of time they may have found it advantageous to improve their status by becoming arms-bearing farmer freemen (Saxon *ceorls*), part of the Saxon social structure. This opportunity may not have been as readily available in the British social structure. Koch suggests that both scenarios could have contributed to the Anglicisation of Britain.

Given the different strands of evidence, the nature of the Saxon takeover is still unclear. The factors operating appear to be the killing and intimidation of the Britons by the Saxon warriors; the Britons' partial evacuation of their territory; the remaining Britons living in virtual slavery; 'acculturation' to Saxon society by the Britons; and (as an underclass) the Britons being outbred by the Saxons. The above elements are not mutually exclusive and may have had different emphases in different parts of Britain.

[19] The *Historia Brittonum* was written in 829-30 (Dumville, 1972-74b) but the main recension, the Harleian, does not include the prologue that attributes the authorship to Nennius. This prologue appears in only five manuscripts, the most important being the Corpus Christi College, Cambridge, MS 139, the source for the other four. Dumville (1972-74a; 1975-6) has shown that it was only late (between 1164-1166) that the prologue, with the name spelt Ninnius, was copied into the Corpus Christi 139 manuscript. He assigns the writing of the prologue and the general fashioning of the recension to which it belongs to the eleventh century (Dumville, 1986).

Dumville thus argues that we have no grounds for believing that Nennius was the author of the *Historia* (Dumville, 1975-6). This has been challenged by Field (1996), who argues that the prologue has linguistic similarities to the main text and also gives an unfavourable portrayal of the Britons which may have caused its omission from the early manuscripts.

[20] Hanning (1966: 120); Dumville (1976-7); Dumville (1986: 5, 15, 26).

[21] Davies (1982: 205); Jackson (1963); Koch (1996); Field (2008).

[22] Three differences between the Vatican and Harleian Arthurian sections will be considered here. Firstly, Breguoin's replacement of Agned does provide a plausible battle site that can be identified. Geoffrey of Monmouth had identified Agned with Edinburgh but no convincing evidence supports this and its location remains unknown. Jackson (1945) could find no British or Welsh meaning for Agned, suggesting that it may be a corruption.

The Vatican also states that Arthur was chosen twelve times as battle leader 'though there were many more noble than himself'. This and other references that do not explicitly call him a king have led some scholars to infer that he was not a king himself. However, he is repeatedly called a king in *Preideu Annwfyn*, a poem centuries earlier than the *Historia*. Gildas refers to the rapid turnover of tyrants, where one would be quickly replaced with another even more brutal (Section 21.4) Arthur may have become a king through popular support, from his success as a battle leader. Chris Snyder (2005) argues that the viewpoint that the *Historia* shows that Arthur was not a king should be abandoned.

Thirdly, the Vatican recension replaces the 960 men killed by Arthur in the Harleian with 940 men.

[23] Chadwick and Chadwick (1932: 155).

[24] Jackson (1949: 46); Jackson (1959a: 6).

[25] Jones (1964: 10).

[26] Dumville (1986: 13).

[27] Williams (1968).

[28] Chadwick and Chadwick (1932); Jones (1964); Bromwich (1975-6); Koch (1985-6; 1996); Dumville (1986) and Field (2008).

[29] Koch (1996: 248).

[30] Padel (1994) and Wood (1999) propose that Badon should be attributed to Ambrosius. Their argument rests on the fact that Winterbottom (1978: 28), in his authoritative translation, started a new paragraph between Ambrosius' initial victory and the battles that led up to Badon, a break that was not in the manuscript. Padel (1994: 17) asserts that if the paragraph break is removed, the text reads 'naturally as the victory that crowned the career of Ambrosius Aurelianus'. However, a full reading of the text does not give this impression and suggests that it is unlikely that Ambrosius won Badon. Gildas clearly idolises Ambrosius, praising him profusely in stark contrast to his slandering of the Britons in general. He emphasises the Roman background of Ambrosius, as if to separate him from the cowardly and sinful Britons. If Ambrosius had won Badon, then Gildas would have trumpeted it to the skies.

It has long been thought that Ambrosius lived too early to be associated with Badon. The *Historia Brittonum* describes Vortigern as living in fear of Ambrosius and also credits Ambrosius with winning the battle of Guoloph, which is thought to be Wallop in Hampshire, and which was dated early to AD 437 (Morris, 1973: 73). If this data is correct, Ambrosius would have been dead or an old man when Badon was fought.

Further, the text of Gildas suggests that Ambrosius led the Britons for only a limited time. He won an initial victory, but then Gildas states that 'From then on victory went now to our countrymen, now to our enemies'. The victories here are attributed to 'our countrymen', not Ambrosius. It would seem that Ambrosius had faded from the picture. It would also seem that a long period of time elapsed between the initial victory of Ambrosius and the battle of Badon, as Gildas implies that the indecisive victories were ordained by God to make the Britons endure a trial to see whether they would return to God. One would also not expect the Anglo-Saxons to cease their raiding and leave the Britons in peace unless a long period of battles had ensued. It would seem that Ambrosius was probably an old man when Badon occurred.

No Welsh or Latin text attributes the Badon victory to Ambrosius while the Welsh poem underlying the *Historia* battle list gives the victory to Arthur. The notion that Ambrosius won Badon but that the Britons forgot this major achievement (the battle having been made famous by Gildas), allowing a later Welsh scholar to replace him with Arthur, seems highly improbable.

[31] Jackson (1945; 1949; 1953-58); Field (2008).
[32] Green (2008); Cessford (1997: 221).
[33] Bachrach (1990: 22).
[34] Jackson (1945: 50).
[35] Leeds (1933); Tolstoy (1960-62); Burkitt and Burkitt (1990).
[36] Jackson (1953-58); Field (2008).
[37] The date given to Badon in the *Annales* (516/518) is often thought to be too late by a few decades, although it is not impossible. Gildas gives a long, convoluted statement (in Section 26) that could potentially help with a dating, but there are several possible interpretations. The translation below refers to the initial victory of Ambrosius with the words 'From that time,...'.

From that time, now our countrymen, now the enemy were victorious...This continued until the year of the Badon Hill siege, virtually the last and not the least slaughter of the villains. And this being the 44th year (as I know), with one month by this time having passed, which was also the year of my birth.

The mainstream view takes the starting point for the 44 years as the year of the Battle of Badon, which was also the year of Gildas' birth, hence his ('as I know') comment. Gildas was writing 44 years later. The one month having passed implies either that he was writing in February or that he was referring to his birth month and it was 44 years and one month after his birthday. Given this view, there is a problem with the 516/518 *Annales* date for Badon as Gildas' time of writing would be 516+44=560 (using the 516 value). But Maglocunus died in 547 giving the absurd scenario of Gildas urging him to repent in 560 when he had died 13 years previously. Thus the 516/518 Badon date is problematic. It is thought that Gildas wrote in circa 540. Then if Badon were 44 years earlier, it would have taken place in c. 496.

A second interpretation takes the victory of Ambrosius ('From that time') as the starting point for the 44 years. Then Gildas was writing 44 years after the victory of Ambrosius, the year of his birth. Although the text does refer to 'the year of the Badon Hill siege', this view does not connect Badon with the start or the finish of the 44 years. Badon can be placed closer to the time of Gildas' writing than 44 years (say 20-30 years). This option addresses a concern raised by Wood (1984: 23) that the language that Gildas uses (*novissimae*) suggests that Badon may have been more recent than 44 years ago. There is also the phrase referring to the battle, 'in our own times', by Gildas in Section 2 which could suggest a more recent Badon. One also wonders whether it is plausible that this battle could keep the Saxons at bay for 44 years. This view allows flexibility for Badon's date. It could well fit a timeframe where Ambrosius initiated the fightback in circa 495 (Dumville, 1984a: 83), which would give a time of writing of c. 539 and allows a date of 516/518 for Badon.

A third view comes from Bede who thought that the battle of Badon had occurred 44 years after the arrival of the Saxons, which he dated approximately to 450. Thus Badon and the year of Gildas' birth would be c. 494. This leaves the time of Gildas' writing as a free parameter. The problem with this approach is that it does not satisfactorily account for the one month passing. It is absurd to date Badon/Gildas' birthday as occurring 44 years and one month after the coming of the Saxons as their arrival date is a subjective one and extremely imprecise. To have a convincing meaning, the 'one month passing' must relate to the *current year*, the time of Gildas writing.

Wiseman (2000) has argued that the 518 date could have been estimated by an eighth-century scholar by using Bede's *Chronica Majora* (c. 725), which dates the victory of Ambrosius to the reign of Zeno (474-491). This requires taking the starting point for the 44 years as the victory of Ambrosius and the ending point as the battle of Badon (and Gildas' birth). This leaves the time of writing as a free parameter, and it also leaves the one month unexplained. It seems unrealistic to regard the victory of Ambrosius as occurring exactly 44 years and one month before Gildas' birthday, a precision that would seem improbable. However, the point is not whether the argument is convincing but whether it could have been adopted by an eighth-century scholar to infer a date. It it were, then as Wiseman argues, he may have taken the earliest date for the reign of Zeno (474) and added 44 years to get 518 for the date of Badon.

[38] Jackson (1959a: 9).
[39] Williams (1972: 5).
[40] Jackson (1953); Koch (1985-6); Sims-Williams (1990); Koch (1996).
[41] Jackson (1959a: 7-8); Bromwich (1975-6: 169); Jackson (1973: 122).
[42] Koch (2006e: 1653).

Chapter 3 Medieval Beliefs in Arthur's Atlantic Voyages

[1] For *Life of Merlin*, see Parry (1925).
[2] Bromwich (2006: 274).
[3] McCone (2000); Meyer (1895); O'Meara (2002).
[4] Perrin (1919: 23).
[5] Parry (1925: 85-6).

[6] The geography of the *Navigatio* is confused and sometimes inconsistent. The 'Promised Land of the Saints' is described as a huge, significant landmass rich in resources, not a tiny island retreat like those on which the monks lived. In the first journey, Barinthus sails *west* from Delightful Island, close to Slieve League, Donegal. Towards the end of their journey they spend an hour in thick fog before reaching the Promised Land (O'Meara, 2002: 26-8).

In the second journey, Brendan leaves from the island of the steward, in the Faroes (O'Meara, 2002: 62). This time the text says they sailed *east* for 40 days and then spend an hour in the thick fog, as in the initial visit. For a historical journey, this can hardly be correct as a boat sailing east from the Faroes would meet the coast of Norway in several days. As the first visit was westward, Ashe (1962: 321-2) and others have argued that 'east' was a mistake for 'west' in the second visit. This would then explain the fog, as 40 days sailing west would bring the boat to near Labrador or Newfoundland, the latter being associated with thick fogs. It is also consistent with features that suggest knowledge of westward sailing such as the Faroes (Isle of Sheep/Birds), Iceland (Isle of Smiths) and an iceberg off Newfoundland (crystal pillar in the sea).

[7] MacMillan and Abeles (2004: 7).
[8] McCarthy (1848); Little (1945); Krenn (1950); Pohl (1961); Ashe (1962); Chapman (1973); Severin (1978).
[9] Wooding (2000: 226-9); Wooding (2002: 20-1).
[10] Parry (1925: 85).
[11] Cunliffe (2001: 84).
[12] Romer (1998: 115).
[13] For *Culhwch and Olwen*, see Ford (1977: 126).
[14] Thorpe (1966: 217).
[15] Thorpe (1978: 281).
[16] The linking of Glastonbury with Arthur is unhistorical. The first source to do so was Caradoc's *Life of Gildas* (written 600 years after Arthur's time) where Melwas carries off Gwenhwyfar to Glastonbury. Gildas then acts as the mediator between Melwas and Arthur. After the publication of Geoffrey's *History*, the Glastonbury monks capitalised on Arthur's fame by faking the discovery of his grave. The catalyst for this was the fire of 1184 which burnt down the sacred wooden church, the most important part of the Glastonbury complex. Funds to rebuild were needed and thus 'discovering' Arthur's grave would give the site publicity for fundraising. The exhumation of some bones (not Arthur's) was real, but the lead cross found in the grave with 'old' writing in the style of the tenth century, mentioning the 'Isle of Avalon', was clearly a fake, the name 'Avalon' first being coined by Geoffrey in his pseudo-history of 1138. See the account by Ronald Hutton (2003: 68-70).
[17] Ashe (2003: 107-8).
[18] Koch and Carey (2003: 406); Coe and Young (1995: 37).
[19] MacMillan and Abeles (2004: 86-7).
[20] Little is known about Jacob Cnoyen and his travels. Mercator states that he came from 's-Hertogenbosch in Holland and that he travelled around the world like Mandeville, but recorded his travels with better judgement. Enterline (2002: 51) indicates that the town archives in 's-Hertogenbosch show that Cnoyen was a

common name in the 1300s and 1400s, with at least two Jacob Cnoyens on record in the 1400s.

[21] For the *Discoveries* version see Taylor (1956: 56-61).

[22] For the *Limits* version see MacMillan and Abeles (2004: 3, 83-5).

[23] Cnoyen relates how an Oxford friar (carrying an astrolabe) explored the northern regions c. 1360 and left the main party of explorers to journey further through the whole of the north. His geographical observations were recorded in *Inventio Fortunatae,* a copy of which was presented to Edward III on returning to England. This text is now lost, but it did exist, as others independently refer to it. Johann Ruysch had quoted from it according to Taylor (1956: 63).

The above story of the friar was told to the King of Norway in 1364 by a priest who now possessed the friar's astrolabe. He stated that he and his seven companions were descended from Arthur's original colonists of the northern regions. The priest had actually met the friar in his travels and had exchanged a testament for the friar's astrolabe.

[24] Nansen (1911: 66-94) and Seaver (2008).

[25] The account of Arthur's two voyages appears in Taylor (1956: 58).

[26] See Note 7 in Taylor (1956: 58). For the *Tytle Royall* estimate of the date of the expeditions see MacMillan and Abeles (2004: 46).

[27] For the 23 people who were not above 4 feet tall, see Taylor (1956: 59).

[28] In *Limits*, John Dee makes unwarranted inferences from Cnoyen's general text and incorporates it into Arthur's first voyage. The priest with the astrolabe claimed to be descended in the 5th generation from a Bruxellensis (possibly a man from Brussels). Dee thought that Bruxellensis was the name of one of Arthur's original colonists and that the 5th generation was a corruption for the 25th generation. He inserted Bruxellensis (conceived as a German follower of Arthur) into the *Limits* narrative of the first voyage, describing him as wintering in the isles of Scotland before crossing to Iceland.

[29] While the notion that ships with iron nails could be wrecked on magnetic rocks is nonsensical to us, the belief has a long history. Ptolemy's *Geographia* (about AD 140-150) mentions ten islands off the coast of India, the Maniolae, where the nearby magnetic stones could attract and wreck boats with iron nails (Nobbe, 1966: 170, in Greek; Stevenson, 1932: 157). This notion also appears in the *Commonitorium Palladii* by Bishop Palladius of Helenopolis, written in the early 400s. The key text is reproduced in Latin in Kübler (1891: 211). It states that magnetic stones that attract iron are found near Taprobane (Sri Lanka) and that ships which travel in this area are built entirely without iron nails.

At some point, the 'magnetic stones' attracting ships changed into a much more formidable object – the 'magnetic mountain'. This change appears in *Book of the Marvels of India* written by Buzurg ibn Shahrijar in c. 950. The text appears in Lecouteux (1984: 36) and refers to 'montagnes d'aimant' preventing ships containing iron from navigating on the stream, for fear that they would be attracted by the mountains. The magnetic mountain appears in the *Arabian Nights* in the *Story of the Third Kalendar* (Lang, 1898) and in *The Adventures of Abulfuaris*, an early Persian tale (Blamires, 1979: 89-90).

In c. 1170, the magnetic mountain that attracted ships appears in the German literature in the story of *Herzog Ernst* (Blamires, 1979). The 16th-century work,

Hortus Sanitatis, contains a woodcut illustration showing a ship crashed against a magnetic mountain, with sailors drowning and iron nails flying through the air, as reproduced in Lecouteux (1984: 41).

This brief survey shows that the threat of magnetic stones wrecking ships was written down about 400 years before Arthur (by Ptolemy) and 100 years before Arthur (by Bishop Palladius). Tuczay (2005: 273) notes that the *Commonitorium Palladii* was a part of the group of legends associated with Alexander the Great, which spread widely and probably reached Britain before Arthur's time. The *Book of Taliesin* has two poems on Alexander the Great by poets adopting the Taliesin persona (Haycock, 2007: 404-32).

[30] Jones (1964: 14) thought that Brân's voyage was based on *Preideu Annwfyn*. For the magnetic rocks under the water in *Branwen*, see Ford (1977: 67).
[31] Charles-Edwards (1970); Sims-Williams (1991b).
[32] See Taylor (1956: 57); MacMillan and Abeles (2004: 46). A 1571 edition of the Ortelius atlas, *Theatrum Orbis Terrarum*, containing his world map is in the Victoria and Albert Museum (Level 2) in London.
[33] For the meaning of Grocland, see Enterline (2002: 65).
[34] National Geospatial-Intelligence Agency (2011: 299).
[35] Carlson (1975: 753-5).
[36] Enterline (2002: 59).
[37] Morison (1971).
[38] In a footnote, Skelton (1965: 244) gives his opinion that Arthur's voyages were reminiscent of Eirík the Red's and were presumably fabricated therefrom. However, a close reading of both accounts indicates that they are so different that it is unlikely that Arthur's voyages were based on Eirík the Red's.

In Eirík's first voyage, he sailed from Iceland to Greenland with his crew in a single boat. He spent three Summers exploring different parts of Greenland and then returned to Iceland. In Arthur's case, the colonisation took place on the first voyage in a single year. Rather than sailing in a single boat, Arthur had a fleet which wintered in the islands of Scotland. In May, his fleet crossed over to Iceland. They were warned about the indrawing seas from four boats returning from the north. No mention of indrawing seas is made in Eirík's journey. Arthur then colonised the islands lying beyond Scotland to Iceland, and also Grocland. Grocland is unlikely to be Greenland, if Enterline's (2002) argument that it means 'wild pasture land' is correct. Arthur's colonisation took place in the one year, over a number of lands, with a fleet of ships. In contrast, Eirík spent three years exploring the single land, Greenland, in one boat. Furthermore, whereas the sailors on Arthur's ships feared the magnetic rocks, this threat is not even mentioned in Eirík's journey.

Eirík's second journey was from Iceland to Greenland. In contrast, Arthur left Iceland to return to Britain, the starting point for his second voyage. Eirík's second journey had 35 ships (or 25) depending on the manuscript (Jones, 1986: 187). Arthur's second voyage had 12 ships. Both expeditions lost ships, either 21 or 11 in Eirík's case; 5 in Arthur's. Details in Arthur's voyage are not copied from Eirík's: the departure date, the crew sizes and the detail of his ships passing through a narrow passage. In addition, Arthur's ships took 44-46 days to get to their destination, which seems to be a different destination to that reached by

Eirík. If the Arthurian voyages were based on Eirík's, they make no use of place names and locations given in the latter.

[39] Masefield (1939: 54-5); MacMillan and Abeles (2004: 57-8).

[40] Liebermann (1894: 91-100). Prior to *Archaionomia*, the Arthurian material also appeared in Latin in the *Miscellanea* of William of Worcestre's *Itineraries* of circa 1480. This is reproduced in Harvey (1969: 390).

[41] Muir (1968: 255-6).

[42] Tschan (1959: 219); Muir (1968: 262).

[43] The Greby graveyard in western Sweden contains some 200 mounds and barrows dating from AD 200 to 600. According to the graveyard's information signs (under the heading 'Scottish raiders defeated') there was a tradition that Scottish raiders had come to plunder Bohuslan but were killed in battle and many were buried there at Greby.

[44] For the hostages taken from *Llychlyn*, see Ford (1977: 124-5).

[45] Tschan (1959: 228); Muir (1968: 257).

[46] Muir (1968: 254, 259).

[47] Geoffrey apparently realised that his northern account was unconvincing, so he met the issue head on by reinforcing it. After Arthur's death, Geoffrey selects four of the five kings reigning simultaneously in Gildas, but he has them reign consecutively, ending in Malgo (Maglocunus). He emphasises the importance of Arthur's conquests by creating a blatantly fictitious tale of Malgo reconquering *exactly* the same six countries: Ireland, Iceland, Gotland, Orkney, Norway and Denmark (Thorpe, 1966: 263).

[48] Thorpe (1966: 248).

[49] Geoffrey used a similar strategy with Arthur's battles which are listed in the *Historia Brittonum*. He chose four names from the *Historia*'s battle list (Dubglas, Linnuis, Celidon and Badon) and then created plausible equivalents – Douglas, Lincoln, Caledon and Bath. He then tried to differentiate his account from the *Historia* by introducing the battle of *Kaerluideoit* (Thorpe, 1966: 214-5) which he seems to have taken from the poem *Marwnad Cynddylan*. Cynddylan fought a battle at *Caer Lwytgoed*, which Geoffrey expresses as *Kaerluideoit* and wrongly attributes to Arthur, as Arthur is mentioned in the poem as a great warrior from the past. In fact, the battle occurred over a century after Arthur's death. Geoffrey also places *Kaerluideoit* in the incorrect location (in Lincoln), probably because the *Historia* places Dubglas in Lincoln.

Ever the inventive, Geoffrey also added York (a siege) and Loch Lomond in Scotland to Arthur's battles. Whereas the *Historia* made Arthur fight four battles at Dubglas, Geoffrey had him fight the four in Scotland, either at or near Loch Lomond. Lewis Thorpe (1966: 213-9) gives Geoffrey's account of these battles. Geoffrey's partial selections, modifications and additions are devices to disguise his reliance on the well-known texts. His skilful dramatic constructions supply the exciting (but fictitious) detail that the other sources lack. This allows Geoffrey to keep up the pretence that he alone has the authentic, fully fledged history of the Britons, of which he is merely the translator.

[50] MacMillan and Abeles (2004: 57-8).

[51] For 'our last king', see MacMillan and Abeles (2004: 58).

[52] Rex (2004: 62).

[53] Rex (2004) chronicles the various elements of the Norse involvement in the English resistance. When William defeated Harold Godwinson at Hastings, there appears to have been a Danish contingent that supported Harold, according to William of Poitiers (Rex, 2004: 95). The Danes became part of the English revolt against William in Northumbria in 1069, when Edgar sought help from Sweyn Estrithson of Denmark who sent his large fleet to Northumbria. The rebels with the aid of the Danes then captured York, before William regained control and the Danes departed. The Danes were later involved in the revolt at Ely, joining forces with Hereward in the attack on Peterborough Abbey in 1071. They also supported Ralph, Earl of East Anglia in the Revolt of the Earls and recaptured York in 1075 after the failure of the revolt. In 1085, the Danes again raided York and captured it (Rex, 2004: 101).

The *Northern Lands List* seemingly names Vinland, which appears in Adam of Bremen's *History of the Archbishops of Hamberg-Bremen*. This was not published until about 1075. However Adam had received his information on Vinland in 1068 or 1069 from the Danish king (Kunz and Sígurðsson, 2008: xxvii). As the author of the *Northern Lands List* appears to be a Norseman (or sympathetic to the Norse), and the Danes were in constant contact with the English, the existence of Vinland may have been known to him by circa 1070.

[54] Thomas (2003: 29).

Chapter 4 Sixth-Century North America

[1] See Woodward and McDonald (2002: 45). Prufer (1964: 93) argues that the term Hopewell 'culture' is inappropriate as the Hopewell beliefs and activities were only one segment of the cultural totality of Native American groups that adopted them. He suggests the word 'cult' rather than 'culture' but his usage has not caught on. The term 'culture' continues to be used by researchers and is used by the US government in naming the *Hopewell Culture National Historical Park*, which comprises five sites around Chillicothe.

[2] The Ohio Woodland Period has three overlapping phases. The Early phase ran from about 1000 BC to 1 AD; the Middle phase from about 250 BC to AD 550, and the Late phase from about AD 550 to 950. See Lepper (2005).

[3] Milner (2004: 11-12).

[4] See Lepper (2011: 7, 17); Milner (2004: 90); Prufer (1964: 98).

[5] This vacant ceremonial centre model was advanced by Olaf Prufer and built on by William Dancey, for example Dancey (2005).

[6] Lepper (2011: 18).

[7] See Yerkes (2005); Yerkes (2006). Cowan (2006) also argues for a mobile Hopewell.

[8] Lepper (2005: 120).

[9] Higley (1996: 45).

[10] Based on National Park Service (2008).

[11] Squier and Davis (1848).

[12] The side midpoint without a mound probably originally had one. A plan of the site by James and Charles Salisbury in the 1860s was recently rediscovered in the 1990s (Lepper, 2005: 153). It appears to show the missing mound.

[13] Hively and Horn (2005: 160-1).

[14] Lepper (1995).
[15] Squier and Davis (1848: 57), Plate XXI, No. 2.
[16] National Park Service (1999).
[17] Greber (1983); Greber and Ruhl (1989); Greber (2005).
[18] Smith (1992); Pacheco (1996); DeBoer (1997); Carr, Goldstein and Weets (2006); Carr and Case (2006b).
[19] Prufer (1964: 98).
[20] Prufer (1964: 93); Lepper (2005: 143).
[21] Prufer (1964: 93).
[22] Prufer (1964: 91, 96); Lepper (2011: 16).
[23] Prufer (1964: 96); Lepper (2011: 11).
[24] Turff and Carr (2006: 670-2); Spence and Fryer (2006: 720).
[25] Lepper (2011: 10).
[26] Glanzman's painting appears in the coloured pamphlet by the *National Park Service* (2008) and in Lepper (2005: 108). Black and white versions of the painting are also reproduced on the front cover of Carr and Case (2006a) and on p.178 of that work.
[27] Carr and Case (2006b: 26).
[28] Hulbert and Schwarze (1910: 12).
[29] Lepper (2005: 113).
[30] Greber (1983: 33).
[31] Squier and Davis (1848: 244).
[32] Hulbert and Schwarze (1910: 12).
[33] Hughes (1998). For atlatl, see Lepper (2005: 60-1).
[34] See Figure 1 in Blitz (1988: 132).
[35] Odell (1988); Bradbury (1997).
[36] Thomas (1978); Bradbury (1997); Shott (1997).
[37] Blitz and Porth (2013).
[38] Both Christenson (1986) and Blitz (1988) comment on the bow and arrow conferring an advantage in warfare.
[39] Mensforth (2001); Mensforth (2007).
[40] Milner (1999: 122).
[41] Lepper (2005: 168-9).
[42] Blitz and Porth (2013: 91).
[43] Prufer (1964: 100-2).
[44] Riordan (1996).
[45] Prufer (1964: 102).
[46] Ruby, Carr and Charles (2006: 154).

Chapter 5   Arthur's American Voyage

[1] *Annwfyn* derives from (*an* + *dwfyn*) where *dwfyn* has the meaning of either 'deep' or 'world'. The *an* part of the name would function as an intensifier as in 'very' or as an opposite as in 'not', being similar to some uses of the English 'in'; e.g. 'invaluable' (intensifier) and 'incomplete' (opposite). Thus one meaning of *Annwfyn* could be 'very deep', while another could be 'opposite world'. It has long been identified with the Celtic Otherworld. The poem's title was only created in the late 16th or early 17th century by John Lewis, taken from Line 7 of the poem

and using the later spelling *Annwn* (Haycock, 2007: 438). For more detailed discussions, see the comments of Haycock (2007: 440), Koch (1996: 265), and Koch (2006a: 75).
[2] Loomis (1956: 141).
[3] *Preideu Annwfyn* has been found difficult to interpret by most commentators. The English historian Sharon Turner (1828: 636) was utterly baffled by it and referred to it as follows: 'Could Lycophron or the Sybils, or any ancient oracle, be more elaborately incomprehensible'.
[4] Squire (1905: 318, 321).
[5] Babcock (1913: 11-12).
[6] The best scholarship available was consulted in providing the translation. Marged Haycock's (2007) *Legendary Poems from the Book of Taliesin* deserves a special mention. This authoritative book with its expert translations and related commentary is an essential aid to research in this difficult area, not only for *Preideu Annwfyn* but for all the legendary poems. Of the modern translations, Loomis (1956) attempted the first four stanzas only, then nearly 30 years elapsed before Haycock provided an expert translation of all stanzas in Haycock (1983-84). Other modern translations have been provided by Budgey (1992), Bollard (1994), Higley (1996) and Koch, in Koch and Carey (2003). Haycock then updated her translation in her 2007 book and has added to our knowledge of the poems with her *Prophecies from the Book of Taliesin* (Haycock, 2013).

John Koch (1984; 1985-6; 1988; 1996; 2006c) provides expert comments on old linguistic forms, which suggest an early dating. Sarah Higley (1996) gives a beautiful translation, elegant and accurate and has made it accessible on the internet with notes and an oral recitation. Due to the research of these scholars, most of the poem can be translated without major disagreement (although there is sometimes a choice of alternatives), the main difficulty being in understanding the ancient allusions made in the poem.
[7] Haycock (2007: 438) notes that *py* ('what', 'why') should be emended to *ry*.
[8] See Higley (1996: 45, 50). Consistent with his mythological view of *Preideu Annwfyn*, John Rhŷs (1891: 282) viewed Pwyll and Pryderi as 'dark divinities'. Kenneth Jackson (1959b: 17) thought Pryderi was an Otherworld divinity.
[9] The name was a common one. Among the possibilities from other Welsh literature is Gweir son of Gweirioedd, listed as a famous prisoner in Triad 52 in *Triads of the Island of Britain* (Bromwich, 2006: 146). Another prospect is Gweir son of Gwystyl, the father's name meaning 'hostage' (Bromwich, 2006: 374). There are also four Gweirs listed as members of Arthur's retinue in *Culhwch and Olwen* (Ford, 1977: 129). Perhaps one of these men was the Gweir who was imprisoned. Rhŷs (1901: 679) states that Lundy Island in the Bristol Channel had the old name of *Ynys Wair* (the Island of Gweir). This data, however, is worthless, merely reflecting the fact that Gweir was considered to have been imprisoned somewhere on an island (from the phrase 'isle of the strong door' in *Preideu Annwfyn*).
[10] Stanza 1 seems a little disjointed, possibly resulting from the transposing of two lines over a long period of oral transmission. Perhaps Lines 5-6 became transposed with Lines 3-4 during this time. Placing Lines 5-6 *before* Lines 3-4 would give a smoother ordering. It would keep the lines referring to the King

together and the lines referring to Gweir together and would provide a suitable introduction to Gweir as a loyal servant before naming him, describing his prison, the report of his capture by Pwyll and Pryderi, and his singing bitterly. This transposition of the two lines is shown below.

1   **Golychaf wledic, pendeuic, gwlat ri,**
    I praise the Sovereign, Prince, King of the land,
2   **py ledas y pennaeth dros traeth mundi.**
    who has enlarged his dominion across the world's shores.
5   **Neb kyn noc ef nyt aeth idi,**
    Nobody before him went into it,
6   **yr gadwyn trom las – kywirwas ae ketwi.**
    into the heavy blue chain – it restrained a loyal servant.
3   **Bu kyweir karchar Gweir yg kaer sidi**
    The prison of Gweir was prepared in the mound fortress
4   **Trwy ebostol Pwyll a Phryderi**
    according to the account of Pwyll and Pryderi.
7   **A rac preideu Annwfyn tost yt geni.**
    And for the sake of the spoils of Annwfyn bitterly he sang.
8   **Ac yt Urawt parahawt yn bardwedi.**
    And till Judgement (Day) our bardic prayer shall endure.
9   **Tri lloneit Prytwen, yd aetham ni idi.**
    Three fullnesses of Prydwen, we went into it.
10 **Nam seith, ny dyrreith o gaer sidi.**
    Except seven, none returned from the mound fortress.

Alternatively, the final form may be the product of a bard whose thoughts dart from one image to another: starting with the King, abruptly mentioning Gweir in prison, darting briefly back to the King, and then returning to Gweir.
[11] Sims-Williams (1982: 244); Jackson (1959b: 16); Bollard (1994: 20).
[12] Higley (1996: 45).
[13] A more radical possibility is that the bard really did mix potions in a cauldron as an aid to obtaining poetic inspiration.
[14] Higley (1996: 50). Jones (1964: 14) also gives the 'four-peaked' option.
[15] Haycock (2007: 442).
[16] See Haycock (2007: 435) and Higley (1996: 50). Haycock emends *pedyr ychwelyt* to *pedrychwelyt* in Line 12.
[17] See Carney (1963: 44); Oskamp (1970: 43); Breatnach (1977: 106) for the dating and Stokes (1889) for a translation.
[18] Cross and Slover (1936: 254).
[19] Lea (1994: 108).
[20] A fourth highly unlikely possibility is that *lluch* ('flashing') is taken to be a person's name which would then produce the name 'Lluch Lleawc'. Roger Loomis (1956: 161-4) takes this view and provides a flawed discussion of other characters based on this phantom character, including his derivation of the name of the knight 'Lancelot of the Lake' (p.163).
[21] Prufer (1964: 64).

[22] Loomis (1927: 350; 1956: 156). Loomis maintained a mythological view of the cauldron and thought that this incident of its capture in *Preideu Annwfyn* represented the earliest stages of the legend of the Holy Grail.
[23] Squire (1905: 317); Jackson (1959b: 16); Ashe (1962: 309); Barber (1986: 15); Coe and Young (1995: 135).
[24] Cross and Slover (1936: 328, 352-3).
[25] Ford (1977: 69).
[26] Ford (1977: 152-3).
[27] Ford (1977: 162-4).
[28] Bromwich (2006: 259-60).
[29] Haycock (1983-4: 71).
[30] Haycock (2007: 436).
[31] Cross and Slover (1936: 352).
[32] That is, Haycock (2007); Budgey (1992); Higley (1996); Koch and Carey (2003). Others interpret *echwyd* as 'noonday' rather than 'flowing (fresh) water', an alternative favoured by Loomis (1956), Jackson (1959b), Bollard (1994) and Green (2009). This could suggest that at noon it was still dark, a circumstance that could exist in Winter if the camp were at a high latitude, around the Arctic Circle, or higher. This interesting scenario is also consistent with the European sources discussed in Chapter 3, that have Arthur exploring the North.
[33] Haycock (2007: 445); Barney et al. (2006: 319-20).
[34] Tschan (1959: 217).
[35] Sims-Williams (1982: 244); Koch and Carey (2003: 310).
[36] Higley (1996: 51-2).
[37] Koch and Carey (2003: 291); O'Meara (2002: 53-4).
[38] Haycock (2007: 446); Jackson (1959b: 17).
[39] Haycock (2007: 183).
[40] Haycock (2007: 433-4); Williams (1899: 21, 45).
[41] Newton (1970: 216); Morison (1971: 90-2); Nansen (1911: 131-2).
[42] Koch and Carey (2003: 365).
[43] Bromwich (2006: 124).
[44] Banfield (1974: 405).
[45] Reynolds, Gates and Glaholt (2003: 1013); Banfield (1974: 405).
[46] Hulbert and Schwarze (1910: 59).
[47] Higley (1996: 52); Koch and Carey (2003: 311).
[48] The 'silvery' descriptor is used on the enature website: Retrieved on 5 July 2015 at: http://www.enature.com/fieldguides/detail.asp?recNum=MA0031
[49] Jackson (1961).
[50] Larivière and Walton (1998).
[51] Gudger (1927: 199).
[52] Squier and Davis (1848: 257).
[53] Higley (1996: 52-3); Jackson (1982: 31).
[54] Haycock (2007: 449).
[55] Winterbottom (1978: 52); Haycock (2007: 450); Schumacher (2004: 701).
[56] Higley (1996: 53). Haycock (2007: 438) takes *bet* to be *pet* ('how many') and *allawr* as 'altar' and gives 'how many saints are in the void and how many altars' which does not make sense in relation to the content of the last two stanzas.

[57] Haycock (2007: 474).
[58] Winterbottom (1978: 153).
[59] Haycock (2007: 295).
[60] Thorpe (1974: 143, 152).
[61] Jones (1967: 126-7).
[62] Coe and Young (1995: 44-7).
[63] Koch (1996: 251).
[64] Bromwich (2006: 167-9); Rivet and Smith (1979: 293-4).
[65] Rhŷs (1888: 248); Squire (1905: 318); Nash (1858: 214).
[66] In four lines, *Golychaf-i Gulwyd* gives a picture of Elffin similar to that in *The Tale of Taliesin*. The poet (a Taliesin persona) goes to Degannwy to dispute with Maelgwn, in order to persuade him to release Elffin. *Kanu y Med* also gives a treatment of Elffin. In eight lines, the poet (a Taliesin persona) implores God to release Elffin from banishment. He recalls how Elffin had given him many fine things, including wine, ale, mead, and powerful horses. He ends the poem with the uncertain and enigmatic line requesting that the 'Elffin rider' should possess the North (see Haycock, 2007: 352). In *Kanu y Byt Mawr*, in the last four lines, the Taliesin persona announces that he is Taliesin, with a wise man's eloquence, and that his praise of Elffin will last until the end of time. All three poems appear to be elaborations on the ending of *Kadeir Teÿrnon*. The Taliesin persona also gives a reference to *Kat Godeu* in Lines 29 and 30 of the later *Book of Taliesin* poem, *Golychaf-i Gulwyd*.
[67] Haycock (1983-4: 65); Haycock (2007: 439).

Chapter 6 Death of Arthur in America

[1] For a translation and notes, see Haycock (2007: 167-239).
[2] Poetic exaggeration of the number of opponents slain is common in Welsh poetry and is not to be taken literally. This large number given could reflect the poet's perception of the many attacks made on the Britons in Annwfyn.
[3] See Koch (1997: 15, 37).
[4] Ford (1977: 186).
[5] See also Haycock (2007: 231) for a discussion of the problems in translation and some suggested options.
[6] Haycock (2007: 184).
[7] Haycock (2007: 231).
[8] Williams (1972: 143), footnote 61. Also Bede's *EH* (Book 2, Ch. 20). See McClure and Collins (1994: 105-6; 384).
[9] Bede's *EH* (Book 3, Ch. 12-13). See McClure and Collins (1994: 129-31).
[10] Dated by Ford (1999: 177, 184-7). Urien fought the Angles with his son Owain during the late 500s. His territory *Rheged* may have stretched west into southern Scotland, but was perhaps centred on Carlisle and the Lake District. Two *Book of Taliesin* poems imply that he was 'Lord of Catraeth', considered to be modern Catterick. He may have taken Catraeth from the Angles with his ally, Gwallawg, who was king of Elmet (around Leeds). The *Historia Brittonum* has them fighting the Anglian king, Theodoric, who took refuge on Lindisfarne. Urien was killed when betrayed by another British ally, Morcant.
[11] Ford (1977: 70).

[12] Jackson (1964: 36-7).
[13] See Chacon and Dye (2007); Mensforth (2001); Mensforth (2007); Schmidt and Sharkey (2012).
[14] See Shetrone and Greenman (1931); Thomas, Carr and Keller (2006: 369).
[15] Dragoo and Wray (1964: 196); Weets et al. (2006: 552); Lepper (2005: 124).
[16] Koch (1990).
[17] Jones (1964: 14).
[18] See Williams (1938) for Line 1242 in *Y Gododdin*. For the Cornish legend, see Chambers (1927: 228-9).
[19] Ford (1977: 69); Koch (2006c: 236).
[20] In *Perceval*, Chrétien de Troyes employed the 'pierced thighs' motif for the Fisher King, an invalid who had been pierced through the thighs by a javelin, perhaps represented by the bleeding lance in the grail procession. Had Perceval asked about the grail and lance, the King would have been cured and calamity for his kingdom averted.
[21] Koch (1991: 116).

Chapter 7 Interpreting the 'Battle of the Trees'

[1] Robert Graves (1961) gives a mysterious but untenable explanation that the tree names correspond to a kind of secret alphabet, spelling out a coded message. See the comments of Haycock (2007: 172-3) which give a valuable and sensible discussion. Haycock (1990; 2007) appears to regard the poem as a parody of epic poems in which the bard was creating a mock-heroic pastiche. However, Benozzo (2004) does not accept Haycock's view of the poem as a parody but instead sees the creative mind of the poet at work, imposing movement on an important part of the landscape.
[2] Lloyd-Jones (1950); Haycock (2007: 170).
[3] Ford (1977: 125).
[4] Benozzo (2004: 111); Green (2007a: 66); Haycock (2007: 169).
[5] Coe and Young (1995: 144-5); Haycock (2007: 175-6).
[6] See Lamberton (1988: 53). West (1966: 381-3) defends the authenticity of the Typhon story as part of the original. Fontenrose (1959: 71) remarks that if it were an interpolation then it was an early one.
[7] Evelyn-White (1914: 139).
[8] Rouse (1940: 39, 41, 63, 73, 83, 91).
[9] Rouse (1940: 3, 19, 21).
[10] Clube and Napier (1990: 189).
[11] Bailey, Clube and Napier (1990: 69).
[12] Baillie (1994); Baillie (1999: 58, 67-8).
[13] Stothers and Rampino (1983); Stothers (1984); Gunn (2000); Keys (2000).
[14] See Clube and Napier (1990: 145-154). The AD 400-600 period is given in Bailey, Clube and Napier (1990: 76).
[15] Larsen et al. (2008); Dull, Southon and Sheets (2001); Rigby, Symonds and Ward-Thompson (2004).
[16] Haycock (2007: 173).
[17] Haycock (2007: 192).
[18] Haycock (1990: 325).

[19] See Lewis (1996: 169-71); the quotation is on p.170. John Lewis provides a table of such events on pp.176-82. An early example comes from China in about AD 476, just before Arthur's time, when 'Thundering Chariots' which were 'like granite' fell to the ground. The largest documented meteorite fall occurred in January 1868, near Pultusk in Poland, in which there fell over 100,000 H-group chondritic meteorites.

[20] Dark (1994b: 188-91; 2000: 36-7) shows that Virgil was well known in the west of Britain in the fifth and sixth centuries. A book now stored in the Vatican Library called *Vergilius Romanus* (Cod. Vat. lat. 3867) contains Virgil's *Georgics*, *Eclogues* and *Aeneid* and is illustrated with colour paintings. Dark states that the Roman art specialist Martin Henig identifies the artwork as probably Romano-British, not Italian. It may have been created c. 500 according to Dark. However, see Wright (2001: 62) who argues for a Rome creation based on the high standard of book production.

[21] Coe and Young (1995: 18-21; 39-43).

[22] Clube and Napier (1990: 284-5).

[23] Williams (1968: xliv).

Chapter 8 The Aftermath of the Voyage

[1] Another approach is given by Haycock (2007: 295) which overcomes these difficulties, but destroys the above pattern of 'and his' or 'with his' and turns three of the lines into questions which are alternatives; e.g. 'is he a famous one, a wise one? or the ruler of Rheon? or is he a royal ruler?'. This pattern of alternatives seems unconvincing and even logically faulty. If Arthur were the 'ruler of Rheon' then he was probably also 'a famous one'. These should not really be alternatives. Despite the difficulties in getting an exact translation, the general heroic picture of Arthur that emerges is not much affected.

[2] For the Barkway plaque see Collingwood and Wright (1995: 70-1; RIB no. 218). For the South Shields altar see Collingwood and Wright (1995: 353; RIB no. 1055). See also Haycock (2007: 300) and Green (2007b).

[3] Haycock (2007: 300).

[4] The Arthurian tapestry is shown in the frontispiece of Loomis (1959).

[5] Koch (1997: 144).

[6] Watson (1926: 34); Crawford (1935: 285); Haycock (2007: 300-1).

[7] See Haycock (2007: 301). It is possible that others have taken *rif* to mean 'number' and thus associated Arthur with a scriptural number, possibly 'three' from the Trinity. The later art often depicts Arthur in garments, armour or with banners, each emblazoned with an image of three crowns.

[8] Jones (1964: 15); Sims-Williams (1991a: 52); Coe and Young (1995: 142).

[9] Haycock (2007: 294). There is one clear instance in the poem where *kadeir* does seem to have the meaning of 'song'. In Line 41 'my brilliant contest-song', 'song' seems to be the only possible interpretation (Haycock, 2007: 297).

[10] Winterbottom (1978: 31).

[11] 'Pale' appears to indicate a favoured colour. In *Y Gododdin*, prized horses appear to be those that are 'pale' (B2.37, A.58), 'very white' (B1.10) or 'the colour of swans' (B1.21).

[12] See Ford (1977: 52, 54); Sims-Williams (1991a: 40).

[13] See Ford (1977: 65-6); Bromwich (2006: 25-6).
[14] Bromwich (2006: 25).
[15] Bartrum (1966: 62).
[16] Bromwich (2006: 1, 35).
[17] The parallels between Arthur and Brân are given in Chapter 6. If Arthur is equated with Brân, then the Triad could be seen as implying that Caradawg was Arthur's son, but this inference is nowhere made in the Welsh literature. The *Dream of Rhonabwy* makes Arthur and Caradawg first cousins, while a 16th-century MS implies that Arthur's mother, Eigyr, was the sister of Caradawg's mother, Tywanedd (Bartrum, 1965: 242-3). The author of the triad may have attempted to create answers to the question of 'who minded the country' without any real knowledge of what happened in Arthur's case.
[18] Alcock (1971: 360).
[19] Haycock (2007: 309).
[20] Haycock (2007: 297-8).
[21] Baillie (1999: 75).
[22] Haycock (2007: 310).
[23] Thorpe (1966: 263-5).
[24] Hieatt (1992: 79).
[25] Elffin appears centuries later in a tale about Taliesin which comprises two parts, *The Tale of Gwion Bach* and *The Tale of Taliesin* (given in Ford, 1977, 159-81). It begins with Ceridwen making a magic brew in her cauldron, intended for her son, Afagddu. However, it was Gwion, the fire stoker, who swallowed some drops of her brew. Gwion, in fleeing from Ceridwen, changed himself into a grain of wheat and was eaten by Ceridwen, who had changed herself into a hen. Nine months later Ceridwen gave birth to a boy, containing the soul of Gwion. She could not bear to harm the baby, but placed him in a small coracle which floated to Gwyddno's weir. It was found by Gwyddno's son, Elffin, who named him Taliesin ('radiant brow') and became his patron. Later in the story, Elffin's boasting had caused him to be imprisoned by Maelgwn (the Maglocunus of Gildas). In several incidents at Maelgwn's court, Taliesin made fools of the other bards and Maelgwn's son, Rhun. He eventually persuaded Maelgwn to release Elffin by singing his inspired poetry.

Kadeir Teÿrnon contradicts this late tale about Taliesin. It seems to imply that Elffin was being held by foreign peoples who came to Britain, rather than by Maelgwn. The last line in the poem is an impassioned plea to release Elffin. If we are to take *Kadeir Teÿrnon* as a source of information on Arthur, then we must accept the implication that the poem treats Elffin as a historical figure who has been captured by foreigners. Elffin's appearance in this late story should not disqualify him from being thought of as a historical figure, any more than it would Maelgwn Gwynedd, the Maglocunus of Gildas. Elffin was a sixth-century name. An Elffin is mentioned in *Y Gododdin*, stanza A.37, where he was a paragon of valour – a warrior's courage is being praised because it was like that of Elffin (Koch and Carey, 2003: 345).

A later storyteller may have understood little more than that Elffin was held prisoner somewhere (and probably also that he was Gwyddno's son), but then used his imagination to compose a tale where Elffin was imprisoned by Maelgwn

Gwynedd and released through the inspirational poetry of Taliesin. That is, the tale can be seen as an embellishment seeking to add detail to the brief enigmatic mention at the end of *Kadeir Teÿrnon*. The incident of Elffin's capture must have been regarded as important, as poets in the *Book of Taliesin* refer to it. It appears in *Golychaf-i Gulwyd* (Lines 23-6), *Kanu y Med* (Lines 15-2) and *Kanu y Byt Mawr* (Lines 60-1).

Chapter 9   Dating the Three Poems

[1] Roberts (1811); Wright (1842).
[2] See Winterbottom (1978: 29-36).
[3] See Ó Faoláin (2006: 621) on the Damnonia pun. Jackson (1982: 30) relates how Gildas plays on the literal meanings of the king's names to create hostile or demeaning interpretations. Gildas also uses a biblical reference to liken each of the kings to an animal – Constantine to a lion, Aurelius 'Caninus' also to a lion, Vortipor to a leopard, Cuneglasus to a bear and Maglocunus to a dragon. Gildas appears to have selected these animals from Revelation 13:2, where they each form part of a horrific biblical beast, a composite of the animals.
[4] Koch (1997: cxxii).
[5] Jackson (1982: 32-3); Winterbottom (1978: 31).
[6] Jackson (1982: 34).
[7] Thorpe (1974).
[8] Williams (1899: 81).
[9] Winterbottom (1978: 34).
[10] Williams (1899: 21, 45).
[11] Winterbottom (1978: 13, 16).
[12] Winterbottom (1978: 52).
[13] Winterbottom (1978: 71).
[14] Haycock (1983-4: 54); Haycock (2007: 433-4).
[15] Haycock (2007: 446).
[16] Dumville (1988b: 101-2).
[17] O'Meara (2002: 53-4).
[18] Koch and Carey (2003: 291).
[19] Meyer (1895: xvi).
[20] Carney (1976: 174); Carney (1983: 178); Breatnach (1977: 101-3); Mac Mathúna (1985: 411); Mac Mathúna (2006: 959).
[21] Based on Cross and Slover (1936: 588-595).
[22] Cross and Slover (1936: 589).
[23] Haycock (2007: 277).
[24] Carey (1995: 41-2); McCone (2000: 29, 45, 47).
[25] Based on McCone (2000: 121-3).
[26] Breatnach (1977: 106).
[27] Cross and Slover (1936: 328); Sims-Williams (1982: 251).
[28] Based on Cross and Slover (1936: 352-3).
[29] Haycock (2007: 436); Cross and Slover (1936: 352).
[30] Cross and Slover (1936: 254, 273).
[31] Stokes (1889: 80-1).
[32] Haycock (2007: 167).

[33] Preideu Annwfyn and Kat Godeu compared

Portraying the Otherworld as a terrible tragedy rather than a paradise
In each of the first six stanzas of *Preideu Annwfyn* the bard laments the few survivors. He calls their experience a 'disastrous visit' and 'woeful conflict', and in the climax announces Arthur's death. In *Kat Godeu*, the bard describes torrid fighting, and comments that he had killed a large number of opponents. He also describes how Arthur (the 'boar') was killed.

Christian beliefs
Both poems express strong Christian beliefs. In *Preideu Annwfyn* the poet prays for Gweir and later turns to Christ for comfort, being distraught over Arthur's death. In *Kat Godeu*, Gwydion asks Christ to save the Britons. The bard twice mentions the three greatest cataclysms in world history, which include Christ's crucifixion and Judgement Day, which he thinks is at hand. He also refers to God's control of earthly events, making and remaking civilisations.

Judgement Day
Both poems mention Judgement Day. In *Preideu Annwfyn* the poet states that he will pray for Gweir until Judgement Day comes, while the *Kat Godeu* poet refers to Judgement Day twice as noted above.

Portraying Arthur as a king
Both poems imply that Arthur was a king. In the first line of *Preideu Annwfyn*, the poet describes Arthur as the sovereign (*wledig*), prince (*pendeuic*) and king (*ri*) of the land. He similarly describes Arthur in the last stanza, calling him 'great prince'. In *Kat Godeu*, the poet has sung before the 'Lord of Britain', who can hardly be anyone other than Arthur, given that the same poet went with Arthur to Annwfyn, as shown in Lines 189-204.

A deep respect for Arthur
In *Preideu Annwfyn* the poet praises Arthur on many occasions. In the first stanza he addresses Arthur as a king in three different ways, states that Arthur has extended his sovereignty across the world's shores and that he was the first to go into this new land. He later refers to the valour of Arthur. In the last stanza, the poet praises Arthur as a great prince and states that he is praising Arthur as a way of preventing himself from grieving. In *Kat Godeu*, the poet finishes the Annwfyn section with a beautiful tribute to Arthur: 'Shining his name, strong of hand: Brilliantly he directed the host'.

The use of the unusual word 'muchyd'
The word *muchyd* refers to the solid coal-like material – lignite, or jet. This quite unusual word occurs in both *Preideu Annwfyn* and *Kat Godeu*. In the former, *muchyd* gives an internal rhyme with *echwyd* and could be used literally for 'jet' or taken as a proxy for something dark (Line 25). In *Kat Godeu*, it appears in a line that translates simply as 'black is jet' (Line 140). This occurrence of the same unusual word could imply a common authorship of the two poems. The word

muchyd does not appear in any of the other legendary poems (as classified by Haycock, 2007) in the *Book of Taliesin*.

Fighting with the Annwfyn people
In *Preideu Annwfyn* there is implied fighting when a cauldron is captured from the inhabitants and Gweir is imprisoned. The bard also comments on the valour of Arthur in Annwfyn, implying heroism in a battle. He also mentions 'woeful conflict' (Line 47). Further, the return to Britain of only a small number of men, when considered jointly with the above, implies large losses in battle.

In *Kat Godeu*, the fighting is made explicit. The people of Annwfyn use the streams of the region to mobilise their forces for battle (Lines 189-90). Then the old bard boasts about the large number of warriors he killed in the fighting and their courage (Lines 191-2).

Noting the bravery of the Annwfyn people
Both poems refer to the great bravery of the Annwfyn inhabitants. In *Preideu Annwfyn*, the poet remarks that the captured cauldron does not boil the food of a coward, a surprising comment on the bravery of the enemy (Line 17). In *Kat Godeu*, the poet notes that the enemy is similar to himself in their aggression and appears to say that they had the passion for battle of one hundred normal warriors (Lines 193-5).

Distress at the death of Arthur
In *Preideu Annwfyn* the bard's distress is evident in the last stanza. In *Kat Godeu*, he takes solace in the fact that God is in charge of worldly events (Lines 201-2).

A statement about the death of Arthur in Annwfyn
In *Preideu Annwfyn*, the bard builds dramatic tension leading to Line 58 where he announces that the grave of the saint (Arthur) is lost/annihilated, both grave and champion. In *Kat Godeu*, he states that a lord he calls the 'boar' was killed by a meek one, interpreted here as a mercy killing of the wounded Arthur by his bard (Lines 197-200).

An interest in the numbers 3, 9 and their multiples
In *Preideu Annwfyn* the poet refers to the three 'fullnesses' of Prydwen in three of the stanzas. He also refers poetically to the nine priestesses who kindle his cauldron of poetic inspiration (Line 14) and the three score hundred men who stood on the wall (Line 31). In addition, his attack on the monks is centred on three stanzas (4-6) which have a parallel structure.

Kat Godeu is a very long poem with many examples of threes, nines and their multiples. In the transmigration of the soul introduction, the poet was a bridge over three score estuaries (Line 12), while he was a string in a harp for nine years (Line 20). He refers to the three greatest catastrophes in the world in Line 69, and repeats these in Lines 243-5. His soul was composed from nine forms of matter (Line 154), while he refers to the power of the ninth wave (Line 162). In battle, he boasts that he had the passion of 900 warriors (Line 196) and killed 900 select warriors (Line 224).

[34] Preideu Annwfyn and Kadeir Teÿrnon compared

An implication that Arthur had been away
Kadeir Teÿrnon does not mention Arthur sailing to Annwfyn but it does imply that Arthur had been away from Britain for an extended period of time. The poet abruptly asks who were the three stewards that minded the country (Lines 23-4). The question is asked without any context, which suggests that no context was actually needed and that the audience were quite familiar with Arthur's absence overseas in Annwfyn.

This unanswered question was later elaborated, becoming one of the *Triads of the Island of Britain* and part of the *Mabinogi* story when Brân the Blessed left Britain for Ireland and placed others in charge. In *Preideu Annwfyn*, the whole poem is about Arthur being away on his expedition to Annwfyn.

The locating of Arthur in northeast Wales
Preideu Annwfyn notes that the inhabitants of Annwfyn do not visit the Defwy (Devwy) meadows in Britain, which would therefore seem to be part of the home territory of the bard. John Koch has tentatively translated 'Devwy' as 'Dee' in the *Spoils of Taliesin*. It is argued that Devwy was probably derived from *Deva* (Chester) and *gwy* (for a river) and that the bard is referring to the meadows along the River Dee which runs through Chester. *Kadeir Teÿrnon* states that Arthur wore the lorica of Lleon, which refers to Caer Lleon (Chester) in particular, or northeast Wales in general.

Christian beliefs
In *Preideu Annwfyn*, the poet shows his Christian beliefs on many occasions, as previously discussed. In *Kadeir Teÿrnon*, Christian belief appears in Lines 33-4 when the poet remarks that it is fine when the True One (God) shines forth and even finer when He pronounces. He also provides a list of Arthur's praiseworthy features, which include his reverence for scripture (Line 8).

Portraying Arthur as a king
It has already been shown that *Preideu Annwfyn* refers to Arthur as a king in multiple ways (*wledic, pendeuic, rî*). *Kadeir Teÿrnon* also refers to Arthur as a king on several occasions. The very title of the poem, *Chair of the Sovereign*, refers to Arthur's kingship and who will fill it now that Arthur is dead. The poem also describes Arthur as governor of Rheon (a region now in southwest Scotland) (Line 6) and refers to his royal sovereignty (Line 7). In Line 65, it also refers to the annihilation of the prince (*pendeuic*), which is a reference to Arthur's death in Annwfyn.

A deep respect for Arthur
As discussed earlier, *Preideu Annwfyn* shows a deep respect for Arthur. So does *Kadeir Teÿrnon*, which describes him as brave and authoritative (Line 3), wise (Line 4), governing in a royal way (Line 7), having a respect for scripture (Line 8), providing protection (Line 9), providing the necessities for his people (Line 16) and having great valour as a warrior (Lines 21-2, Line 66).

The use of questions
In *Preideu Annwfyn*, the poet refers to incidents and things that Arthur's men have encountered in Annwfyn and which the monks do not know. This listing of ignorance represents implied questions that the monks cannot answer. In addition, direct questions are posed: 'the cauldron of Annwfyn's chieftain: what is its form?' (Line 15). There are also questions near the end of the poem designed to delay the climax and build suspense: 'Is the wind of one path? Is the sea of one water?' (Line 51); 'Is the invincible fire of one spark?' (Line 52).

In Kadeir Teÿrnon, the bard asks his audience some questions which are very specifically focused: 'Who were the three stewards that minded the country?' (Lines 23-4); 'Who were the three wise ones that guarded the portent?' (Lines 25-6); 'What are the names of the three forts that are now covered by the sea flood?' (Lines 44-5). These items would seem to reflect real questions about a region of Britain after Arthur's death.

This use of questions is one of the hallmarks of the 'mythological Taliesin', the series of later poets who adopted the Taliesin persona. It is the viewpoint expressed here that *Preideu Annwfyn, Kat Godeu* and *Kadeir Teÿrnon* were probably the work of Arthur's bard, a sixth-century poet. Later poets adopting the Taliesin persona imitated features of these genuine sixth-century poems, one of which was the use of questions. A reading of these later poems shows that they are usually very inferior and they can generally be identified as spurious without difficulty.

Inspiration from the cauldron
In *Preideu Annwfyn*, the poet refers to the inspired nature of his poetry. It is as though it were conjured from a cauldron kindled by nine maidens skilled in magic (Lines 13-14). Stories about such maidens must have been familiar to the audience, as noted from the work of Pomponius Mela in AD 44. In *Kadeir Teÿrnon*, the poet expresses a similar view of the cauldron with the lines: '(it is) fine when came from the cauldron, the threepart inspiration' (Lines 35-6).

Distress at the death of Arthur
The distress at Arthur's death is strongly evident in the last stanza of *Preideu Annwfyn*. In *Kadeir Teÿrnon*, the bard laments that his men are bereft (Line 63) and that he himself is similarly distressed at Arthur's death (Line 64).

Use of same word 'diua' for the death of Arthur
In both *Preideu Annwfyn* and *Kadeir Teÿrnon* the same word for the death of Arthur is used. In *Preideu Annwfyn* the line is translated as 'The grave of the saint is lost/annihilated', which implies that the grave has effectively been obliterated and cannot be found (Line 58). In *Kadeir Teÿrnon* the appropriate line is translated as 'the annihilation of the prince', a devastating term for Arthur's death (Line 65). The same word (*diua*) also appears a second time in *Preideu Annwfyn* in Line 57, where it refers to the utter destruction of places by the strong winds. This common usage could imply that the same bard composed both poems or it could imply one author copying the language of the other. Unfortunately, the same term has also been used by much later and inferior poets in the *Book of*

Taliesin. The same word also appears in the later poems *Prif Gyuarch Geluyd* (Line 40), *Angar Kyfundawt* (Line 127), *Cunedaf* (Line 50), *Marwnat Vthyr Pen* (Line 10) and *Kanu y Byt Bychan* (Line 13) which removes the uniqueness of the word linkage between *Preideu Annwfyn* and *Kadeir Teÿrnon*. So this argument, although interesting, is hardly conclusive.

An interest in the numbers 3, 9 and their multiples
The use of the numbers three, nine and their multiples in *Preideu Annwfyn* has already been discussed. In *Kadeir Teÿrnon* the poet consistently uses three or its multiples as follows – he refers to the third profound song of the wise one (in Line 17), Arthur's trampling over nine opponents at once (Line 22), the three stewards who minded the country (Line 23), the three wise ones who guarded the portent (Line 25), the three part inspiration from the cauldron (Line 36) and the three fortresses now under flooding (Line 43).

[35] Jackson (1945: 48).
[36] Koch (1984; 1985-6; 1988; 1996; 2006d).
[37] Koch (1985-6: 57).
[38] Jackson (1953: 293-4); Koch (1985-6: 59).
[39] Koch (1996: 265).
[40] Koch (2006e: 1653).
[41] Koch (1991: 116).
[42] Koch (1985-6: 55, 59); Koch (1991: 112).
[43] Haycock (2007: 226).
[44] Haycock (1990: 307); Haycock (2007: 172, 206).
[45] Koch (1997: 144).
[46] Koch (1988: 27).
[47] Koch (1997: cxxviii).

Chapter 10   An Attempt to Reconstruct the Voyage
[1] Park (2008: 191).
[2] Ingstad and Ingstad (1986).
[3] The L'Anse aux Meadows site is not now considered to be Vinland itself but a staging post that allowed easy access to it (Kunz and Sígurðsson, 2008: xxvi; Wallace, 2008: 610). Vinland was probably the good lands on the shores of New Brunswick, the northern limit for the growth of wild grapes, and south of this. Radiocarbon dating of the L'Anse aux Meadows site yields a date range of AD 975-1020 (Nydal, 1989).
[4] For example, Stefánsson (1942); Whitaker (1981-2); Cunliffe (2001: 130).
[5] Little (1945); Ashe (1962); Chapman (1973); Severin (1978).
[6] Morison (1971: 25).
[7] Jones (1986: 33-4).
[8] Sharpe (1995: 118, 127, 196-8, 219).
[9] Young (2009: 131-9).
[10] Campbell (1987); Ahronson (2000); Ahronson (2003).
[11] Eldjárn and Fridriksson (2000); Magnússon (1973).
[12] Alonso-Núñez (1986).

[13] See Tierney (1967: 75). The notion that it was light during the night in midsummer in northerly regions occurs in these other ancient writers: Pliny (*Natural History*, II), Isidore of Seville (*Etymologies*, XIV) and in Bede (*In Regum Librum XXX Quaestiones*).
[14] Jones (1986: 144).
[15] Foley and Holder (1999: 129-30); dating in Meyvaert (1999: 275).
[16] Tierney (1967: 76-7).
[17] Cunliffe (2001: 132-3).
[18] Hammond (1996: 58, 60-3).
[19] McGrail (2006: 39-43); Nayling and McGrail (2004).
[20] McGrail (2006: 42).
[21] Barney, Lewis, Beach and Berghof (2006: 10, 373-6).
[22] Stefánsson (1947: 43).
[23] Lehn (2000). Also Lehn and Schroeder (1979); Sawatzky and Lehn (1976).
[24] Diemand (2001: 1255-6).
[25] Marko et al. (1994: 1336).
[26] Schell (1962: 162).
[27] Diemand (2001: 1256); Marko (1996: 553).
[28] Ebbesmeyer, Okubo and Helseth (1980: 976).
[29] Diemand (2001: 1257).
[30] Marko et al. (1994: 1338).
[31] Ebbesmeyer, Okubo and Helseth (1980: 977).
[32] Diemand (2001: 1261-2).
[33] Marko et al. (1994: 1338).
[34] Morison (1971: 392).
[35] Morison (1971: 401).
[36] Morison (1971: 405).
[37] Morison (1971: 415).
[38] Feininger and Goodacre (1995: 1351).
[39] Morison (1971: 410-11).
[40] Morison (1971: 390).
[41] Cunliffe (2001: 133).
[42] Morison (1971: 418).
[43] Squier and Davis (1848: 3).
[44] The Cedar Bank Works contained a mound in the shape of a rectangular pyramid which was truncated at the top to form a platform. It was about five miles north of Chillicothe, east of the Scioto (Squier and Davis, 1848: 52). It had a large rectangular enclosure of earthen walls, with one wall not built on the open western side which fell away steeply in a terrace bank. Inside this large enclosure was an earthen mound shaped like a rectangular pyramid, with a flat top, 250 ft long by 150 ft wide. Access to this top was gained by earthen ramps on the north and south sides. The axis of symmetry passing lengthwise through the top platform was aligned with these ramps and with openings in the walls of the rectangular enclosure.

The Marietta Earthworks, at the join of the Muskingum and Ohio Rivers, also contained examples of truncated rectangular pyramids inside a square enclosure. These two large pyramids had earthen ramps on all four sides of the rectangle to

allow access to the platform top (Squier and Davis, 1848: 73). The Pinson Mounds site in Tennessee also contained five large platform mounds, radiocarbon dated to about AD 1-500 (Mainfort, 1988).
[45] Lepper (2005: 148).
[46] The High Bank Works was about five miles southeast of Chillicothe, east of the Scioto (Squier and Davis: 50). It featured a large octagon which enclosed eight mounds. Each mound was perfectly positioned inside the octagon next to each point of the octagon. Attached to the octagon's northern edge was a large circular enclosure that encompassed 20 acres, joined to the octagon by a short section of parallel walls.

This octagon, its internal mounds and circle were similar to those of the Newark Earthworks, west of Columbus. The axis of symmetry passing through the octagon, through the parallel walls and through the attached circle was at 90 degrees to the corresponding axis of symmetry in the Newark works, a considerable achievement (Hively and Horn, 2005: 161).
[47] Prufer (1964: 93); Lepper (2005: 143).
[48] Lepper (2005: 120).
[49] Prufer (1964: 94).
[50] Spence and Fryer (2006: 724).
[51] See McHugh (1972) and Lott (2002). The two bison types are recognized as subspecies by many scholars (see the discussion in Reynolds, Gates and Glaholt (2003: 1009). However other scholars consider them as ecotypes, their physical differences being attributed to living in different environments instead of being genetically caused (for example, Geist, 1991).
[52] Lott (2002: 71); Reynolds, Gates and Glaholt (2003: 1012).
[53] Prufer (1964: 90).
[54] Hulbert and Schwarze (1910: 59).
[55] Reynolds, Gates and Glaholt (2003: 1013).
[56] Banfield (1974: 405).
[57] Moore (1961: 90).
[58] Larivière and Walton (1998).
[59] Lepper (2005: 127).
[60] Gudger (1927).

Chapter 11 A Reappraisal of the Traditional Arthurian Evidence
[1] Chadwick and Chadwick (1932: 161-2).
[2] In discussing the four men named 'Arthur', the work of Bromwich (1975-6) is misinterpreted by Green (2007a). Bromwich (p.178-9) says that the naming of the men after Arthur '*would be a type of commemoration for which Celtic tradition offers no other parallel, as far as I know*'. That is, Bromwich is stating that the naming is unique, as far as she is aware.

Nevertheless, she regards it as a possible argument for Arthur's historicity and goes on to say 'All of these instances [the northern Arthurs] could reflect, directly or indirectly, the fame of an Arthur who was renowned locally, wherever he may have lived' (p.179). Further, she notes that there are grounds for accepting the proposition for a 'common 'pool' of knowledge about Arthur among the Britons of Strathclyde between the seventh and ninth centuries' (p.180). She speculates that Arthur was a historical figure who could have been associated with the East Riding of Yorkshire (p.180).

Green (2007a: 49) misinterprets the italicised Bromwich statement above as implying that it would seem to be 'untenable' that the four were named after Arthur. However, this implication that 'unique' means 'untenable' does not follow and is also inconsistent with Bromwich's further arguments. Having dismissed a naming after the historical Arthur, Green then presents her desired 'solution' – that the naming of the four men was based on a mythical folkloric figure instead. This would be far less likely than a naming after a historical Arthur. A historical figure is localised in time, as Arthur was to the early sixth century. Hence it makes perfect sense for children to be named after this famous figure in the later sixth century. Belief in a folkloric figure, on the other hand, can extend for thousands of years which makes the sudden appearance of the Arthur names, clustered in a short time segment, difficult to explain.

[3] Chadwick (1949: 152); Jackson (1959a: 3-4).
[4] Bannerman (1974: 91); Anderson and Anderson (1961: 45-6).
[5] Meyer (1895: 84); also Zimmer (1893: 284); Bromwich (1975-6: 178).
[6] Meyer (1905: 17).
[7] Bartrum (1966: 4, 10).
[8] Watson (1926: 34); Crawford (1935: 285); McCarthy (2004: 125); Haycock (2007: 300-1).
[9] Koch (1997: lii, lxxiii).
[10] Alcock (1983: 15-17); Wilson et al. (1996: 50-4).
[11] Koch (1997: lxxx); Cessford (1997: 218); Dumville (1988a: 2, 13).
[12] Koch (2006b: 119).
[13] Koch (1997: 147).
[14] Koch (1997: 8-9; 22-3). For the Welsh text, see Evans (1908: 35, 37).
[15] Koch (1997: xlviii).
[16] Poems addressed to the northern British king, Urien, could also imply a circa 550 date for the battle of Catraeth, if at least one were composed in Urien's time. These are *Gweith Gwen Ystrat* (Battle of the Blessed/White Valley) and *Spoils of Taliesin*. They praise Urien as 'Lord of Catraeth' and his men as 'men of Catraeth', implying that he and his ally, Gwallawg, took control of Catraeth in the late 500s. Gwallawg's victory there is also implied by a third poem, *Moliant Cadwallon* (Praise of Cadwallon). In the *Historia Brittonum*, Urien and Gwallawg fought the Anglian chief, Theodoric, forcing him to take refuge on Lindisfarne Island. Theodoric's floruit was c. 572-579, according to the *Moore Memoranda*.

Urien's extensive lands appear to have included parts of Ayrshire, Galloway, Carlisle, the Lake District and east to Catraeth (see Laing and Longley, 2006: 161). Given this huge area, it is very interesting that the poems twice focus on Catraeth. It suggests that Catraeth was notorious at the time the poems were composed and that his title 'Lord of Catraeth' was all the more prestigious for being contrasted with an earlier British failure.

It is possible that the Gododdin defeat at Catraeth did not take place about 600 (as is often stated) but preceded Urien. However, there are doubts about the poems. Dumville (1988a) has reservations about them, while Isaac (1998) argues that *Gweith Gwen Ystrat* was composed much later than the sixth century. If these are genuine sixth-century poems, they suggest that the Gododdin defeat took place around AD 550.

[17] Charles-Edwards (1978; 1991). Also Charles-Edwards (2013: 364-78).
[18] Green (2007a: 51).
[19] Koch (1997: 148).
[20] Jarman (1988: lxiv).
[21] Barber (1986: 14).
[22] Green (2007a) has argued that Arthur was a folkloric figure or Celtic god who became 'historicized'. She thus treats the *Y Gododdin* Arthurian reference in a grossly exaggerated fashion, making inferences that can hardly be justified – '*Y Gododdin*... very clearly possesses a concept of Arthur as a mythical 'superhero', not a historical figure' (p.36). She also states that Arthur is 'portrayed as superhuman, not human' by the Arthurian clause (p.52). She remarks: 'Arthur was clearly viewed by the poet as 'the impossible comparison', a 'Brittonic superhero' and legendary paragon of valour to whose heights of valour not even a man who killed 300 could compare' (p.52).

Despite Green's use of 'clearly' she is in error, both in her assertion that Arthur was regarded as a 'mythical superhero' and in her view that Gorddur had killed 300 men. To consider the latter first, John Koch (1997: 23) translates the first line of the stanza as 'More than three hundred of the finest were slain'. The warriors slain here are the Britons, the Gododdin force, not the enemy. No British bard would refer to the enemy, the despised Angles, as being among 'the finest' (*echassaf*) warriors. Ifor Williams (1968: 106) also translates *echassaf* as 'most valiant'. Koch discusses the suppression of the prefixed pronoun *ef* on p.148. The number slain in the first line corresponds to the total losses suffered by the Gododdin force, which is not a coincidence. For the stanzas giving the number of men in the Gododdin force see Koch (1997: 35, 37, 49, 61, 73, 77, 109). The poet is really saying that the Gododdin lost over 300 of the finest warriors, of whom Gorddur was one.

Green is also incorrect in her assertion that the poet regarded Arthur as a 'mythical superhero' in the stanza. The implausibility of this assertion may be illustrated from examples. Suppose an old boxing aficionado comments on the latest champion: 'He is a great champion but he is not as good as Joe Louis'. This statement would be unobjectionable as Joe Louis was regarded as the paragon of excellence in boxing. It is comparable to the 'though he was not Arthur' reference. However, if he said: 'He's a great champion but he is not as good as a mythical opponent with super powers', this would surely provoke derision. The possession of super powers by one of the contestants would thus render the comparison invalid and therefore utterly pointless. Similarly, if one said 'Our priest is a holy man, but not as holy as God', a similar contemptuous reaction would ensue. In order to make sense, the two things being compared must be sufficiently similar so as to make a comparison at least conceivable, even if it were a very unequal one. For the poet to state that Gorddur was not as good as a mythical superhero, as a way of praising him, is extremely implausible.

[23] Rowland (1990: 180).
[24] Bromwich (1975-6: 177).
[25] Green (2007a: 53).

[26] The text requires that '*Artir*' be emended to '*Artur*', first proposed by Ifor Williams (1932-33: 140), the editor of *Marwnad Cynddylan*. This emendation is supported by Bromwich (1975-6: 177), Gruffydd (1982: 23), Bromwich et al. (1991: 5, 13), Koch and Carey (2003: 379) and Green (2007a: 252). Rowland (1990: 186) however proposes the emending of *artir wras* to *arddyrnfras*, meaning 'strong-handed', but this is a more extensive emendation. It also leaves the whelps without an origin and creates an incongruity as to how people who were defeated in battle could be described as 'a mighty fortress'.

[27] Green (2007a: 49-54) also uses the *Marwnad Cynddylan* reference to Arthur in attempting to show that Arthur was viewed as a mythical superhero. The reference states that the warriors in the poem showed such great valour that they may be regarded as 'descendants of great Arthur, a mighty fortress'. Green however states that the poem refers to 'the praising of Cynddylan and his brothers as being of comparable valour to Arthur's children – note, but not Arthur himself' (p.53). Green's interpretation is not correct. The warriors are being compared to Arthur, not Arthur's children, as is clear from the poem's text. It would make no sense for the poem to compare the warriors to Arthur's children in valour, rather than the more illustrious Arthur.

Green is also incorrect in stating that this reference implies Arthur was seen as 'a mythical 'superhero', not a historical figure' (p.36). This conclusion simply does not follow from the evidence. As can be seen, the imagery 'a mighty fortress' represents conventional praise imagery – there is nothing in it to imply that the warriors were being compared to a mythical superhero.

[28] Rowland (1990: 459, 505).

[29] Sims-Williams (1991a: 47-8).

[30] Green (2007a: 79).

[31] A Gerennius (Geraint), a Cornish king, appears in the *Life of St Teilo*, a sixth-century saint, in *The Book of Llandaff* (Rees, 1840: 345-51). This account contains fantastic features typical of those found in the lives of saints – in this case, a floating stone coffin containing the body of Geraint. A second Geraint (apparently sixth century) appears in *Y Gododdin* in the *A* text, where he raises the battle cry against the south and is described as 'a generous nobleman' (Koch and Carey, 2003: 354). Are we to assume this Geraint died with the other warriors at Catraeth or is this just a stanza honouring a notable (non-participant) warrior which was included in the compilation? From these two cases, we may infer that the name Geraint was not uncommon in the sixth century and if the hero were not one of these two, he may have been another sixth-century person with the same name.

[32] Morris (1973: 104).

[33] Bartrum (1993: 415).

[34] Charles-Edwards (2013: 176).

[35] Sharpe (1995: 111).

[36] Selmer (1959: xviii); Sharpe (1995: 55).

[37] Rowland (1990: 389); Koch (1994: 1127).

[38] Green (2007a) uses a Procrustean vigour to force the mythological model onto the *Geraint son of Erbin* poem. Taking Sims-Williams' (1991a: 48) view as the most probable, it appears that Arthur's brave men were being slain as they

hewed with steel in battle. Arthur himself is described as 'emperor, director of the toil (of battle)'. This reference places Arthur in his usual setting as a battle commander, directing the course of battle while his men were being killed. Green (2007a: 79) sees this as 'another reference to Arthur as the great 'military superhero' of British legend'. However, this viewpoint conflicts with what is actually happening in the poem. If the poet were really depicting Arthur and his men as superheroes, one may enquire why Arthur's 'superhero' men were dying. A more straightforward reading of the stanza would be that Arthur was directing the battle while his men were suffering heavy losses.

[39] Bromwich (1975-6: 172). See also Lloyd (1911); Crawford (1935); Jackson (1945); Jones (1964); Higham (2002); Green (2007a).

[40] See Peter Field (2008). Bromwich (1975-6) presents as evidence a battle at Pencoed fought by Urien, a battle she relates to the battle of Pencon (emended to Pencoed) among the southern Britons in 722 (listed in the *Annales Cambriae*). Another case concerns Arthur's battle at Bregion and Urien's battle at Brewyn, which appear to be the same place at High Rochester. Field (2008) reveals the limitations of this argument. It rests on the untenable assumption that two different battles are unlikely to be fought at the same place. Yet as Field shows, there are many cases of multiple battles that were fought on the same site. In particular, some strategic locations attract multiple battles, as capture of the site confers a clear military advantage. Field argues that High Rochester was one such strategic site. Furthermore, he points out that the *Pencoed* name could exist in many places in Britain (as Bromwich herself suggested) so that the *Annales* entry mentioning *Pencoed* in the south ('southern Britons') may have been trying to distinguish that location from other *Pencoed* locations.

[41] See Koch (2006b: 120-1).

[42] Alcock (1971: 45-9).

[43] Hughes (1980a; 1980b); Dumville (1977; 1984b; 1984c); Charles-Edwards (2013: 346-59).

[44] Carnhuanawc (1842: 260); Stephens (1849: 17).

[45] Kampen (2009: 124); Berger (1981).

[46] Barber (1972: 101-3).

[47] Ashe (1982: 142-3) argues that a passage in *The Ruin of Britain* (28.1) could imply the existence of a British Marian shrine in the sixth century. It refers to Constantine's murder of two young princes at the altar of a church in Dumnonia. The princes were caught off guard as they had placed their trust in (amongst other things) Constantine's oath and the Mother (*genetrix*), the latter having Ashe's capitalisation. Ashe notes that in Christian Latin up to AD 600, *genetrix* was used for the Mother of God (Mary) while *mater* was used for Mother Church. It is not impossible that Ashe is correct, which would give the first example of a British church devoted to Mary. However, as he points out, such a dedication seems to have been unique or rare.

Chapter 12 Who was Arthur?

[1] The location in Britain where Arthur was thought to have been based varies greatly according to different researchers, as shown below:

- Caerleon (on Usk) – Geoffrey of Monmouth (c. 1138)
- Cornwall – Ritson (1825)
- South Scotland/North England – Jones (1964); Bromwich (1975-6)
- Dalriada, Scotland – Chadwick (1953); Barber (1972)
- Carlisle, Cumbria – Goodrich (1986)
- English Lowlands, east of Wales – Morris (1973)
- South Cadbury hillfort, Somerset – Alcock (1971); Ashe (1981)
- Wroxeter, Shropshire – Phillips and Keatman (1992)
- SE Wales – Barber & Pykitt (1997); Gilbert, Wilson & Blackett (1998)
- North Wales – Blake and Lloyd (2004).

Apart from Arthur's home area, researchers have made 'identifications' of his battle sites that have varied enormously across Britain. Jackson (1945) points out several examples of theories based on slender foundations that have biased the identifications of his battle locations. He notes the work of the Scottish historian Skene (1868) who identified Arthur as a warrior of the North and hence 'discovered' that all of his battles were in Scotland, including the implausible location of Bouden Hill as the site for Badon. A second example is Anscombe (1904) who was convinced that all the battles were in the Midlands of England (because Chester appeared to be a certain location) and thus found all of the battles there. A third example is Collingwood (1929) who believed that Arthur was fighting the Jutes of Kent, from the *Historia Brittonum* line that preceded the battle list. He therefore 'discovered' that all of Arthur's battles were in southeastern England.

[2] Some attempts to identify Arthur with known historical figures from the fifth and sixth centuries are given below.

Artur son of Aedán of Dalriada
Of these historical figures, only Artur (son of Aedán) has an equivalent name to Arthur. This prince has been discussed in Chapter 11 where it has been argued that he was one of the four people named after Arthur. He is a minor figure who lived too late to be Arthur and died relatively young at the battle of Miathi, c. 590. Ziegler (1999) convincingly argues that Artur is unlikely to be Arthur. Bromwich (1975-6: 179) also notes that Aedán was remembered in Welsh tradition as the 'treacherous' or 'wily', making it unlikely that his obscure son should have become the epic hero of the Britons.

Owain Ddantgwyn
Owain Ddantgwyn is highly unlikely to be Arthur. He was the son of Einion Yrth, who was the son of Cunedda Wledig, thus coming from the leading family in north Wales. Phillips and Keatman (1992) argue that he was 'the Bear' of Gildas, on the grounds that he was the father of Cuneglasus. However Owain has the double disadvantage of having a different name to Arthur and being a figure about whose deeds we know virtually nothing. He appears to be the uncle who was killed by Maglocunus when the latter was in the 'first years of his youth' (from *The Ruin of Britain*, Section 33).

Riothamus
In identifying Riothamus with Arthur, Ashe (1981; 1995) can account for an Arthurian campaign in Gaul, something that was a prominent part of Geoffrey of Monmouth's pseudo-history. On the positive side, Riothamus was said to have commanded 12,000 men and so was a powerful king. It is uncertain whether he was a Briton or a Breton. Putting aside this uncertainty, his name was not 'Arthur' and he did not enjoy the appropriate success, being defeated probably at Bourges in Gaul and fleeing into anonymity. There is also no connection with the Welsh Arthurian material. However, it is possible that Geoffrey used information from Riothamus' life, along with that from the *Life of St Goeznovius*, to justify giving Arthur his fictitious campaign in Gaul.

Athrwys son of Meurig
The identification of Athrwys (son of Meurig) with Arthur was given in 1591 by Sir Edward Mansel, with Mansel's text being reproduced in Matthews (1903). It also appears in Owen (1803), Parry (1834) and in the *Iolo Manuscripts* of 1848, a collection of manuscripts assembled by Iolo Morganwg (Edward Williams), which was translated and edited by Iolo's son, Taliesin Williams. In one of the genealogies in this book, Athrwys has been falsely replaced by Arthur in the line 'Morgan, the son of Arthur, had the cantrev of Gwent' (Williams and Williams, 1848: 550). This identification has been made in modern times by Barber and Pykitt (1997) and Gilbert, Wilson and Blackett (1998).

The first problem with the identification is that 'Athrwys' is not a form of 'Arthur'. It is a different name that is spelt and pronounced quite differently. In the ancient Welsh poems, *Preideu Annwfyn*, *Kat Godeu* and *Kadeir Teÿrnon* (dated previously to the sixth century), Arthur is always called 'Arthur', but never 'Athrwys'. Further, *Y Gododdin* distinguishes the two names, referring to Arthur as the paragon of military valour in stanza B2.38 (Koch and Carey, 2003: 326). It also refers to an Athrwys (not the son of Meurig) who was killed by Cadwal, in stanza A19 (Koch and Carey, 2003: 341). Both names are sixth-century names and are distinguished in the poem.

Secondly, Athrwys appears to be a sixth-century prince but a little after the time of Arthur. In *The Book of Llandaff* (Rees, 1840: 386), it refers to the time of Athrwys as being after the Yellow Pestilence. The latter disease is said to have killed Maglocunus (p.343). In the *Annales Cambriae* dates, Maglocunus died in about 549, implying that the time of Athrwys was in the 550s, after the death of Arthur in about 539. Inasmuch as these dates can be trusted, it appears that Arthur was dead before Athrwys came to power.

Finally, the Athrwys son of Meurig appears to be just a minor prince. There is no record of him fighting any battles. In *The Book of Llandaff* his greatest claim to fame is by association with Gwrgan, being described as the 'grandson of Gwrgan the Great' (Rees, 1840: 387) suggesting that he was hardly famous in his own right. Wendy Davies (1979: 76) argues that Athrwys died early in Meurig's reign. The 19th-century historian Sharon Turner (1852: 246) was aware of the theory identifying Athrwys with Arthur but rejected it, stating that he 'seems to have been too petty a personage, and too obscure for his greater namesake', a view with which it is difficult to disagree.

[3] Anderson (1928: 404-5); Bachrach (1990: 26); Phillips and Keatman (1992: 127-34, 160-4).
[4] Morris (1973: 116); Winterbottom (1978: 28).
[5] Winterbottom (1978: 26); Dumville(1977: 183-4).
[6] Winterbottom (1978: 29).
[7] Bede's *Ecclesiastical History*, Bk. 3, Ch. 9; McClure and Collins (1994: 124).
[8] Winterbottom (1978: 31).
[9] Koch (1997: 24, 68).
[10] Jones (1964: 3).
[11] Winterbottom (1978: 36).
[12] Lapidge (1984: 50).
[13] Triad 20 in Bromwich (2006: 39-40).
[14] There is another Dinarth in Ceredigion (Dumville, 1984b: 58). However, Ken Dark (1994a: 126) remarks that this small fort above an inland river confluence is 'not a good contender' for Gildas' *receptaculi ursi*.
[15] Jackson (1982: 34); Longley and Laing (1997: 90).
[16] Williams (1899: 77).
[17] Dark (2000: 144).
[18] For example, Thorpe (1974: 128-9, 171-2, 180-1).
[19] Gruffydd (1989-90: 7).
[20] Williams (1899: 55).
[21] Winterbottom (1978: 36).
[22] Barbieri (2002, Book 1.6); Gidlow (2004: 104).
[23] Jackson (1982: 34-5); Dark (2000: 178).
[24] Gruffydd (1989-90: 7).
[25] Williams (1899: 319-20, 322); Winterbottom (1978: 149); Bromwich (2006: 41); Ford (1977: 127); Haycock (2007: 295).
[26] Jackson (1953: 42).
[27] Williams (1899: 403). The *Life* by Caradoc states that Gildas was a son of Nau, a scribal mistake for Cau (Williams, 1899: 388; Bromwich, 2006: 307) and a brother to Huail. Enmity between Arthur and Huail appears in *Culhwch and Olwen* (Ford, 1977: 128) and in *Chwedl Huail ap Caw ac Arthur* (Jones, 1968).
[28] Thorpe (1978: 259).
[29] Giles (1841: 24).
[30] Williams (1899: 67).
[31] Williams (1968: xxviii); Koch and Carey (2003: 365).
[32] Haycock (2007: 309).
[33] Jackson (1945: 50).
[34] Higham (2002); Green (2007a).
[35] Dumville (1984a: 74).
[36] Bromwich (2006: 164).
[37] Jones (1967: 114-5, 130-3).
[38] Bromwich (2006: 432).
[39] Jones (1967: 114).
[40] Bromwich (2006: 1); Sims-Williams (1991a: 41); Ford (1977).
[41] Bromwich (2006: 3); Padel (1994: 12).
[42] Watson (1926: 16).

[43] The naming of the British tribes called Cornovii after a 'horn' of land is also supported by Watts (2004: 158). A different viewpoint is that the Cornovii tribe received their name from their worship of the horned god *Cernunnos* (Ross, 1996: 189). The peninsula bounded by Degannwy (to the west) and Dinarth (to the east) was apparently not occupied by the Cornovii tribe that had Deva in its territory. The Deceangli tribe were in this region. However, if the peninsula were called *kernyw*, this name may have been derived the two 'horns' of the Great and Little Orme, independent of the Deva Cornovii.
[44] Bartrum (1966: 85).
[45] See Ford (1977: 127) for the *Culhwch and Olwen* reference. See Bromwich and Evans (1992: 77) for the comment on Arthur's in-laws.
[46] Ford (1977: 91).
[47] Dark (2000: 175-7).
[48] Snyder (1998: 167).
[49] Dark (1994a; 2000); Longley (1997).
[50] Longley and Laing (1997: 88-91); Denison (1997).
[51] Laing (2006: 34-5).
[52] Although 'the Bear's Stronghold' is the best interpretation of *receptaculi ursi*, others have been made. Anderson (1928) argues that Gildas used 'the Bear' as a metaphor for Arthur but his interpretation of *aurigaque currus receptaculi ursi* was implausible, differing from those of Williams (1899) and Winterbottom (1978). The above refers to a chariot (*currus*) and a stronghold (*receptaculum*). Williams and Winterbottom keep them distinct, both giving similar translations. Anderson merges them into one ('the Waggon') with his 'driver of the Waggon, which holds the Bear' (p.404) and then suggests that Gildas was referring to the star constellation Ursa Major. However it seems weird that Gildas would mention a star constellation, something of beauty, in denouncing the sins of Cuneglasus. This would have mystified readers who were not as learned as Gildas. Three other kings are given names for which star constellations could have been used: Maglocunus ('dragon'); Constantine and Aurelius 'Caninus' ('lion'). The Draco (dragon) and the Leo constellations are mentioned by Ptolemy, along with Ursa Major. Had Gildas referred to Ursa Major it would be odd that he did not continue the 'stars' theme with the other kings by referring to the heavens.

Higham (2002: 78) suggests that Gildas could be translating the name of a defended settlement, Dineirth, into Latin as a bilingual pun. He states that this name 'has nothing to do with the question of an historical Arthur figure, except as possible evidence that an Arth- place-name may have existed when he wrote, which might or might not derive from a personal name'. There is zero evidence for this strong statement that it has 'nothing to do' with an historical Arthur. On the contrary, the Dineirth location in Rhos is consistent with data from a number of sources that locate Arthur in northeast Wales. There is no evidence that Dineirth was a formal name in c. 540. The most likely possibility is that it was an informal descriptor reflecting the settlement's current function, being occupied by a powerful figure whose name was sufficiently close to the word for 'bear' (*Arth*) for Gildas to make a pun. Although there are other names that begin with *Arth*, Arthur's name is more suitable for a pun, differing from the word for 'bear' by adding only two letters.

[53] Alcock (1967).
[54] Dark (1994a: 128).
[55] Gardner and Savory (1964); Savory (1971); Guilbert (1980).
[56] Gardner and Savory (1964: 216); Dark (2000: 170).
[57] Savory (1960).
[58] Dark (1994a: 133).
[59] Blake and Lloyd (2004: 92-3).
[60] Dark (1994a: 134); Rhian Andrews in Andrews and McKenna (1996: 619).
[61] Nieke and Duncan (1988: 11-12).
[62] Longley (1997: 41-2).
[63] Gruffydd (1989-90: 7).
[64] Jackson (1959a: 9).
[65] Winterbottom (1978: 19).
[66] Geoffrey of Monmouth has Uthyr Pendragon as Arthur's father, but this is not his invention as it is implied in *Marwnat Vthyr Pen*. In his pseudo-history, Geoffrey has Merlin change the shape of Uthyr to resemble Gorlois. He may have derived the name Gorlois from *Gorlassar* ('armed in blue') which is applied to Uthyr in Line 3 of the poem. The 'voice' of the poem is Uthyr's, who refers to 'a vigorous swordstroke against the sons of Cawrnur' (Line 12). From *Kadeir Teÿrnon* and Caradoc's *Life of Gildas*, Arthur was also in conflict with Cawrnur and his sons. In Line 14, Uthyr says that he had a ninth share of Arthur's valour. That is, while he was not Arthur's equal in valour, he was comparable to Arthur. In Line 24, he says that there would not be life (for the Britons) if not for his offspring. These three poetic lines (12, 14, 24) form the argument for thinking that Arthur was Uthyr's son.

However the poem is dubious in that it is a deathsong to celebrate the life of Uthyr, but the 'voice' of the poem is that of the dead king himself, not his bard. It also attracts suspicion in Line 38, in its mention of the Virgin Mary, suggesting it is ninth century or later. Further, in Line 27 it mentions Afagddu, from *The Tale of Gwion Bach*, a late tale of magic and shape-shifting, showing how little Gwion was reborn as Taliesin. Uthyr Pendragon appears in *Pa Gûr* which is late (c. 1100, Sims-Williams, 1991a: 39) and contains many fantastic elements. Unfortunately, the above poetic data is too dubious to carry any weight. The idea that Uthyr was Arthur's father is almost certainly pre-Galfridian but it still occurs in late and doubtful sources.

It is sometimes claimed that Uthyr Pendragon is only a title (e.g. Barber and Pykitt, 1997: 54) which would obscure the real name. This device allows some enthusiasts to claim that X was the real Arthur even though X's father was not named Uthyr Pendragon. However the argument that Uthyr Pendragon is a title is unconvincing. The 'Pendragon' part does means 'foremost warrior' or 'chief of warriors' and by itself could be used as a title or epithet. 'Uthr' or 'Uthyr' can also be the adjective 'terrible' (inspiring terror) which could in theory give a title like 'terrible chief of warriors'. However Uthyr is used as a personal name in Welsh poetry. For example, in the poem *The Colloquy of Arthur and the Eagle* Eliwlat is given as the son of Madawc, who was the son of Uthyr. Further, in the *Book of Taliesin* poem *Madawc Drut*, this same Madawc is given as the son of Uthyr. Bromwich (2006: 513) gives other examples of Uthyr being used as a personal name. On balance, Uthyr Pendragon is more likely a name (Uthyr) and an epithet (Pendragon), which was not an uncommon practice.

[67] Bartrum (1966: 39, 93).
[68] Bartrum (1966: 9-10, 94).
[69] Dumville (1977: 182); Gruffydd (1989-90: 13-14).
[70] Thornton (2003: 80-2).
[71] Miller (1975-6: 108).
[72] Bartrum (1965: 242); Padel (1994: 24); Green (2007a: 241).
[73] Baillie (1999).
[74] Rees (1840: 343-6, 371-2).
[75] Arthur may have had four sons. His best-known son, Llacheu, appears in Triad 4 as one of three princes well qualified to rule (Bromwich, 2006: 9-10). In *Pa Gûr*, Llacheu fights alongside Cai (Sims-Williams, 1991a: 43). His death is described in the poem *Mi a wum* ('I have been...') where the ravens 'croaked over blood' (p.44). A second son, Gwydre, appears in *Culhwch and Olwen* where he was killed by foreigners who are represented as boars (Ford, 1977: 154). A third son, Amr, appears only in the *Mirabilia* of the *Historia Brittonum* and may not have been historical. Arthur may have also have had a son, Cydfan, to Eleirch, as discussed earlier. The *Bonedd y Saint* pedigree (No. 85) also gives Arthur a daughter, Archfedd, who was the mother of Efadier and Gwrial, their father being Llawfrodedd (Bartrum, 1966: 66).
[76] One wonders whether parts of the *Mabinogi* and other such tales retain significant bits of information that relate to what happened in Annwfyn. For example, did Pwyll actually live among the Native Americans for an extended period as implied by the first tale in the *Mabinogi*? If he did become accepted by them, he may even have taken a Native American wife.

There is an old folk tale intended to explain the name *Ryd-y-gyfarthfa* ('Ford of the Barking') recorded in Koch and Carey (2003: 369-70) which could suggest interbreeding between the Annwfyn people and the Britons. It tells how Urien of Rheged arrives at a ford where some dogs used to bark and sees a young woman washing herself. At this point, the dogs cease barking and the two have sexual intercourse. The woman tells Urien that she is the daughter of the King of Annwfyn and to return after a year to get their new son. As it turns out, she has twins, a boy Owain (a historical son of Urien) and a girl, Morfydd. This tale gives a curious mixture of historical persons and a daughter of the King of Annwfyn. It makes one wonder as to whether there was interbreeding between the Britons and the Native Americans and whether any of them were taken to Britain. About 1000 years after Arthur's time, Jacques Cartier took the two teenage sons of Chief Donnaconna back to France at the end of his First Voyage. There they lived for a year before being returned to Canada on the Second Voyage. Then Cartier did the unthinkable by kidnapping Donnaconna himself, his two sons and others totalling ten people and took them to France. Donnaconna was there introduced to the King of France (Francis I) and enjoyed life at the court but after four years there he died.

The original stories behind the 'Ford of the Barking' tale are very old. Koch and Carey (2003) argue that the oldest version is from 400 BC with the king-to-be of the Parisi tribe of Gaul meeting the Celtic goddess Matrona at the ford. In

Triad 70 and its variants, the mother of Owain and Morfydd is Modron (from Matrona), daughter of Avallach. In the 'Ford of the Barking' story the daughter of the King of Annwfyn has replaced Modron, daughter of Avallach. See Bromwich (2006: 195-8: 449-51).
[77] Ford (1977: 52, 54); Sims-Williams (1991a: 40); Rhŷs (1891: 283).
[78] Ford (1977: 57).
[79] Watson (1926: 34); Crawford (1935: 285); McCarthy (2004: 125); Haycock (2007: 300-1).
[80] Bromwich (2006: 4); Haycock (2007: 300).
[81] Haycock (2007: 170).
[82] Jackson (1945: 48).
[83] Watson (1926: 156).
[84] McCarthy (2004: 122-5).
[85] Laing and Longley (2006: 157).
[86] Watson (1926: 156); McCarthy (2002); Williams (1968: xxxvi-xlvii); Laing and Longley (2006: 161). Laing and Longley (2006: 164) suggest that Dunragit could derive from the word *gwaragedd* 'women' instead of Rheged, the fort being called 'fort of the women'.
[87] Watson (1926: 157-8).
[88] Toolis and Bowles (2012).
[89] Cessford (1994); Dark (2000: 209).
[90] McCarthy (2004: 128); Alcock (1983: 4); Laing and Longley (2006).
[91] Williams (1971: 121).
[92] See Dark (2000: 209); McCarthy (2002: 369).
[93] McCarthy (2002: 363) calls it the Carrick Forest.
[94] See Koch (1997: 144); Winterbottom (1978: 148); Koch (1988: 27).
[95] Dark (1992: 116, 118); McCarthy (2002: 367).

Chapter 13 Who was Arthur's Bard?
[1] Huws (2000: 79).
[2] Haycock (2007: 117).
[3] Lewis (1968: 298); Koch (2006e: 1653).
[4] Williams (1968: lix-lxii).
[5] Isaac (1998: 67-8) argues that if the poem were originally sixth century, then the prosthetic vowels would not have been present in the Neo-Brittonic text (e.g. the 'y' in *ystrat*). He argues that removing the prosthetic vowels from the text gives an unsatisfactory syllable count, implying that the composition of the poem postdates the introduction of the prosthetic vowel.
[6] Dumville (1988a: 3).
[7] Koch (2006e: 1653).
[8] Williams (1968: xii).
[9] Koch and Carey (2003: 359-61); Williams (1968: l-li).
[10] For the *magi* of Vortigern, see Koch and Carey (2003: 295-6); for *Echtrae Chonnlai*, see McCone (2000: 175-81).
[11] For example, Layton (1989); Lampe (2003: 292-318); Head and Cranston (1961: 35-6); Trumbower (2001: 109-25); Heine (2002: 48-9).
[12] Hefele (1895: 336-7); Hutton (1897: 156-79).

[13] Corning (2006: 4-14, 73-9).
[14] Hefele (1895: 342).
[15] Koch and Carey (2003: 301).
[16] Footnote 8 in Williams (1972: 44).
[17] Gruffydd (1989-90: 10).
[18] Jackson (1963: 29).

Chapter 14 Review of the Claims
[1] For example, Jones (1964: 13); Jarman (1988: lxiv).
[2] Koch (1997: xlviii).
[3] Koch (1994: 1127).
[4] Chadwick and Chadwick (1932: 161).
[5] Jones (1964: 10).
[6] Roberts (1811).
[7] Koch (1985-6: 63).
[8] Jackson (1953: 42).
[9] Koch and Carey (2003: 365).
[10] Gruffydd (1989-90: 10).
[11] Haycock (2007: 446).
[12] Higley (1996: 45).
[13] Jackson (1959b: 16); Bollard (1994: 20).
[14] Rhŷs (1891: 282).
[15] Prufer (1964: 93).
[16] Prufer (1964: 90); Hulbert and Schwarze (1910: 59).
[17] Lepper (2005: 127).
[18] Prufer (1964: 102).
[19] Loomis (1956: 165-7).
[20] One would usually expect that prose works, such as *Historia Brittonum* and the *Navigatio*, would describe icebergs by using the appropriate words for 'ice'. That these prose works use the 'glass tower' imagery suggests that they were being influenced by an important earlier work that used this imagery. It has been argued previously that the *Historia* incident is a garbled derivative of Lines 30-2 from *Preideu Annwfyn*, which would explain why the same imagery is used. The *Navigatio* of St Brendan is prose and gives an extended description of the glass tower which seems to be a clear description of an iceberg. It appears that the *Preideu Annwfyn* lines and their derivative (which was later written into the *Historia*) came first and influenced the author of the *Navigatio* to use the same imagery even though it was evident that the object was an iceberg.
[21] Wood (2001: 59).

REFERENCES

Ahronson, K. (2000). Further Evidence for a Columban Iceland: Preliminary Results of Recent Work. *Norwegian Archaeological Review, 33*, 117-124.

Ahronson, K. (2003). The crosses of Columban Iceland: a survey of preliminary research. In S. Lewis-Simpson (ed.) *Vínland revisited: the Norse world at the turn of the first millennium*. St. John's, N.L.: Historic Sites Association of Newfoundland and Labrador; 75-82.

Alcock, L. (1967). Excavations at Degannwy Castle, Caernarvonshire, 1961-6. *Archaeological Journal, 124*, 190-201.

Alcock, L. (1971). *Arthur's Britain: History and Archaeology AD 367-634*. Harmondsworth: Penguin.

Alcock, L. (1983). Gwŷr y Gogledd: an archaeological appraisal. *Archaeologia Cambrensis, 132*, 1-18.

Alonso-Núñez, J.M. (1986). A note on Roman coins found in Iceland. *Oxford Journal of Archaeology, 5*, 121-122.

Anderson, A.O. (1928). Varia. 1. The dating passage in Gildas's *Excidium*. 2. Gildas and Arthur. *Zeitschrift für Celtische Philologie, 17*, 403-406.

Anderson, A.O. and Anderson, M.O. (1961), eds. and trans. *Adomnan's Life of St Columba*. London: Thomas Nelson and Sons.

Andrews, R.M. and McKenna, C. (1996). Gwaith Bleddyn Fardd. In R.M. Andrews, N.G. Costigan (Bosco), C. James, P.I. Lynch, C. McKenna, M.E. Owen and B.F. Roberts (eds.) *Gwaith Bleddyn Fardd a Beirdd Eraill Ail Hanner y Drydedd Ganrif ar Ddeg*. Vol. 7, Poets of the Princes Series. Cardiff: University of Wales Press; 519-663.

Anscombe, A. (1904). Local names in the 'Arthuriana' in the 'Historia Brittonum'. *Zeitschrift für Celtische Philologie, 5*, 103-123.

Ashe, G. (1962). *Land to the West*. London: Collins.

Ashe, G. (1981). 'A Certain Very Ancient Book': Traces of an Arthurian Source in Geoffrey of Monmouth's History. *Speculum, 56*, 301-323.

Ashe, G. (1982). *Avalonian Quest*. London: Methuen.

Ashe, G. (1995). The Origins of the Arthurian Legend. *Arthuriana, 5*, 1-24.

Ashe, G. (2003). *The Discovery of King Arthur*. Thrupp, Stroud: Sutton.

Babcock, W.H. (1913). *Early Norse Visits to North America. Smithsonian Miscellaneous Collections, 59* (19). Washington: Smithsonian.

Bachrach, B.S. (1990). The Questions of King Arthur's Existence and of Romano-British Naval Operations. In R.B. Patterson (ed.) *The Haskins Society Journal, 2*, 13-28.

Bailey, M.E., Clube, S.V.M. and Napier, W.M. (1990). *The Origin of Comets*. Oxford: Pergamon Press.

Baillie, M.G.L. (1994). Dendrochronology raises questions about the nature of the AD 536 dustveil event. *The Holocene, 4*, 212-217.

Baillie, M.G.L. (1999). *Exodus to Arthur: Catastrophic Encounters with Comets*. London: B.T. Batsford.

Banfield, A.W.F. (1974). *The mammals of Canada*. Toronto, Ontario: University of Toronto Press.

Bannerman, J. (1974). *Studies in the History of Dalriada*. Edinburgh: Scottish Academic Press.
Barber, C. and Pykitt, D. (1997). *Journey to Avalon: the Final Discovery of King Arthur*. York Beach, Maine: Samuel Weiser, Inc.
Barber, R.W. (1972). *The Figure of Arthur*. London: Longman.
Barber, R.W. (1986). *King Arthur: Hero and Legend*. Woodbridge: Boydell.
Barbieri, F.P. (2002). *History of Britain, 407 – 597*. Retrieved 21 June 2015 from: http://www.facesofarthur.org.uk/fabio/book1.6.htm
Barney, S.A., Lewis, W.J., Beach, J.A. and Berghof, O. (2006), eds. and trans. *The Etymologies of Isidore of Seville*. Cambridge: Cambridge UP.
Bartrum, P.C. (1965). Arthuriana from the genealogical manuscripts. *National Library of Wales Journal, 14*, 242-245.
Bartrum, P.C. (1966), ed. *Early Welsh Geneaological Tracts*. Cardiff: University of Wales Press.
Bartrum, P.C. (2009). *A Welsh Classical Dictionary: People in History and Legend up to about A.D. 1000*. Aberystwyth: National Library of Wales.
Benozzo, F. (2004). *Landscape Perception in Early Celtic Literature*. Aberystwyth: Celtic Studies Publications.
Berger, P.C. (1981). *The Insignia of the Notitia Dignitatum*. New York: Garland.
Biddle, M. (2000). *King Arthur's Round Table: an archaeological investigation*. Woodbridge, England: Boydell and Brewer.
Blake, S. and Lloyd, S. (2004). *The Lost Legend of Arthur*. London: Rider.
Blamires, D. (1979). *Herzog Ernst and the Otherworld Voyage*. Manchester: Manchester University Press.
Blitz, J.H. (1988). Adoption of the Bow in Prehistoric North America. *North American Archaeologist, 9*, 123-145.
Blitz, J.H. and Porth, E.S. (2013). Social Complexity and the Bow in the Eastern Woodlands. *Evolutionary Anthropology, 22*, 89-95.
Bollard, J.K. (1994). Arthur in the early Welsh tradition. In J.J. Wilhelm (ed.) *The Romance of Arthur*. New York: Garland Publishing; 11-23.
Bradbury, A.P. (1997). The Bow and Arrow in the Eastern Woodlands: Evidence for an Archaic Origin. *North American Archaeologist, 18*, 207-233.
Breatnach, L. (1977). The Suffixed Pronouns in Early Irish. *Celtica, 12*, 75-107.
Brett, C. (2011). Soldiers, Saints and States? The Breton Migrations Revisited. *Cambrian Medieval Celtic Studies, 61*, 1-56.
Bromwich, R. (1975-6). Concepts of Arthur. *Studia Celtica, 10-11*, 163-181.
Bromwich, R. (1991). First transmission to England and France. In R. Bromwich et al. (eds.) *The Arthur of the Welsh*. Cardiff: University of Wales Press; 273-298.
Bromwich, R. (2006), ed. and trans. *Trioedd Ynys Prydein: The Welsh Triads (3rd edition)*. Cardiff: University of Wales Press.
Bromwich, R. and Evans, D.S. (1992), eds. *Culhwch ac Olwen: An Edition and Study of the Oldest Arthurian Tale*. Cardiff: University of Wales Press.
Bromwich, R., Jarman, A.O.H., Roberts, B.F. and Huws, D. (1991). Introduction. In R. Bromwich et al. (eds.) *The Arthur of the Welsh*. Cardiff: University of Wales Press; 1-14.

Budgey, A. (1992). "Preiddeu Annwn" and the Welsh Tradition of Arthur. In C.J. Byrne, M. Harry and P. Ó Siadhail (eds.) *Celtic Languages and Celtic Peoples*. Halifax, Nova Scotia: Saint Mary's University; 391-404.

Burgess, R.W. (1990). The Dark Ages return to fifth-century Britain: the 'Restored' Gallic Chronicle exploded. *Britannia, 21*, 185-195.

Burkitt, T. and Burkitt, A. (1990). The Frontier Zone and the Siege of Mount Badon: a Review of the Evidence for their Location. *Proceedings of the Somerset Archaeological and Natural History Society, 134*, 81-93.

Campbell, E. (1987). A cross-marked quern from Dunadd and other evidence for relations between Dunadd and Iona. *Proceedings of the Society of Antiquaries of Scotland, 117*, 105-117.

Capelli, C., Redhead, N., Abernethy, J.K., Gratix, F., Wilson, J.F., Moen, T., Hervig, T., Richards, M., Stumpf, M.P.H., Underhill, P.A., Bradshaw, P., Shaha, A., Thomas, M.G., Bradman, N., and Goldstein, D.B. (2003). A Y Chromosome Census of the British Isles. *Current Biology, 13*, 979-984.

Carey, J. (1995). The Rhetoric of Echtrae Chonlai. *Cambrian Medieval Celtic Studies, 30*, 41-65.

Carlson, J.B. (1975). Lodestone Compass: Chinese or Olmec Primary? *Science, 189*, 753-60.

Carney, J. (1963). Review of *Navigatio Sancti Brendani Abbatis* edited with Introduction and Notes by Carl Selmer. *Medium Aevum, 32*, 37-44.

Carney, J. (1976). The Earliest Bran Material. In J.J. O'Meara and B. Naumann (eds.) *Latin Script and Letters AD 400–900: Festschrift presented to Ludwig Bieler on the Occasion of his 70th Birthday*. Leiden: Brill; 174-193.

Carney, J. (1983). The Dating of early Irish Verse Texts, 500–1100. *Éigse, 19*, 177-216.

Carnhuanawc [Thomas Price] (1842). *Hanes Cymru*. Crickhowell: T. Williams.

Carr, C. and Case, D.T. (2006a), eds. *Gathering Hopewell: Society, Ritual, and Ritual Interaction*. New York: Springer.

Carr, C. and Case, D.T. (2006b). The Gathering of Hopewell. In C. Carr and D.T. Case (eds.) *Gathering Hopewell: Society, Ritual, and Ritual Interaction*. New York: Springer; 19-50.

Carr, C., Goldstein, B.J. and Weets, J. (2006). Estimating the Sizes and Social Compositions of Mortuary-Related Gatherings at Scioto Hopewell Earthwork-Mound Sites. In C. Carr and D.T. Case (eds.) *Gathering Hopewell: Society, Ritual, and Ritual Interaction*. New York: Springer; 480-532.

Cessford, C. (1994). Pictish Raiders at Trusty's Hill? *Transactions of the Dumfriesshire and Galloway Natural History and Antiquarian Society, 69*, 81-88.

Cessford, C. (1997). Northern England and the Gododdin poem. *Northern History, 33*, 218-222.

Chacon, R.J. and Dye, D.H. (2007), eds. *The Taking and Displaying of Human Body Parts as Trophies by Amerindians*. New York: Springer.

Chadwick, H.M. (1949). *Early Scotland: the Picts, the Scots and the Welsh of southern Scotland*. Cambridge: Cambridge University Press.

Chadwick, H.M. and Chadwick, N.K. (1932). *The Growth of Literature, 1*. Cambridge: Cambridge University Press.

Chadwick, N.K. (1953). The Lost Literature of Celtic Scotland: Caw of Pritdin and Arthur of Britain. *Scottish Gaelic Studies*, 7, 115-183.

Chambers, E.K. (1927). *Arthur of Britain*. London: Sidgwick & Jackson.

Chapman, P.H. (1973). *The Man Who Led Columbus to America*. Atlanta, Georgia: Judson Press.

Charles-Edwards, T.M. (1970). The Date of the Four Branches of the Mabinogi. *Transactions of the Honourable Society of Cymmrodorion*, 263-298.

Charles-Edwards, T.M. (1978). The Authenticity of the Gododdin: an Historian's View. In R. Bromwich and R.B. Jones (eds.) *Astudiaethau ar yr Hengerdd: Studies in Old Welsh Poetry*. Caerdydd: Gwasg Prifysgol Cymru; 44-71.

Charles-Edwards, T.M. (1991). The Arthur of History. In R. Bromwich et al. (eds.) *The Arthur of the Welsh*. Cardiff: University of Wales Press; 15-32.

Charles-Edwards, T.M. (2013). *Wales and the Britons 350-1064*. Oxford: OUP.

Christenson, A.L. (1986). Projectile Point Size and Projectile Aerodynamics: An Explanatory Study. *Plains Anthropologist, 31*, 109-128.

Clube, S.V.M. and Napier, W.M. (1990). *The Cosmic Winter*. Oxford: Blackwell.

Coates, R. (2007). Invisible Britons: the view from linguistics. In N.J. Higham (ed.) *Britons in Anglo-Saxon England*. Woodbridge: Boydell; 172-191.

Coe, J.B. and Young, S. (1995), eds. and trans. *The Celtic Sources for the Arthurian Legend*. Felinfach: Llanerch Publishers.

Collingwood, R.G. and Wright, R.P. (1995), eds. *Roman Inscriptions of Britain, I:Inscriptions on Stone. Addenda and Corrigenda*, R.S.O. Tomlin. Stroud: Sutton.

Collingwood, W.G. (1929). Arthur's battles. *Antiquity, III*, 292-298.

Corning, C. (2006). *The Celtic and Roman Traditions: Conflict and Consensus in the Early Medieval Church*. New York: Palgrave Macmillan.

Cowan, F.L. (2006). A Mobile Hopewell? Questioning Assumptions of Ohio Hopewell Sedentism. In D.K. Charles and J.E. Buikstra (eds.) *Recreating Hopewell*. Gainesville: University Press of Florida; 26-49.

Crawford, O.G.S. (1935). Arthur and his battles. *Antiquity, IX*, 277-279.

Cross, T.P. and Slover, C.H. (1936), eds. *Ancient Irish Tales*. New York: Holt.

Cunliffe, B. (2001). *The Extraordinary Voyage of Pytheas the Greek*. London: Penguin.

Cunliffe, B. and Koch, J.T. (2010), eds. *Celtic from the West: alternative perspectives from Archaeology, Genetics, Language and Literature*. Oxford: Oxbow Books.

Dancey, W.S. (2005). The Hopewell of the Eastern Woodlands. In T.R. Pauketat and D. DiPaolo Loren (eds.) *North American Archaeology*. Oxford: Blackwell; 108-137.

Dark, K.R. (1992). A Sub-Roman Re-defence of Hadrian's Wall. *Britannia, 23*, 111-120.

Dark, K.R. (1994a). *Discovery by Design: the identification of secular elite settlements in western Britain A.D. 400-700*. BAR 237. Oxford: Hadrian.

Dark, K.R. (1994b). *Civitas to Kingdom: British Political Continuity 300–800*. London: Leicester University Press.

Dark, K.R. (2000). *Britain and the End of the Roman Empire*. Brimscombe Port, Stroud, Gloucestershire: Tempus.

Davies, W. (1979). *The Llandaff Charters*. Aberystwyth: National Library of Wales.

Davies, W. (1982). *Wales in the Early Middle Ages*. Leicester: Leicester UP.

DeBoer, W.R. (1997). Ceremonial Centers from the Cayapas (Esmeraldas, Ecuador) to Chillicothe (Ohio). *Cambridge Archaeological Journal, 7*, 225-253.

Denison, C. (1997). *British Archaeology: News*, No 29. Retrieved 21 June 2015: http://www.archaeologyuk.org/ba/ba29/ba29news.html

Diemand, D. (2001). Icebergs. In J. Steele, S. Thorpe and K. Turekian (eds.) *Encyclopedia of Ocean Sciences*. London: Academic Press; 1255-1264.

Dragoo, D.W. and Wray, C.F. (1964). Hopewell figurine rediscovered. *American Antiquity, 30*, 195-199.

Dull, R.A., Southon, J.R. and Sheets, P. (2001). Volcanism, Ecology and Culture: A Reassessment of the Volcán Ilopango Tbj eruption in the Southern Maya Realm. *Latin American Antiquity, 12*, 25-44.

Dumville, D.N. (1972-74a). The Corpus Christi 'Nennius'. *Bulletin of the Board of Celtic Studies, 25*, 369-380.

Dumville, D.N. (1972-74b). Some aspects of the chronology of the Historia Brittonum. *Bulletin of the Board of Celtic Studies 25*, 439-445.

Dumville, D.N. (1975-6). 'Nennius' and the Historia Brittonum. *Studia Celtica 10/11*, 178-195.

Dumville, D.N. (1976-7). On the North British section of the Historia Brittonum. *The Welsh History Review, 8*, 345-354.

Dumville, D.N. (1977). Sub-Roman Britain: history and legend. *History, 62*, 173-192.

Dumville, D.N. (1977-8). The Welsh Latin Annals. *Studia Celtica, 12/13*, 461-467.

Dumville, D.N. (1984a). The chronology of De Excidio Britanniae, Book 1. In M. Lapidge and D.N. Dumville (eds.) *Gildas: New Approaches*. Woodbridge, Suffolk: Boydell Press; 61-84.

Dumville, D.N. (1984b). Gildas and Maelgwn: Problems of Dating. In M. Lapidge and D.N. Dumville (eds.) *Gildas: New Approaches*. Woodbridge, Suffolk: Boydell Press; 51-59.

Dumville, D.N. (1984c). When was the 'Clonmacnoise Chronicle' created? The evidence of the Welsh annals. In K. Grabowski and D.N. Dumville (eds.) *Chronicles and Annals of Mediaeval Ireland and Wales: the Clonmacnoise-group texts*. Woodbridge: Boydell; 209-226.

Dumville, D.N. (1986). The historical value of the Historia Brittonum. *Arthurian Literature, 6*, 1-26.

Dumville, D.N. (1988a). Early Welsh poetry: problems of historicity. In B.F. Roberts (ed.) *Early Welsh Poetry: Studies in the Book of Aneirin*. Aberystwyth: National Library of Wales; 1-16.

Dumville, D.N. (1988b). Two approaches to the dating of the 'Nauigatio Sancti Brendani'. *Studi Medievali, 29*, 87-102.

Ebbesmeyer, C.C., Okubo, A. and Helseth, J.M. (1980). Description of iceberg probability between Baffin Bay and the Grand Banks using a stochastic model. *Deep-Sea Research, 27A*, 975-986.

Eldjárn, K. and Friðriksson, A. (2000). *Kuml og haugfé úr heiðnum sið á Íslandi (2nd ed., revised by Friðriksson)*. Reykjavík: Mál og menning.

Enterline, J.R. (2002). *Erikson, Eskimos and Columbus*. Baltimore: The John Hopkins University Press.

Evans, J.G. (1908), ed. *Facsimile and Text of the Book of Aneirin*. Pwllheli: J.G. Evans.

Evelyn-White, H.G. (1914), trans. *Hesiod: the Homeric Hymns and Homerica*. Cambridge, Massachusetts: Harvard University Press. Reprinted 1982.

Feininger, T. and Goodacre, A.K. (1995). The eight classical Monteregian hills at depth and the mechanism of their intrusion. *Canadian Journal of Earth Sciences, 32*, 1350-1364.

Field, P.J.C. (1996). Nennius and his History. *Studia Celtica, 30*, 159-165.

Field, P.J.C. (2008). Arthur's battles. *Arthuriana, 18*, 3-32.

Foley, W.T. and Holder, A.G. (1999), eds. & trans. *Bede: a Biblical Miscellany*. Liverpool: Liverpool University Press.

Fontenrose, J. (1959). *Python: a study of Delphic Myth and its Origins*. Berkeley: University of California Press.

Ford, P.K. (1977), ed. and trans. *The Mabinogi and other Medieval Welsh Tales*. Los Angeles: University of California Press.

Ford, P.K. (1999), trans. *The Celtic Poets: Songs and Tales from Early Ireland and Wales*. Belmont, Massachusetts: Ford and Bailie.

Frappier, J. (1959). Chrétien de Troyes. In R.S. Loomis (ed.) *Arthurian Literature in the Middle Ages*. Oxford: Clarendon Press; 157-191.

Gardner, W. and Savory, H.N. (1964). *Dinorben: a hill-fort occupied in early Iron Age and Roman times*. Cardiff: National Museum of Wales.

Geist, V. (1991). Phantom subspecies: The wood bison *Bison bison athabascae* Rhoads 1897 is not a valid taxon, but an ecotype. *Arctic, 44*, 283-300.

Gidlow, C. (2004). *The Reign of Arthur: from History to Legend*. Thrupp, Stroud, Gloucestershire: Sutton Publishing.

Gilbert, A., Wilson, A. and Blackett, B. (1998). *The Holy Kingdom*. London: Bantam Press.

Giles, J.A. (1841), trans. The Works of Gildas, surnamed the Wise. In J.A.Giles, *The Works of Gildas and Nennius*. London: James Bohn; 1-103.

Goodrich, N.L. (1986). *King Arthur*. New York: Franklin Watts.

Graves, R. (1961). *The White Goddess: A Historical Grammar of Poetic Myth*. London: Faber & Faber.

Greber, N. (1983). Recent Excavations at the Edwin Harness Mound, Liberty Works, Ross County, Ohio. *Mid-Continental Journal of Archaeology*, Special Publication 5. Kent OH: Kent State University Press.

Greber, N. (2005). The Edwin Harness Big House. In B.T. Lepper (ed.) *Ohio Archaeology*. Wilmington OH: Orange Frazer Press; 132-134.

Greber, N. and Ruhl, K. (1989). *The Hopewell Site: A Contemporary Analysis based on the Works of Charles C. Willoughby*. Boulder: Westview Press.

Green, T. (2007a). *Concepts of Arthur*. Chalford, Stroud: Tempus Publishing.

Green, T. (2007b). A note on Aladur, Alator and Arthur. *Studia Celtica, 41*, 237-241.

Green, T. (2008). The British Kingdom of Lindsey. *Cambrian Medieval Celtic Studies, 56*, 1-43.

Green, T. (2009). An Alternative Interpretation of Preideu Annwfyn, Lines 23-8. *Studia Celtica, 43*, 207-213.

Gruffydd, R.G. (1982). Marwnad Cynddylan. In R.G. Gruffydd (ed.) *Bardos.* Cardiff: University of Wales Press; 10-28.

Gruffydd, R.G. (1989-90). From Gododdin to Gwynedd: reflections on the story of Cunedda. *Studia Celtica, XXIV/XXV*, 1-14.

Gudger, E.W. (1927). Fishing with the Otter. *The American Naturalist, 61*, 193-225.

Guilbert, G.C. (1980). Dinorben C14 dates. *Current Archaeology, 70*, 336-38.

Gunn, J.D. (2000), ed. *The Years without Summer: tracing A.D. 536 and its aftermath.* Oxford: Archaeopress.

Hammond, C. (1996), trans. *Caesar: The Gallic War.* Oxford: Oxford University Press.

Hanning, R.W. (1966). *The Vision of History in Early Britain.* New York: Columbia University Press.

Harvey, J.H. (1969), ed. and trans. *Itineraries: William Worcestre.* Oxford: Clarendon Press.

Hawkes, S.C. (1989). The south-east after the Romans: the Saxon settlement. In V. Maxfield (ed.) *The Saxon Shore.* Exeter: University of Exeter; 78-95.

Haycock, M. (1983-4). 'Preiddeu Annwn' and the Figure of Taliesin. *Studia Celtica, 18-19*, 52-78.

Haycock, M. (1990). The Significance of the 'Cad Goddau' Tree-List in the Book of Taliesin. In M.J. Ball, J. Fife, E. Poppe and J. Rowland (eds.) *Celtic Linguistics: Readings in the Brythonic Languages for T. Arwyn Watkins.* Amsterdam: Benjamins; 297-331.

Haycock, M. (2007), ed. and trans. *Legendary Poems from the Book of Taliesin.* Aberystwyth: CMCS Publications.

Haycock, M. (2013), ed. and trans. *Prophecies from the Book of Taliesin.* Aberystwyth: CMCS Publications.

Head, J. and Cranston, S.L. (1961), eds. *Reincarnation: an East-West Anthology.* New York: The Julian Press.

Hefele, C.J. (1895). *A History of the Councils of the Church, Vol. IV.* Edinburgh: T. & T. Clark. Reprinted in 1972 by AMS Press, New York.

Heine, R.E. (2002). *The Commentaries of Origen and Jerome on St Paul's Epistle to the Ephesians.* Oxford: Oxford University Press.

Hieatt, A.K. (1992). King Arthur in William Lambarde's *Archaionomia* (1568). *ANQ: A quarterly journal of short articles, notes and reviews, 5*, 78-82.

Higham, N.J. (1992). *Rome, Britain and the Anglo-Saxons.* London: Seaby.

Higham, N.J. (1993). Gildas and 'Agitius': a comment on De Excidio XX, 1. *Bulletin of the Board of Celtic Studies, 40*, 123-134.

Higham, N.J. (2002). *King Arthur: Myth-making and History.* London and New York: Routledge.

Higley, S.L. (1996). The Spoils of Annwn: Taliesin and Material Poetry. In K.A. Klar, E.E. Sweetser and C. Thomas (eds.) *A Celtic Florilegium. Studies in Memory of Brendan O Hehir*. Lawrence, Massachusetts: Celtic Studies Publications; 43-53.

Hills, C. (2003). *Origins of the English*. London: Duckworth.

Hines, J. (1990). Philology, Archaeology and the Adventus Saxonum vel Anglorum. In A. Bammesburger and A. Wollman (eds.) *Britain 400-600: Language and History*. Heidelberg: Carl Winter; 17-36.

Hively, R.M. and Horn, R.L (2005). Ohio Archaeoastronomy. In B.T.Lepper (ed.) *Ohio Archaeology*. Wilmington OH: Orange Frazer Press; 160-161.

Hodges, R. (1989). *The Anglo-Saxon Achievement: Archaeology and the Beginnings of English Society*. Ithaca, NY: Cornell University Press.

Hughes, K. (1980a). The Welsh Latin chronicles: *Annales Cambriae* and related texts. In K. Hughes, *Celtic Britain in the Early Middle Ages* (ed. D.N. Dumville). Woodbridge: Boydell; 67-85. Originally published in *Proceedings of the British Academy*, 1973, 59, 233-258.

Hughes, K. (1980b). The A-text of *Annales Cambriae*. In K. Hughes, *Celtic Britain in the Early Middle Ages* (ed. D.N. Dumville). Woodbridge: Boydell; 86-100.

Hughes, S.S. (1998). Getting to the Point: Evolutionary Change in Prehistoric Weaponry. *Journal of Archaeological Method and Theory*, 5, 345-408.

Hulbert, A.B. and Schwarze, W.N. (1910), eds. and trans. *David Zeisberger's History of the northern American Indians*. Columbus, OH: F.J. Heer.

Hunter Blair, P. (1963). *Roman Britain and Early England 55BC – AD871*. London: W.W. Norton.

Hutton, R. (2003). *Witches, Druids and King Arthur*. London: Hambledon Continuum.

Hutton, W.H. (1897). *The Church of the Sixth Century: Six Chapters in Ecclesiastical History*. London: Longmans, Green and Co.

Huws, D. (2000). *Medieval Welsh Manuscripts*. Cardiff: University of Wales Press and The National Library of Wales.

Ingstad, A.S. and Ingstad, H. (1986). *The Norse Discovery of America*, 2 Vols. V.1: *Excavations at L'Anse aux Meadows, Newfoundland* 1961-1968). V.2: *The Historical Background and the Evidence of the Norse Settlement Discovered in Newfoundland*. Oslo: Norwegian University Press.

Isaac, G. (1998). Gweith Gwen Ystrat and the northern Heroic Age of the sixth century. *Cambrian Medieval Celtic Studies*, 36, 61-70.

Jackson, H.H.T. (1961). *Mammals of Wisconsin*. Madison, Wisconsin: The University of Wisconsin Press.

Jackson, K.H. (1945). Once again Arthur's battles. *Modern Philology*, 43, 44-57.

Jackson, K.H. (1949). Arthur's battle of Breguoin. *Antiquity*, 23, 48-49.

Jackson, K.H. (1953). *Language and History in Early Britain*. Edinburgh: Edinburgh University Press.

Jackson, K.H. (1953-58). The Site of Mount Badon, *Journal of Celtic Studies*, 2, 152-155.

Jackson, K.H. (1959a). The Arthur of History. In R.S. Loomis (ed.) *Arthurian Literature in the Middle Ages*. Oxford: Clarendon Press; 1-11.

Jackson, K.H. (1959b). Arthur in Early Welsh Verse. In R.S. Loomis (ed.) *Arthurian Literature in the Middle Ages*. Oxford: Clarendon Press; 12-19.

Jackson, K.H. (1963). On the northern British section in Nennius. In N.K. Chadwick (ed.) *Celt and Saxon: Studies in the Early British Border*. Cambridge: Cambridge University Press; 20-62.

Jackson, K.H. (1964). *The Oldest Irish Tradition: a Window on the Iron Age*. Cambridge: Cambridge University Press.

Jackson, K.H. (1973). The British languages and their evolution. In D. Daiches and A. Thorlby (eds.) *The Medieval World*. London: Aldus Books; 113-126.

Jackson, K.H. (1982). Varia: II. Gildas and the Names of the British Princes. *Cambridge Medieval Celtic Studies, 3*, 30-40.

Jarman, A.O.H. (1988), ed. and trans. *Aneirin: Y Gododdin, Britain's Oldest Heroic Poem*. Llandysul: Gomer Press.

Jarman, A.O.H. (1989-90). The Arthurian allusions in the Book of Aneirin. *Studia Celtica, 24-25*, 15-25.

Jarman, A.O.H. (1991). The Merlin legend and the Welsh tradition of prophecy. In R. Bromwich et al. (eds.) *The Arthur of the Welsh*. Cardiff: University of Wales Press; 117-145.

Jones, G. (1986), ed. and trans. *The Norse Atlantic Saga*. Oxford: Oxford University Press.

Jones, M.E. (1996). *The End of Roman Britain*. Ithaca, NY: Cornell University Press.

Jones, M.E. and Casey, J. (1988). The Gallic Chronicle restored: a chronology for the Anglo-Saxon invasions and the end of Roman Britain. *Britannia, 19*, 367-398.

Jones, T. (1964). The early evolution of the legend of Arthur. *Nottingham Medieval Studies, 8*, 3-21.

Jones, T. (1967). The Black Book of Carmarthen 'Stanzas of the Graves'. *Proceedings of the British Academy, 53*, 97-137.

Jones, T. (1968). Chwedl Huail ap Caw ac Arthur. In T. Jones (ed.), *Astudiaethau Amrywiol a gyflwynir i Syr Thomas Parry-William*. Cardiff: University of Wales Press; 48-66.

Kampen, N.B. (2009). *Family Fictions in Roman Art*. Cambridge: Cambridge University Press.

Kendrick, T.D. (1950). *British Antiquity*. London: Methuen and Co.

Keys, D.P. (2000). *Catastrophe: an Investigation into the Origins of the Modern World*. New York: Ballantine.

Koch, J.T. (1984). 'gwydanhor, gwydyanhawr, clywanhor'. *Bulletin of the Board of Celtic Studies, 31*, 87-92.

Koch, J.T. (1985-86). When was Welsh Literature first written down? *Studia Celtica, XX/XXI*, 43-46.

Koch, J.T. (1988). The Cynfeirdd Poetry and the Language of the Sixth Century. In B.F. Roberts (ed.) *Early Welsh Poetry: Studies in the Book of Aneirin*. Aberystwyth: National Library of Wales; 17-41.

Koch, J.T. (1990). Brân, Brennos: an Instance of Early Gallo-Brittonic History and Mythology. *Cambridge Medieval Celtic Studies, 20*, 1-20.

Koch, J.T. (1991). Gleanings from the Gododdin and other Early Welsh texts. *Bulletin of the Board of Celtic Studies, 38*, 111-118.
Koch, J.T. (1994). Review of R. Bromwich et al. (eds.) The Arthur of the Welsh. *Speculum, 69*, 1127-1129.
Koch, J.T. (1996). The Celtic Lands. In N.J. Lacy (ed.) *Medieval Arthurian Literature: a Guide to Recent Research.* New York: Garland; 239-322.
Koch, J.T. (1997), ed. and trans. *The Gododdin of Aneirin: Text and Context from Dark-Age Northern Britain.* Cardiff: University of Wales Press.
Koch, J.T. (2006a). Annwfyn. In J.T. Koch (ed.) *Celtic Culture: A Historical Encyclopedia.* Santa Barbara & Oxford: ABC-CLIO; 75.
Koch, J.T. (2006b). Arthur, the historical evidence. In J.T. Koch (ed.) *Celtic Culture: A Historical Encyclopedia.* Santa Barbara & Oxford: ABC-CLIO; 117-122.
Koch, J.T. (2006c). Brân fab Llŷr/Bendigeidfran. In J.T. Koch (ed.) *Celtic Culture: A Historical Encyclopedia.* Santa Barbara & Oxford: ABC-CLIO; 236-238.
Koch, J.T. (2006d). Preiddiau Annwfn. In J.T. Koch (ed.) *Celtic Culture: A Historical Encyclopedia.* Santa Barbara & Oxford: ABC-CLIO; 1456.
Koch, J.T. (2006e). Taliesin (1) the Historical Taliesin. In J.T. Koch (ed.) *Celtic Culture: A Historical Encyclopedia.* Santa Barbara & Oxford: ABC-CLIO; 1652-1653.
Koch, J.T. and Carey, J. (2003), eds. and trans. *The Celtic Heroic Age: Literary Sources for Ancient Celtic Europe and Early Ireland and Wales* (4th edition). Aberystwyth: Celtic Studies Publications.
Krenn, E. (1950). Wer hat Amerika zuerst entdeckt? *Petermanns geographische Mitteilungen, 94*, 207-211.
Kübler, B. (1891). Commonitorium Palladii. *Romanische Forschungen, 6,* 203-237.
Kunz, K. and Sígurðsson, G. (2008), trans. and ed. *The Vinland Sagas: The Icelandic Sagas about the First Documented Voyages across the North Atlantic.* London: Penguin.
Lacy, N.J. (1991), ed. *The New Arthurian Encyclopedia.* New York: Garland.
Laing, L. (2006). *The Archaeology of Celtic Britain and Ireland c. AD 400–1200.* Cambridge: Cambridge University Press.
Laing, L. and Longley, D. (2006). *The Mote of Mark: a Dark Age Hillfort in South-West Scotland.* Oxford: Oxbow.
Lamberton, R. (1988). *Hesiod.* New Haven: Yale University Press.
Lampe, P. (2003). *From Paul to Valentinus: Christians at Rome in the First Two Centuries.* Minneapolis: Fortress Press.
Lang, A. (1898), ed. *The Arabian Nights Entertainments.* London: Dover.
Lapidge, M. (1984). Gildas's education and the Latin culture of sub-Roman Britain. In M. Lapidge and D.N. Dumville (eds.) *Gildas: New Approaches.* Woodbridge, Suffolk: Boydell Press; 27-50.
Larivière, S. and Walton, L.R. (1998). Lontra Canadensis. *Mammalian Species, No. 587*, 1-8.

Larsen, L.B., Vinther, B.M., Briffa, K.R., Melvin, T.M., Clausen, H.B., Jones, P.D., Siggaard-Andersen, M.-L., Hammer, C.U., Eronen, M., Grudd, H., Gunnarson, B.E., Hantemirov, R.M., Naurzbaev, M.M. and Nicolussi, K. (2008). New ice core evidence for a volcanic cause of the A.D. 536 dust veil. *Geophysical Research Letters, 35*, 1-5.

Layton, B. (1989). The Significance of Basilides in Ancient Christian Thought. *Representations, 28*, 135-151.

Lea, A.E. (1994). Beyond Boasting: Táin Bó Cúailnge and Le Voyage de Charlemagne. In J.P. Mallory and G. Stockman (eds.) *Ulidia: Proceedings of the First International Conference on the Ulster Cycle of Tales*. Belfast: December Publications; 107-113.

Lecouteux, C. (1984). Die Sage vom Magnetberg. *Fabula, 25*, 35-65.

Leeds, E.T. (1933). The Early Saxon Penetration of the Upper Thames Area. *Antiquaries Journal, 13*, 229-251.

Le Gentil, P. (1959). The Work of Robert de Boron and the *Didot Perceval*. In R.S. Loomis (ed.) *Arthurian Literature in the Middle Ages*. Oxford: Clarendon Press; 251-262.

Lehn, W.H. (2000). Skerrylike Mirages and the Discovery of Greenland. *Applied Optics, 39*, 3612-3619.

Lehn, W.H. and Schroeder, I.J. (1979). Polar Mirages as Aids to Norse Navigation. *Polarforschung, 49*, 173-187.

Lepper, B.T. (1995). Tracking Ohio's Great Hopewell Road. *Archaeology, 48*, 52-56.

Lepper, B.T. (2005), ed. *Ohio Archaeology*. Wilmington: Orange Frazer Press.

Lepper, B.T. (2011). *People of the Mounds: Ohio's Hopewell Culture*. (Ohio Historical Society). Eastern National.

Lewis, C.W. (1976). The historical background of Early Welsh verse. In A.O.H. Jarman and G.R. Hughes (eds.) *A Guide to Welsh Literature, Volume 1*. Swansea: Christopher Davies; 11-50.

Lewis, J.S. (1996). *Rain of Iron and Ice: the very real Threat of Comet and Asteroid Bombardment*. New York: Helix Books.

Lewis, S. (1968). The Tradition of Taliesin. *Transactions of the Honourable Society of Cymmrodorion*, 293-298.

Liebermann, F. (1894). *Über die Leges Anglorum saeculo xiii. ineunte Londoniis collectae*. Halle: Max Niemeyer.

Little, G.A. (1945). *Brendan the Navigator: An Interpretation*. Dublin: Gill.

Lloyd, J.E. (1911). *History of Wales from the Earliest Times to the Edwardian Conquest*, Vol. 1. London: Longmans, Green and Co.

Lloyd-Jones, J. (1950-2). Nefenhyr. *Bulletin of the Board of Celtic Studies, 14*, 35-37.

Longley, D. (1997). The Royal Courts of the Welsh Princes of Gwynedd, AD 400–283. In N. Edwards (ed.) *Landscape and Settlement in Medieval Wales*. Oxford: Oxbow; 41-54.

Longley, D. and Laing, L. (1997). Bryn Euryn Hillfort, Llandrillo-yn-Rhos. *Archaeology in Wales, 37*, 88-91.

Loomis, R.S. (1927). *Celtic Myth and Arthurian Romance*. New York: Columbia University Press.

Loomis, R.S. (1956). *Wales and the Arthurian Legend*. Cardiff: University of Wales Press.

Loomis, R.S. (1959), ed. *Arthurian Literature in the Middle Ages*. Oxford: Clarendon Press.

Lott, D.F. (2002). *American Bison: A Natural History*. Berkeley: University of California Press.

Mac Mathúna, S. (1985). *Immram Brain: Bran's Journey to the Land of the Women*. Tubingen: Max Niemeyer Verlag.

Mac Mathúna, S. (2006). Immram Brain maic Febail. In J.T. Koch (ed.) *Celtic Culture: A Historical Encyclopedia*. Oxford: ABC-CLIO; 959.

MacMillan, K and Abeles, J. (2004), eds. *John Dee: The Limits of the British Empire*. Westport, Connecticut: Praeger.

Magnússon, Þ. (1973). Sögualdarbyggð í Hvítárholti. *Árbók hins Íslenzka Fornleifafélags* (1972), 5-80.

Mainfort, R.C. (1988). Middle Woodland Ceremonialism at Pinson Mounds, Tennessee. *American Antiquity, 53*, 158-173.

Marko, J.R. (1996). Small Icebergs and Iceberg Fragments off Newfoundland: Relationships to Deterioration Mechanisms and the Regional Iceberg Population. *Atmosphere-Ocean, 34*, 549-579.

Marko, J.R., Fissel, D.B., Wadhams, P., Kelly, P.M. and Brown, R.D. (1994). Iceberg Severity off Eastern North America: Its Relationship to Sea Ice Variability and Climate Change. *Journal of Climate, 7*, 1335-1351.

Masefield, J. (1939). *Voyages. Vol. 1* (by Richard Hakluyt). London: Dent (Everyman's Library).

Matthews, J.H. (1903), ed. The winning of Glamorgan: Documents. *Cardiff Records, Vol. 4*; 6-47. Retrieved 21 June 2015 from: http://www.british-history.ac.uk/cardiff-records/vol4/pp6-47

McCarthy, D.F. (1848). The voyage of St. Brendan. *Dublin University Magazine, 16*, 60-74.

McCarthy, M. (2002). Rheged: an Early Historic Kingdom near the Solway. *Proceedings of the Society of the Antiquaries of Scotland, 132*, 357-381.

McCarthy, M. (2004). Rerigonium: a lost 'city' of the Novantae? *Proceedings of the Society of the Antiquaries of Scotland, 134*, 119-129.

McClure, J. and Collins, R. (1994), eds. *Bede: The Ecclesiastical History of the English People*. Oxford: Oxford University Press.

McCone, K. (2000), ed. *Echtrai Chonnlai*. Maynooth: An Saggart.

McGrail, S. (2006). *Ancient Boats and Ships*. Princes Risborough: Shire Publications.

McHugh, T. (1972). *The Time of the Buffalo*. New York: Alfred A. Knopf.

Mensforth, R.P. (2001). Warfare and Trophy Taking in the Archaic. In O. Prufer, S.E. Peede and R.S. Meindl (eds.) *Archaic Transitions in Ohio and Kentucky Prehistory*. Kent, OH: Kent State University Press; 110-138.

Mensforth, R.P. (2007). Human Trophy Taking in Eastern North America During the Archaic Period: Its Relationship to Warfare and Social Complexity. In R.J. Chacon and D.H. Dye (eds.) *The Taking and Displaying of Human Body Parts as Trophies by Amerindians*. NY: Springer; 218-273.

Meyer, K (1895), ed. and trans. *The Voyage of Bran son of Febal*. London: Nutt.

Meyer, K. (1905), ed. and trans. *Cáin Adamnáin: an Old-Irish Treatise on the Law of Adamnan*. Oxford: Clarendon Press.

Meyvaert, P. (1999). "In the Footsteps of the Fathers": The Date of Bede's Thirty Questions on the Book of Kings to Nothelm. In W.E. Klingshirn and M. Vessey (eds.) *The Limits of Ancient Christianity: Essays on Late Antique Thought and Culture in Honor of R.A. Markus*. Ann Arbor: University of Michigan Press; 267-86.

Micha, A. (1959). The Vulgate *Merlin*. In R.S. Loomis (ed.) *Arthurian Literature in the Middle Ages*. Oxford: Clarendon Press; 319-324.

Miller, M. (1975-6). Date Guessing and Pedigrees. *Studia Celtica 10-11*, 96-109.

Miller, M. (1978). The last British entry in the 'Gallic Chronicles'. *Britannia, 9*, 315-318.

Milner, G.R. (1999). Warfare in Prehistoric and Early Historic Eastern North America. *Journal of Archaeological Research, 7*, 105-146.

Milner, G.R. (2004). *The Moundbuilders: Ancient Peoples of Eastern North America*. New York: Thames & Hudson.

Moore, J.H. (1961). The Ox in the Middle Ages. *Agricultural History, 35*, 90-93.

Morison, S.E. (1971). *The European Discovery of America: The Northern Voyages*. New York: Oxford University Press.

Morris, J. (1973). *The Age of Arthur*. London: Weidenfield & Nicholson.

Muhlberger, S. (1983). The Gallic Chronicle of 452 and its authority for British events. *Britannia, 14*, 23-33.

Muir, L. (1968). King Arthur's northern conquests in the Leges Anglorum Londoniis Collectae. *Medium Aevum, 37*, 253-262.

Myres, J.N.L. (1969). *Anglo-Saxon Pottery and the Settlement of England*. Oxford: Oxford University Press.

Myres, J.N.L. (1986). *The English Settlements*. Oxford: Oxford University Press.

Nansen, F. (1911). *In Northern Mists: Arctic Exploration in Early Times (Vol II)*. New York: Frederick A. Stokes Company.

Nash, D.W. (1858), ed. and trans. *Taliesin; or The Bards and Druids of Britain: a translation of the remains of the earliest Welsh bards, and an examination of the Bardic mysteries*. London: John Russell Smith.

National Geospatial-Intelligence Agency (2011). *Sailing Directions (Enroute) Newfoundland, Labrador, and Hudson Bay* (13th ed.) Bethesda: NGIA.

National Park Service (1999). *A Walking Tour of Mound City*. Chillicothe OH: Hopewell Culture National Historical Park.

National Park Service (2008). *The Hopewell World*. Chillicothe OH: Hopewell Culture National Historical Park.

Nayling, N. and McGrail, S. (2004). *The Barland's Farm Romano-Celtic Boat*. York: Council for British Archaeology.

Newton, A.P. (1970). *The Great Age of Discovery*. New York: Burt Franklin.

Neyman, J. and Pearson, E.S. (1967). The testing of statistical hypotheses in relation to probabilities a priori. *Joint Statistical Papers*. Cambridge: Cambridge University Press; 186-202.

Nickel, H. (1983). About Arms and Armor in the Age of Arthur. *Avalon to Camelot, 1*, 19-21.

Nickel, H. (1991). Arms and Armor. In N.J. Lacy (ed.) *The New Arthurian Encyclopedia*. New York: Garland Publishing; 12-15.

Nieke, M.R. and Duncan, H.B. (1988). Dalriada: the establishment and maintenance of an Early Historic kingdom in North Britain. In S.T. Driscoll and M.R. Nieke (eds.) *Power and Politics in Early Medieval Britain and Ireland*. Edinburgh: Edinburgh University Press; 6-21.

Nobbe, C.F.A. (1966), ed. *Claudii Ptolemaei Geographia*. Vol.2. Hildesheim: George Olms. (A 1966 reprint of a work written in 1843-5).

Nydal, R. (1989). A Critical Review of Radiocarbon Dating of a Norse Settlement at L'Anse aux Meadows, Newfoundland Canada. *Radiocarbon, 31*, 976-985.

Odell, G.H. (1988). Addressing Prehistoric Hunting Practices through Stone Tool Analysis. *American Anthropologist, 90*, 335-356.

Ó Faoláin, S. (2006). Dumnonia. In J.T. Koch (ed.) *Celtic Culture: A Historical Encyclopedia*. Santa Barbara & Oxford: ABC-CLIO; 619-621.

O'Meara, J.J. (2002). The Latin Version: Translation. In W.R.J. Barron and G.S. Burgess (eds.) *The Voyage of Saint Brendan: Representative Versions of the Legend in English Translation*. Exeter: University of Exeter Press; 26-64.

Oskamp, H.P. (1970), ed. and trans. *The Voyage of Mael Dúin*. Groningen: Wolters-Noordhoff.

Owen, D.D.R. (1987), trans. *Chrétien de Troyes: Arthurian Romances*. London: Dent.

Owen, W. (1803). *The Cambrian Biography*. London: E. Williams.

Pacheco, P.J. (1996). Ohio Regional Settlement Patterns. In P.J. Pacheco (ed.) *A View from the Core: A Synthesis of Ohio Hopewell Archaeology*. Columbus, OH: Ohio Archaeological Council; 16-35.

Padel, O. (1994). The nature of Arthur. *Cambrian Medieval Celtic Studies, 27*, 1-31.

Padel, O. (2006). Geoffrey of Monmouth and the Development of the Merlin Legend. *Cambrian Medieval Celtic Studies, 51*, 37-65.

Padel, O. (2007). Place-names and the Saxon conquest of Devon and Cornwall. In N.J. Higham (ed.) *Britons in Anglo-Saxon England*. Woodbridge: Boydell Press; 215-230.

Park, R.W. (2008). Contact between the Norse Vikings and the Dorset culture in Arctic Canada. *Antiquity, 82*, 189-198.

Parry, J.H. (1834). *The Cambrian Plutarch*. London: Simpkin and Marshall.

Parry, J.J. (1925). The Vita Merlini: Geoffrey of Monmouth. *University of Illinois Studies in Language and Literature, 10* (3).

Parry, J.J. and Caldwell, R.A. (1959). Geoffrey of Monmouth. In R.S. Loomis (ed.) *Arthurian Literature in the Middle Ages*. Oxford: Clarendon Press; 72-93.

Pattison, J.E. (2008). Is it necessary to assume an apartheid-like social structure in early Anglo-Saxon England? *Proceedings of the Royal Society B, 275*, 2423-2429.

Perrin, B. (1919), ed. and trans. *Plutarch's Lives* (Vol. VIII). Cambridge, Massachusetts: Harvard University Press.

Piggott, S. (1941). The sources of Geoffrey of Monmouth: I The 'pre-Roman' King-list. *Antiquity, 15*, 269-286.

Phillips, G. and Keatman, M. (1992). *King Arthur: the True Story*. London: Century Random House.

Pohl, F.J. (1961). *Atlantic Crossings Before Columbus*. New York: W.W. Norton.

Prufer, O.H. (1964). The Hopewell Cult. *Scientific American, 211*, 90-102.

Pryor, F. (2004). *Britain AD: a Quest for Arthur, England and the Anglo-Saxons*. London: HarperCollins.

Raffel, B. (1999), trans. *Perceval, the Story of the Grail: Chrétien de Troyes*. London: Yale University Press.

Rees, W.J. (1840), trans. *The Liber Landavensis*. Llandovery: Welsh MSS. Soc.

Rex, P. (2004). *The English Resistance: the Underground War against the Normans*. The Mill, Stroud, Gloucestershire: The History Press.

Reynolds, H.W., Gates, C.C. and Glaholt, R.D. (2003). Bison (*Bison bison*). In G.A. Feldhamer, B.C. Thompson, and J.A. Chapman (eds.) *Wild Mammals of North America: Biology, Management, and Conservation* (2nd ed.). Baltimore: John Hopkins University Press; 1009-1060.

Rhŷs, J. (1888). Lectures on the Origin and Growth of Religion. *The Hibbert Lectures, 1886*. London: Williams and Norgate.

Rhŷs, J. (1891). *Studies in the Arthurian Legend*. Oxford: Clarendon.

Rhŷs, J. (1901). *Celtic Folklore: Welsh and Manx* (Vol. 2). Oxford: Clarendon.

Rigby, E., Symonds, M. and Ward-Thompson, D. (2004). A comet impact in AD 536? *Astronomy and Geophysics, 45*, 23-26.

Riordan, R.V. (1996). The Enclosed Hilltops of Southern Ohio. In P.J. Pacheco (ed.) *A View from the Core: a Synthesis of Ohio Hopewell Archaeology*. Columbus: Ohio Archaeological Council; 242-256.

Ritson, J. (1825). *The Life of King Arthur from Ancient Historians and Authentic Documents*. London: William Nicol.

Rivet, A.L.F. and Smith, C. (1979). *The Place-Names of Roman Britain*. London: B.T. Batsford.

Roberts, B.F. (1991). Culhwch ac Olwen, The Triads, Saints' Lives. In R. Bromwich et al. (eds.) *The Arthur of the Welsh*. Cardiff: University of Wales Press; 73-95.

Roberts, P. (1811), trans. *The Chronicle of the Kings of Britain; translated from the Welsh copy attributed to Tysilio*. London: E. Williams.

Rodway, S. (2005). The Date and Authorship of Culhwch ac Olwen: A Reassessment. *Cambrian Medieval Celtic Studies, 49*, 21-44.

Romer, F.E. (1998), trans. *Pomponius Mela's Description of the World*. Ann Arbor: University of Michigan Press.

Ross, A. (1996). *Pagan Celtic Britain*. Chicago: Academy Chicago Publishers.

Rouse, W.H.D. (1940), trans. *Nonnos Dionysiaca: Books 1–15*. (The Loeb Classical Library). Cambridge, Massachusetts: Harvard University Press.

Rowland, J. (1990), ed. and trans. *Early Welsh Saga Poetry: a Study and Edition of the Englynion*. Cambridge: Cambridge University Press.

Rowland, J. (1995). Warfare and horses in the Gododdin and the problem of Catraeth. *Cambrian Medieval Celtic Studies, 30*, 13-40.

Ruby, B.J., Carr, C. and Charles, D.K. (2006). Community organizations in the Scioto, Mann, and Havana Hopewellian regions: a comparative perspective. In C. Carr and D.T. Case (eds.) *Gathering Hopewell: Society, Ritual, and Ritual Interaction*. New York: Springer; 19-50.

Russo, D.G. (1998). *Town Origins and Development in Early England, c. 400-950 AD*. Westport, CT: Greenwood Press.

Savory, H.N. (1960). Excavations at Dinas Emrys, Beddgelert (Caernarvonshire), 1954-6. *Archaeologia Cambrensis, 109*, 13-77.

Savory, H.N. (1971). *Excavations at Dinorben, 1965-9*. Cardiff: National Museum of Wales.

Sawatzky, H.L. and Lehn, W.H. (1976). The Arctic Mirage and the Early North Atlantic. *Science, 192*, 1300-1305.

Schell, I.I. (1962). On the iceberg severity off Newfoundland and its prediction. *Journal of Glaciology, 4*, 161-172.

Schmidt, C.W. and Sharkey, R.A.L. (2012). Ethical and Political Ramifications of the Reporting/Non-Reporting of Native American Ritualized Violence. In R.J. Chacon and R.G. Mendoza (eds.) *The Ethics of Anthropology and Amerindian Research: Reporting on Environmental Degradation and Warfare*. New York: Springer; 27-36.

Schumacher, S. (2004). *Die keltischen Primärverben: ein vergleichendes, etymologisches und morphologisches Lexikon*. Innsbruck: Institut für Sprachen und Literaturen der Universität Innsbruck.

Seaby, W.A. and Woodfield, P. (1980). Viking stirrups from England and their background. *Medieval Archaeology, 24*, 87-122.

Seaver, K.A. (2008). "Pygmies" of the far north. *Journal of World History, 19*, 63-87.

Selmer, C. (1959), ed. *Navigatio Sancti Brendani Abbatis*. South Bend, Indiana: University of Notre Dame Press.

Severin, T. (1978). *The Brendan Voyage*. New York: McGraw-Hill.

Sharpe, R. (1995), trans. *Adomnán of Iona: Life of St. Columba*. London: Penguin.

Shetrone, H.C. and Greenman, E.F. (1931). Explorations of the Seip group of prehistoric earthworks. *Ohio Archaeological and Historical Quarterly, 40*, 343-509.

Shott, M.J. (1997). Stones and Shafts Redux: The Metric Discrimination of Chipped-Stone Dart and Arrow Points. *American Antiquity, 62*, 86-101.

Sims-Williams, P. (1982). The Evidence for Vernacular Irish Literary Influence on Early Mediaeval Welsh Literature. In D. Whitelock, R. McKitterick, and D. Dumville (eds.) *Ireland in Early Mediaeval Europe: Studies in Memory of Kathleen Hughes*. Cambridge: Cambridge University Press; 235-257.

Sims-Williams, P. (1983). Gildas and the Anglo-Saxons. *Cambridge Medieval Celtic Studies, 6*, 1-30.

Sims-Williams, P. (1990). Dating the transition to Neo-Brittonic: phonology and history, 400-600. In A. Bammesburger and A. Wollman (eds.) *Britain 400-600: Language and History*. Heidelberg: Carl Winter; 217-261.

Sims-Williams, P. (1991a). The early Welsh Arthurian poems. In R. Bromwich et al. (eds.) *The Arthur of the Welsh*. Cardiff: Univ. of Wales Press; 33-71.

Sims-Williams, P. (1991b). The Submission of Irish Kings in Fact and Fiction: Henry II, Bendigeidfran, and dating of the Four Branches of the Mabinogi. *Cambridge Medieval Celtic Studies, 22*, 31-61.

Sims-Williams, P. (2006). *Ancient Celtic Place-Names in Europe and Asia Minor*. Oxford: Blackwell Publishing.

Sims-Williams, P. (2012). Celtic Civilization: Continuity or Coincidence? *Cambrian Medieval Celtic Studies, 64*, 1-45.

Skelton, R.A. (1965). *The Vinland Map and the Tartar Relation*. New Haven: Yale University Press.

Skene, W.F. (1868), ed. & trans. *The Four Ancient Books of Wales*. Edinburgh: Edmonston and Douglas.

Smith, B.D. (1992). Hopewellian Farmers of Eastern North America. In B.D. Smith, M.P. Hoffman and C.W. Cowan (eds.) *Rivers of Change: Essays on Early Agriculture in Eastern North America*. Washington, DC: Smithsonian Institution Press; 201-248.

Snyder, C.A. (1998). *An Age of Tyrants: Britain and the Britons A.D. 400-600*. Thrupp, Stroud, Gloucestershire: Sutton.

Snyder, C.A. (2003). *The Britons*. Malden, MA: Blackwell Publishing.

Snyder, C.A. (2005). Arthur and Kingship in the Historia Brittonum. In N.J. Lacy (ed.) *The Fortunes of King Arthur*. Woodbridge: Brewer; 1-12.

Spence, M.W. and Fryer, B.J. (2006). Hopewellian Silver and Silver Artifacts from Eastern North America: Their Sources, Procurement, Distribution, and Meanings. In C. Carr and D.T. Case (eds.) *Gathering Hopewell: Society, Ritual, and Ritual Interaction*. New York: Springer; 714-733.

Squier, E.G. and Davis, E.H. (1848). *Ancient Monuments of the Mississippi Valley*. Washington DC: Smithsonian Institution.

Squire, C. (1905). *The Mythology of the British Islands, and Introduction to Celtic Myth, Legend, Poetry and Romance*. London: Blackie and Son.

Stancliffe, C. (1997). The Thirteen Sermons attributed to Columbanus and the question of their Authorship. In M. Lapidge (ed.) *Columbanus: Studies on the Latin Writings*. Woodbridge, Suffolk: Boydell Press; 93-202.

Stefánsson, V. (1942). *Ultima Thule: Further Mysteries of the Arctic*. London: Harrap.

Stefánsson, V. (1947). *Greenland*. New York: Doubleday, Doran & Co.

Stenton, F.M. (1947). *Anglo-Saxon England. The Oxford History of England*. Vol. 2. Oxford: Clarendon Press.

Stephens, T. (1849). *Literature of the Kymry*. Llandovery: William Reese.

Stevens, C.E. (1941). Gildas Sapiens. *English Historical Review, 56*, 353-373.

Stevenson, E.L. (1932), ed. and trans. *Claudius Ptolemy: The Geography*. New York: New York Public Library. (Reprint, 1991, New York: Dover).

Stokes, W. (1888-1889), ed. and trans. The Voyage of Mael Duin. *Revue Celtique, 9*, 1888: 447-495, and *Revue Celtique, 10*, 1889: 50-95.

Stothers, R.B. (1984). Mystery cloud of AD 536. *Nature, 307*, 344-345.

Stothers, R.B. and Rampino, M.R. (1983). Volcanic Eruptions in the Mediterranean before A.D. 630 from Written and Archaeological sources. *Journal of Geophysical Research, 88*, 6357-6371.

Tatlock, J.S.P. (1950). *The Legendary History of Britain*. New York: Gordian.

Taylor, E.G.R. (1956). A letter dated 1577 from Mercator to John Dee. *Imago Mundi, 13*, 56-68.

Thomas, C.R., Carr, C. and Keller, C. (2006). Animal-Totemic clans of Ohio Hopewellian peoples. In C. Carr and D. T. Case (eds.) *Gathering Hopewell: Society, Ritual, and Ritual Interaction*. New York: Springer; 339-385.

Thomas, D.H. (1978). Arrowheads and Atlatl Darts: How the Stones got the Shaft. *American Antiquity, 43*, 461-472.

Thomas, H.M. (2003). *The English and the Normans: Ethnic Hostility, Assimilation, and Identity 1066-c. 1220*. Oxford: Oxford University Press.

Thomas, M.G., Stumpf, M.P.H. and Harke, H. (2006). Evidence for an apartheid-like social structure in early Anglo-Saxon England. *Proceedings of the Royal Society B, 273*, 2651-2657.

Thomas, M.G., Stumpf, M.P.H. and Harke, H. (2008). Integration versus apartheid in post-Roman Britain: a response to Pattison. *Proceedings of the Royal Society B ,275*, 2419-2421.

Thompson, E.A. (1977). Britain, A.D. 406-410. *Britannia, 8*, 303-318.

Thornton, D.E. (2003). *Kings, chronologies, and genealogies: studies in the political history of early medieval Ireland and Wales*. Oxford: Unit for Prosopographical Research, Linacre College.

Thorpe, L. (1966), trans. *Geoffrey of Monmouth: The History of the Kings of Britain*. Harmondsworth: Penguin.

Thorpe, L. (1974), trans. *Gregory of Tours: the History of the Franks*. Harmondsworth: Penguin.

Thorpe, L. (1978), trans. *The Journey through Wales and The Description of Wales*. Harmondsworth: Penguin.

Tierney, J.J. (1967), ed. and trans. *Dicuili: Liber de mensura orbis terrae*. Dublin: Dublin Institute for Advanced Studies.

Tolstoy, N. (1960-62). "Nennius, Chapter Fifty-Six." *Bulletin of the Board of Celtic Studies, 19*, 118-62.

Toolis, R. and Bowles, C. (2012). *The Galloway Picts Project: Excavation and Survey of Trusty's Hill. Summary Report*. Dumfries: The Dumfriesshire and Galloway Natural History and Antiquarian Society.

Topf, A.L., Gilbert, M.T.P., Dumbacher, J.P. and Hoelzel, A.R. (2006). Tracing the Phylogeography of Human Populations in Britain Based on 4th-11th Century mtDNA Genotypes. *Molecular Biology and Evolution, 23*, 152-161.

Trumbower, J.A. (2001). *Rescue for the Dead: The Posthumous Salvation of Non-Christians in Early Christianity*. Oxford: Oxford University Press.

Tschan, F.J. (1959), trans. *History of the Archbishops of Hamburg-Bremen, by Adam of Bremen*. New York: Columbia University Press.

Tuczay, C.A. (2005). Motifs in the Arabian Nights and in Ancient and Medieval Literature: a Comparison. *Folklore, 116*, 272-291.

Turff, G. and Carr, C. (2006). Hopewellian Panpipes from Eastern North America: Their Social, Ritual, and Symbolic Significance. In C. Carr and D.T. Case (eds.) *Gathering Hopewell: Society, Ritual, and Ritual Interaction*. New York: Springer; 648-695.

Turner, S. (1828). *History of the Anglo Saxons*, Volume III (5th edition). London: Longman, Rees, Orme, Brown and Green.

Turner, S. (1852). *History of the Anglo Saxons*, Volume I (7th edition). London: Longman, Brown, Green and Longmans.

Wallace, B.L. (2008). The Discovery of Vinland. In S. Brink and N. Price (eds.) *The Viking World*. New York: Routledge; 604-612.

Watson, W.J. (1926). *History of the Celtic Place-Names of Scotland*. Edinburgh: Blackwood and Son. Reprinted by Simon Taylor (Edinburgh, 2004).

Watts, V. (2004), ed. *The Cambridge Dictionary of English Place-Names*. Cambridge: Cambridge University Press.

Weale, M.E., Weiss, D.A., Jager, R.F., Bradman, N. and Thomas, M.G. (2002). Y chromosome evidence for Anglo-Saxon Mass Migration. *Molecular Biology and Evolution, 19*, 1008-1021.

Weets, J., Carr, C., Penney, D. and Carriveau, G. (2006). Smoking Pipe Compositions and Styles as Evidence of the Social Affiliations of Mortuary Ritual Participants at the Tremper Site, Ohio. In C. Carr and D.T. Case (eds.) *Gathering Hopewell: Society, Ritual, and Ritual Interaction*. New York: Springer; 533-552.

Welch, M. (1992). *Anglo-Saxon England*. London: B.T. Batsford.

West, M.L, ed. (1966). *Hesiod: Theogony*. Oxford: Clarendon Press.

Whitaker, I. (1981-82). The Problem of Pytheas' Thule. *The Classical Journal, 77*, 148-164.

White, L. (1962). *Medieval Technology and Social Change*. Oxford: Oxford University Press.

Williams, E. and Williams, T. (1848), eds. *The Iolo Manuscripts*. Llandovery: William Rees.

Williams, H. (1899), ed. and trans. *Gildas: Cymmrodorion Record Series No. 3*. London: David Nutt.

Williams, I. (1932-3), ed. Marwnad Cynddylan. *Bulletin of the Board of Celtic Studies, 6*, 134-141.

Williams, I. (1938), ed. *Canu Aneirin*. Caerdydd: Gwasg Prifysgol Cymru.

Williams, I. (1968). *The Poems of Taliesin*. Trans. J.E.C. Williams. Dublin: The Dublin Institute for Advanced Studies.

Williams, I. (1972). *The Beginnings of Welsh Poetry*. Ed. and trans. R. Bromwich. Cardiff: University of Wales Press.

Williams, J. (1971). A Crannog at Loch Arthur, New Abbey. *Transactions of the Dumfriesshire and Galloway Natural History and Antiquarian Society, 48*, 121-124.

Williams, J.E.C. (1991). Brittany and the Arthurian legend. In R. Bromwich et al. (eds.) *The Arthur of the Welsh*. Cardiff: University of Wales Press; 249-272.

Wilson, P.R., Cardwell, P., Cramp, R.J., Evans, J., Taylor-Wilson, R.H., Thompson, A., and Wacher, J.S. (1996). Early Anglian Catterick and Catraeth. *Medieval Archaeology, 40*, 1-61.

Winterbottom, M. (1978), ed. and trans. *Gildas: the Ruin of Britain and other works*. London: Phillimore and Co.

Wiseman, H. (2000). The derivation of the date of the Badon entry in the *Annales Cambriae* from Bede and Gildas. *Parergon, 17*, 1-10.

Wood, I. (1984). The end of Roman Britain: Continental evidence and parallels. In M. Lapidge and D.N. Dumville (eds.) *Gildas: New Approaches*. Woodbridge, Suffolk: Boydell Press; 1-25.

Wood, M. (1999). *In Search of England: Journeys into the English Past*. London: Viking.

Wood, M. (2001). *In Search of the Dark Ages*. London: BBC Worldwide Ltd.

Wooding, J.M. (2000). Monastic Voyaging and the Nauigatio. In J.M. Wooding (ed.) *The Otherworld Voyage in Early Irish Literature: An Anthology of Criticism*. Dublin: Four Courts Press; 226-245.

Wooding, J.M. (2002). The Latin Version: Introduction. In W.R.J. Barron and G.S. Burgess (eds.) *The Voyage of Saint Brendan: Representative Versions of the Legend in English Translation*. Exeter: University of Exeter Press; 13-64.

Woodward, S.L. and McDonald, J.N. (2002). *Indian Mounds of the Middle Ohio Valley*. Blacksburg, Virginia: McDonald & Woodward Publishing.

Wright, D. (2001). *The Roman Vergil and the Origins of Medieval Book Design*. London: The British Library.

Wright, N. (1982). Geoffrey of Monmouth and Gildas. *Arthurian Literature, 2*, 1-40.

Wright, N. (1984). Geoffrey of Monmouth and Gildas Revisited. *Arthurian Literature, 4*, 155-163.

Wright, N. (1986). Geoffrey of Monmouth and Bede. *Arthurian Literature, 6*, 27-59.

Wright, T. (1842). *Biographia Britannica Literaria: Anglo Saxon Period*. London: John W. Parker.

Yerkes, R.W. (2005). Bone Chemistry, Body Parts, and Growth Marks: Evaluating Ohio Hopewell and Cahokia Mississippian Seasonality, Subsistence, Ritual, and Feasting. *American Antiquity, 70*, 241-265.

Yerkes, R.W. (2006). Middle Woodland Settlements and Social Organization in the Central Ohio Valley. In D.K. Charles and J.E. Buikstra (eds.) *Recreating Hopewell*. Gainesville: University Press of Florida; 5-61.

Young, S. (2009). *The Celtic Revolution*. London: Gibson Square.

Ziegler, M. (1999). Artúr mac Aedán of Dalriada. *The Heroic Age*, Issue 1, Spring/Summer 1999.

Zimmer, H. (1893). *Nennius Vindicatus: Über Entstehung, Geschichte und Quellen der Historia Brittonum*: Berlin: Weidmannsche Buchhandlung.

INDEX

A

Aberffraw, 131, 204, 219, 246
Adena culture, 47
Adomnán, 155, 182–83, 192, 197, 242
Aedán of Dalriada, 182, 184, 197, 229, 242, 299
Aëtius, 229, 266
Afagddu, 75, 286, 303
Afon Gamlan, 89
Afon Gell, 212, 246
Agned, battle, 19, 21, 271
Ahronson, K., 155, 292
Akpatok Island, 36
Aladur (equated with Mars), 115, 117
Alaric, 16
Alban, St, 88, 217
Alcock, L., xi, 264–65, 267–68, 286, 295, 298–99, 303, 305
Alexander the Great, 37, 41, 276
Alonso-Núñez, J.M., 156, 292
Ambrosius, xiv, 4–5, 17, 198, 200, 215, 247, 262, 264–65, 271–73
Anderson, A., 295, 301–2
Andrews, R., 303
Aneirin, xiii, 184–85, 237–38, 262
Angar Kyfundawt, 238, 292
Anglesey, 15, 131, 204, 209, 215–17, 219, 246
Annales Cambriae, 3, 5, 13–15, 17, 21, 27, 88–89, 125, 127, 193–96, 198, 242, 244, 298, 300
Annals of Tigernach, 154, 182
Annwfyn, meaning of, 65, 279
Anscombe, A., 299
Anticosti Island, 164
Antonine Wall, 266
Appalachian Mountains, 82, 169
Arawn, 221
Archfedd, 304
Arctic Circle, 155, 282
Arctic Mirage, 161
Arecluta, 119, 126, 205
Arfon, 213, 216, 245
Arth, xv, 200, 205, 218, 243–44, 258, 302
Arthur
  battles, 19–23, 191–93, 196–97, 242
  as 'the Bear', xv, xviii, 199–202, 204–6, 208, 211–12, 214, 218–19, 228, 243–44, 258, 299, 302
  bogus Glastonbury grave, 31, 274
  children, 213, 245, 304
  death date, 14–15, 27, 89, 125, 127, 154, 182–83, 193–94, 196, 204, 220, 234, 300
  fighting Cawrnur, 116, 119, 126, 303
  governance of Rheon, xix, 115, 117–19, 126, 129, 148, 184, 197, 223–24, 226–29, 246–47, 259, 285, 290
  killing Huail, 205–7, 244
  location, xv, 9, 38, 40, 44, 124, 213–16, 238, 245, 258
  men named after Arthur, 182–84, 197, 229, 242, 299
  pedigree, 217–18, 286, 303
  in poem *Geraint son of Erbin*, 4, 181, 190, 197, 242, 297–98
  in poem *Marwnad Cynddylan*, 189, 192, 197, 242, 277
  in poem *Y Gododdin*, 185–89, 196, 241, 257, 300
  reverence for scripture, 88, 115, 118, 127, 148, 235, 290
  round table, 7
  weapons, 8, 30, 194–95
Arthurian tapestry, 285
Ashe, G., 109, 140, 264, 274, 282, 292, 298–300
Athrwys, son of Meurig, 300
atlatl (dart thrower), 61–62, 279
Augustine, 237
Aurelius Caninus, xiv, 15, 85, 130, 133, 202, 233, 287, 302
Avallach, 305
Avalon, 8–9, 27–30, 44, 220, 274

B

Babcock, W., 67, 280
Bachrach, B., 22, 199, 272, 301
Badbury hills, 22
Badon, battle, xi, 14–15, 21–23, 117, 127, 195–96, 217, 242, 244, 247, 271–73, 277, 299
Báetán, 155
Baffin Island, 35–36, 162
Bailey, M.E., 109–10, 284
Baillie, M., 14, 109, 125, 127, 265, 284, 286, 304
Bamburgh, 102
Banfield, A., 82
Bannerman, J., 295
Barber, R., 188, 195, 282, 296, 298–99
Barbieri, F., 204, 301
Barinthus, 9, 28–29, 44, 274
Barney, S.A., 261, 282, 293
Bartrum, P., 191, 218–19, 286, 295, 297, 302, 304
Basilides, 237

Bassas, battle, 19, 21–22
Bath, 22–23, 277
Bedd Geraint (grave of Geraint), 191
Bede, xv, 5, 155, 157, 195, 200, 203, 206, 211, 243, 245, 266–68, 273, 293, 301
Benozzo, F., 108, 284
Bernicia, 187, 241
Biddle, M., 264
Bleddyn Fardd, 216
Bollard, J., xvi, 261, 280–82, 299, 306
Bonedd y Arwyr, 213, 217–18, 221
Bonedd y Saint, 121, 304
Book of Aneirin, 185, 238, 262
Book of Taliesin. See Taliesin's Poems
Boron, Robert de, 8
Bradbury, A., 279
Bran son of Febal, 66, 129, 139–41, 146
Brân the Blessed, 35, 91, 102–5, 120–21, 215, 222, 253–54, 286, 290
Branwen daughter of Llŷr, 35, 74, 102, 104–5, 276
Breatnach, L., 142, 281, 287
Bregion (Breguoin, Breuoin, Bregomion), battle, 19, 21–23
Brendan, St, xvii, 8–9, 28–29, 44, 78, 95, 137, 154–55, 255–57, 274, 306
Brennos, 102, 104
Bricriu's Feast, 73, 129, 144–46
brindled ox, 80, 82, 92, 95, 173–75, 251, 256
Bromwich, R., 75, 82, 89, 120–22, 189, 192, 212–13, 261, 271, 273, 280, 282–83, 286, 294–99, 301–5
Bruxellensis, 275
Bryn Euryn, 202, 208, 214, 225
Bryn Seith Marchawg, 120, 215
Brytanici Imperii Limites, 32
Buffalo (American bison), 82, 170, 173
Burgess, R.W., 267–68
Bwrdd Arthur, 214–15

C

Cabot, John, 36–37
Cabot Strait, 164, 249
Cadwallon, 23, 102, 192, 197, 217, 242, 295
Cadwallon Llawhir, 218–19
Caer Dathl in Arfon, 213
Caer Gai, 210
Caerleon, 7, 40, 217, 299
Caernarfon Bay, 213, 245
Caer Nefenhyr, 107, 113, 119, 148, 223–24, 226, 235
Caesar, Julius, 157–58
Cai (Sir Kay), 210, 304

Cáin Adamnáin, 183
Caledonian Forest (Coit Celidon), 19, 21–23, 114, 118, 193, 224, 226, 246, 277
Camelot, xi, 7
Camlann, battle, xi, 8, 13, 27, 29, 31, 44, 89, 193–94, 196
Capelli, C., 269
Caradawg, 120–21, 286
Carannog, St, 113, 263
Carey, J., 261–62, 274, 280, 282, 286–87, 297, 300–301, 304–6
Carlisle, 22, 148, 224–26, 283, 295, 299
Carney, J., 281, 287
Carr, C., 57–58, 60, 63, 103, 279, 284
Cartier, Jacques, 36–37, 160, 164–66, 168–70, 304
Casey, P.J., 267
Catraeth, battle, 184, 268, 295, 297
Cawrdaf son of Caradawg, 121
Cawrnur (Caw), 116, 119, 126, 205, 244, 301, 303
Ceredigion, 191, 301
Ceridwen, 75, 91, 286
Cernunnos (horned god), 302
Cessford, C., 225, 272, 295, 305
Chadwick, H., 4, 20, 182, 261, 271, 294, 306
Chambers, E., 104, 261, 265, 284
Chapman, P.H., 274, 292
Charles-Edwards, T., 188, 261, 276, 296–98
Charles Island, 36
Chester, xv, 22–23, 81, 95, 124, 127, 193, 210–11, 213–14, 216–17, 245, 258, 290, 299
Chillicothe, 47–49, 52, 55, 103, 171–72, 278, 293–94
Christian cross carvings, 155, 157
Chronicum Scotorum, 154, 182
Clube, V., 109–10, 113, 284–85
Cnoyen, Jacob, 9, 32–33, 44, 274–75
Coats Island, 36
Coe, J., 108, 274, 282–85
Columba, St, 155, 157, 182–83, 192, 197, 242
Colwyn Bay, xv, 199, 208, 243
comets, 109–10, 145
Connlae, 65, 141, 235
Constantine, xiv, 15, 130, 202, 212, 246, 287, 298, 302
Conwy, river, 204
Cormac, 155, 157
Corning, C., 237
Cornovii, 213, 302
Cornwall, 15, 27, 89, 104, 203, 212–13, 216, 246, 299

Cross, T., 73–74, 142, 144
'Crystal pillar' in the sea, xvii, 95, 137, 255, 257, 274
Cú Chulainn, 74, 76, 142–43, 145
Culhwch and Olwen, 5, 8, 30, 70, 75, 107, 205, 212–13, 223–24, 226, 262–63, 274, 280, 301–2, 304
Cunedda, 16, 211, 218–19
Cuneglasus, xiv–xv, 15, 130–31, 133, 200–202, 204, 218–19, 243–44, 258, 287, 299, 302
Cunliffe, B., 30, 154, 157, 169, 265, 274, 292–93
Cú Roí, 73–74, 87, 142, 144
Cynan Garwyn, 21
Cynddylan, 4, 181, 189–90, 197, 277, 297

D

Dark, K., 18, 113, 202, 213–15, 225, 228–29, 266–68, 285, 301–3, 305
Davies, W., 18, 300
Davis Strait, 36, 162, 164
DeBoer, W., 57, 279
Decapitated Heads, 102–3
Dee, river, xv, 81, 95, 124, 127, 160, 210, 216, 245, 258, 290
Dee, John, 9, 28–29, 32, 34–35, 38–39, 44, 275
Defwy meadows, 65, 80–81, 92, 95, 124, 127, 210, 245, 251, 256, 290
Deganwy, 204, 211, 214, 219, 243, 245–46, 283, 302
Denmark, 16, 38, 40–41, 43, 269, 277–78
Dicuil, 156–57
Diemand, D., 293
Dinarth, xv, xix, 204, 208–9, 211–12, 214, 218–19, 225, 228, 238, 243–46, 258, 261, 301–2
Dinas Emrys, 214–15, 245
Dionysiaca by Nonnos, 108
Dragons, 5, 108, 112–13, 145–46, 219, 262–63, 287, 302
Druids, 112, 141, 232, 235–36
Dubglas, river, 19, 21–22, 277
Dumbarton, 161, 182
Dumnonia, 15, 130, 195, 204, 212, 217, 246, 298
Dumville, D., xi–xiv, 18, 261, 265–66, 268, 270–71, 273, 287, 295, 298, 301, 304–5
Dunragit, 224–25, 305
Dún Scáith, 11, 74, 129, 142–46
Dyfed, 119, 183, 221–22

E

Eastern Woodlands, xvii, 47, 62, 170, 232, 249, 254–55
Ebbesmeyer, C., 163
Echtrae Chonnlai, 28, 65–66, 129, 141–42, 146, 305
Ecumenical Council (in AD 553), 237
Edinburgh, 5, 142, 150, 161, 184–85, 187–90, 223, 241, 271
Edwin's head, 102
Einion Yrth, 218, 299
Eiríksson, Leif, 153
Eldjárn, K., 155–56, 292
Eleirch, 213, 245, 304
Elffin, 91, 125–26, 283, 286–87
Elizabeth I, Queen, 9, 28, 32, 38–39, 44
Elwy, river, 212, 238, 245–47
Enterline, J.R., 264, 274, 276
Environmental crisis, 109–10, 125, 127, 220–21
Euflamm (Efflam), St, 113, 263
Evelyn-White, H., 109, 284
Exodus, xv, 203, 218

F

Fairies, xvi, xviii, 66–67, 69, 75, 79, 81, 95, 100, 220, 250–51, 253, 255, 257
False Negative (Type 2 error), xii–xiii, 181, 261
Faroes, 29, 157, 160, 249, 274
Feininger, T., 293
Field, P., 191, 271–72, 298
Findabair, 215
Fisher King, 8, 284
Foley, W., 293
Folkloric theories, xiii–xiv, 66, 181, 198, 295–96
Ford, P., 274, 276–77, 280, 282–86, 301–2, 304–5

G

Gallic Chronicles, 266–67
Galloway, xix, 184, 199, 223–24, 228–29, 258, 295
Gardner, W., 212, 215
Garwen, xv, 211, 215, 243, 245
Gelliwig (Celliwig), 121, 212, 246
Geoffrey of Monmouth, xi, xiii, 5–10, 25, 27–31, 33, 37–41, 43–44, 196, 198, 264, 274, 277, 299–300, 303
Geraint son of Erbin, 190–92, 197, 297
Gerald of Wales, 6, 31, 205
Gestae Arthuri, 9, 33, 35, 41, 44–45, 160, 162
Gidlow, C., 204, 301

Gildas
  brother of Huail, 119, 200, 205–8, 222, 244, 301
  date of death, 15, 265
  date of writing, 14, 204
  location, 15
  punster, xv, 85, 130, 200–201, 205, 212, 218, 243, 246, 258
  sophisticated Latin, 201
  suppression of names, xv, 199–200, 206, 243–44
Gildas: *Lives* of
  by Caradoc, 119, 205, 222, 244, 274, 301, 303
  by monk from Rhuys, 119, 126, 205, 244
Gildas' *Ruin of Britain*
  Advent of the Saxons, 16–17, 266–70
  Ambrosius, 17, 271–72
  Badon, 17, 119, 272–73
  Bear's Stronghold, xv, 200–202, 214, 218, 228, 243–44, 302
  British military are cowards, xvii, 14, 132, 205–6, 244, 271
  Chariot driver, xv, 140, 200–201, 204–5, 218, 243, 258, 302
  The Five Kings, xiv, 15, 85–86, 130–31, 200–202, 204, 243–44
  The Pharaoh overking, xiv–xv, xviii, 199–201, 203–4, 206, 217–18, 243–44, 258
'Glass' fortress, xvi–xvii, 2, 78–79, 92, 95, 137–38, 141–42, 146, 161, 232, 248, 255–57
Gododdin, Y, xix, 4, 150, 181, 184–90, 192, 196–97, 229, 238, 241–42, 247, 257, 284–86, 295–97, 300
Golychaf-i Gulwyd, 90, 98, 140, 283, 287
Gorddur, 184, 186–88, 241, 247, 296
Gotland, 38, 40–41, 277
Greber, N., 57, 279
Green, C., 191, 261–63, 272, 282, 284–85, 294–98, 301, 304
Greenland, 9, 35–36, 38, 44, 81, 110, 161–62, 249, 276
Grocland, xviii, 9, 32–33, 35–37, 44, 276
Gruffydd, R.G., 265, 297, 301, 303–4, 306
Gudger, E., 84, 176, 252, 282, 294
Guinevere (Gwenhwyfar), xiii, 7, 27, 89, 196, 215
Guinnion fort, battle, 19, 21–22, 195
Gwallawg, xiii, 21, 193, 233–34, 265, 283, 295

Gweir, xvi–xvii, 68–70, 90–93, 97, 100, 134, 136, 171, 179, 221, 232, 235, 250–51, 280–81, 288

H
Hadrian's Wall, xix, 23, 118, 126, 192, 217, 227, 229, 247, 259, 267
Haycock, M., 72, 76–80, 86–88, 91, 107–8, 111, 117–18, 124–26, 137–38, 148–49, 223, 261, 280–87, 292, 305–6
Hefele, C., 237, 305–6
Hennin, father of Garwen, xv, 211–12, 215, 243, 245
Hieatt, K., 126, 286
Higham, N., 266, 269, 298, 301–2
High Rochester, 19, 22–23, 229, 298
Higley, S., 2, 48, 69, 72, 78, 82, 85, 87, 249, 261, 278, 280–82, 306
Historia Brittonum
  academic criticism, 18–19
  Ambrosius and Vortigern, xiv, 4–5, 198, 215, 262
  Arthur's battles, 18–23
  Cunedda's migration, 16, 211, 218, 229
  Famous sixth-century bards, 27, 237, 248
  'Glass tower' in the sea, xvii, 2, 78–79, 95, 137–39, 248, 255
  Mirabilia, xiv, 4, 198, 261–62, 304
Holy Grail, 8, 282
The Hopewell
  appearance, 59–61
  artifacts, 47, 57–59, 103, 171–72
  central location, 49–50, 84, 170, 232
  communities, 47–48
  Great Hopewell Road, 52, 103
  prolific use of pearls, xvii, 2, 58, 74, 94, 134, 143, 170–72, 251
  under threat, 62–63, 252
  weapons, 61–62
Hopewell Earthworks
  Hopewell site, 54
  Marietta, 293
  Mound City, 49, 55–58, 60–61, 84, 171, 175
  Newark, 49, 51–53, 63, 171, 294
  Pinson, 294
  Seip, 55–56, 58, 60, 103, 172
  Tremper, 85, 176
Huail, brother of Gildas, 119, 205–8, 222, 244, 301
Hudson Strait, 36, 162
Hughes, K., xii, 194, 298
Hughes, S., 61, 279
Hulbert, A., 60, 173, 261, 279, 282, 294, 306

I

Icebergs, 2, 78–79, 137–38, 140, 142, 146, 161–64, 249, 256–57, 274, 306
Île Ste-Hélène, 166, 168
Indrawing seas, 33, 36, 276
Ingstad, H., 153, 292
Innermessan, 224, 246
Insule Brittannie, 40
International Ice Patrol (IIP), 163
Inventio Fortunatae, 33, 275
Iona, 155, 182–83
Iron Brow, xix, 247–48, 258
Isaac, G., 233, 295, 305
Isidore of Seville, 3, 77, 156, 159, 293
Íslendingabók, 155–56

J

Jackson, K., xvi, 3, 18–20, 22–23, 69, 78, 85, 148–49, 202, 206, 211, 217, 239, 244, 249
Jarman, A.O., 262, 264, 296, 306
Jones, G., 154, 156–57, 292–93
Jones, T., 89, 261, 271, 276, 281, 283–85, 298–99, 301, 306
Judgement Day, 2, 69–70, 91, 93, 97, 111–12, 134, 145, 147, 171, 179, 235, 250–51, 288

K

Kadeir Teÿrnon, xv–xvi, 23–25, 117, 120–23, 125–27, 129, 147–48, 150, 231–32, 235–36, 238–39, 247–48, 257–59, 286–87, 290–92
Kaer sidi, xvi–xvii, 2, 68–69, 90–91, 93, 97, 99, 134, 141, 171, 177, 179, 249–50, 281
Kat Godeu, xvi–xvii, 11, 64, 66, 97–98, 105, 107–16, 118, 126–27, 129, 145–51, 235–36, 255, 257–59, 288–89
Kernyw, 121, 199, 212, 238–39, 246
Koch, J., 105–6, 148–50, 185, 187–88, 241–42, 261–62, 265–66, 270–71, 273–74, 280, 282–87, 292, 295–98, 300–301, 304–6
Kunz, K., 278, 292

L

Labrador, 35, 161–62, 164, 249, 274
Lachine Rapids, 153, 166, 170, 249, 254
Lailoken, 5, 226, 264
Laing, L., 202, 214, 224–25, 261, 295, 301–2, 305
Lake Erie, 49, 170, 177–78
Lambarde, William, 9, 38
Lamberton, R., 108, 284
Lancelot, 7, 264, 281
Landnámabók, 155
L'Anse aux Meadows, 153, 292
Lapidge, M., 201, 301
Lapland, 39–40
Larivière, S., 175, 282, 294
Larsen, L.B., 110, 284
Layton, B., 305
Leedham-Green, E., 42
Leges Anglorum, 38–40, 42, 125–26
Lehn, W., 161, 293
Lepper, B., 48, 52, 58–59, 61–62, 103, 172, 176, 251, 278–79, 284, 294, 306
Lewis, J.S., 111, 284–85
Liebermann, F., 38–39, 42, 277
Life of St Columba, by Adomnán, 155, 182, 192, 197, 242
Life of St Goeznovius, 31, 217, 300
Life of St Oudoceus, 221
Life of St Teilo, 221, 297
Lignite, 77, 288
Linnuis (Lindsey, Lincoln), 19, 22–23, 193, 217, 258, 277
Little Ormes Head, 209, 211, 213
Llacheu, 304
Llanborth, Ceredigion, 191
Llandrillo-yn-Rhos, 202
Llandudno, xv, 199, 204, 208, 211, 243–45
Llanfair Talhaiarn, 238–39, 247
Llangernyw, 212–13, 238–39, 246–47, 258
Llangollen, 215
Lleawc, 71, 73–74, 92, 94
Lleminawc, 71, 73–75, 92, 94, 143
Lleon, xv, 123–24, 126–27, 210, 245, 258, 290
Llongborth, battle, 190–91, 193, 197, 242
Llychlyn (Norway), 39, 277
Llŷn Peninsula, 216, 245
Llyn Tegid (Bala Lake), 210, 216, 245
Llywarch Hen, 102
Loch Arthur, 225
Loch Ryan, xix, 118, 126, 148, 184, 197, 199, 223–25, 227–29, 242, 246–47, 258–59
Longley, D., 202, 214, 216, 224–25, 261, 295, 301–3, 305
Loomis, R.S., 65, 280–82, 285, 306
Lott, D., 173, 294
Luce Bay, 224, 229, 259

M

Mabinogi, 35, 45, 74, 91, 102, 104, 119–20, 122, 221, 254, 304
Mac Mathúna, S., 287
MacMillan, K., 38, 41–42, 264, 274–77
Mael Dúin, 72–73, 129, 142, 144–46
Maglocunus (Maelgwn Gwynedd), xiv, 131, 133, 202–5, 211, 216, 218–19, 238, 243–44, 246, 272, 277, 287, 299–300, 302
Magnetic rocks (magnetini), 33–36, 41, 45, 275–76
Magnus Maximus (Maxen Wledig), 90, 121
Mainfort, R.C., 294
Marko, J., 162–63, 293
Marwnad Cynddylan, 189, 191–92, 197, 242, 297
Marwnat Corroi, 87–88
Marwnat Vthyr Pen, 217, 292, 303
Masefield, J., 38, 277
McCarthy, M., 223–24, 228, 274, 295, 305
McClure, J., 261, 266, 283, 301
McCone, K., 141, 273, 287, 305
McGrail, S., 158–59, 293
Menai Strait, 213, 216, 245
Mensforth, R.P., 279, 284
Mercator, Gerard, xviii, 9, 32–36, 44, 274
Mercator's Letter to John Dee, 32–35, 275
Mercy Killings, 101–2, 222, 289
Merlin (Myrddin), 5, 8–9, 27–31, 44, 198, 264, 273, 303
Meurig, King, xiv, 300
Meyer, K., 273, 287, 295
Meyvaert, P., 157, 293
Miathi, battle, 182, 299
Middle Woodland period, 47, 61–62
Milner, G., 278–79
Moel Arthur, 215–16
Mommsen, T., 200, 265
Mongán, 139–40, 182
Montreal, 2, 49, 73, 76, 94, 153, 165–70, 232, 249, 254
Mont Rougemont, 2, 166–67
Mont Royal, 2, 166–67, 249
Mont St-Bruno, 2, 166–67
Mont St-Hilaire, 2, 166–67
Moore Memoranda, 234, 295
Mordred (Medraut), 7, 13, 27, 89, 193–94, 196
Morfa Rhianedd, 211, 243, 245
Morgan le Fay, 30
Morison, S., 276, 282, 292–93
Morris, J., xi, xiii, xv, 3, 14, 191, 261, 265, 272, 297, 299, 301
Morris-Jones, J., 238
mound fortress, xvi, 2, 68–70, 92, 94, 232, 249, 256, 281
Muir, L., 9, 38–40, 264, 277
Muskingum, river, 49, 82, 95, 171, 173, 177, 251, 293
Myres, N., 3, 261, 267

N

Nansen, F., 275, 282
National Geospatial-Intelligence Agency, 36, 276
National Park Service, 278–79
Navigatio Sancti Brendani Abbatis. See Brendan
Nefenhyr, 107, 148, 223, 226
Neo-Brittonic, xv–xvi, 10, 21, 23–24, 85, 105, 117, 129–30, 149, 185, 200, 205, 228, 243, 258
Newark, 47, 51–53, 103, 171
Newton, A., 81, 282
Nieke, M., 216, 303
Nonnos of Panopolis, 108–9, 145
Northern Lands List, 9–10, 38–42, 278
Notitia Dignitatum, 195
Novantae tribe, 107, 148, 223–24, 226, 246

O

Odell, G., 61, 279
O'Meara, J., 261, 273–74, 282, 287
Origen, 237
Orkney, 40–41, 155, 157, 160, 249, 277
Ortelius, Abraham, 33, 35, 44, 276
Oskamp, H., 281
Oswald, 102, 192, 197, 242
Oswiu, 102, 189, 197
Otherworld, xvi, 65–67, 73–74, 77, 81, 140, 142, 147, 220–21, 232, 235, 255, 257, 280, 288
Otter effigy pipe, 57, 84–85, 103, 175–76
Owain Ddantgwyn, 218–19, 299
Owain son of Urien, xiii, 121, 233–34, 305
Oxford friar, 33, 275

P

Pacheco, P., 57, 279
Padel, O., 3, 212, 219–20, 261, 264, 270–71, 301, 304
Pa Gûr, 22, 210, 263, 303–4
Palladius, Bishop, 34, 36, 275–76
Park, R., 153, 292
Parry, J.J., 264, 273–74

Penbryn Beach, 191–92
Pen Rhionydd, 148, 197, 223, 226
Perceval, 8, 284
Phantom Chariot of Cú Chulainn, 74, 76, 142
Phillips, G., 199, 299, 301
Picts, xix, 13, 15–16, 23, 25, 132, 200, 203, 227, 229, 247, 262, 266–67
Polydore Virgil, 264–65
Pomponius Mela, 30–31, 72, 94, 236, 291
Pope Leo, 14
Portpatrick Bay, 224–25
Preideu Annwfyn, xvi–xviii, 28–31, 63–68, 72–76, 90–91, 97–100, 126–27, 129, 132–34, 137–48, 150–51, 165–69, 171–73, 255–58, 288–92
Prufer, O., 2, 48, 58, 63, 74, 172, 251–52, 261, 278–79, 281, 294, 306
Pryderi, xvi–xvii, 35, 68–69, 75, 92–93, 104, 119, 221–22, 250, 280–81
Prydwen, 30, 68–70, 76–79, 92, 165, 281, 289
Ptolemy, 34, 213, 224, 246, 275–76, 302
Puffin Island, 209, 215, 217
Pwyll, 119, 221–22
Pytheas, 154, 156–57, 161, 169

R

Rechtur, 115, 117, 150, 223, 228, 246–47
Rees, W., 221, 297, 300, 304
Rerigonium, 224–25, 229, 246
'Revolving' fort, 72–73, 94, 144–46
Rex, P., 42, 277–78
Reynolds, H., 173–74, 282, 294
Rheon, 115, 117–19, 126, 148, 184, 223–24, 226–28, 246–47
Rhiannon, 221–22
Rhinns of Galloway, 224–25
Rhŷs, J., xiii–xiv, 261, 280, 283, 305 6
Rigby, E., 110, 284
Riothamus, 300
Rivet, A.L.F., 89, 283
Roberts, B., 263, 287, 306
Ross, A., 302
Rouse, W., 109, 284
Rowland, J., 6, 189–90, 192, 264, 296–97
Ruby, B., 63, 279
Ruthin, 206–8, 244

S

Sanant, 211, 243
Savory, H., 215, 303

Schmidt, C.W., 103, 284
Scioto, river, 173, 177, 251, 293–94
Seaby, W., 6, 264
Selmer, C., 297
Severin, T., xviii, 29, 154, 274, 292
Sharpe, R., 292, 297
Shott, M., 62, 279
Sims-Williams, P., 77, 263, 265, 270, 273, 276, 281–82, 285, 287, 297, 301, 303–5
Smith, B., 57, 279
Snyder, C., 265, 271, 302
Solway Firth, xix, 199, 224, 229, 258
South Cadbury hillfort, xi, 299
Spence, M., 58, 172, 279, 294
Squier, E., 49, 51, 54–55, 60–61, 63, 85, 171, 278–79, 282, 293–94
Squire, C., 66–67, 90, 261, 280, 282–83
Stancliffe, C., 265
Stanzas of the Graves, xv, 88, 211, 243, 259
Stefánsson, V., 292–93
Stevens, C.E., 266, 268
Stilicho, 194
St Illtud, xiv
St Lawrence River, 2, 49, 76, 94, 143, 153, 164–65, 167–70, 178–79, 249, 254
Stone of Huail, 207
Stornoway, 160
Stothers, R.B., 284
St Patrick, 141–42, 235
Strait of Belle Isle, 162–64, 249
Stranraer, 223–25
Strathclyde, 119, 126, 182, 184–85, 223, 226, 294
strong door, 76, 94, 143, 168, 170
Sūlis (equated with Minerva), 117
Sweyn Estrithson, 278

T

Táin Bó Cuailnge, 8
Talhaearn
  'father of inspiration', xix, 237–40, 247–48, 258
  'greatest sage', 238
  'iron brow', 238–39
  placenames in north Wales, 238, 247
Taliesin
  historical bard, xiii, 21, 184, 193, 231, 233–34, 237–40, 247–48, 265
  legendary figure, 27–29, 31, 35, 44, 75, 104

Taliesin's Poems
  historical poems, 21, 81, 193, 210, 231, 233–34, 245, 265, 268, 283, 290, 295
  by Taliesin personae, 87–88, 90, 136, 147, 150, 228, 231, 238–39, 265, 276, 283, 291
Tatlock, J.S.P., 264
Taylor, E., 9, 32, 34, 36, 264, 275–76
Tees, river, 187
Teÿrnon Twrf Liant, 119, 221–22
Theodoric, 234, 283, 295
Theogony by Hesiod, 108
Thomas, C.R., 103
Thomas, H., 43, 278
Thornton, D.E., 304
Thorpe, L., 264–65, 274, 277, 283, 286–87, 301
Thule, 154, 156–57, 161, 169
Tierney, J.J., 293
Timaeus by Plato, 65
Tonsure, British, 237
Transmigration of soul, 98, 107, 117, 122–23, 126, 148, 231, 234, 236–37, 289
Tribruit, battle, 19–21, 195
Troyes, Chrétien de, xi, 7–8, 105, 284
Tschan, F., 77, 277, 282
Turff, G., 58, 279
Turner, S., 280, 300
Typhon, 108–9, 237

U
Ulster Cycle, 8, 142, 144
Urien Rheged, 21, 102, 193, 224, 233–34, 240, 247–48, 265, 268, 283, 295, 298, 304
Ursa Major, star constellation, 302
Uthyr Pendragon, 5–6, 217–18, 303–4

V
Veneti, 3, 157–58
Vergilius Romanus, 112, 285
Vinland, 9, 38–39, 44, 153, 278, 292
Virgil, 112, 237, 285
Virgin Mary, 20, 194–95, 303
Vortigern, xiii, xv, 5, 16, 198–201, 203, 235, 243, 262, 266, 268, 271, 305
Vortipor, xiv, 15, 118, 130, 183, 202–3, 287
Votadini, 184

W
Wallace, B.L., 292
Watson, W., 118, 212, 223–24, 285, 295, 301, 305
Watts, V., 302

Weets, J., 57, 103
Welsh Triads, xv, 6, 82, 118, 120–22, 148, 184, 197, 202, 212, 223, 246, 258, 280, 290
Wheeler, M., xi
Whitaker, I., 292
Williams, H., 131, 202, 205–6, 261, 265, 282, 287, 301–2
Williams, I., 21, 24, 102, 114, 193, 210, 226, 233–34, 238, 270–71, 273, 283–85, 296–97, 301, 305–6
Williams, J.E.C., 4
Winterbottom, M., 63, 131, 200, 205, 261–62, 265, 271, 282–83, 285, 287, 301–3, 305
Winwaed, battle, 189, 197, 242
Wiseman, H., 273
wledic, 86, 90–91, 290
Wooding, J., 29, 274
Woodward, S., 47, 278
Wray figurine, 103, 284
Wulfstan, 187, 241
Wynelandiam, 9, 38–39

Y
Yellow Pestilence, 220, 300
Yerkes, R., 48, 278
Young, S., 108, 155
Yrfai, 185–87, 189, 196, 241

Z
Zeisberger, D., 2, 60, 82, 173, 251
Ziegler, M., 299
Zimmer, H., 295
Zosimus, 267

www.ingramcontent.com/pod-product-compliance
Lightning Source LLC
Chambersburg PA
CBHW071151300426
44113CB00009B/1170